MW01057116

The Ho 9/Ho 229:
Retrospective

The Horten Ho 9/Ho 229: Retrospective

David Myhra

Schiffer Military History
Atglen, PA

Dedication

Gerhard Hopf
1921-1987

This manuscript benefitted tremendously by the running commentary of former *Luftwaffe* pilot/engineer *Gerhard Hopf*. Born in Dresden in 1921, *Gerhard* graduated in 1944 with a degree in aviation engineering. He immediately went into the *Luftwaffe* and was in training to be an *Messerschmitt Me 163* pilot. Postwar, late 1945, *Gerhard* was offered employment at the Wright-Patterson Air Force Base, Dayton, Ohio. He accepted and came to the United States with his wife Marianne, daughter and two sons in "*Operation Paperclip*." I later had the good fortune to meet him in 1982 in Naples, Florida where he and his wife were living in retirement. I have benefitted greatly by knowing him. Once, when I was about to leave for then West Germany, he asked a favor.

David, is it possible for you to venture into Communist East Germany during your upcoming trip to West Germany?
Yes, I responded, I have been inside the DDR several times.
You have no trouble at the border with the Eastern German Police?
No, not yet.
Is it then possible for you, to go to the City of Dresden and seek out the site of my ancient family home?
Yes, of course. In fact I'm going to Bitterfeld and talk with aviation designers who were taken to the USSR in 1946 to work on the *DFS 346*. Bitterfeld is only a couple of hours northwest of Dresden. I'd be happy to do it, I told *Gerhard*.

Armed only with a hand-drawn map, *Gerhard* wished to know what might have become of the family house given the two-night fire-bombing of Dresden in mid February 1945. Although I found the street with the help of many passers-by there were no longer any houses. The street was still there, however, where houses once stood up until February 1945 there now was a city park. I telephoned *Gerhard* from the *DDR* that he now owned a piece of a city park in Dresden. I brought back photographs to show him. He was overjoyed.

That you *Gerhard* for your patience with me especially with my all questions usually beginning with "I don't understand," and "what is this person talking about?" You enlightened me on the *Luftwaffe* and how things really were...how things really worked. Thanks for your running commentary on the *Horten* interviews. This book is for you.

Gerhard Hopf (1921-1987). Photo by author.

Book Design by: Joseph M. Riggio Jr.

Library of Congress Catalog Number: 2002111336

Printed in China.
ISBN: 0-7643-1666-4

We are interested in hearing from authors with book ideas on related topics.

Published by Schiffer Publishing Ltd.
4880 Lower Valley Road
Atglen, PA 19310
Phone: (610) 593-1777
FAX: (610) 593-2002
E-mail: Schifferbk@aol.com.
Visit our web site at: www.schifferbooks.com
Please write for a free catalog.
This book may be purchased from the publisher.
Please include $3.95 postage.
Try your bookstore first.

In Europe, Schiffer books are distributed by:
Bushwood Books
6 Marksbury Avenue
Kew Gardens
Surrey TW9 4JF
England
Phone: 44 (0) 20 8392-8585
FAX: 44 (0) 20 8392-9876
E-mail: Bushwd@aol.com.
Free postage in the UK. Europe: air mail at cost.
Try your bookstore first.

Acknowledgments

In most acknowledgments an author will state that his or her book-writing project could not have been achieved without the help of this person or persons. In most cases the author is not really so indebted but it sounds nice. However, in the case of my long association with *Walter* and *Reimar Horten* it truly would not have been possible without *Robert "Bob" Storck*. He was the archivist for the Vintage Sailplane Association (VSA). Back in the early 1980's very few people knew where in the world the *Horten* brothers lived. It was known that I was seeking their postal addresses and I was having an impossible time obtaining this information from a few people who knew but were unwilling to share it with me. One day, while I was doing research work at the National Air Space Museum (NASM) Library, a man with a full, dark beard walked past my desk dropping a folded yellow piece of paper and without speaking walked on by. Upon opening the folded paper I discovered to my astonishment two hand-written addresses: *Reimar Horten* in Argentina and *Walter Horten* in West Germany. That bearded man was *Robert "Bob" Storck.*

It was *Bob Storck*, too, who later arranged for me to get up close to the *Horten Ho 229 V3* in storage at that time in Silver Hill, Maryland. For an entire morning and part of an afternoon one very cold day in February 1982 *Bob* locked me in a windowless corrugated metal quonset hut. It was housing the *Horten Ho 229 V3* and the only light available come through two small snow-covered skylights in its metal roof.

"I'll be back after lunch. Myhra, will you be okay?" he called back before pulling the door shut made difficult by all the snow which had drifted up against it.

"Sure, sure," I replied, barely raising my voice.

I doubt that *Bob* heard me because by that time my eyes were focused on the world's most exotic flying machine of World War II sitting forlornly in the northeast corner of this metal hut. I was completely alone with this machine and my heart stood still. May God bless you always *Bob Storck*.

David Myhra

Fort Myers, Florida, USA
September 2002

Bob Storck, Washington, D.C., 1982. Photo by author.

Introduction

In the early 1980s, I was doing research and collecting material on German proposed turbojet- powered and bi-fuel liquid rocket driven fighters, interceptor, and bomber aircraft. This material would later be published by *Schiffer Publishing Limited* in 1998 as the "*Secret Aircraft Designs of the Third Reich*" (ISBN 0-7643-0564-6).

At that time, my research failed to reveal the origins of two projects: The *DFS 346* bi-fuel liquid rocket-driven speed of sound research airplane. The second project was the twin-turbine, all-wing *Horten Ho 229* fighter/fast bomber. A pre-production example, the *Horten Ho 229 V3*, existed in storage at the National Air & Space Museum (NASM) *Paul Garber Restoration Facility* in Washington, D.C. It may have been taken to Wright-Patterson Army Airfield near Dayton, Ohio, by the Army Air Corps who apparently intended at that time to make this twin *Junkers Jumo 004B*-powered all-wing airworthy and test fly it. It was thought that the *Horten Ho 229 V3* had come to the United States from England in May 1946 after spending approximately one year at the Royal Aircraft Establishment RAE) Farnborough, England. But this did not happen. *Phil Butler* in his 1994 book *War Prizes* (ISBN 0-904597 86-5) wrote that "the US Air Force estimated that the *Horten Ho 229 V3* would require approximately 15,000 man hours to bring the flying machine up to aircraft standards from its metal pipe and plywood spar and wing covering." They obviously felt that the *Horten Ho 229 V3* wasn't worth the expenditure of time and materials and it was restored sufficiently to museum display conditions.

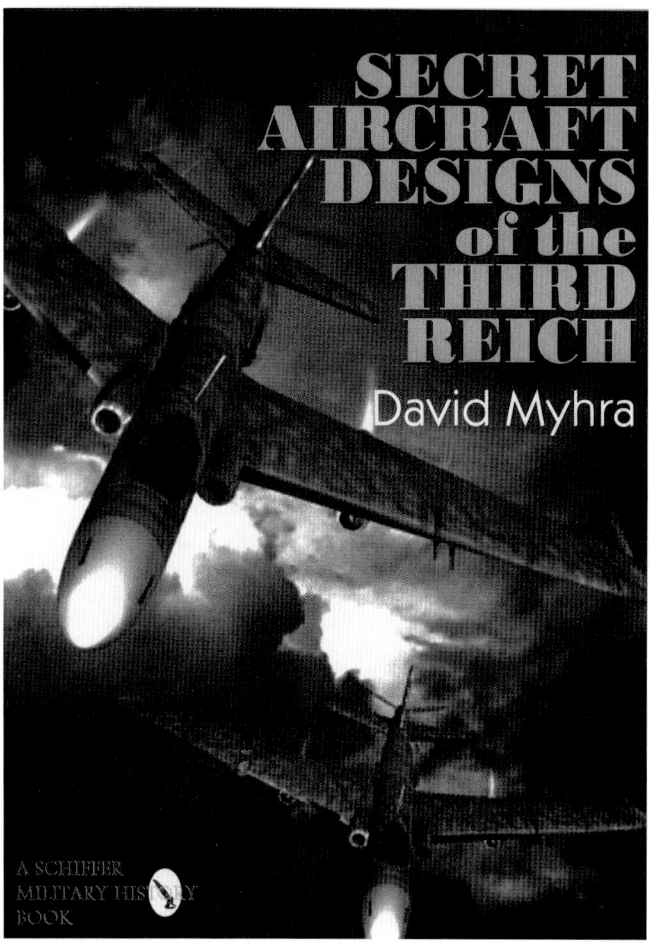

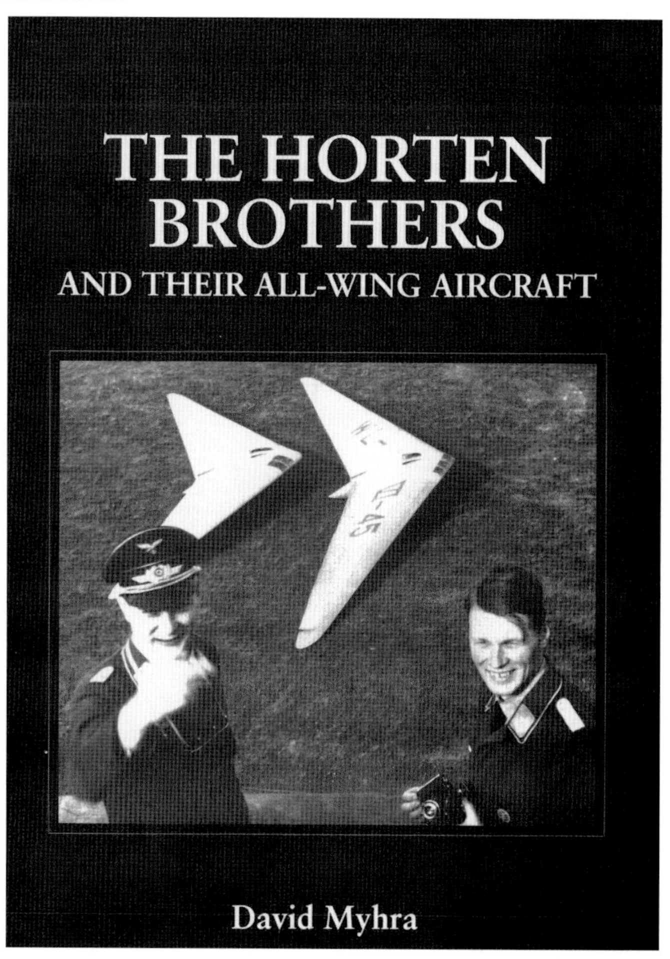

Eventually the *Horten Ho 229 V3* lost its indoor hangar space at Wright-Patterson and was moved outdoors. Years later, the NASM became the owner of the badly deteriorated *Horten Ho 229 V3*. After its many years of storage outdoors, exposed to the elements, the *Horten Ho 229 V3* was back indoors again, although in an unheated, windowless Quonset hut at Silver Hill, Maryland. Here was one of the most exotic war birds of all time, yet virtually nothing was known about its origin and developmental history. Also, very little was known in this country about its builders, *Walter* and *Reimar Horten*. It was known that the *Horten* brothers were highly active in German sailplaning at the *Rhön/Wasserkuppe* with their all-wing aircraft, beginning in the mid-1930s. But where, when, and how could a twin turbine-powered fighter project such as the *Horten*

Geoff Steele, Washington, District of Columbia

Margarita Reck, Salem, West Germany, 1982. Photo by author.

Ho 229 V3 be connected with people who built and competitively flew these unusual, light weight sailplanes built out of wood? About the *Horten* brother's personal lives, almost nothing was known. For example, it was uncertain if they had survived the war. Were they alive in the early 1980s....and if so, where were they living? I needed to find out. Through a considerable amount of effort and with the help of many people, I learned that two of the three *Horten* brothers were indeed alive and well. *Walter Horten*, the one who organized the secret production of this aircraft, was living in Baden Baden, West Germany. *Reimar Horten*, the young genius behind the *Horten Ho 229 V3's* design, lived on a ranch outside Córdoba, Argentina. I had found the *Horten* brothers! I wrote to them both, describing the information I needed to complete my "*Secret Aircraft Designs of the Third Reich*" manuscript. The *Horten* brothers proved to be excellent, supportive letter writers and after months of corresponding with them, I was invited to come and visit them personally. This I did immediately and during the ensuing years, we became good friends. *Walter* and *Reimar Horten* shared their memories with me on the history of development of their series of all-wing aircraft. At that time I was particularly interested in their *Horten Ho 9 V1* and *Horten Ho 9 V2.* They told me all they remembered and gave me numerous photos from their private collections. My collection of photos on the *Horten Ho 9/229* is substantial, thanks in great part to the *Horten* brothers. In addition to speaking with *Walter* and *Reimar Horten*, I was — through their help — able to contact and speak with several former *Horten Flugzuegbau GmbH* workers who were willing to share their memories of the *Horten Ho 9* project. Everyone I consulted was willing to give generously of his time to supply me with historical material, personal recollections (via cassette taped interviews), drawings, and photographs...many of these from private collections and never before seen. These men poured much additional information into my funnel, leaving me the job of trying to organize

Rich Horrigan, NASM's master aircraft restoration craftsman, with a pen and ink drawing of the Museum's *Horten Ho 229 V3* by *Arthur Bentley* in the background. Silver Hill, Maryland

Rich Horrigan, NASM, with the Museum's *Horten Ho 229 V3* in the background as seen from its rear port side. Silver Hill, Maryland.

An overhead view of the *Horten Ho 229 V3* all-wing as seen from its port side rear. Digital image by *Marek Rys*.

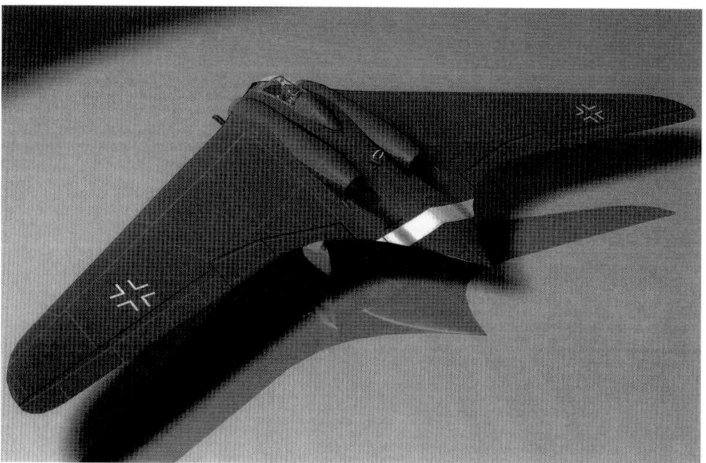

and make sense of it all. This was not an easy task. After forty years, the memories of many of the principals in this story have faded. Some activities and incidents, remembered by one commenter, may be forgotten all together by the others. A historian also is confronted with conflicting stories of events....requiring a careful sifting of accounts to try and discern the truth of what actually happened. Why, for example, was this twin turbine-powered all-wing, first placed under construction in 1943 and one of the few turbojet-powered aircraft to be built in Germany prior to war's end, lost in a crash landing in February, 1945. The really significant facts in the history of the pioneering *Horten Ho 9* were recorded primarily in the memories of the men who designed and organized its construction: *Walter* and *Reimar Horten*. The story of the *Horten* brother's accomplishments was more than just the culmination of their efforts in development of the turbojet powered *Horten Ho 9*. These two men, who started building their jet-powered *Horten Ho 9* in 1943, traced their beginnings to their first primitive wood and fabric sailplane built in 1933 - - the *Horten Ho 1*. All their lives, these remarkable brothers sought to find ways to perfect the all-wing design concept. This wasn't an easy task. In 1997, *Peter Schiffer* published my biography of these remarkable brothers from Bonn, titled "*The Horten Brothers and their All-Wing Aircraft*" (ISBN 0-7643-0441-0). It was designed to show the remarkable energy and resourcefulness of these brothers during their youthful years in the 1930s, then the difficulties they encountered later, during the difficult and dangerous years of World War Two. Because this new book on the *Horten Ho 9/229* is drawn from numerous taped interviews with both *Horten* brothers and several of their friends and workers, the reader will find that a number of the same questions appear to be asked several times. Also, questions directed to one individual also may have been answered by another interview subject, but at a later date. Or, the same question will be put to all, especially to ensure the right sequence of events, or attempt to ferret out all the details of an issue. These interviews took place over a period of more than two years. I have gone through more than four hundred pages of transcribed text of the interviews to select and organize the material for this volume. Naturally it would have been much easier for the reader to have duplicate questions and answers removed. My favorite interviewing technique is known as the "snowball approach" in which a general question is put to the interviewee in such a manner that it cannot be easily answered with a simple yes or no. As each interviewee begins recalling people and events, I merely let the person continue talking and talking,

An overhead view of the *Horten Ho 229 V3* as seen from its starboard side nose. Digital image by *Marek Rys*.

recording the answers on tape, and gently asking leading questions at appropriate moments. So the volume of material and information obtained just grows and grows and duplication sometimes is difficult to avoid when presenting all perspectives. Throughout these interviews, the reader will notice that several individuals were quite candid in their beliefs and sentiments of what caused the death of test pilot *Erwin Ziller*. Some individuals are singled out for criticism, such as those who were the major supporters of the all-wing planform concept and others who were its major detractors. Such adverse comments, as spoken to me, have not been altered here. Each person I interviewed was aware that his comments were being tape-recorded and that they might be published in the years to come. *Heinz Scheidhauer*, the *Horten Flugzeugbau's* principal test pilot, put it quite bluntly when he said:

"You can print all these conversations because in ten years time or so, we'll all be dead and it won't matter anymore what this person says about that person."

Thus the reader will find, scattered throughout these interviews, old jealousies, dislikes, and character assassinations of people connected somehow to the *Horten Ho 9/229* all-wing development project. Today, as I re-read these interviews, I find myself wishing that I could have more fully pursued several threads of this history. There are many additional questions I'd like to ask these gentlemen. One in particular comes to mind. *Theodore Rosarious* knew a great deal about his late friend *Siegfried Knemeyer* who wished to build a bomber capable of carrying a radioactive spreading device to the United States. I wish now that I could go back and have him talk more about *Knemeyer* who inherited *Udet's* job as well as Rosarius' own so-called "*Flying Circus*." I also wish that I had questioned *Walter* and *Reimar* more about their proposed *Horten Ho18* intercontinental jet bomber design and *Knemeyer's* deadly cargo it was supposed to transport to America — radioactive materials or chemical weapons. Acknowledgments... I am especially pleased to thank several good friends who have made this book a pleasure for me to write. During the development of this manuscript, my work benefitted greatly by the running commentary of *Gerhard Hopf*. He graduated in 1943 with a degree in aviation engineering. He

The *Horten Ho 229 V3* moments after lift off - a ground level view featuring its port side. Digital image by *Marek Rys*.

The *DFS 346* in the former USSR mounted under the starboard wing of an interned *USAAF Boeing B-29* bomber, Summer of 1947.

The *DFS 346-P* sailplane in the former USSR. Spring 1946.

The 3rd *Horten Ho 9 V2* center section with *Junkers Jumo 004Bs* installed in place of former *BMW 003s*. The *Horten Ho 9 V2's* center section frame is being assessed to determine the modifications required to make these *Junker Jumo 004Bs* with all their accessories fit entirely beneath the center section's surface covering with only the jet exhaust tube protruding. Göttingen, October, 1944.

immediately went into the *Luftwaffe* and was in training to be a *Messerschmitt Me 163* pilot. Born in Dresden, his family home was totally destroyed in the Allied fire-bombing in February, 1945. In late 1945, he was offered employment at Wright-Patterson Army Airfield here in the United States. *Gerhard* accepted and came to the United States, with his family, as part of "*Operation Paperclip*." I later had the good fortune to meet him in 1980, in Naples, Florida, where he and his wife lived in retirement. I benefitted greatly by knowing him.

My publisher *Peter Schiffer* wanted these *Horten Ho 9/229* photos made available to others throughout the world who are interested in this period of aviation history. But I wanted the interviews with the *Hortens* and the others who significantly contributed to the development of this aircraft included, too. How best to present all the photos and the information from many interviews was a problem. *Ian Robertson, Peter Schiffer's* very able military book editor, suggested that one way to describe the origin and development of the *Horten Ho 9/229* was to systematically present the photos from my collection wrapped around these word-by-word accounts from my several interviews. Now, in this way we believed, the reader could study the interviews, observe the photos, and draw their own conclusions on how this highly unusual aircraft evolved and how its jet-powered prototype, the *Horten Ho 9 V2*, crashed with test pilot *Erwin Ziller* at the controls on a cold winter day in February, 1945. The marvelous computer-generated images of some advanced variations of the *Horten Ho 7*, *Horten Ho 9*, and *Horten 229* were created by my friend *Mario Marino* of Garland,

Horten Flugzeugbau Horten Ho 9 V2 test pilot *Leutnant Erwin Ziller*, Göttingen, 1944.

The *Horten Ho 9 V2* shown at Oranienburg Air Base, February, 1945. *Horten* ground crew chief, *Walter Rösler*, in white coveralls, is carefully watching the *Horten Ho 9 V2s* as its starboard *Junkers Jumo 004B* is being started by *Horten Flugzeugbau* test pilot *Erwin Ziller*, with help from a *Jumo 004B* specialist from *Junkers Jumo*.

A pen and ink drawing of the *Luftwaffe's* very secret Orainenburg Air Base which was located northwest suburbs of Berlin. Courtesy: *JV44: The Galland Circus*, Robert Forsyth, Classic Publications, Great Britain.1996.

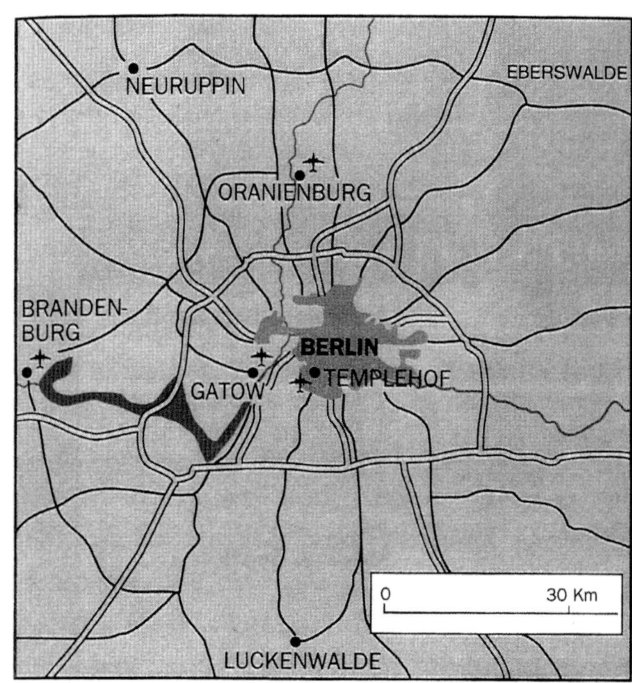

The *Horten Ho 9 V2* seen in a landing approach a couple of meters from touch down with landing gear extended at the Oranienburg Air Base, February, 1945.

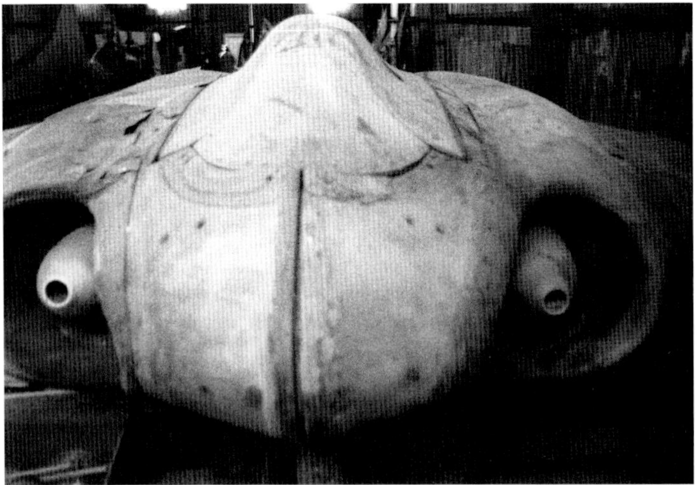

Front-on view of the thick dust-covered *Horten Ho 229 V3* center section seen in storage at NASM's *Paul E. Garber Facility*, Silver Hill, Maryland, early 1982. Photo by author.

Front-on view of the *Horten Ho 229 V3* center section as delivered to Freeman Field, Seymour, Indiana, about September, 1945. Some superficial damage appears on the outer edges of both air intakes, especially the port side air intake, perhaps encountered during the aircraft's long adventure from *Gothae Waggonfabrik's* Friedrichsroda workshop to Freeman Field.

The *Horten 229 V3* center section on public display at Wright-Patterson Air Force Base, Dayton, Ohio. Notice that its two damaged air intake fairings have been repaired. This was done post war in Germany.

A rear-view of the plywood-covered *Horten Ho 229 V3's* center section looking forward as seen at NASM's *Paul E. Garber Facility*, Silver Hill, Maryland, early 1982. Its center section trailing edge would likely had carried a single *Halkenkreuz* (*swastika*) instead of the two painted on forward the trailing edge post-war. Perhaps no *Halkenkreuz*! Photo by author.

The *Horten Ho 229 V3* seen from the rear as delivered to Freeman Field, Seymour, Indiana, about September, 1945. Notice, too, when it was delivered it came without a *Halkenkreuzs*. The *swastika's* were added to the center section's trailing edge some time when it was at Freeman Field or Wright-Patterson Air Force Base.

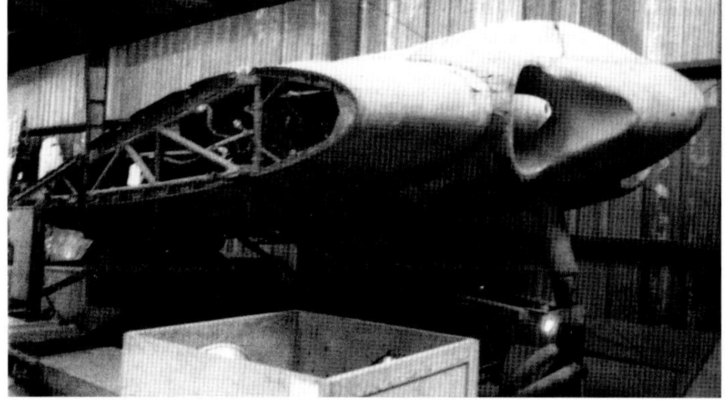

The *Horten Ho 229 V3* featuring a view of its front and starboard side in 1982. The flying machine was photographed as it sat in storage at NASM's *Paul E. Garber Facility*, Silver Hill, Maryland. Photo by author.

The *Horten Ho 229 V3* featuring its port side and shown as delivered to Freeman Field, Seymour, Indiana, about September, 1945. No photos of the *Horten Ho 229 V3* with its outer wings attached are known to exist to this author.

A view of the *Horten Ho 229 V3* featuring its rear port side, as delivered to Freeman Field, Seymour, Indiana, about September, 1945. The aircraft in the background appears to be the four-engined *Junkers Ju 290* nicknamed "*Alles Kaput*" by its American pilots who flew it to the United States from Europe in mid 1945. It was the only German heavy bomber to make it to America although *Göring*, *Himmler*, *Knemeyer*, the *Horten* brothers, *Wernher von Braun*, *Eugen Sänger*, and others might have wished that it would have been prior to Germany's unconditional surrender in early May, 1945.

It is not known to this author which vessel brought the *Horten Ho 229 V3* to the United States from Europe about August/September, 1945. It was certainly not the Royal Navy aircraft carrier *HMS Reaper* featured in this photo as it is sometimes written, although it did bring numerous *Luftwaffe* aircraft to America in mid to late1945. Dock workers are seen off-loading 30 types of German aircraft at the Port of Newark, New Jersey, July, 1945. The *Horten Ho 229 V3* came about two months later (September) and probably by an American Liberty transport ship. This author has searched historical documents in England as well as in the United States. Other aviation historians have looked, too, such as *Arthur Bentley*. No satisfactory explanation can be found explaining why the *Horten Ho 229 V3* came later, what merchant ship/military transport carried it to America, nor how it happen to show up one day at Freeman Field apparently without any documentation. The documentation must be out there, however. For now it is a mystery but one day it will be solved and this is what makes aviation history so interesting.

Three American *USAAF* officers looking over a *Junkers Jumo 004B* turbojet engine on the port side of a *Messerschmitt Me 262* somewhere in Germany post war. Left to right: *General Carl Spaatz*, *Colonel Harold Watson*, and *Director of Army Air Intelligence, General George C. McDonald*. About May 1945. It was *General McDonald* who played a major role in gathering up the *Horten Ho 9 V1*, *Horten Ho 229 V3*, and *Horten Ho 229 V4*, for their technical intelligence value. It is not known what eventually happen to the *Horten Ho 9 V1*, even the remains of the *Horten Ho 9 V2*, the *Horten Ho 229 V4*, and their final disposition. RAE-Farnborough may have received the gathered up remains of the *Horten Ho 9 V2* that had crashed at Oranienburg Air Base, killing Erwin Ziller, as for a time, they were considering the possibility of reconstructing the all-wing flying machine.

CONFIDENTIAL COPY NO._

AIR TECHNICAL INTELLIGENCE SECTION
OFFICE OF THE DIRECTOR OF INTELLIGENCE
HEADQUARTERS; USSTAF
APO 633, US ARMY

TECHNICAL INTELLIGENCE)
REPORT NO ...... A-383)

10 May 1945

SUBJECT: Inspection of Enemy Airfield

1. On 6 May 1945 the airfield at Leipzig/Brandis, Germany, MA Rx/4214, was inspected. All of the aircraft on this field had been destroyed by fire or demolition. It is believed this was a station for training and experimentation.

2. The following aircraft and components were inspected:

Aircraft

Type	Condition
2 x Ju 187 (287???)	Burnt out.
14 x He 177	Destroyed by demolition.
10 x Ju 88	Destroyed by demolition.
2 x Ju 188	Burnt out.
1 x Ju 86 M2	Fuselage only.
1 x Ju 34	Burnt out.
33 x Me 163	Destoyed by demolition.
4 X Me 109 G-14	Burnt out.
22 x Me 110	Burnt out.
5 x Me 410	Burnt out.
1 x Me 108	Burnt out.
3 x Do 217M	Burnt out.
1 x FW 190	Destroyed by demolition.
2 Ar 96	Destroyed by demolition.
1 x Hs 130A	Burnt out.
28 Si 204	Destroyed by demolition.

Components

1 x Ho IX Glider Wing, dismantled, slightly damaged.
4 x DB 610 engines, good condition.
2 x DB 610 engines, damaged.
7 x DB 605A engines, used.
2 x BMW 801 engines, used.
17 x 109-500A0, ATO units, used.
32 x 109-501, ATO units, used.

3. The Ho IX Glider Wing is believed to be of good technical value and the necessary arrangements have been made for removal to Merseburg. Six each of the ATO units have been received at Merseburg.

Basic report prepared by Thomas Wigglesworth, Capt., AC, Millard H. Hall, 1st Lt., AC, approved by John O. Gette, Jr, Lt. Col., AC, Chief of Section.

GEORGE C. McDONALD
Brig. Gen., U.S.A.
Director of Intelligence

A reproduced word-for-word copy of *Brigadier General George C. McDonald's* May 6, 1945, memo to Army Air Intelligence Headquarters, *USSTAF* reporting the finding of the *Horten Ho 9 V1* sailplane. It was found at Brandis/Leipzig Air Field and removed to an American captured *Luftwaffe* aircraft collection center, near the village of Merseburg for further evaluation and safe keeping. In the end it would not leave Merseburg as a complete aircraft. It was torn down for its salvageable metal.

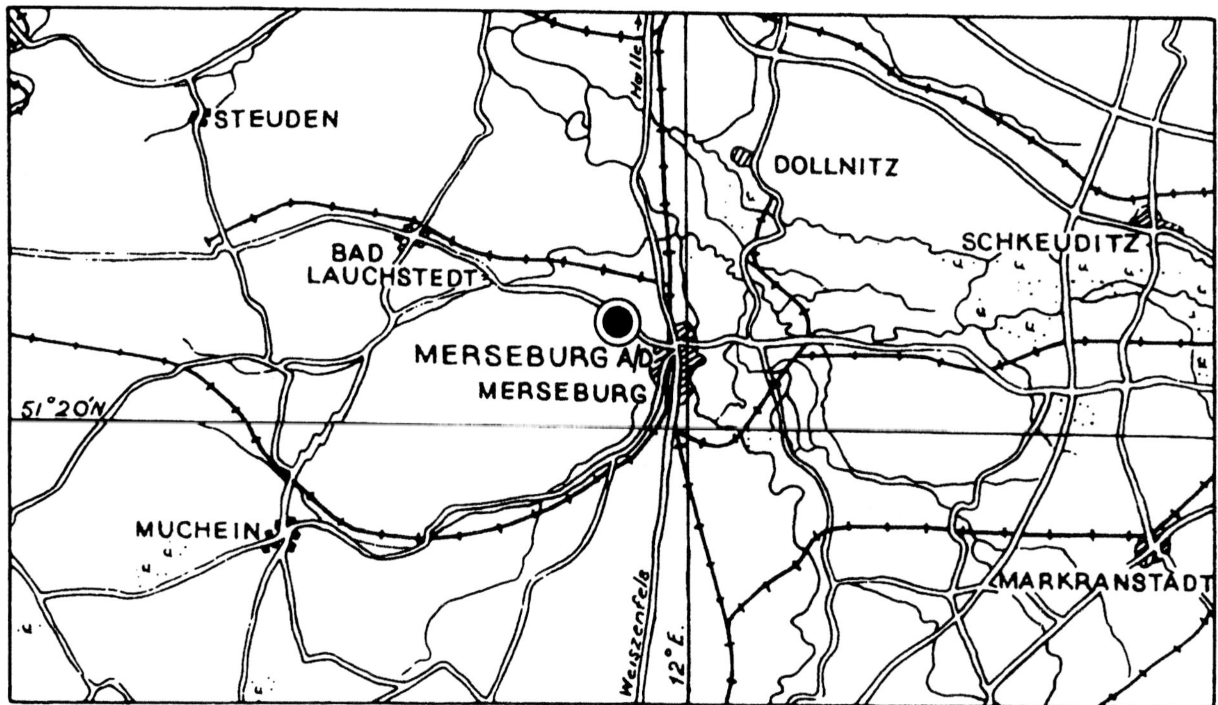

A pen and ink drawing featuring the general location of the former *Luftwaffe* Air Field at Merseburg, north east of Munich. Merseburg was one of the several American collection centers for captured *Luftwaffe* aircraft, such as the *Horten Ho 9 V1,* established by *Brigadier General George C. McDonald*, Chief of Army Air Intelligence in May 1945.

A pen and ink drawing featuring the layout of the former *Luftwaffe* Air Field at Merseburg where *Brigadier General George C. McDonald* established an American captured *Luftwaffe* aircraft collection/storage area. The *Horten Ho 9 V1* had been taken to Merseburg from *Gothaer Waggonfabrik*-Fredrichroda to await technical evaluation and final disposition.

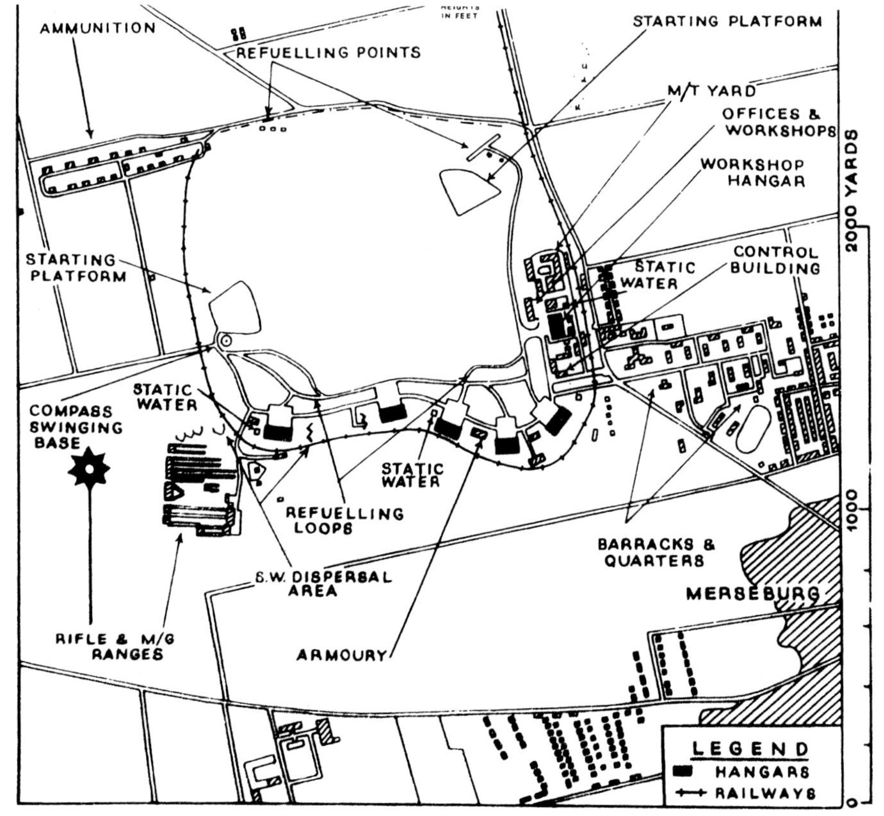

The new-looking *Horten Ho 9 V1* seen parked out front of its hangar. Göttingen about 1944.

The *Horten Ho 9 V1* (port side) seen gliding down in its landing approach with its nose wheel fully extended. *Horten Flugzeugbau* test pilot *Heinz Schiedhauer* is at the controls. Göttingen about 1944.

The *Horten Ho 9 V1*, seen about April 1945 at the Brandis/Leipzig Air Field. Its outer wings were separated from the center section and the three sections were being supported by sawhorses when discovered by *Brigadier General C. McDonald's* Army Air Intelligence team. The *Horten Ho 9 V1* had been at Göttingen and it is not entirely clear who, when, how, and why the *Horten Ho 9 V1* sailplane was taken to Brandis/Leipzig. Other than what appears to be damage to its nose wheel, the *Horten Ho 9 V1* appears to be in good condition. Retreating *Luftwaffe* personnel at Brandis/Leipzig sought to destroy all of their aircraft left behind, especially *Messerschmitt Me 163's*. Apparently no one bothered to attend to the *Horten Ho 9 V1* even through it was stored outside close to a hangar wall. Perhaps none cared enough to set it afire as everyone was retreating..

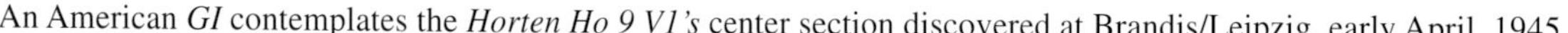

An American *GI* contemplates the *Horten Ho 9 V1's* center section discovered at Brandis/Leipzig, early April, 1945.

The center section of the *Horten Ho 9 V1* seen months after its arrival at the American captured *Luftwaffe* collection/storage area at Merseburg in April 1945. The *Horten Ho 9 V1's* technical value appears to have been heavily discounted as nothing more valuable than scrap as it sits in the grass in early summer, deteriorating and waiting to be recycled. Its port wing can be seen lying in the grass in the background to the left of the photo.

A view of the abandoned Brandis/Leipzig Air Field in mid April, 1945. In the foreground is a *Junkers Ju 88*. The Air Field is quiet now and littered with former *Luftwaffe* aircraft destroyed by retreating *Luftwaffe* officers and personnel..

Up until its abandonment, the Brandis/Leipzig Air Field was home of *JG/400* piloting the *Messerschmitt Me 163* rocket interceptor. *Hauptmann* (later) *Major Wolfgang Späte* was its commander between November, 1944 and April, 1945. Shown is *Major Späte* wearing his *Ritterkreutz*.

Two *Messerschmitt Me 163's* flown by *JG/400* stationed at Brandis/Leipzig Air Field about August, 1944. Their tail control surfaces and cockpit plexiglass are covered to due to rain which has already formed puddles on the tarmac.

Classification Cancelled
Changed to
Auth: S & R 1/22/46
fr TSNTE-1
By B L Masterson

COPY NO.

HEADQUARTERS
UNITED STATES STRATEGIC AIR FORCES IN EUROPE
Office of Asst. Chief of Staff A-2

D52.1
Horton /3

AAF Station 379
APO 633, U S Army
12 May 1945.

TECHNICAL INTELLIGENCE)
REPORT NO..........I-4)

SUBJECT: Horton 229 Bat Wing Ship Construction.

1. Pursuant to instructions from Operations Officer, ATI-Roth, R-46 the undersigned investigated subject target this date and interrogated the German civilian Engineer detained therewith at target location. As a result the following preliminary report is submitted.

a. Report

(1) NAME OF TARGET: Horton 229 Bat Wing Ship Construction.

(2) LOCATION: 45th ADG, code name-"Gunfire"- situated in town of Wolfgang, GSGS 4346, M-872-694 (near Hanau) (Airplane picked up by 45th ADG at Fredrichroda, R/5 090550).

(3) DESCRIPTION: Twin jet propelled bat wing constructed airplane, tricycle landing gear. The airplane is of steel and plywood construction and this particular ship has never been flown. It is presently disassembled in three major sections namely the right and left wing sections, and the center section consisting of the nose-jet engines-landing gear. The center section cannot be disassembled because of welded construction.

Size disassembled, center section--24' long, 10'-8" wide.
Wing panels--12' wide, 28' long.
Size assembled, wing span approximately 65', length 24'.
Weight, approximately 5 ton.

(4) INTERROGATION OF ENGINEER: Herr Eckhardt Kaufmann, civilian, resident of Fredrichroda, Germany claims to be the supervisor of construction and assembly of this airplane. He states that a Major Horton of the German Luftwaffe is the inventor and designer of this ship and that he is supposed (by Kaufmann) to be a PW at present; that he was ordered to build three of such airplanes at the Gotha W.F. (Car Foundry) of which a Dr. Berthold is director; that the ship was designed as a fighter with provisions made in plans for wing guns; that its maximum speed was to be 900 km/hr; that one ship was built, test flown at 300 km/hr and landed safely but on the second flight, the left engine burned up and the ship crash landed. Upon further questioning Herr Kaufmann admitted that practically all the materials used in construction of this ship are too heavy and improper, and are not in keeping with materials currently used in aircraft construction but that aluminum, dural, etc. were not available and that he was to use whatever material he could find. He further claims that on or about March 15, 1945, General Young, in charge of jet airplanes, came to him and offered proper materials, stating that airplane production in Germany had stopped, but that it was too late because construction had progressed to it's present status. Herr Kaufmann claims that plans in our possession incorporate improvements over this airplane.

(5) Herr Kaufmann has expressed a desire to work with American Engineers in America toward completion and perfection of this plane. He claims that with his knowledge and existing plans he could, with proper materials, build even a better plane without the use of the present prototype. Herr Kaufmann also expressed a desire that his family accompany him if he went elsewhere to work on these plans for fear of reprisals against them in Germany.

-1-

Photo-copy of page one of a memo from *Brigadier General George C. McDonald* to United States Strategic Forces In Europe dated May 12th 1945, regarding the final disposition of the *Horten Ho 229 V3* and *Horten Ho 229 V4 "Bat-Wings"* to the American captured *Luftwaffe* aircraft collection center near the village of Wolfgang near Hanau. *General McDonald* goes on to report that a metal locker containing complete plans for construction of the *Horten Ho 229* series accompanies his report. A near complete copy of these plans are known to exist at the *Deutsches Museum*, Munich, Germany. No memo is available regarding the disposition of the crashed *Horten Ho 9 V2's* remains left at Oranienburg have yet to be located. Perhaps none will be since this entire area was occupied by Red Army troops after their taking of Berlin in March, 1945. Then, again, RAF *Captain Eric Brown* believed that the *Horten Ho 9 V2's* remains were removed to RAF-Farnborough thanks to the American Army, which is thought to have picked up the pieces. Later the *Horten Ho 229 V3* was removed from Friedrichnada to the American captured former *Luftwaffe* aircraft collection/storage center by Merseburg.

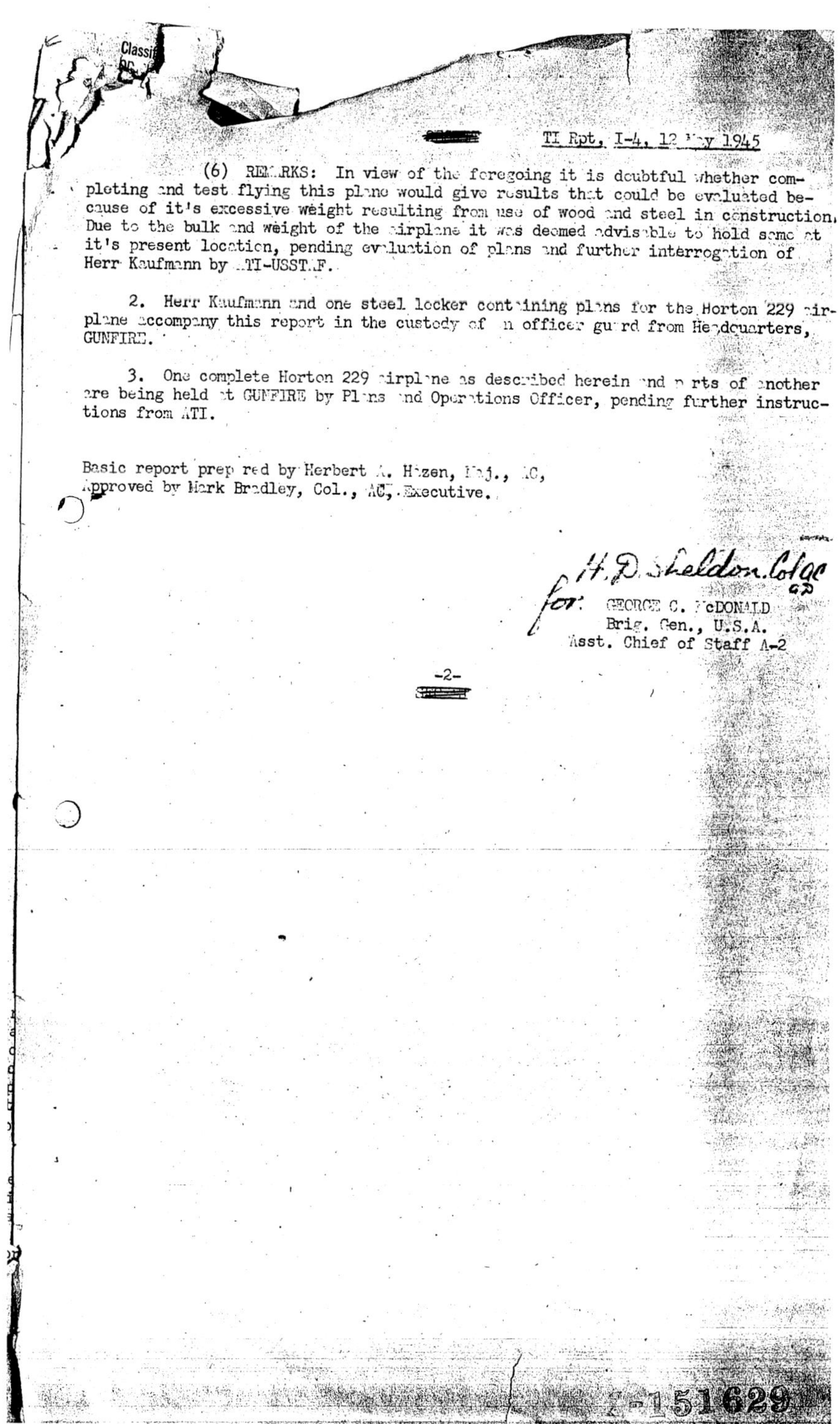

TI Rpt, I-4, 12 May 1945

(6) REMARKS: In view of the foregoing it is doubtful whether completing and test flying this plane would give results that could be evaluated because of it's excessive weight resulting from use of wood and steel in construction. Due to the bulk and weight of the airplane it was deemed advisable to hold same at it's present location, pending evaluation of plans and further interrogation of Herr Kaufmann by ATI-USSTAF.

2. Herr Kaufmann and one steel locker containing plans for the Horton 229 airplane accompany this report in the custody of an officer guard from Headquarters, GUNFIRE.

3. One complete Horton 229 airplane as described herein and parts of another are being held at GUNFIRE by Plans and Operations Officer, pending further instructions from ATI.

Basic report prepared by Herbert A. Hazen, Maj., AC,
Approved by Mark Bradley, Col., AC, Executive.

H. D. Sheldon, Col GSC
for: GEORGE C. McDONALD
Brig. Gen., U.S.A.
Asst. Chief of Staff A-2

-2-

151629

Photo-copy of page two of *Brigadier General George C. McDonald's* May 12th 1945, memo.

A popular photograph of the *Horten Ho 229 V3* in its ex-*Gothaer Waggonfabrik* workshop. Historians reproducing this photo claim this is the way the *Horten Ho 229 V3* was found with its starboard air intake fairing almost complete while its port air intake was unfinished as shown. Not so. The *Horten Ho 229 V3* in this widely circulated photo is in the process of being readied for removal and shipped to Freeman Field United States via the American captured *Luftwaffe* collection aircraft center at Wolfgang. *Brigadier General C. McDonald* ordered former *Gothaer* workers supervised by *Eckhardt Kaufmann* to complete the center section's leading edge nose panels before removing the prototype all-wing flying machine to the captured *Luftwaffe* aircraft collection center near the village of Wolfgang. In this photo it appears that ex-*Gothaer* workers have at least completed the fairing around the starboard air intake but have yet to complete the port air intake fairing.

Texas. He is a first-rate craftsman at producing digital images of these design concepts of the *Horten* brothers. Though the aircraft depicted in *Mario's* images were never built, they reflect the innovative thinking in the minds of *Reimar Horten* and other designers, made possible by the startling advent of the new gas turbine powerplants, something we take for granted in today's jet air travel. *Mario's* contributions appear frequently in my books published by *Schiffer Publishing*, and I'm grateful for his friendship. My friend *Geoff Steele* took considerable time away from his own personal schedule in Arlington, Virginia, to read the entire manuscript, view the photographs, and provide suggestions for improvement of this book. A glider and power pilot himself, *Geoff* was among the seven founding members of the Vintage Sailplane Association in 1974. As first editor of VSA's newsletter, "*Bungee Cord*," he produced a two-part article on the *Horten* brothers and their series of sailplanes that jump-started a new wave of interest in these aircraft among VSA members and others around the world. *Russell Lee*, a curator on the Aero Department Staff of the NASM in Washington, D.C., provided technical and historical backup to *Geoff* during the review process. *Russ* is a *Horten* aircraft expert and currently leads a project for restoration — by a museum in Germany—of several *Horten* sailplanes from NASM's collection. Some of these ultimately will be displayed, with the *Horten Ho 229*, at the new Dulles Airport Museum facility of NASM, west of Washington, DC, which is scheduled to open in early 2002. *Al Bowers* is a very talented aeronautical engineer at the National Air and Space Administration's Dryden Research Facility at Edwards Air Force Base in California. A hang glider pilot, he is

An extremely poor quality photograph of the starboard air intake on the *Horten Ho 229 V3*, yet a very important photo in establishing the sequence of events regarding the *Horten Ho 229 V3* post war. When the *Ho 229 V3* was first discovered by the U.S. Army, the *Horten Ho 229 V3's* fairing around its starboard circular air intake was unfinished, too, but not as incomplete as the port side fairing.

Another extremely poor quality photograph of the port air intake on the *Horten Ho 229 V3*. Its port air intake was finished by *Eckhardt Kaufmann* and a few former *Gothaer Waggonfabrik* workers post war. The photo shows the *Horten Ho 229 V3's* port side air intake in the same condition when it was found.

The finished work by *Eckhardt Kaufmann* and his ex-*Gothaer Waggonfabrik* workers. Both air intakes are now complete although unpainted and the *Horten Ho 229 V3* was ready to be removed to the United States. But before it would be shipped to the United States, probably by a Liberty transport ship, *Kaufmann* and his work force requested that they be allowed to make the *Horten Ho 229 V3* airworthy. *Kaufmann* believed that this would take only a short time, but *Brigadier General McDonald* refused, believing that a flight ready *Horten Ho 229 V3* would not give much information because the *Horten Ho 229 V3* had been built out of non-regulation aircraft material such as metal alloy pipe and plywood. He recommended that it never be made flight ready due to safety reasons...and it wasn't.

deeply interested in flying wing design evolution and has spoken about the *Horten Brothers'* concepts at several important aviation forums. Via email, *Al* joined in the review of the textual material, in an effort to ensure that the context of *Reimar's* comments about flight characteristics and performance of the *Horten* brothers' various designs was correctly presented here. *Rich Horrigan*, Chief of the talented restoration staff at NASM's *Paul Garber Restoration Facility* in Suitland, Maryland, worked to identify and clarify specific terms used in the many photo captions. *Rich* also is a power and glider pilot and has owned and flown a *Marske "Pioneer"* flying wing. He was involved in restoration of the Museum's *Arado Ar234B* jet bomber and *Messerschmitt Me 262A-1A* jet fighter, as well as several of the German missiles in NASM's collection, including one of *Wernher von Braun's V2* rocket missiles. Hopefully he will soon be providing leadership in the restoration of the *Horten Ho 229 V3* at NASM's new Dulles Airport Museum Restoration Facility. Thank you *Gerhard, Peter, Ian, Mario, Geoff, Russ, Al,* and *Rich* for your important devotion and individual contributions to this project. Thank you *Walter* and *Reimar Horten*, and your many associates, relatives and friends for so willingly giving your time and resources to bring more of this important history to the public. I am a better person for having met and known each and every one of you. Thank you *Betsy Hertel* — my wife, confidant, best friend, and the love of my life. Were it not for your generous and loving support, dear, you know that this book would not have been easily written.

David Myhra

An American Army Infantry soldier looks over a bare *Horten Ho 229* center section frame. It appears to be a single-seat center section frame and it is quite possibly the *Horten Ho 229 V5*. Several such bare center section frames were found at *Gothaer's* small Friedrichroda *Horten Ho 229* workshop and it is believed that all bare metal alloy frames were left behind when the U.S. Army vacated the area to the Soviets on July 1st 1945.

This *Horten Ho 229* pictured is thought to be the *Horten Ho 229 V4.* It was photographed by U.S. Army Intelligence. According to *General George C. McDonald's* May 12th 1945 memo to Headquarters, he reports that a second *Horten Ho 229* was gathered up along with the *Horten Ho 229 V3* and both removed to the village of Wolfgang for safe-keeping. What happen to the *Horten Ho 229 V4* after it was taken to Wolfgang is unknown. We know that its sister center section, the *Horten Ho 229 V3* was removed and transported to the United States directly from Merseburg. A *Horten Ho 9* is alleged to have been given to *Captain Eric Brown* representing the RAE-Farnborough. Could it have been the bits and pieces of the former *Horten Ho 9 V2?* This is what *Captain EricBrown* told this author that the machine they received back in England appeared that it had been in a crash! But as of December 1998 no documents/memos/reports have been located in America or British archives and/or museums regarding the fate of the *Horten Ho 229 V4* and whether the crashed *Horten Ho 9 V2* was taken to RAE-Farnborough, England as stated in a letter to this author by legendary *Eric Brown,* was in fact, the *Horten Ho 9 V2.*

A port side rear view of the yet to be covered (sheet plywood) center section of what is believed to be the *Horten Ho 229 V4* at *Gothaer Waggonfabrik* and photographed by U.S. Army Intelligence. *Gothaer* pretty much followed the *Horten Ho 9 V2's* basic design making changes only when it would expedite series production by its semi skilled work force. The *Horten Ho 229 V4,* pictured, would have differed considerably from the *Horten Ho 9 V2.* In order to bury the *Junkers Jumo 004Bs* the *Hortens* placed the turbines as far aft as practical. *Gothaer* placed the nose of the *Junkers Jumo 004B's* right up to the wing's leading edge. As a result, *Gothaer* had to remove the gasoline fuel tank for the *Riedel* starter engine from each *Junkers Jumo 004B.* They then put a small single fuel tank in the apex of the center section's nose with feeder lines to both *Junkers Jumo 004Bs.*

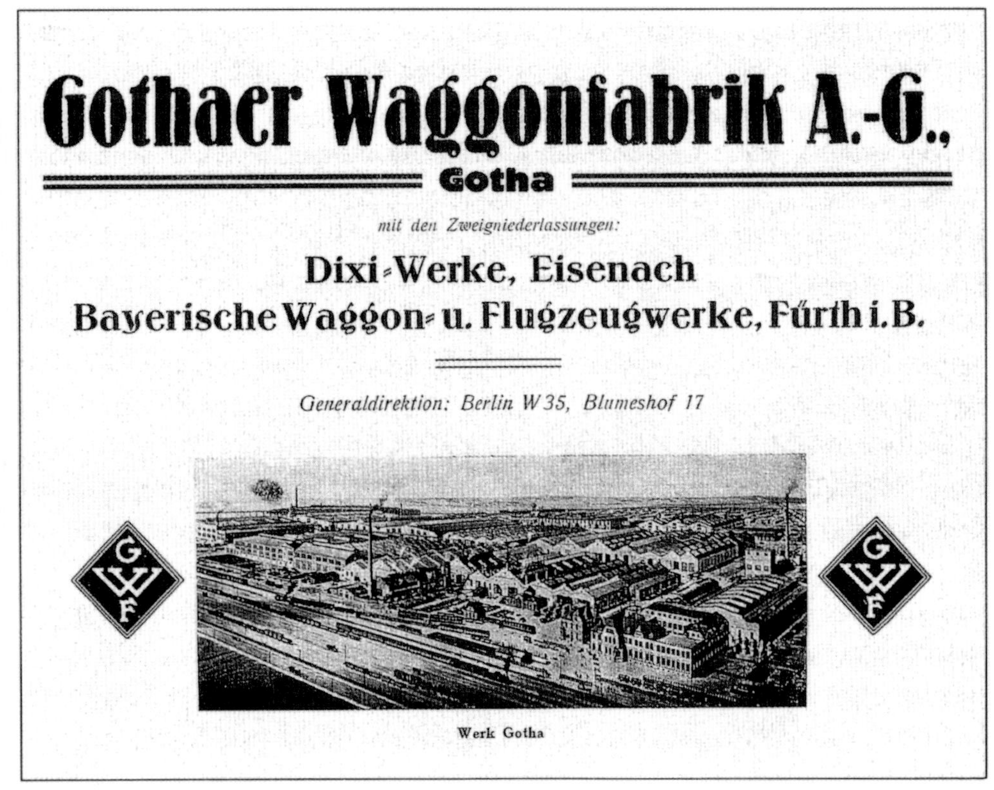

Gothaer Waggonfabrik AG's manufacturing complex in the city of Gotha.

Gothaer Waggonfabrik's business headquarters building in the city of Gotha.

In the upper portion of the photo is the single-story Gothaer Waggonfabrik garage-like building at Friedrichroda where the U.S. Army found the prototype Horten *Ho 229 V3,* Horten Ho *229 V4, and several* welded-up bare center section Horten Ho 229 metal alloy pipe welded frames. Th*e Gothaer work shop buildings are s*imilar in appearance to those buildings w*here the* Hor*t*en Ho 9 V1 and Horten Ho 9 V2 were as*sembled* at Grome, near Göttingen.

Bob Sotrck on the left with the legendary *Paul E. Garber* on the right. Washington, D.C., 1982. Photo by author.

Horten Ho 2 in flight at the *Rhön/Wasserkuppe* Summer Competitions of 1937.

Horten Ho 4A. Göttingen, summer 1943.

Walter Horten age 32 years. Göttingen. 1944.

Reimar Horten age 29 years. Göttingen. 1944.

Walter Horten age 70 years. Baden Baden, West Germany. 1982. Photo by author.

Reimar Horten age 68 years. *Horten Ranch*, outside the Villa General Belgrando, Argentina. 1982. Photo by author.

Sabrina Horten, left, former personal secretary of the late *Ernst Udet* and ex-wife of *Walter Horten*. Göttingen. About Spring, 1944.

Ernst Udet, left, popular female aerobatic pilot *Thea Rasche*, and airplane designer/constructor *Gerhard Fieseler (Fieseler Fi 156 Storch"* and the *Fieseler Fi 103 V1* flying bomb). Germany mid 1930s.

Heinz Scheidhauer. Freiburg, West Germany. 1982. Photo by author.

Oberst Siegfried Knemeyer, head of *RLM's* planning and development group (*Ernst Udet's* old job). Oranienburg Air Base. *Knemeyer* is about to take a test flight (right) in the motorized sailplane *Horten Ho 3G*. Autumn, 1944. Before doing so he is showing the controls to his long-time colleague *Theordore Rosarious* (left) leader of *Circus Rosarious*. *Knemeyer* was a powerful backer of the *Horten* all- wing flying machines in the *RLM*.

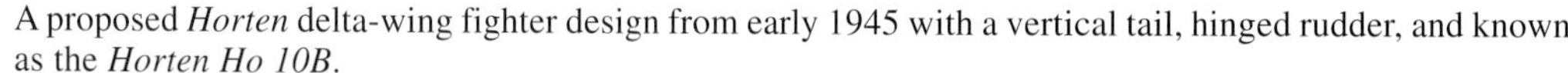

A proposed *Horten* delta-wing fighter design from early 1945 with a vertical tail, hinged rudder, and known as the *Horten Ho 10B*.

Reimar and *Walter Horten,* Fall 1944. *Walter* (right) is holding *Heinz Scheidhauer's* dog named "*Purzel,*" or elf.

A proposed *Horten* tailless fighter design from early 1945, the *Horten Ho 13B* and looking surprisingly similar to the tailless designs of *Alexander Lippisch* from 1944/1945. Air brush by *Gert Heumann*.

Fritz Sauckel recruited millions of slave labor which his boss *Albert Speer* needed in the German armaments factories. Many died due to maltreatment. *Sauckel* was hanged at Nuremburg on October 16th 1945 after being found guilty of crimes against humanity. *Sauckel* would have provided the slave labor for constructing the *Horten Ho 18B* in the giant underground concrete hangar under construction in late 1944 at Muhldorf near Landsberg.

A rendering of the six turbojet engine powered *Horten Ho 18A "Amerika Bomber"* by artist *Richard Keller* of the *Horten Flugzeugbau*. December 1944.

A pen and ink 3 view illustration from the *Horten Flugzeugbau* of their proposed *Horten Ho 18A "Amerika Bomber."* December 1944.

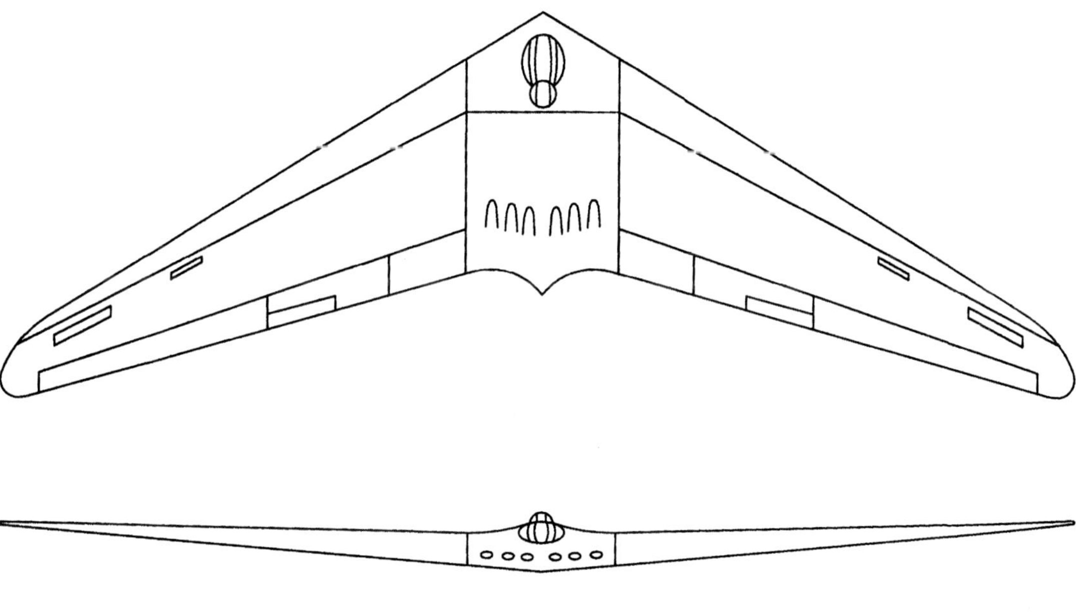

Rendering by Richard Keller of the four turbojet powered *Horten Ho 18B "Amerika Bomber*." This was long-range bomber aircraft *Hermann Göring* told *Walter* and *Reimar Horten* to build in the quickest manner possible. This flying machine, powered by four *Heinkel-Hirth HeS 011* turbojet engines, was to have been constructed by slave labor to be furnished by *Fritz Sauckel* who was from the *Speer*-run *Armament Ministry*.

A pen and ink 3-view illustration from the *Horten Flugzeugbau* of their proposed *Horten Ho 18B "Amerkia Bomber*." February 21st 1945.

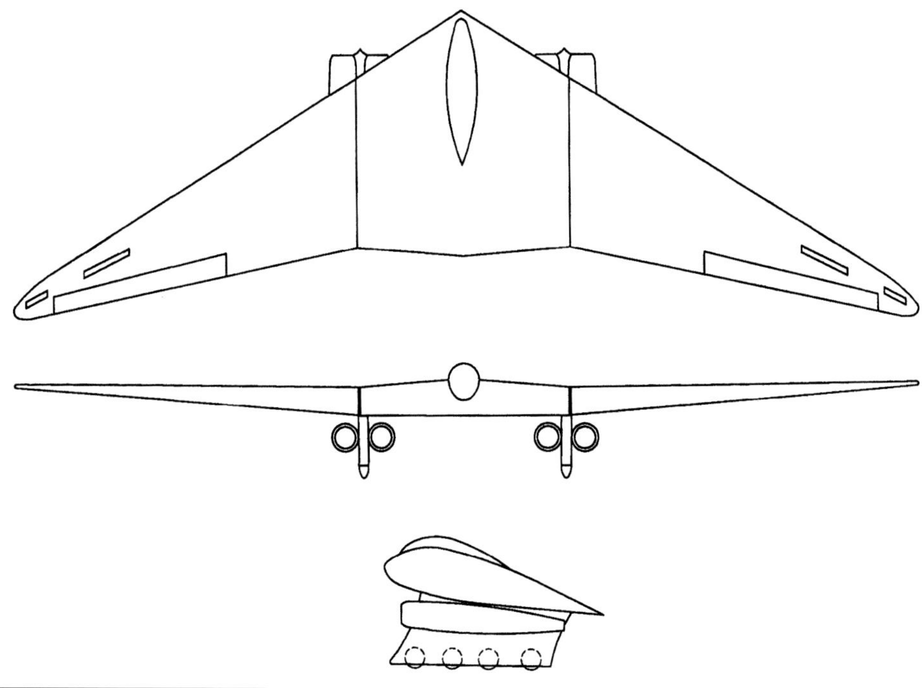

Hermann Göring. Found guilty at Nuremburg for complicity in *Nazi* mass atrocities and war crimes, especially the "Final Solution." He was sentenced to be hanged on October 15th 1945, however, committed suicide three hours before the event by swallowing a cyanide capsule which he had hidden in his teeth. Thus ended the life of one of the *Horten* brother's most powerful supporters in *Nazi* Germany of their all-wing concept. The other was *Siegfried Knemeyer*, who came to America post war via "Operation Paper Clip." He never spoke to the Horten brothers again.

Reichsführer SS Heinrich Himmler. He committed suicide while being interrogated by British Colonel *Michael Murphy*, Field Marshall *Montgomery's* Intelligence Chief, on May 23rd 1945, after a failed attempt to escape Germany through British lines even though he was in disguise. His suicide came quickly after he swallowed a cyanide capsule which he had hidden in his teeth...the same way *Hermann Göring* died.

Architect *Albert Speer*, left, with *Adolf Hitler*. *Speer* had an important position in the *Third Reich*. He was the minister of Armament Production.

Albert Speer, right, with *Hilde* his daughter and her husband *Ulf*. This photo was taken upon *Speer's* midnight release from Spandau Prison on September 30th 1966 after serving his twenty year sentence to the day for consenting to the use of slave labor in German armament factories, including the series production of *Wernher von Braun's A-4* (*V2*) rocket missile in the caves of the Harz Mountains.

Classification Cancelled
OR Changed to
Auth: R & R 1/22/46
W TSNTE-1
By B L Masters

COPY NO.

HEADQUARTERS
UNITED STATES STRATEGIC AIR FORCES IN EUROPE
Office of Asst. Chief of Staff A-2

AAF Station 379
APO 633, U S Army
19 May 1945

TECHNICAL INTELLIGENCE)
REPORT NO.........I-3)

D52.1
Horten

SUBJECT: Interrogation of Herr Eckhardt Kaufmann Concerning Ho 229 Aircraft.

1. Herr Eckhardt Kaufmann, who stated that he was supervisor of construction and assembly of the Ho 229 aircraft for Gotha Waggenfabrik A.G. in the plant at Friedrichroda (50°48'N/10°33'E), had been sent back to USSTAF (Main) by ATI personnel. He was interrogated 14 May 1945 at Chateau du Grand Chesnay, near Headquarters, SHAEF (Main), by Lt. Col. A. B. Deyarmond and Capt. S. Litton of the Office of the Asst. Chief of Staff, A-2, USSTAF.

2. Digest of statements by Herr Kaufmann.

a. The Gotha Waggenfabrik A.G. of Gotha ordinarily builds railroad cars, but during the war about half of their capacity was devoted to aircraft manufacture. They built Me 110 aircraft in quantity, attaining a peak production of about 120 in September, 1944. They had started work on FW-152's and had partially constructed five (5) which were about ready for assembly. Because of lack of progress by Horten in the development of the Ho 229 this job was turned over to Gotha W.F. They had partially completed three and had a contract for another ten, after which they were supposed to go into quantity production. This product was considered a very high priority job and they all worked very hard and very long hours on it.

b. The key personnel of this company who were involved in the Ho 229 project were:

(1) Dr. Berthold, Director.

(2) Herr Huehnerjaeger, Chief Engineer. Under him were:

(a) Herr Mueller in charge of control systems; formerly with Junkers.

(b) Herr Schaupp in charge of power plant.

(c) Herr Hermann in charge of body design.

(d) Herr Freitag in charge of landing gear.

(e) A fifth engineer, whose name Herr Kaufmann did not remember, was in charge of design of skin and covering.

(f) About fifteen draftsmen.

(3) Herr Kaufmann was supervisor of construction and assembly and directly responsible to Dr. Berthold.

c. There were no resident government inspectors on the project but a district inspector visited there periodically to check the parts being manufactured.

d. There was also one Aluis Boensch, a Junkers employee, who was a specialist on the engines. He was in the Army but placed in an inactive status in order to do that work. When the district was taken by the Americans he was sent to a P/W camp at Laucha. ATI personnel visited the location of this camp but it had been moved and they could not trace Boensch.

e. Other companies associated with Gotha in the manufacture of this aircraft were:

(1) Hartweg in Sonneberg (about 80 km. from Gotha) made the wings.

-1-

Page one of the interrogation of *Gothaer Waggonfabrik's Horten Ho 229* series construction supervisor *Eckhardt Kaufmann* who is commenting on the history of *Gothaer* and key personnel involved in the production of the *Horten Ho 229 V3.*

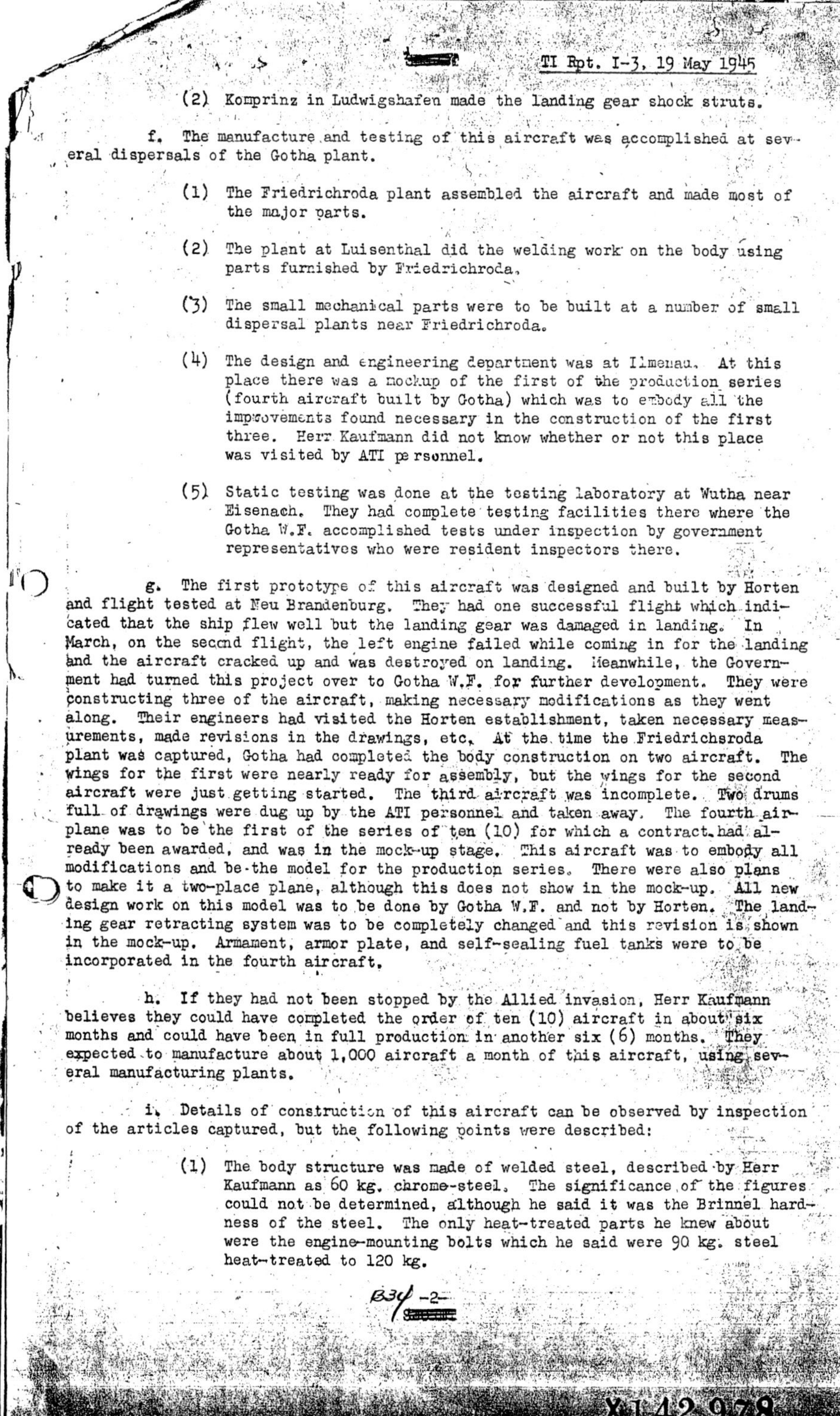

TI Rpt. I-3, 19 May 1945

(2) Komprinz in Ludwigshafen made the landing gear shock struts.

f. The manufacture and testing of this aircraft was accomplished at several dispersals of the Gotha plant.

(1) The Friedrichroda plant assembled the aircraft and made most of the major parts.

(2) The plant at Luisenthal did the welding work on the body using parts furnished by Friedrichroda.

(3) The small mechanical parts were to be built at a number of small dispersal plants near Friedrichroda.

(4) The design and engineering department was at Ilmenau. At this place there was a mockup of the first of the production series (fourth aircraft built by Gotha) which was to embody all the improvements found necessary in the construction of the first three. Herr Kaufmann did not know whether or not this place was visited by ATI personnel.

(5) Static testing was done at the testing laboratory at Wutha near Eisenach. They had complete testing facilities there where the Gotha W.F. accomplished tests under inspection by government representatives who were resident inspectors there.

g. The first prototype of this aircraft was designed and built by Horten and flight tested at Neu Brandenburg. They had one successful flight which indicated that the ship flew well but the landing gear was damaged in landing. In March, on the second flight, the left engine failed while coming in for the landing and the aircraft cracked up and was destroyed on landing. Meanwhile, the Government had turned this project over to Gotha W.F. for further development. They were constructing three of the aircraft, making necessary modifications as they went along. Their engineers had visited the Horten establishment, taken necessary measurements, made revisions in the drawings, etc. At the time the Friedrichsroda plant was captured, Gotha had completed the body construction on two aircraft. The wings for the first were nearly ready for assembly, but the wings for the second aircraft were just getting started. The third aircraft was incomplete. Two drums full of drawings were dug up by the ATI personnel and taken away. The fourth airplane was to be the first of the series of ten (10) for which a contract had already been awarded, and was in the mock-up stage. This aircraft was to embody all modifications and be the model for the production series. There were also plans to make it a two-place plane, although this does not show in the mock-up. All new design work on this model was to be done by Gotha W.F. and not by Horten. The landing gear retracting system was to be completely changed and this revision is shown in the mock-up. Armament, armor plate, and self-sealing fuel tanks were to be incorporated in the fourth aircraft.

h. If they had not been stopped by the Allied invasion, Herr Kaufmann believes they could have completed the order of ten (10) aircraft in about six months and could have been in full production in another six (6) months. They expected to manufacture about 1,000 aircraft a month of this aircraft, using several manufacturing plants.

i. Details of construction of this aircraft can be observed by inspection of the articles captured, but the following points were described:

(1) The body structure was made of welded steel, described by Herr Kaufmann as 60 kg. chrome-steel. The significance of the figures could not be determined, although he said it was the Brinnel hardness of the steel. The only heat-treated parts he knew about were the engine-mounting bolts which he said were 90 kg. steel heat-treated to 120 kg.

B34 -2-

X142978

Page two of the interrogation of *Gothaer Waggonfabrik's Horten Ho 229* series construction supervisor *Eckhardt Kaufmann* who is commenting on the various component assembly manufacturers on the *Horten Ho 229 V3.*

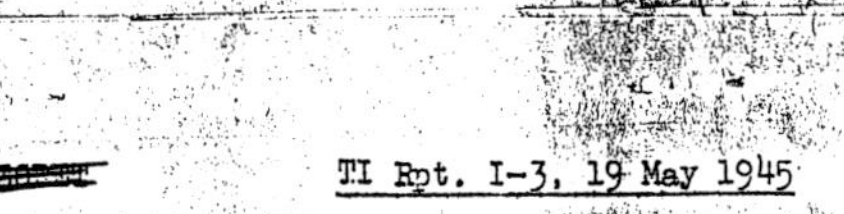

TI Rpt. I-3, 19 May 1945

(2) The covering of the body was plywood six mm. thick at the rear, twelve mm. in the middle and sixteen mm. at the nose. Behind the jets is a mild steel plate covering over the wood. Casein glue was used in joining the wood.

(3) The wings were made of wood. He did not know the details of construction as another company made these parts. However, he did say the spars were made of vertical laminations. He thought that fir, beech, and birch wood were used in various parts. The covering was plywood.

(4) The largest wheel of the tricycle landing gear is the nose wheel.

(5) There are three trailing edge moveable control surfaces on each wing. The two inboard acted as elevators and the outboard as ailerons and elevators. Spoiler flaps, top and bottom, at the wing tips were used for directional control. The details of use of controls could not be checked as Herr Kaufmann was not familiar with them. Lower surface flaps near the center could be used in landing or pulling out of a dive. A decceleration parachute was available for emergency use.

(6) The fuel tanks, four in each wing, had a total capacity of 3,000 liters. Herr Kaufmann thought the aircraft would have an endurance of three quarters of an hour to one hour at 20,000 to 25,000 feet.

(7) The armament was to be four Mk 108 or two Mk 103 cannons. The armor plate was to be 10 mm. thick.

(8) A catapult type seat was provided using an explosive propellant.

(9) The first ship was tail heavy and used about 800 kg. of nose ballast. Mr. Kaufmann thought the installation of armament and armor would make up for this. The ballast was 200 kg. in the very nose and 600 kg. in two places about 1600 mm. back. It could be replaced by a total of 438 kg. in the nose.

j. Herr Kaufmann knew nothing of aerodynamic details or of the strength design of the aircraft. He did not have with him a detail weight breakdown.

k. Herr Kaufmann brought with him a box of documents which did not seem to be very important. Some of the correspondence indicated that the government wanted this project rushed. This box of documents is being held by Exploitation Division, Office of the Assistant Chief of Staff, A-2, US Strategic Air Forces in Europe, pending further disposition. One interesting item was an illustrated parts list for the Jumo 004 engine.

3. Recommendations.

a. That the appropriate ATI Collection Point investigate the design and engineering establishment of Gotha W.F. at Ilmenau, inspect the mock-up and take necessary photographs.

b. That an attempt be made to find aerodynamic and performance reports on this aircraft. Copies may be at Ilmenau.

c. That engineering personnel of Gotha W.F. and of Horten be questioned if available, but not brought to USSTAF for this purpose.

d. That the static test laboratory at Wutha be inspected by ATI personnel from the appropriate Collection Point, to determine whether anything more of value can be learned.

X142978

Page three of the interrogation of *Gothaer Waggonfabrik's Horten Ho 229* series construction supervisor *Eckhardt Kaufmann* who is commenting on the general details of the *Horten Ho 229 V3* such as landing gear, armament, control surfaces, and so on.

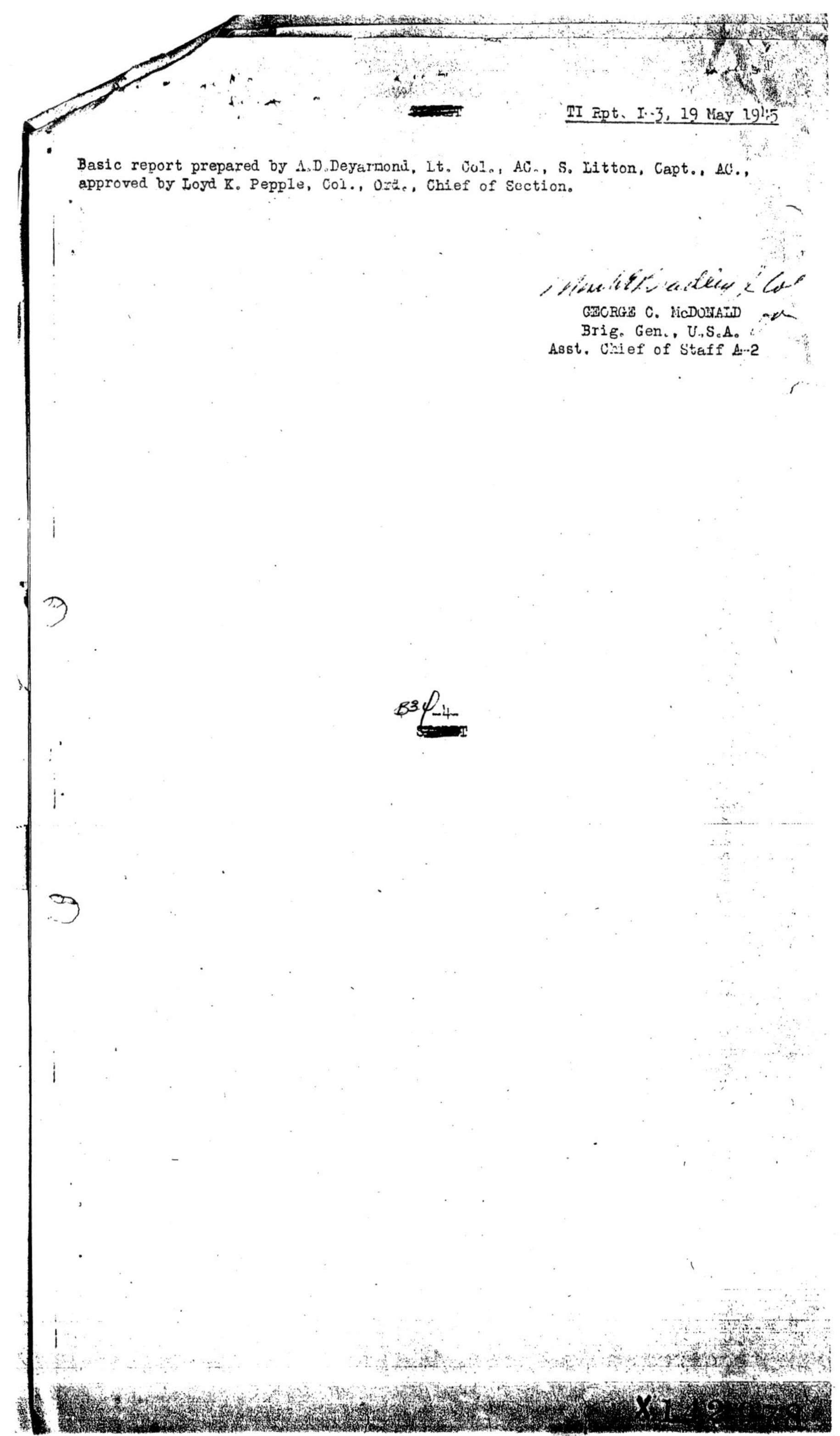

SECRET TI Rpt. I-3, 19 May 1945

Basic report prepared by A.D.Deyarmond, Lt. Col., AC., S. Litton, Capt., AC., approved by Loyd K. Pepple, Col., Ord., Chief of Section.

GEORGE C. McDONALD
Brig. Gen., U.S.A.
Asst. Chief of Staff A-2

-4-
SECRET

Page four of the interrogation of *Gothaer Wagonfabrik's Horten Ho 229* series construction supervisor *Eckhardt Kaufmann* who is commenting that he has a large box of documents and that the *Horten* brothers should be interrogated, too, about their *Horten Ho 229 V3.*

Garber, NASM Archives Division, Bldg. 12, Freeman Field Reports

ARMY AIR FORCES
HEADQUARTERS OF THE MATERIEL COMMAND
HEADQUARTERS
AIR TECHNICAL SERVICE COMMAND

IN REPLY ADDRESS BOTH COMMUNICATION AND ENVELOPE TO ATTENTION OF FOLLOWING OFFICE SYMBOL: TSVMP

FOR VICTORY BUY UNITED STATES WAR BONDS AND STAMPS

TSVMP/PGF/ehb
WRIGHT FIELD, DAYTON, OHIO
28 JAN 1946

Subject: Availability of Glider

To: Commanding Officer
Freeman Field
Seymour, Indiana

1. It is requested that this office be notified when the Horten 9 Jet Glider will be completed and ready for flight.

2. It is desired to take aerial and ground shots of this glider, when it is available, for use at this Command.

BY COMMAND OF LIEUTENANT GENERAL TWINING:

Henry G. Ross
for RICHARD J. CUNNINGHAM
Lt. Colonel, Air Corps
Chief, Photographic Intelligence (T2)

Henry G. Ross,
Major, Air Corps,
Chief, Motion Picture Section,
Photographic Office,
Intelligence (T2)

1st Ind. FFE/CHB/abc

HEADQUARTERS, FREEMAN FIELD, ATSC, Seymour, Indiana. 30 January 1946.

TO: Commanding General, ATSC, Wright Field, Dayton, Ohio. ATTN: TSVMP

1. The Horten 9 jet propelled flying wing is not being considered for restoration to flight condition. A portion of the center section and one incomplete wing panel are available at Freeman Field. The other wing panel is not available.

2. During a visit of Colonel Celik (TSITO) to Freeman Field on 25 January a visual inspection of the Horten 9 was conducted. There was complete concurrence in the fact that reconstruction is not feasible and is impossible without a re-design of the basic aircraft.

H. C. DORNEY
Colonel, Air Corps
Commanding

EHB TSVMP 2/1/46

125
AAFMC-304-WF-8-22-44-300M

A poor quality reproduction of a January 28th 1946 memo from the Army Air Forces, Headquarters regarding the final disposition of the *Horten Ho 229 V3* then at Freeman Field, Seymour, Indiana. The Photographic Office at Wright Field, Dayton, Ohio, wishes to know when this *Horten Ho 229* turbojet propelled flying wing will be ready for flight testing. When it is ready, they would like to be present to take aerial and ground photos. *Colonel H.C. Dorney* of Freeman Field responds in a January 30th 1946 memo saying that the *Horten Ho 229 V3* is not being considered for restoration to flight condition because based on recent (January 25th 1946) visual inspection of the machine that it had been determined that a reconstruction was not feasible and impossible without a total re-design of the basic aircraft.

Chapter 01

WALTER HORTEN Interview

Date: October, 1982
Location: Baden-Baden, West Germany
Language: English

Background:
Walter Horten was the second of four children born to *Professor Dr. Max* and *Elizabeth Horten* on November 13th 1913 in Bonn, Germany. *Wolfram Horten*, the eldest was born in 1912. *Reimar Horten*, the all-wing sailplane design genius, was born March 2nd 1915. Their sister *Gunhild Horten*, was born in 1921. Without question it was Walter's influence on Reimar which led to the *Horten's* experimentation in burrying piston engines and turbines inside the airfoil of their all-wing designs.

Walter Horten was first and foremost a highly skilled pilot. He began with gliders and earned the coveted soaring badge, the "Silver C". He joined the clandestine Luftwaffe before its existence was unveiled to the world and trained first as a bomber pilot but subsequently transferred to fighters, becoming a polished aerobatic pilot. He was the Technical Officer (TO) for *JG/26* but was assigned the task of protecting *Adolf Galland* as his wingman...a very dangerous job because *Galland* had by then lost twelve wingmen and few if any wanted to fly with him. *Walter Horten* survived the experience and scored 7 confirmed victories before receiving a direct order to cease all combat flights. The *Luftwaffe* did not want to lose their *TOs* in combat but *Walter* laughed. He wasn't afraid of the *Supermarine Spitfire* but he did respect the machine and its highly trained pilots. Nonetheless, Walter was *Galland's* only wingman to score any kills. He claimed, perhaps rightly, that he was a better pilot than *Galland*. Walter scored 2 more unconfirmed victories before he transferred to Berlin and the *JagdFlugInspektion* (*JFI*) or Inspectorate of Fighters under the direction of *General von Döring*, a pre-war *kommodore* of *JG/26*. The experience of the Battle for Britain and the painful loss of so many colleagues made a deep and lasting impression.

Walter Horten aged 70 years. Baden Baden, West Germany. 1982. Photo by author.

Walter realised that the *Luftwaffe* required a better fighter than the legendary *Messerschmitt Bf 109* and the later *Focke-Wulf Fw 190*. The *Luftwaffe's* best fighter and bomber pilots were dwindling day-by-day and he believed that his *Luftwaffe* could only regain superiority in the skies with twin-engine all-wing fighter.

Walter was very bright, an extrovert, an excellent conversationalist, and was so very convincing. People sought him out and wanted to be his friend. We see *Walter* in photographs conversing with *Hermann Göring*, *Werner Molders*, and *Erhard Milch*. *Ernst Udet* sought his advice and *Walter* gave honest answers. He loved his brother *Reimar* and the highest priority in his life in war-time Germany was to keep *Reimar* out of harm's way - and that he did. Whatever it took, bluff, deception, falsifying *Udet's* signature on documents, hiding the existence of their *Horten Ho 9* all-wing fighter/fast bomber - he did it. *Walter* would have given his life to save his brother from being harmed in any way. We see in *Walter* an exceptional organizer, administrator, networker, and someone highly goal oriented. He had outwitted the *RLM* (Reichsluftfahrtministerium) in *Nazi*-controlled Germany where individual inititative was largely forbidden and aircraft development tightly controlled. To look back at what *Walter Horten* accomplished in this climate is amazing. He managed to protect his brother and keep him working on aircraft design. Though a network of friends in high-places he obtained work space, manpower, equipment, tools and an unending supply of materials to construct some twenty five aircraft and sailplanes during the war years. Ultimately he managed to acquire one of the scarecest aero engines in all of Germany...the *Junkers Jumo 004B* turbojet. Doing this in America today as a member of the U.S. Air Force would be considered impossible. So how did *Walter* accomplish what he did? I can't fully explain it. I did not have the opportunity to speak with any of *Walter's* contempories to get their opinions. But it appears that

Walter Horten aged 32 years. Göttingen, Germany. 1944.

Walter had an extraordinary ability to interest people in the work he pursued with his brother.... that if they would just help in some way with a vacant building, warehouse, unused hangar, and so on, *Reimar* would produce something extraordinary. But, of course, there is more to it than a promise of good things to come. What is so extraordinary, is that these events took place in *Nazi* Germany. A totalitarian state where unauthorised and unorthodox behaviour risked jail or the firing squad ! Why were so many individuals in high places willing to take the chance...the risk? I don't know.

Interview:

Walter Horten (W. Horten). Adolf Gallund had no interest in my idea of an all-wing fighter. I could not talk to him about its dog-fighting abilities compared to an *Messerschmitt Bf 109* or an *Focke-Wulf Fw 190*. My brother *Reimar* was more interested in high performance sailplanes and soaring. What was I to do? But I thought that if we are to win the war against the Americans, as yet we do not have an aircraft capable of doing the job. Even in 1940 I felt strongly that war with America was bound to come. And the potential for producing aircraft in the USA was awesome, as *Ernst Udet* had said many times after his visits there in the 1930s. *Udet* had frequently stated that if America entered the war, their ability to produce large quantities of fighters and bombers would surpass any other country in the world. If America entered the war on the side of England, then we would eventually lose.

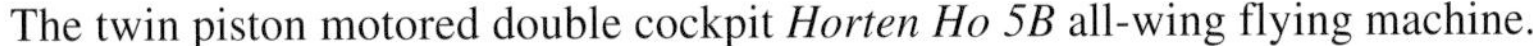

The twin piston motored double cockpit *Horten Ho 5B* all-wing flying machine.

The twin piston motored single seat *Horten Ho 5C* as seen in flight and from its starboard side.

David Myhra (Myhra): As a person what was *Adolf Galland* like?

W. Horten: Being a wing man for *Adolf Galland* was very difficult because the wing man had to fly better than he did. *Galland* was a difficult person. Look, in no book is it written that *Galland* lost twelve wing men just during August and September, 1940. I was assigned as his thirteenth. I knew that I could fly better than *Galland*. I was *Galland's* only wing man to score a kill. I managed nine victories - all while protecting *Galland* plus two more which we couldn't count. I laughed that I was able to finish the war alive after protecting *Galland*. I'll tell you something else...no one wanted to fly with him, because it was very dangerous to be *Galland's* wing man. He did not protect his wing men, but we had to try to protect him. We all watched carefully to see that he was not shot down. After I stopped flying with him, because I had been transferred to the *Inspectorate of Fighters* in Berlin, I learned that he had lost yet another wing man. That made thirteen in all during our Battle for Britain.

Myhra: Why were so many of *Adolf Galland's* wing men lost?

W. Horten: *Adolf Galland* always wanted to fly at maximum speed. If you had to follow him and *Galland* had the better and faster *Messerschmitt Bf 109,* then you were always left some distance behind. Whenever we received new aircraft in *JG/26,* he looked for the best and fastest aircraft and reserved those for himself. It would have been better to give the faster *Messerschmitt Bf 109s* to *Galland's* wing men.

Adolf Galland at the time *Walter Horten* received permission to leave *JG/26* to join *General Pascha von Döring* at the *JadgFlugInspektion* or *JFI* (Inspection of Fighters Command), Berlin. 1941.

Myhra: What would *Galland* do if he learned that his wing men were under attack?

W. Horten: First of all we two wing men would attack the enemy. But most of the time *Galland* was flying so far out front that we couldn't see him anymore, although we were also flying fast just trying to keep up with him. So when British *Supermarine Spitfires* or *Hawker Hurricanes* came down, it was these two lonely wing men flying far back behind *Galland* who were always attacked first. If we saw the *Spitfires* coming down, in time, the wing men could turn toward them shooting. If we had sufficient time after first seeing them, we knew that they would lose their wings if they went into a dive and picked up too much speed. So if I saw *Spitfires* coming down and turned to engage them, then I would frequently lose sight of *Galland,* for he would be too far ahead of us, I'd go into a power dive. Sometimes, if *Galland* saw *Spitfires*, he would dive and I'd be alone. I'd call out to him "I have lost you." Once this happened and in looking around, I saw two *Supermarine Spit-*

fires diving on me and attacking. At that moment I had only two possibilities. One was to turn against them firing, but it was already too late. I quickly took the other choice and dove straight down away from the *Spitfire's*...one of which carried a squadron leader's markings. I was going straight down and the *Spitfire's* began following but they had to turn away because during the dive they would be going too fast and their wings might break loose from the high speed.

Myhra: What was the diving speed limit for a *Supermarine Spitfire* compared to the *Messerschmitt Bf 109?*

Adolf Galland on the lecture tour. He died February 9th 1996, age 84 years.

Walter Horten. Photo by author.

W. Horten: For a *Supermarine Spitfire,* it was between 500 and 600 km/h (311 and 373 mph). In a *Messerschmitt Bf 109* I once made a dive up to 900 km/h (559 mph); it was a very strong aircraft. The end of the scale on my air speed indicator was 700 km/h (435 mph) and the needle went completely around and I estimated that my speed had reached about 900 km/h (559 mph). All in all, I flew forty-five sorties with *Adolf Galland*. I shot down nine enemy fighters. Then in September, 1940 an order was issued forbidding *TOs*, such as myself, to go on raids over England. Nevertheless, I flew ten more sorties with *Galland* before I was told via a direct order to stop - and if I didn't stop, then I'd have the pleasure of facing a court martial. About this time, I received a telephone call from *General Kurt von Döring* in Berlin. In World War One, he had been a member of the original *Richthofen Squadron* and he was one of the founding fathers of *3/JG/26* in December, 1939. "*Horten*, I have to build up a general staff here for our fighter wings and I have no one here who knows anything of fighter techniques. Will you come to Berlin to help me?" I told him that if the time came when I could no longer fly sorties with *Major Galland*, then I would accept his offer. So as soon as the order came which stopped me flying as a wing man, I thought I might be able to realize a long-time wish I'd had about working with my brother to build a fighter aircraft which would be better than all others...an all-wing fighter. I wanted to build a twin-engined all-wing fighter. So, in April, 1941, I left *JG/26*. Then in Berlin, as a *TO* in the *Inspectorate of Fighters Command* office, I had to ensure that the aircraft produced by our factories were better, in terms of service-ability, fly-ability, than those of our enemies. We had learned that the Americans had a projected production rate of 3,000 fighters per month and they also could build an equal number of bombers, such as the *Boeing B-17*. We had a production rate at that time of 300 new fighter aircraft per month and to repair a further 80. We were producing between 400 and 500 twin engine bombers per month. England at that time was producing about 500 fighters and 600 bombers per month. So when we put all these production figures together (as well as those aircraft being produced in the USSR for the Russian Front), you can see the number of potential aircraft which we would have to face in combat. These were not very good odds for us. Later the Soviets entered the war but at the beginning, they didn't have very many aircraft. But the Americans gave them considerable numbers of aircraft through the *Lend-Lease* program, such as the *Bell P-39 "Aircobra."* We also saw the *Bell P-39* and the *Curtiss P-40* in North Africa. But at the end of the war in mid 1945, the Soviets were producing 5,000 fighter aircraft per month.

Walter Horten on the starboard wing-root of his *Messerschmitt Bf 109E* during the Battle of Britain. Coastal France location, 1940.

General Pascha von Döring, right, a *Luftwaffe* fighter pilot of World War One with 11 air victories and *Reimar Horten* (with his back to the camera). September, 1940.

A British *Supermarine F.24 "Spitfire"* in your face.

Consolidated Vultee B-24 "*Liberator*" bomber production in the USA. Series production reached 7,800 units. German aircraft leaders such as *Focke-Wulf's Kurt Tank* mistakenly believed that this type of heavy bomber production was impossible by any country including the United States.

Boeing B-17 "*Flying Fortress*" heavy bomber series production. Towards war's end a *Boeing B-17* was coming off the production line every thirty minutes. *Ernst Udet's* comments to *Kurt Tank* were correct that America would mass produce flying machines just as they did automobiles.

Walter Horten as he appeared in 1934 while he was a member of the *Wehrmacht's* 17th Infantry Regiment commanded by *Erwin Rommel*. Photo taken at Goslar, Harz Mountains.

They weren't producing any bombers as such; only fighter bombers and ground attack aircraft. Their entire air force was mainly one for ground support for their troops. That is why *Erich "Bubi" Hartmann* shot down so many enemy aircraft (352); they were mostly all Soviet aircraft. *Hartmann* specialized in attacking Soviet aircraft and the Soviet pilots were typically not that well trained. Their aircraft at the end of the war were good, fast fighters. Plus they were light, pretty well-armed with cannons, and maneuverable, built mainly out of wood. The Soviet designers made them all very simple to operate and maintain in the field, so these aircraft tended to perform well. In general the *Messerschmitt Bf 109* could not reach more than 9,500 meters (31,168 feet) altitude. The *Supermarine Spitfire* had the advantage of reaching a higher altitude. That's a big advantage. The *Supermarine Spitfires* were directed, too, by radio controlx plus with their advantage of more height they were good. Our *Messerschmitt Bf 109's* were not that good in maneuverability in terms of climb. If a maneuver was necessary to gain additional altitude, let's say 1,000 meters (3,281 feet) plus an 360 degree turn, we'd lose 1,000 meters. Those *Spitfire* pilots, I believe, were smiling when they saw our situation. The *Spitfire* pilot could dive faster, and could zoom back up better than our *Messerschmitt Bf 109*. We had a smaller wing area and that was a very big disadvantage for us. This is why *Galland* once said to *Göring* "Give me *Spitfires*." *Galland* knew that the *Supermarine Spitfire* climbed faster to achieve altitude. I know this, too, because we had made all-wing sailplanes which always had a lower wing-loading than our competitors. Our aircraft were all wing surface and that was very good for achieving altitude. But *Galland* misunderstood. I told him that we have a modified version of the *Messerschmitt Bf 109* which is as good as a *Supermarine Spitfire*. It's great at high altitudes. This was our *Messerschmitt Bf 109T-2 "Traeger"* (aircraft carrier) which had been designed for use on our (never completed) aircraft carrier the *Graf Zeppelin*. To get this *Messerschmitt AG* had taken an *Messerschmitt Bf 109E* and modified its center section making it wider. For example, the *Messerschmitt Bf 109 "Emil"* had about a 10 meter (32 foot 8 inch) wing span while the *Messerschmitt Bf 109T-2* had a wing span of 13.8 meters (45 feet 3 inches). All in all it had more wing area and that was better. It was clear to me that the *Messerschmitt Bf 109T-2* would be better at higher altitudes and would also be faster compared to the *Messerschmitt Bf 109E*. It would have a lower stall speed due to the fact that with more wing area you will be in a situation where the aircraft will not stall as easily as before because of the lower wing loading.

Myhra: How much more higher altitude would the *Messerschmitt Bf 109T-2* have given you over the *Messerschmitt Bf 109E*?

W. Horten: From 9,500 meters to about 12,000 meters (31,168 to 36,000 feet) total altitude. It would have been better than the *Supermarine Spitfire*. But *Adolf Galland* didn't understand all this wing-span talk because he felt that any aircraft with a longer wing span would have to be slower in forward speed. But *Galland* seldom flew at high altitudes. Most of his flying was at medium altitudes such as 4,000 meters (13,123 feet). At that height the *Messerschmitt Bf 109E* was a littler faster but at higher altitudes...but with more span, wing area and consequently a higher aspect ratio...this *Messerschmitt Bf 109T-2* would have been very fast. The *Messerschmitt Bf 109E* was not very maneuverable at high altitudes, where it would stall out. I would say that a fighter squadron which needed high altitude cover would have benefitted from the *Messerschmitt Bf 109T-2*. The dive bomber wings would have had better protection with the *Messerschmitt Bf 109T-2*, too. We had flown an *Messerschmitt Bf 109T-2* in Norway and this is how we learned about its far better performance over the *Messerschmitt Bf109E*. Most of the *Messerschmitt Bf 109T-2s* built were assigned to *2/JG/11* and *1/JG/77*. *Galland* called me "*Langer* who has dreams" (tall one who has dreams). In other words he felt that my belief in the *Messerschmitt Bf 109T-2* was dream-like and not real. *Galland* believed that the *Messerschmitt Bf 109T-2* would not be faster than the *Messerschmitt Bf 109E*. While that may have been correct in medium heights, it was not so at higher altitudes. *Galland* just couldn't understand this because he was not an engineer nor a statistician. *Galland* hadn't done performance calculation in different altitudes. He didn't understand no matter what I'd tell him, it just didn't matter. I just couldn't reach him. Yet *Galland* admitted

PRODUCTION CHART of GOODS and MANPOWER–WORLD WAR II

	Year	USA	Britain	Germany	Japan	USSR
Tanks				Tanks, self-propelled guns, and assault-guns	Medium and light tanks	
	1940	300	1,400	1,600	Not available	2,800
	1941	4,100	4,800	3,800	1,000	6,400
	1942	25,000	8,600	6,300	1,200	24,700
	1943	29,500	7,500	12,100	800	24,000
	1944	17,600	4,600	19,000	300	29,000
	1945	12,000	Not available	3,900 (Jan-Mar)	100 (Apr-July)	15,400 (Jan-June)
Warships			Displacement tons	Submarines only. Few major surface vessels were built during the war	Fiscal year	
	1940	52,600 (July-Dec)	263,200	23,800 tons	94,700	Not available
	1941	210,300	437,200	147,800	225,200	
	1942	859,500	481,400	193,000	254,000	
	1943	2,667,400	609,600	211,400	230,100	
	1944	3,176,800	583,400	275,300	468,400	
	1945	1,190,000 (Jan-June)	312,800 (Jan-Sept)	54,900 (Jan-May)	66,700 (Apr-July)	
Merchant ships		Gross tons (ships of 2,000 tons and over)	Gross tons (ships of 100 tons and over)	Figures not available; production probably negligible	Gross tons (ships of 500 tons and over)	
	1940	444,700	810,000		293,600	Not available
	1941	749,100	1,156,000		210,400	
	1942	5,392,800	1,301,000		260,100	
	1943	12,485,600	1,204,000		769,100	
	1944	11,403,200	1,014,000		1,699,200	
	1945	7,614,900	856,000 (Jan-Sept)		559,600 (Jan-Aug)	
Aircraft	1940	6,100	15,000	10,200	4,800	7,000
	1941	19,400	20,100	11,000	5,100	12,500
	1942	47,800	23,600	14,200	8,900	26,000
	1943	85,900	26,200	25,200	16,700	37,000
	1944	96,300	26,500	39,600	28,200	40,000
	1945	46,000 (Jan-Aug)	12,100	Not available	11,100	35,000
Manpower		On June 30 of each year		On May 31 of each year		
	1940	458,300	2,212,000	5,600,000	1,723,200	2,500,000
	1941	1,795,000	3,278,000	7,200,000	2,411,400	4,207,000
	1942	3,844,500	3,784,000	8,600,000	2,829,400	9,000,000
	1943	8,918,600	4,300,000	9,500,000	3,808,200	10,000,000
	1944	11,241,200	4,500,000	9,100,000	5,365,000	12,400,000
	1945	11,858,500	4,653,000	Not available	7,193,200 (Aug 1945)	10,800,000

Production chart of goods and manpower by major countries in World War Two. For example, the United States had a total aircraft production of 86,900 aircraft of all types in 1943 and 96,300 aircraft in 1944. Germany had a total of 25,200 aircraft of all types in 1943 and 39,600 aircraft in 1944. Thus, the United States produced 183,200 aircraft of all types 1943-1944 while Germany produced a total of 64,800 aircraft for the same period of time.

Front row left to right: *Majors Adolf Galland* and *Gotthardt Handrick*. Summer, 1940. *Handrick* was lost over England on August 21st 1940.

Conference about 1938: left *Wilhelm Keitel*, *Adolf Hitler*, *Hermann Göring*, and *Ernst Udet*. At war's end *Keitel* had been hanged by order of the Nuremburg Tribunal after being convicted of war crimes. He was hanged on October 16th 1945. The other three in the photograph committed suicide, too.

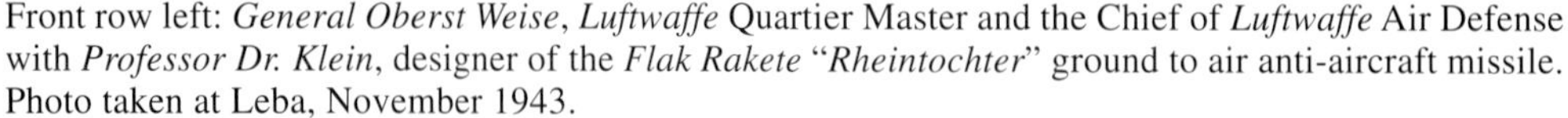

Front row left: *General Oberst Weise*, *Luftwaffe* Quartier Master and the Chief of *Luftwaffe* Air Defense with *Professor Dr. Klein*, designer of the *Flak Rakete "Rheintochter"* ground to air anti-aircraft missile. Photo taken at Leba, November 1943.

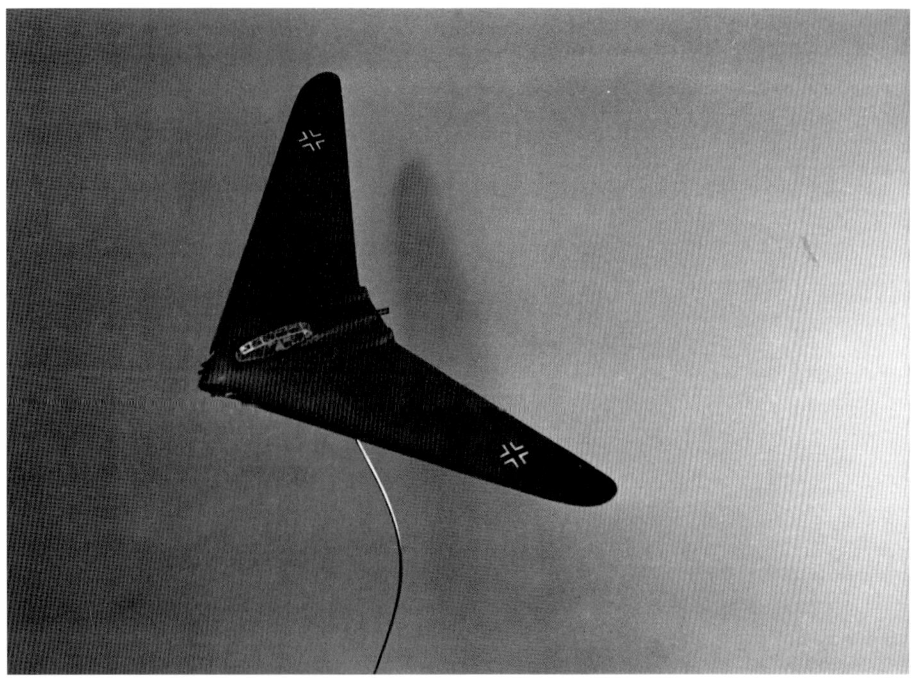

The initial turbojet powered fighter concept design for what was being called the *Horten Ho 9*. Scale model by the *Horten Flugzeugbau*. Early 1940s. It was really a *Horten Ho 7* with turbojet engines instead of twin propellers.

A pen and ink general arrangement drawing of the initial *Horten Ho 9* turbojet powered fighter concept design from the *Horten Flugzeugbau*. Early 1940s.

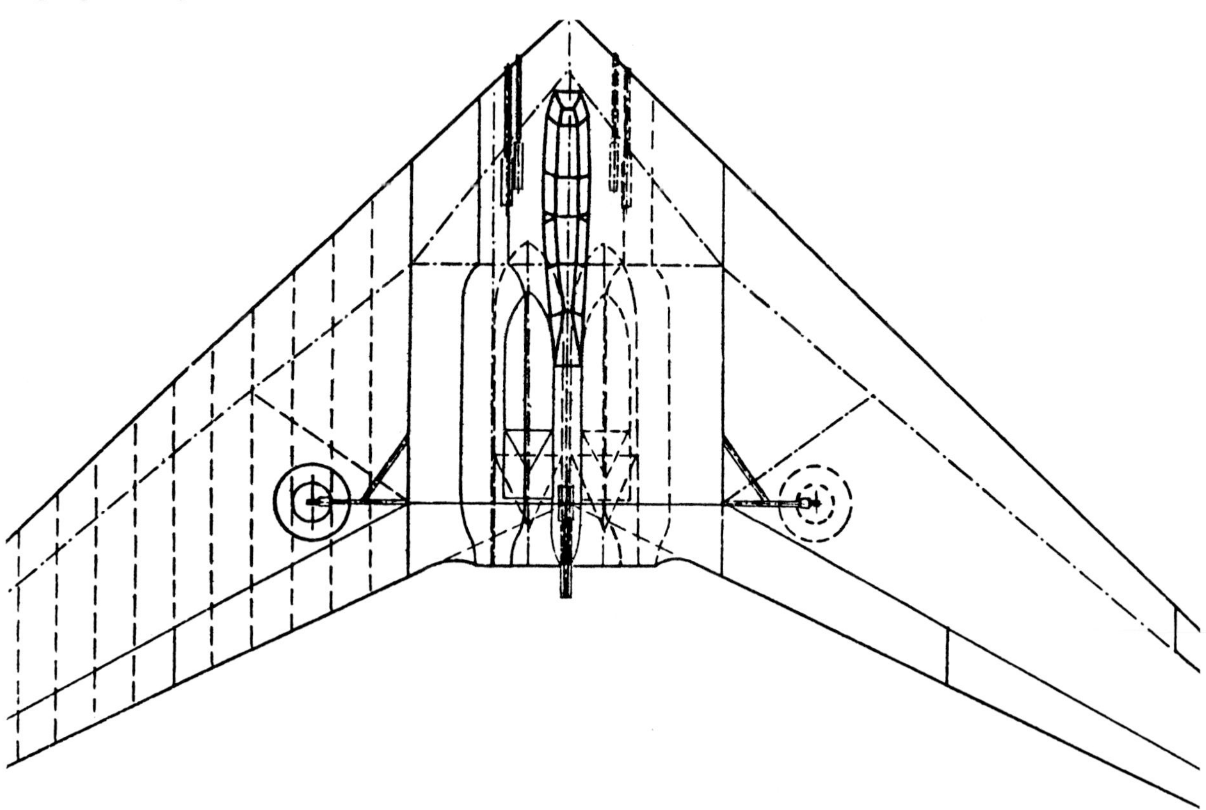

Front-on view of an early *Horten Ho 9* turbojet-powered fighter concept design. Scale model built by the *Horten Flugzeugbau* in the early 1940s.

A pen and ink drawing by *Horten Flugzeugbau* of their proposed turbojet powered fighter concept *Horten Ho 9*. Featured is the nose of the fighter's center section.

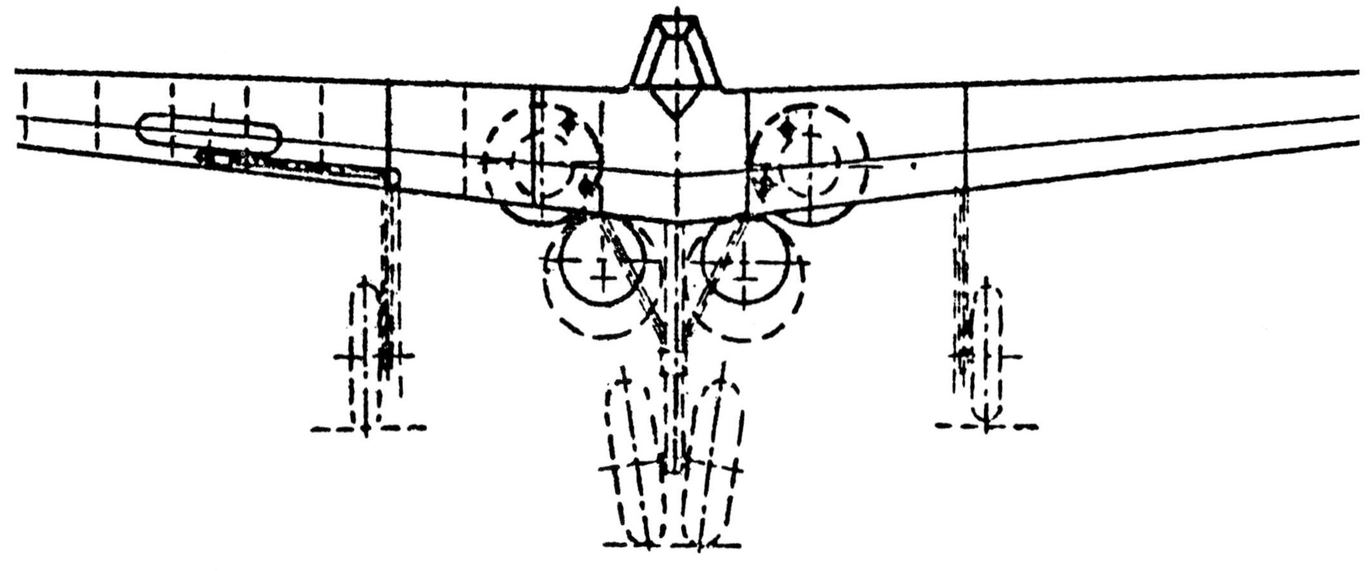

Bramo/BMW P.3302 (*002*) turbojet engine project of 1940 seen from its port side. Its air intake is left and the exhaust nozzle right. The *Horten's* were planning on installing two of these early turbojet engines in their *Horten Ho 9* fighter concept, however, *BMW* abandoned work on this engine for its failure to achieve design thrust. This decision would produce severe strain on the *Horten* Flugzeugbau as they waited for *BMW* to redesign their *BMW 3302* into what would be called the *BMW 003*. Finally, the *Horten's* would have to use the larger diameter *Junkers Jumo 004*. All this caused delays and continuous re-engineering.

Pen and ink starboard side view drawing of the *Horten Ho 9* turbojet-powered evolving fighter concept design of 1941/1942. Also featured in this drawing is the rear gunner's position. Beneath the aircraft hang two 551 pound (*SC* 250 kilogram) bombs.

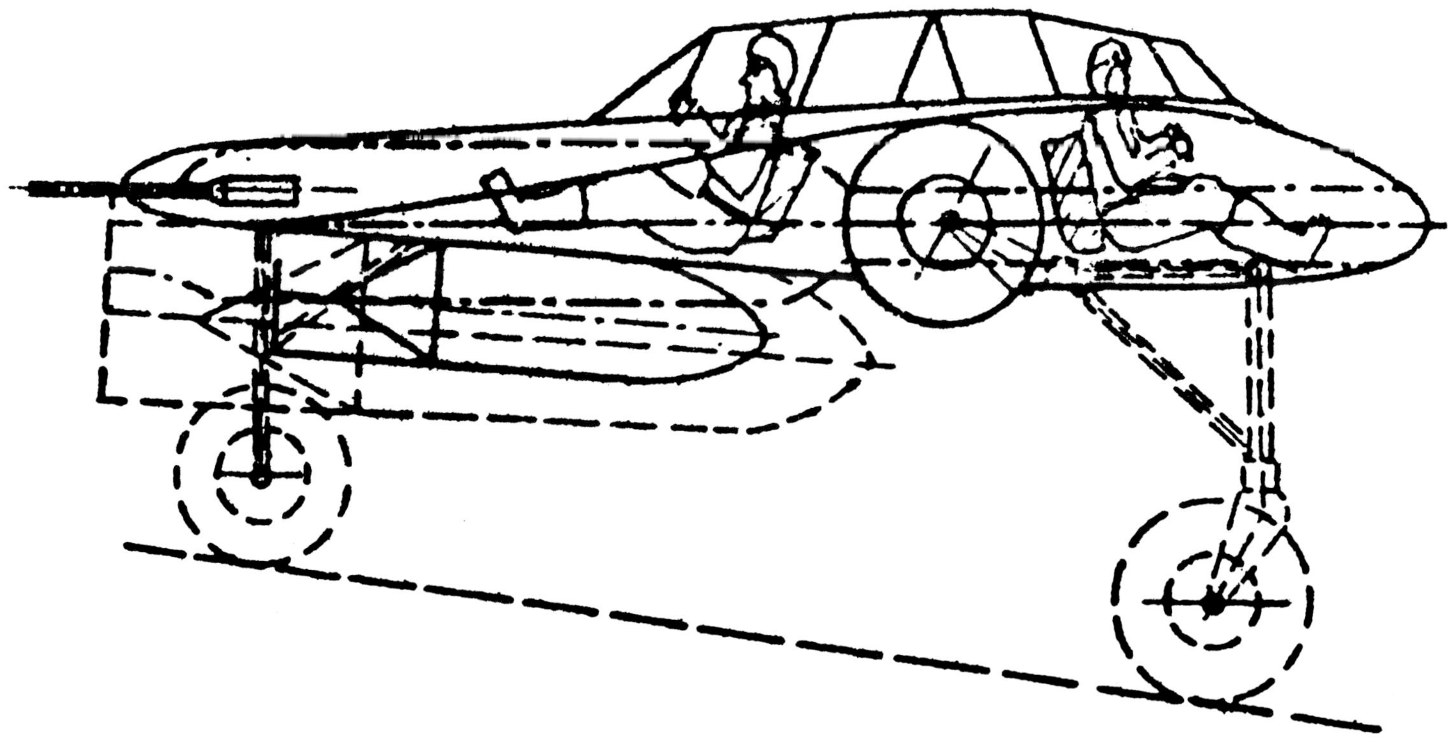

A *Messerschmitt Bf 109* shot down over England during the Battle for Britain and its pilot captured. This *Messerschmitt Bf 109* is seen on public display in the main square at Bolton, Lancashire, England. 1941.

A *Luftwaffe* pilot, pulled from the English Channel during the Battle for Britain, arrives in England as a POW. He was lucky; many *Luftwaffe* pilots who found themselves in the English Channel drowned before they could be rescued....by the British or their *Luftwaffe* sea rescue teams.

General von Döring, front, and *Major Witt* wait in the snow under the port wing of a *Junkers Ju 52/3m*. Dortmund, February 1940.

that the poor performance of the *Messerschmitt Bf 109E* had caused *JG/26* much blood and the loss of many, many of our pilots. In *JG26* we had lost many of our pilots when they were diving down from 8,500 meters (27,887 feet) when the Spitfire reached much higher speeds. It was then that *Galland* went to see *Göring* and said "give us *Spitfires*" and *Göring* replied that *JG/26* should go over to England and get them. Therefore, I was coming to believe more and more that a much better airplane would be an all-wing with the entire wing span as lift area. It would have been a much better aircraft for high altitudes. At that time we did not have pressurized cockpit cabins and we could not fly above 12,000 meters (39,370 feet) because our blood would boil and then the pilot would black out and die. We later experimented with pressure suits at our *Horten Flugzeugbau*-Göttingen because our all-wing with its large wing area could approach 12,000 meters in height and beyond. The *Supermarine Spitfires* would be below us, way below and ending up stalling trying to reach us. But *Galland* didn't understand all this. It was awful that he didn't at least listen to some of this talk. *Galland* seldom picked up advice from other people. He also rejected my gunnery technique which I used to shoot-down English aircraft. During my short career as a fighter pilot with *JG/26* I was officially credited with seven kills but actually had nine.

Myhra: Why did *Adolf Galland* wait so long to test-fly the *Messerschmitt Me 262?* He didn't fly it until 1944. When he did he reported that he felt that he "was being pushed by angels."

W. Horten: He would only act on his own ideas. Never ideas from other people. *Adolf Galland* was the first combat-pilot to flight test the *Messerschmitt Me 262*. He flew this machine as soon as possible and was very excited about it. But afterward, it was demonstrated before *Adolf Hitler*. He asked *Willy Messerschmitt* if it was possible for this aircraft to carry a bomb? *Messerschmitt* said, "Well, yes, this aircraft can do it." Upon hearing this *Hitler* said we'll get this aircraft to a bomber wing because the *Heinkel He 111* was no good and neither was the *Junkers Ju 88. Hitler* wanted the *Messerschmitt Me 262* to be his "*Blitzbomber*" to counter the Allied invasion. At the time *Galland* flew the *Messerschmitt Me 262 it had only just* appeared and was not yet armed. I think that *Galland* suggested that the *Messerschmitt Me 262* be armed with four *MK 108* short-barrel 30 mm caliber cannons which was only good for short-distance shooting. At the same time *Galland* stated that he was only interested in close-in dog-fighting, directly behind the enemy so he didn't need high-velocity guns.

Myhra: Why do you believe *Adolf Galland* didn't want the *Messerschmitt Me 262* sooner?

Horst Geyer, center, *Walter Horten's JG/26 Technical Officer* replacement approved by *Galland. Geyer* was *Ernst Udet's* personal pilot and after his suicide in November 1941 *Guyer* was assigned duties on the Russian *Front*. Left, *Fritz Wendel, Messerschmitt AG* test pilot and right, *Adolf Galland.*

W. Horten: Well now *Adolf Galland* was fighting against the decision made by *Adolf Hitler* who wanted to give this aircraft to bomber pilots and if this happened it would have no impact on the *Boeing B-17* bomber streams. Bomber pilots could not use the *Messerschmitt Me 262* like fighter pilots could. I know this because initially I had been trained as a bomber pilot. Therefore this fine aircraft was not initially used against American bombers. Fighter wing *JG/400* was later scheduled to receive the *Horten Ho 229* because the *Messerschmitt Me 163* was no good being too light, couldn't dive quickly away fast enough from *North American P-51s*, plus they could also catch up with it. Therefore, the *Quartier Meister* of the *Luftwaffe* said that our *Horten Ho 229* would be a better aircraft for bringing down *Boeing B-17* bombers.

Oberst Siegfried Knemeyer, left, an aid, an aid, and *Reimar Horten*. Oranienburg Air Base. August 1944.

A *Messerschmitt Bf 109-T-2*. This particular machine belonged to *2nd/JG/11* or *1st/JG/77*.

The December 8th 1938 launching of the German aircraft carrier *Graf Zeppelin* at the Kiel shipyard.

Myhra: What was the *Quartier Meister's* name?

W. Horten: *General Weise*. He wanted to equip *JG/400* with our *Horten Ho 229* as the successor to the *Messerschmitt Me 163*. He had ordered that we build up this new fighter group. *Wolfgang Späte* was to be the leader of this group. Previously he had commanded the *Test Wing 16* (EK16) which was the training unit, working the Me163 up to operational standard. I had command of over 1,000 soldiers. The "devil's tail" of the *Kommando* unit was not included and this was a special team from Rechlin to help EK *16* to get the *Messerschmitt Me 163* flightworthy. The aerodrome, the hangars, and accommodation was only to be occupied by my new fighter group. *JG/400*, which was to be just the beginning. The development of new fighters to replace the *Messerschmitt Me 163* was very slow so we were going to install in its place the *Horten Ho 229*. The first group was to be IV/*JG/54*. But *Wolfgang Späte* could not have known about this decision of *General Weise*. At that time, too, *Galland* was not yet General of the fighter-wing. It was *General Gallop* and he was all right. *Gallop* would have accepted our *Horten Ho 229*. I knew *Gallop* personally and he told me that if the *Horten Ho 229* functioned well, handled well, and was a good gun platform, then he'd take it. Remember the *Horten Ho 229* was a *1000x1000x1000* fighter-bomber. One thousand *kilometers* per hour

Walter Horten's Messerschmitt Bf 109E of *JG/26* and showing seven of his nine kills on the rudder.

speed, one thousand kilometer range and return, and one thousand kilometer bomb load (621 mph, 621 miles, 2,205 pounds). This bomb load might be two 500 kilogramme (1,102 pound) bombs which is a good load. Then you could put external tanks on, too, giving you even more range. The *Horten Ho 229* would have a range which would have allowed you to roam all across the British Isles where there were more than 2,000 to 3,000 Allied fighters and bombers stationed. The whole British Isles was like an aerodrome or a giant aircraft carrier.

Myhra: What is the difference between *JG/400* and *JG/54?*

W. Horten: The *RLM* was changing numbers. I have never found out exactly what was planned for fighter wing *JG/400* but it was not to be whatever was initially proposed. The *RLM* was planing first that it be a fighter group and if that functioned well, then the *RLM* was planning to expand it into a wing made up of three or four groups.

Myhra: What about *JG/54?*

W. Horten: This would have been the IV group of fighter wing *JG/54*. *Wolfgang Späte* was commander then of *JG/400* and would have also been commander of *JG/54*. Later it was...it got a different name...only the first group, a smaller group, *JG/54*. In reality it was the same organization, pilot training, and carrying out acceptance tests on newly delivered aircraft. It was only a different name. It would be interesting to find out when the *RLM*-people realised that the *Messerschmitt Me 163* was useless. Escort fighters flying

General of Fighters Adolf Galland listening intently to his *führer Adolf Hitler*.

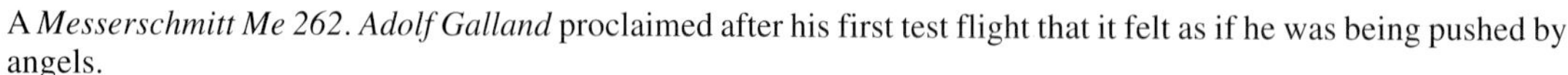

A *Messerschmitt Me 262*. *Adolf Galland* proclaimed after his first test flight that it felt as if he was being pushed by angels.

Ernst Udet doing what he liked best – piloting an airplane. He was the wrong man for a desk job. Being placed as technical director in the *RLM* was a disaster...for the *Luftwaffe* and *Udet* personally.

with the *Boeing B-17* ,especially the *North American P-51,* were a real threat to the *Messerschmitt Me 163* when this rocket-powered interceptor had used all its fuel...when it was completely light and empty. The *Messerschmitt Me 163* couldn't then dive as quickly as the *North American P-51's*. The *Messerschmitt Me 163* was absolutely helpless and it was real nonsense to make a wing or group out of them. (Unsurprisingly an inaccurate recollection, Spate was with JG54, transferred to the group which became EK16 and was later drafted back to JG54 before being returned to JG400 which he left to fly Me.262's with JG7… PW)

Myhra: Who decided to establish an *Messerschmitt Me 163 wing ?*

W. Horten: *Adolf Galland*. Before all of this wing nonsense originated, the *Messerschmitt Me 163* was only intended as a research aircraft to find out about the problems in reaching the speed of sound and then to test the ability of this aircraft to go through the so-called sound barrier. The *Messerschmitt Me 163* made a world's speed record and after this *RLM*-people were so enthusiastic that they said "it could be an interceptor." But they did not think it through to the end. It couldn't intercept beneath a bomber group. If it came near one it faced strong anti-aircraft fire, intensive fire, and then *North American P-51s*. If all this happened then the *Messerschmitt Me 163* flew out to the bomber pack, flew back, and thus all its fuel was consumed with nothing achieved. Once they were on their way back to their grass-strip runway, the *North American P-51s* went right down after them. Later after the Allied invasion we couldn't even operate them effectively. We always had to change over to other bases. This aircraft was not truly operational. *Wolfgang Späte* left it to go to *JG/400*. *JG/400* was not real but existed only on paper. *Späte* was used as a group commander for *JG/54.* He stayed with this fighter group until the end of the war. *Späte* also flew some *Messerschmitt Me 262s*. The *Messerschmitt Me 163s* aerodrome was Brandis/Leipzig. I had seen *Späte* there because I had gone there to investigate the possibility of moving our Göttingen *Horten Ho 9* workshop to Brandis/Leipzig. This was in the last minutes of the war.

Myhra: A *Horten Ho 7* was found at Brandis/Leipzig by the American Army.

W. Horten: Oh sure, that is possible and we had other *Horten* allwings there as well.

Myhra: The *Horten Ho 9 V1* sailplane was found there, too.

W. Horten: The *Horten Ho 9 V1* had been at the Oranienburg Air Base. I don't recall when it was taken to Brandis but it was scrapped by the Americans. Late in the war we had to protect the airdromes containing the *Messerschmitt Me 163* with *Focke-Wullf Fw 190's*. It was also necessary to protect the *Messerschmitt Me 163* when it came down to land. *North American P-51s* tried to catch the *Messerschmit Me 163* in their final landing approach. *JG/400*, the test wing for the *Messerschmitt Me 163*, was to build up a IV fighter group known as *JG/54* with *Focke-Wulf Fw 190s* to protect the aerodromes. When the *Messerschmitt Me 163s* were found to be too little and too small to accomplish much of anything, *JG/54* used their *Focke-Wulf Fw 190s* in raids against the Allies. A problem with the *Messerschmitt Me 262* is that you needed much longer runways that the existing aerodromes had. Only three aerodromes had sufficient length for the *Messerschmitt Me 262* to take-off and these were bombed by the Americans. If we filled in all the bomb craters we could only use them for two or three days and reconnaissance photos brought the bombers back again with more bombs. So we had to place the *Messerschmitt Me 262s* outside the aero-

Erhard Milch (left) and *Ernst Udet* (right), two rivals for control of aircraft development within the *RLM...Milch* was victorious.

The *RLM* building in Berlin. By war's end it would be turned into rubble.

Oberst Artur Eschenauer. He was the *Horten* brothers strong, creative supporter throughout the war within the *Luftwaffe's Quarter Masters Office.*

dromes, out in the woods next to *Autobahns* where they could use the *Autobahn* as their run way.

Myhra: What year was it when *General von Döring* called you to join his staff at the *Inspection of Fighters Command* in Berlin?

W. Horten: That was in April, 1941, when he telephoned me. I went to join him at *RLM*-Berlin in May, 1941. As you know all *Technical Officers* (TO's) in the fighter groups were forbidden to do any combat flying by general order in September, 1940. I had first met *General von Döring* in 1937, or 1938. He was the leader of III/*JG/26* and probably joined *JG/26* at the end of 1939. Once, during the Battle of Britain when the squadron leader of I/*JG/26 Major Gotthardt Handrick* failed to return, *Papi Cousine*, a friend of mine came to me and asked if I wanted to take over *Handrick's* squadron? "I'm a *TO*; how can that be," I asked him? Think it over and tell me tomorrow," he told me. It was a really big decision I had to make. Either remain on the Western Front as a squadron leader, or go to Berlin with *von Döring* and maybe work with my brother *Reimar* on developing a twin-engine all-wing fighter. I decided to go on to Berlin and remain in the technical role of things, to see if we could create an aircraft which would be more effective in our war effort. I was thinking at that time of an aircraft with two high-velocity cannons with about 1,100 meters (3,609 feet) per second velocity. Such cannons were needed in order to effectively bring down a *Boeing B-17* because these huge aircraft began shooting at you when you came within 800 meters (2,625 feet). Each *Boeing B-17* had twelve .50 caliber machine guns, so if you had a squad-

The world's first turbojet-powered aircraft – the experimental *Heinkel He 178*.

ron of 40 *Boeing B-17* bombers tightly grouped together in a bombing raid, you had the effective fire power of between 400 and 500 guns!

Myhra: You said "no," then, to taking over *Handrick's* group *I/JG/ 26?*

W. Horten: Yes. I decided that if I did take *I/JG/26,* then I might not be able to develop the all-wing fighter I had been thinking about. I felt that I could do only one of two things. My choice had to be what would be better for me in our war effort. If I joined the *Inspection of Fighters Comannd*, would *von Döring* allow me to build the all-wing fighter I was thinking about? *Ernst Udet* was *von Döring's* boss. I decided to accept *von Döring's* offer in Berlin. I thought, too, that if I continued flying against the British, *I* might lose my life in the process. Our older brother *Wolfram* already had died in his *Messerschmitt Bf 110* (actually this was in an He.111) off the coast of France while dropping sea mines; one accidently blew up when it hit the water. *Ernst Udet* had pretty much protected me and *Reimar* since the time we first met on the *Rhön/ Wasserkuppe* and he became aware of our efforts to prefect a design for an all-wing sailplane. So because *Udet* was in Berlin at the *RLM,* I thought if I had the opportunity to go to work for *von Döring,* then *Udet* might continue to help us realise our all wing fighter. With *Udet's* help, perhaps *von Döring* could arrange for its acceptance within the *RLM*.

Myhra: At this time were you already thinking of building an all-wing fighter?

W. Horten: Yes

Myhra: What type of engines would have powered your all-wing...piston?

W. Horten: No, turbines.

Myhra: How did you become aware of the German turbines—weren't these advanced engine developments highly secret in early 1940?

W. Horten: *Heinkel AG* produced the first aircraft turbines in 1938. *Bramo, Junkers Jumo,* and *BMW* followed and by 1940 each company had a working turbojet engine under development.

Myhra: Tell me about the choice of a turbojet engine for use in the *Horten Ho 9*.

W. Horten: My first choice had been to use *Bramo/BMW P*.3302 (*002*) turbines because they had a smaller overall diameter than the *Junkers Jumo 004*. Plus I was told by *Dr.-Ing. Hermann Oestrich* that his *Bramo/BMW 002s* might be available before the *Junkers Jumo 004Bs* of *Dr.-Ing. Anselm Franz*. So by using the *BMW* model, we would not need to have so thick of a wing root and center section as well. I knew *Dr. Oestrich* at *BMW* better than *Franz* and he was going to give us two *Bramo/BMW 002s*. This was in late 1941. Later, after the war, *Dr. Oestrich* went to France. I think he has since died. I had heard about all the research going in to turbojet engines as part of my job in the *Inspectorate of Fighters Command* from *General Diesing*. I did not have any trouble meeting the people out in industry who were developing turbine engines, for the *Horten* brothers were well-known throughout the German aircraft industry from our all-wing aircraft experiments at the *Rhön/Wasserkuppe*. Also, I had let it be known that my brother and I would like to develop a turbine-powered all-wing aircraft. *Dr. Oestrich*, also thought that it would be a good idea. He was willing to give us two of his *Bramo/BMW 3302* turbojet engines once he had these powerplants certified for aircraft use.

Myhra: The *Bramo/BMW P.3302* small diameter turbine program was abandoned. Then *BMW* started development on a six-stage compressor turbine known as the *Bramo/BMW 003*. It was abandoned in favor of a seven-stage compressor known also as the *BMW 003A*. Tell me how you obtained those *004B* turbines from *Junkers Jumo*?

W. Horten: Well, after the *Bramo/BMW P.3302* was canceled we received two empty 6-compressor stage *003* engines from *BMW*. After a while we learned from *Dr. Oestrich* that their *003* turbojet project, too, had to be redesigned and so their engines would not be available on time as we all had planned. *Dr. Oestrich* suggested that we go and see *Dr. Franz* at *Junkers Jumo* because he believed that their turbine program was proceeding at a faster rate than his at *BMW*. I went over to Dessau and met with *Dr. Franz* to see if we might obtain two of his *Junkers Jumo 004B* turbines at a future date? He said yes, we could. However, there would be a major problem for us in switching turbines. It appeared that *Franz's Junkers Jumo 004Bs* had a larger diameter that *Dr. Oestrich's BMW 003s*. *Reimar* already had cut and welded up a center-section frame for the *Horten Ho 9* to hold two turbines with an outside diameter with the measurements of the 6-stage compressor *BMW 003*. In order to use the *004B* from *Junkers Jumo,* we would have to modify the center section significantly. It had to become thicker in order to install *Dr. Franz's Junkers Jumo 004Bs*. I think the turbines from *Dr. Oestrich* were about 10 centimeters (4 inches) smaller in diameter. This modification took considerable time.

Myhra: Why did you seek out *Bramo/BMW 002s* then *BMW 003s* in the first place? Why not *Junkers Jumo 004Bs*?

W. Horten: The *Bramo/BMW 002* turbojet engine program was the first one I learned about upon my arrival at the *Inspectorate of Fighters Command*. In fact *Dr. Oestrich* was the first turbine manufacturer I met at the *RLM* because he frequently came in the building. His offices were not too far away at Berlin-Spandau. After the first time meeting him, he and I talked often. I liked him and he was a nice person, friendly, helpful, and excited about our proposed turbojet-powered all wing fighter idea. This is how the *Hortens* obtained two empty *Bramo/BMW 003* turbines in late 1941. It was because of *Dr. Oestrich's* enthusiasm for us that he allowed me to study the various secret specifications of the *BMW 003*, its physical dimensions, its power curve, fuel consumption at various altitudes, and so on. I immediately passed my hand-drawn copies on to *Reimar* for use in his planning our *Horten Ho 9*. This is how we got started on the *Horten Ho 9* in 1941 thanks in great measure to *Dr. Oestrich*. What I did in the early 1940's to develop support and obtain components for my German "*Mosquito*" is today called "networking."

Myhra: Were your *Horten Ho 5* and *Horten Ho 7* machines considered by you and your brother to be future fighter designs?

W. Horten: No. These aircraft were small piston-engined all-wings mainly for testing and experimentation. Our *Horten Ho 7*, for example had more powerful engines than the *Horten Ho 5,* but the *Horten Ho 7* was only thought of as a trainer type for pilots going on to fly the *Horten Ho 229*.

Myhra: So you were thinking of an entirely new all-wing design for your fighter, then?

W. Horten: Yes, but it was not a new idea for me. *Ernst Udet*, who was the person protecting us and our all-wing ideas, also followed our progress. Later in Berlin, I got in touch with *General Kurt Diesing* and *Oberst Siegfried Knemeyer*. Both of these men were general staff within the *RLM* Department of Technical Development of Aircraft and Armament. *General Diesing* was the man who headed up the *RLM's* technical staff. Later *Oberst Knemeyer* became chief of the technical staff after *Udet's* suicide in November, 1941. *Knemeyer* was very important and he flew several of our sailplanes and powered aircraft, including the *Horten Ho 7*. He generally found them to be satisfying and pleasing to fly. *Knemeyer* told me several times that our all-wing was the "right layout" for a long-range bomber.

Myhra: Wasn't *Oberst Siegfried Knemeyer* heavily involved in the "*Amerkia Bomber Project*?" He was working very hard in 1944 to obtain a long range bomber to carry a radiation-spreading device or a biological weapon to the United States and return non stop. Both items were anti-population weapons for mass destruction with minimal physical damage. (A so called "dirty bomb" where radio active material is packed around a conventional bomb, causing death by radiation – rather than a nuclear explosion – because the Nazi's had failed to develop a true nuclear weapon PW)

W. Horten: Yes. But at that time, neither *Reimar* or I had any thoughts of a long-range bomber project. Instead we were struggling to finish our *Horten Ho 9 V2* fighter with its promised *3x1000* performance. *Oberst Siegfried Knemeyer* was not interested much in fighter aircraft, but late in 1944 around Christmas time, he began talking to us about an all-wing with 11,000 kilometer (6,835 mile) range! We could not understand why he was talking of bombers when we desperately needed better and faster fighters. Well, when he asked me if the *Hortens* could build a long-range all-wing bomber, I didn't ask him why it was needed now. Only later did we receive an explanation. *General Diesing* told me that *Adolf Hitler* wanted a long-range bomber aircraft with outstanding operational requirements able to fly to *America* and return without refueling. But the mystery was that this aircraft was only to carry only one 1,000 kilograms (2,205 pound) bomb! One bomb? My brother and I couldn't understand why only one bomb? What could one bomb accomplish? It was later that we learned that *Oberst Knemeyer* was thinking of two types of bombs: some sort of radiation-spreading device or possibly a type of biological weapon, too. We were even strictly forbidden to use the term "atomic bomb." At one time *Siegfried Knemeyer*, *Hermann Göring*, *Karl-Otto Saur*, *Fritz Sauckel*, and so on wanted to use a two stage version *A-4* (*V2*) rocket developed by *Wernher von Braun* to carry radioactive or biological weapons to a target, but the standard *V2* would have only reached London and not the USA. For this reason, *Reichsmarshall Göring* wanted to have a long-range bomber. And this was near the end of the war. We never heard anything about an atomic bomb. But *Knemeyer* had received an order to develop and build an aircraft capable of delivering a radiation/biological spreading device to the United States. (Plans for a modified V2 with its "warhead bay" in its mid section, rather than the nose, were later discovered PW)

Myhra: Tell me about your work within the *JagdFlugInspektion (Inspectorate of Fighters Command)*?

W. Horten: My job was to take a look at all new aircraft related developments throughout the German aircraft industry. These included aircraft under development such as the *Messerschmitt Me 163* and the *Messerschmitt Me 262*. After I left *Adolf Galland* and *JG/26* and went to Berlin, my general task was to review the overall suitability of these new developments to the *Luftwaffe* for potential fighter development. I had to look at the value that all these new projects would bring to our shooting war. This included new weapons, new facilities, new faster aero engines, and so on. About the time I joined the *Inspecorate of Fighters Command* there was considerable interest and activity in developing the turbojet engine for fighter aircraft use and to a lesser extent, in bombers and reconnaissance aircraft. In 1942 I went over to Göttingen to establish a *Sonder Kommando* for the *Horten Ho 9*. I had been thinking that an all-wing design like ours would make a good fast fighter ever since our experience in loosing the Battle for Britain. *Ernst Udet*, of course, had talked a lot about America's huge potential for mass producing fighters and bombers. So I believed along with many other people that Germany needed to develop many fast fighters in order to avoid being bombed and losing the war. At first when I mentioned this proposed aircraft to *Major Galland*, he didn't see any reason for its construction. When I told him I was going to Berlin and possibly develop our *Horten Ho 9* fighter, all he said was okay but you'll have to find me another *TO* before you go. I found him a good man by the name of *Horst Geyer*. He had been *Udet's* personal pilot and when *Udet* died *Geyer* was transferred to the Russian Front. He shot down 36 Soviet aircraft. I contacted him and asked if he'd like to take my place as *TO* for *JG/26*. He agreed. *Udet* had been anxious to continue development of new aircraft ideas as well as turbojet powered fighters, although *Hitler* had issued an order in November, 1940 saying that all development which could not be completed within one year's time had to be stopped immediately. At the end of the war with France at Dunkirk, *Hitler* believed that we had now won the war. So he gave the *Englander's* his hand and freed several hundred thousand Englishmen stranded on Dunkirk. *Hitler* let them all go. It was his gift to Great Britain for their impending surrender. However, the English did not agree nor accept any surrender. The English had refused. The American's refused, too, saying that they would have nothing to do with *Hitler*. Dunkirk was the real turning point of *Hitler's* good fortune in winning victories. After *Hitler's* ban on any new weapons development, *Udet* thought it over privately and suggested to *BMW* and *Junkers Jumo* that they continue their development of the turbines but to keep it quiet and not to advertise. But even by the end of the war in May, 1945 the turbojet engine had still not been perfected. Fuel flow was one of their major problems especially at high speed. Many flame-outs occurred and many pilots lost their lives due to engine flame-out.

Myhra: I recall reading an accident report on the *Messerschmitt Me 262* post-war. Well, the American intelligence mission was questioning ex-*Messerschmitt AG* people about what appeared to be a high percentage of fatal accident rates with the *Messerschmitt Me 262*. The American mission told these ex-*Messerschmitt AG* people that the *Messerschmitt Me 262* suffered 15 fatal accidents during its flight development. *Messerschmitt AG* told interviewers yes, this was correct, but this rate was no higher than on other interceptor fighters. The American's suggested that this statement was contradictory unless the German's accepted an appreciably higher accident rate than they did. Of these 15 accidents, a few were never explained, but the remainder were attributed to the following two causes: (a) stalling of engines and subsequent failure to restart it. (b) engine catching fire, due to incomplete combustion of the fuel in the combustion chamber. In your job with the *Inspectorate of Fighters Command* did your duties include reviewing turbojet engine development and its operating problems in the field?

W. Horten: No, not directly because turbojet engine development came under the General of Fighters as well as under the General of Bombers. All turbine engine work at this time was very secret. However, I was aware of the different stages of development between *Heinkel AG*, *BMW*, and *Junkers Jumo*.

Myhra: Tell me about your long friendship with *Ernst Udet*.

W. Horten: Our initial acquaintance with *Ernst Udet* came about through the National Socialist Flying Corps (*NSFK)-Its Führer* was *Friedrich Christiansen, a holder of the Pour le Merite* from the First World War, who was quite active in gliding. He witnessed our work at the *Rhön/Wasserkuppe* and told *Udet* about these two brothers who were building all-wing sailplanes which seemed to soar better than anything else he'd seen. Later *Christiansen* became a general of the *NSFK* in Berlin. *Udet* and *Christiansen* were good friends and their relationship went back to World War One when they were fighter aces. Apparently we were amongst the subjects about which *Christiansen* spoke to *Udet* during their socializing as old flyers often do. I first met *Ernst Udet* when *Reimar* and I were studying at the Technical High School in Berlin in 1938. This was part of our *Lilienthal Prize*. Afterwards, *Udet* wanted to know if we wished to work for *Heinkel AG*. At this time I made the acquaintance of *Udet's* personal secretary *Sabrina von der Groeben*. *Sabrina* would frequently accompany *Udet* to Paris on official business in the early 1940's. In May, 1941 when I officially joined the *Inspectorate of Fighters Command* I was able to see *Sabrina* more often and we eventually fell in love. We married in 1943 and divorced about ten years later. My job as a *TO* on *General von*

Döring's staff was to submit to his staff various questions of material as it related to the *Luftwaffe's* fighter squadrons. Also development of new aircraft, engine systems, capabilities, and so on. I even had the opportunity in 1941 to fly the *Messerschmitt Me 163* although not with *Helmuth Walter's HWK 509* bi-fuel rocket engine operating. I had been towed up to a high altitude behind an *Messerschmitt Bf 110* aircraft. My opinion was that its handling and flight characteristics were very satisfying.

Myhra: Describe *Ernst Udet*.

W. Horten: *Ernst Udet* was a World War One flying ace, in fact the fourth highest scoring ace in the world and the second highest in Germany. *Hermann Göring* had appointed him head of the *Luftwaffe's* Technical Department. He had been at one time a close friend of *Erhard Milch* and had taken over many of *General Milch's* former responsibilities, as Inspector General of the *Luftwaffe*. However, as *Milch* stated, "*Adolf Hitler* recognized in *Udet* one of our greatest pilots," and he was right. But *Hilter* also saw him as one of the greatest technical experts, but in this *Hitler* was mistaken. *Udet* became the head of a vast bureaucracy, but he did not exercise sufficient control over aircraft production. *Udet* was blamed for equipping the *Luftwaffe* with tactical rather than strategic aircraft and placing emphasis on the *Messerschmitt Bf 109*. *Udet* was very well known in the USA. Older aviation people knew him, but the young people perhaps not as much. *Udet* was put in competition with *Milch*. *Udet* was very successful in his development of the *Junkers Ju 87* dive-bomber, which made the invasion of Poland very speedy. The fall of France, too, was credited to the use of the dive-bomber, but all the dive bombers -whether in Poland, or in France—had been heavily protected by *Messerschmitt Bf 109s*. The big success with dive bombers came to an end in our Battle for Britain after July, 1940 because they could no longer be protected by *Messerschmitt Bf 109s*. The English, with their radar and *Hawker Hurricanes*, destroyed most of our *Junkers Ju 87 "Stuka"* dive bombers which flew there. After our Battle for Britain, everyone said that it was all *Udet's* fault because he had failed make the right kind of aircraft selections and consequently he was responsible for all of Germany's losses. They blamed him, too, for the poor rates of aircraft production and delays in the production of faster bombers and fighters. For example they called the *Heinkel He 177* , "*Udet's Folly*" because it was so wrong. Then there was the *Focke-Wulf Fw 190* fighter, designed by *Adolf Galland* (sic) and *Kurt Tank* and considered by many to be a flawed design. The overall poor showing of this aircraft, too, was blamed on *Udet*. But it wasn't these aircraft design failures which caused his death. *Udet* had frequent quarrels with *General Milch*. *Milch* was a Jew. *Udet* sometimes said to *Göring* "what will *Milch* do with me? Why does he speak so badly of me?" *Milch* believed that *Udet* had friends in the United States and that he was helping them to win the war. *Udet* had traveled to the United States in the early 1930s and made movies there. He was a friend of American World War One flying ace *Captain Eddy Rickenbacker*. He believed that Germany could never win the war once America got into it. Given America's vast natural resources and production capacity -well, no nation could match America's industrial might. No one wanted to believe *Udet*. Then we had the *Goebbels'* propaganda machine saying that all America was good for was making good quality and inexpensive razor blades. But bombers and fighters ? - no. *Udet* told *Joseph Goebbels* that he'd been there many times and they will make bombers, too, you will see. *Milch* also told the *SS* this nonsense and mentioned, too, that *Udet* thought the *NAZIs* were swine and a bunch of criminals. So *Udet* had no friends among the *NAZIs* who then were able to claim that all these aircraft failures were proof that *Udet* was seeking to sabotage Germany's war effort. *Udet* was really losing his respect. He started drinking more and more heavily, becoming very nervous and paranoid. It was his drinking that really did him in - in the end he just couldn't take it anymore and killed himself. On his bathroom mirror *Udet* had written "*Göring*, why did you let this happen to me?" There were too many quarrels between *Milch* and *Udet* and *Göring* didn't try to stop them. After the Battle for Britain and all our losses, *Göring* needed to shift the blame from himself on to others, especially *Udet*, who then became the reason for our failure to defeat the English. The campaign then waged against *Udet* by people looking for a scape-goat just grew and grew. By this time, even *Göring* couldn't win back *Udet's* lost respect. One night after *Udet* had thrown one of his famous parties and everyone had left, he picked up his service pistol. Five shots he fired into a dart board at the end of his study. The sixth he put into his brain. That was November 17th 1941.

Myhra: Did you give any consideration to using one of *Helmuth Walter's HWK 109-509* bi-fuel rocket drive or other advanced jet or rocket engines on your proposed all-wing fighter?

W. Horten: I had heard about *Hellmuth Walter's HWK 509* bi-fuel rocket engine, but I felt that it was not directly suitable for use in a fighter aircraft. I personally did not see any value in the *Messerschmitt Me 163* in the role of a fighter aircraft because its endurance was too short. We in the *Inspecorate of Fighters Command* never considered using the *HWK 509* rocket engine in any of our proposed *Horten* fighters. We did, however, see the benefit of using *HWK 509* solid fuel rocket engines as a booster for take-off assist. I was able to witness some of the first test flights of *von Braun's A-4 (V2)* rocket missile, as well as *Heini Dittmar's* flight in the *Messerschmitt Me 163* when he broke the air-speed record. I had picked up my brother *Reimar* and we both flew to Peenemünde to witness this flight of *Dittmar* in the *Messerschmitt Me 163*.

Myhra: What was *Reimar's* attitude about these unconventional sources of power and how they might be applied to aircraft?

W. Horten: *Reimar* was very excited about all the new propulsion systems I told him about. For example, I recall discussing the possibility of placing one or two *Schmitt-Argus As 014* pulse jets on one of our all-wing aircraft, like the *Horten Ho 7*. We were wondering if the *Schmitt-Argus* intermittent engine, the same engine used to power the *Fieseler Fi 103V1* flying bomb, might work on a fighter aircraft. We didn't get very far with this idea, because the pulse jet required the aircraft to be accelerated up to its operating speed of 241 km/h (150 mph). The only way to achieve this was with a piston engine and propeller, or some form of solid-fuel rockets. *Reimar* felt that all this was just far too complicated and the engines could only work at certain speeds. The *HWK 509* bi-fuel liquid rocket engine used in the *Messerschmitt Me 163* as just too dangerous and too technically complicated for us to consider.

Myhra: Would any type of *Horten* all-wing aircraft have been powered by a *Schmitt-Argus As 014* pulse jet engine?

W. Horten: We did not have any specific design in mind, for we merely thought about trying the pulse jet -only to learn that it would be a very inappropriate engine for a fighter of any kind. However, it might have been used on the wing tips or under the wing but, not within the wing, for it would have been far too dangerous. One of the reasons is that its operating temperature was very, very high. Also, we decided that if we placed these pulse jets on the outer wings, it would ruin the wing-lift distribution we had designed, so we determined to place the engines as close to the center line as possible. We wanted to enclose them inside the wing if possible to cut down on any drag. Once we considered that a *Schmitt-Argus As 014* pulse jet might be attached to something like the *Horten Ho 5B* in addition to its twin propeller engines. But idea was dropped because the pulse jets engine would have to be located outside of the propeller radius. Or we were thinking about placing one or more pulse jets under the wing on the center line. Once the all-wing was airborne, then its piston engines could be shut down, their propellers folded and the two pulse jet engines used to provide the power. These are the designs we finally considered as the most practical way of using these engines of *Dr. Paul Schmitt*.

Myhra: But you never did place an *Argus As 014* pulse jet on either a *Horten Ho 5* or *Horten Ho 7* did you?

W. Horten: No, instead we found that we might be able to obtain turbojet engines from *Dr. Hermann Oestrich* at *BMW* so we dropped any further consideration of *Dr. Schmitt's* pulse jets. Later we had to accept the *Junkers Jumo 004B* because the *BMW 003s* were not ready. The *Junkers Jumo 004* also had a wider diameter than the *BMW 003* and this created a considerable amount of problems and lost man hours for us.

Myhra: Did you ever consider placing one or more turbines on a *Horten Ho 7*—just for the experience?

W. Horten: Yes we did at one time, but then I learned that the turbine should run at nearly full-power most of the time and our *Horten Ho 7* did not have enough strength in its center section to take all this stress. When the *Horten Ho 7* was designed, the turbojet was not available and we decided that it would be better to have an all new design capable of handling all the forces the turbojet engine would produce. This is why we designed and built the *Horten Ho 9*. Later on we had the idea of building other turbojet-powered fighters, but when the *RLM* gave us a contract to design and build the *Horten Ho 18B*, we were told by *Saur* "no more fighter designs, you now concentrate only on the *Horten Ho 18B*."

Myhra: How were you able to obtain these turbines, when so few were being made and a number of airframes were waiting, such as the *Messerschmitt Me 262*, *Arado Ar 234B*, *Heinkel He 162*, *Junkers Ju 287*, *Henschel Hs 132*, and so on?

W. Horten: I arranged for them through the *RLM*. We had obtained some sample *BMW 003* model turbojet casings from *BMW* for use in our *Horten Ho 9* as mockups.

Myhra: Who paid for these turbines? The *Horten* brothers?

W. Horten: Nobody. Well, the *RLM* paid for them. Actually in time of war the people pay for all the military equipment. I had a contract with *Hellmut Schelp*, director of Turbojet Development at the *RLM* and had asked him for two turbines for use in our *Horten Ho 9*. After that *Schelp* saw to it that *Junkers Jumo* provided us with two brand new *Jumo 004Bs*. There are no problems in war time because everybody obeys orders, so all I had to do was make out an order for the *Sonder Kommando #9* to receive two *Junkers Jumo 004B* turbojets and our order was complied with. This was because the staff of the *RLM's* Technical Development office, through *General Diesing*, had a number of special projects and our *Sonder Kommando* x9 was only one of them. Most of these special projects were top-secret, so that very few people were able to investigate the reasons why various pieces of equipment, labor, supplies, facilities, and so on were provided for these projects. Our *Sonder Kommando #9* was no different. So when an order went out to *Junkers Jumo* for two *Jumo 004Bs* the engines were delivered and the *RLM* paid for them with no questions asked.

Myhra: Tell me about your experiments with the high altitude pressure suit.

W. Horten: We had tried some experiments with a pressure suit. It had been designed and developed by *Noble-Dynamit AG*. They were the same people who supplied us with plastic material for use on our *Horten Ho 5A*. One of our workers tried it on and then sat in the *Horten Ho 9 V1*. We all had a very difficult time with that suit. It was especially troublesome when our worker was wearing it in the *Horten Ho 9 V1's* cockpit. I remember that it was big and bulky and left no room for the man to even move. It was developed too late in the war effort to make any difference. Anyway we found it to be no good. We received the suit long after we had designed either our *Horten Ho 9 V1* or *Horten Ho 9 V2* and there was no way we were going to modify the *Horten Ho 9 V2* to make it a more comfortable fit for the pilot. Everything would have had to be extended, such as the controls. This would have been necessary so the pilot could reach them with his heavy-gloved hands. It did not work at all, so it wasn't even tried out in the *Horten Ho 9 V1* sailplane in flight. Maybe it would have been used once *Gothaer Waggonfabrik* had made modifications to our *Horten Ho 229*, once they got into series production. (In fact the production Ho.229 was to have been fitted with a pressure cabin – PW) I think that these pressure suits were designed by a company called *"Dragger,"* the same people who manufactured oxygen masks and flight suits for the *Luftwaffe*.

Myhra: Tell me about the fire power planned for the *Horten Ho 9 V2*.

W. Horten: When we flew the *Horten Ho 9 V1* glider to study its handling characteristics, we saw that the small landing strip at Göttingen was inappropriate and we transferred to Oranienburg Air Base. Later the *Horten Ho 9 V2* with its twin *Junkers Jumo 004Bs* was flight tested there, too. I had intended that the *Horten Ho 9 V2* would carry two 3 centimeters (1˘ inch) cannons. I wanted to shoot precisely at *Boeing B-17*'s from 2,000 meters (6,562 feet) distance with a 1,100 meter (3,609 feet) per second velocity from a gun platform with superior speed. When I requested these cannons for our *Horten Ho 9,* I was told that they were not going into production. So I had to choose between the *MK 103* or the *MK 108* cannons. The barrels on the *MK 108* cannons were very short and their muzzle velocity was only 420 meters (1,378 feet) per second. They were good only for shooting from 200 to 300 meters (656 to 984 feet) distance and to me this was awful. The *Boeing B-17*'s began shooting at us from about 800 meters (2,625 feet). If we stood by at 1,000 to 1,500 meters (3,281 to 4,921 feet), then the *Boeing B-17* gunners didn't shoot. So I asked how can we expect to shoot down a *Boeing B-17* when our cannons are only effective at 200 to 300 meters (656 to 984 feet) distance from a *Boeing B-17*? There was no answer. Instead I was told that they couldn't make a 3 centimeters (1˘ inch) cannon for us because they didn't have the capability, therefore, we had to chose the small version which was cheaper and with shorter gun barrels. I had to decide also if I took two *MK 108s* or if we took the *MG 151* with its 2 centimeters (0.78 inch) shell and place either two or four of them in our *Horten Ho 9*. In the end I felt that it would be better to take two *MG 151s*. Each of these cannons had a firing rate of 15 shells per second, so if one had two cannons, we then had a firing rate of 30 shells per second. In tests which had been conducted at *E-Stelle* Rechlin, I found that one needed only six hits on a *Boeing B-17* with the 2 centimeters (0.78 inch) *TNT* to bring it out of formation. But I felt that if our pilots were taught to fire their 2 centimeters cannons at 1,000 to 1,500 meters (3,281 to 4,921 feet) with a proper 'lead'—a technique I had developed back in France during our Battle for Britain, then perhaps our *Horten Ho 9* would be a capable fighter. I wanted our pilots to be able to fire ahead of the *Boeing B-17* as it was coming across the *Horten Ho 9's* nose so that we could give them plenty of windage (i.e. deflection) from a distance of 1,000 to 1,500 meters (3,281 to 4,921 feet) and yet still bring them down.

Myhra: Tell me about the flight tests of your *Horten Ho 9 V2* at the Oranienburg Air Base.

W. Horten: Well, neither *Reimar* or I was at Oranienburg. It was *Heinz Scheidhauer*, our top test pilot, who agreed that we use *Erwin Ziller* to test the *Horten Ho 9 V2. Ziller* had some training as a fighter pilot while *Scheidhauer* had none. *Ziller* was engaged to test our *Horten Ho 9 V2* in high-speed taxi runs, as well as short hops in the air and back down again onto the runway. He was not supposed to fly the *Horten Ho 9 V2* in free flight until these taxi runs and hops were completed. I also wanted *Ziller* to wait before taking the *Horten Ho 9 V2* into the open air until I was there in person. But in the meantime we got the task of designing the *Horten Ho 18B* from *Oberst Knemeyer*. Everyone of power such as *Karl-Otto Saur, Fritz Sacukel, Hermann Göring*, and so on wanted to know if our *Horten Ho 18B* was capable of a round-trip flight to America without refueling. It was a very important question to these people. *Adolf Hitler* was waiting for an immediate answer, so we couldn't go to Oranienburg Air Base until we gave these powerful people an answer. Our people at Oranienburg were waiting for us to come so that they could get on with the *Horten Ho 9 V2's* flight testing program. But we didn't come and didn't come, while they were impatiently waiting to fly the *Horten Ho 9 V2*. I think that *Ziller* made several proper flights anyway and without permission. One instance I recall happened like this - the runway at the end of one of *Ziller's* test hops came up all of a sudden and *Ziller* couldn't stop the *Horten Ho 9 V2* in sufficient time, so he just lifted off and into the open air. This is what we heard back in Göttingen. We were told that if he had tried to stop the *Horten Ho 9 V2* so near the end of the runway, he would have severely damaged the aircraft, so I guess he decided that it would be better to lift off and go around and then land. This is what we've been told.

Myhra: Were the *Horten Ho 9 V2's* rear main wheels damaged, requiring about three weeks of repair about this time?

W. Horten: I cannot say exactly when the damage to the *Horten Ho 9 V2* occurred. Whether it happened on *Erwin Ziller's* first flight or second flight. *Heinz Scheidhauer* was there and he would know better. The loss of the *Horten Ho* 9 *V2* came as a result of a failed turbojet engine during a landing approach.

Myhra: Are you referring to *Erwin Ziller's* fatal crash with the *Horten Ho 9 V2* on February 18th 1945?

W. Horten: Yes. It is my understanding that the accident was caused by an engine failure during the landing approach. I heard that one engine was not functioning properly, so *Erwin Ziller* began his approach long before entering the airfield boundary. It was reported to me that *Ziller* had engine trouble and was unable to obtain sufficient thrust with the other engine and that he was coming in at only about 1 or 2 meters (3 feet 2 inches to 6 feet 6 inches) above the ground. It was an awful crash and *Ziller* died. We received the news immediately at Göttingen. Thus all our work was over at that moment. But by this time series production of our *Horten Ho 229* had been started at *Gothaer Waggonfabrik* as requested by the *RLM*. One problem continued to plague the development of our *Horten Ho 9 V2* and that was its *Junkers Jumo 004B* turbojet engines. They were prone to fail without any warning, or they could just flame out due to poor fuel flow/circulation. The turbines were a constant problem for us. The turbojet engine was simply not ready for use in fighter aircraft destined for the Front. They were barely able to power an aircraft on an experimental basis. So I guess when one of *Ziller's* turbines failed, he lost too much power and air speed during his approach to Oranienburg Air Base. *Ziller* was losing altitude rapidly until a wing tip dug into the ground spinning him around in front of a small railroad embankment and crashed. I had the opportunity to speak with the first mechanic of the *Horten Ho 9 V2* recently. His name is *Walter Rösler*. He claims that he was the last person to see *Ziller* alive. Plus *Rösler* was the first person to reach *Ziller* as he lay on ground after being thrown out of the *Horten Ho 9 V2*. *Rösler* released *Ziller* from his seat belts.

Myhra: Was *Erwin Ziller* dead at this time?

W. Horten: I think so. *Walter Rösler's* story about *Erwin Ziller's* last flight is most interesting. According to him, *Ziller* had made three passes over the Oranienburg Air Base for the measuring team from the *Luftwaffe* Test Center-Rechlin. These experts from Rechlin were seeking to obtain his average speed based on the three passes. Then *Ziller* came back to land. According to *Rösler*, at about 150 meters (492 feet) *Ziller* dropped the landing gear and immediately the *Horten Ho 9 V2* began making a wide, sweeping, right-hand turn. But the *Ho 9 V2* didn't touch the ground. When I head this I thought that *Ziller* may have "blacked out" shortly after he put out the undercarriage. Mechanics at the crash site said that one of the turbines was frozen meaning that it may have run hot and seized. *Ziller* had trouble with one of the turbines, that much is clear. It is possible that this frozen turbine while it had been running began giving off fumes and that these fumes entered into the cockpit causing *Ziller* to black out. It is a fact that *Ziller* didn't make a control correction...he didn't move the control stick...nothing. This aircraft with one engine out appears to have been running in idle (And the other engine idling ? *–Author*) when it came down and there was no reaction by *Ziller* to line himself up with the runway during his final approach. He had the opportunity to do so but did not and the *Horten Ho 9 V2* continued to make this wide right-handed circle. I had seen something like this before in our Battle for Britain. It was my last air sortie, my last air victory. I had this English *Hurricane* at about 800 meters (2,625 feet) distance and shot at it using what you American's call "*Kentucky windage*." (deflection) I hit his radiator and it exploded. Right below the pilot was the radiator...the coolant area and this blew up. I saw it. There was this cloud of cooling water and anti-freeze, this stuff under great pressure and when it escaped at a height of 700 meters (2,297 feet) a cloud of steam surrounded the *Hurricane*. After it all escaped the engine was still idling. I only shot at it for a few seconds with a small caliber gun...our two machine guns over the engine. Each gun put out 30 shells per second and 60 shells went into the *Hurricane's* engine cowling and cockpit area. It was a lot. Then I thought that if the *Hurricane's* radiator blew up then the pilot, too, must have been hit and perhaps he is dead. But the aircraft was now flying level making a wide circle. A few seconds later I approached this idling *Hurricane*, in fact, got quite near it and saw that its pilot and he was dead hanging in his straps and belts. He did not make any reaction to regain control of his aircraft for he appeared to be unconscious or dead. This *Hurricane* was flying along quite the same as our *Horten Ho 9 V2* has been described. Thus, I can only assume from by dog-fighting experience over England that *Ziller* was either unconscious or dead.

Myhra: You believe, then, that *Erwin Ziller* may have wanted to continue making his final approach but blacked out instead?

W. Horten: Yes. There are many possibilities. But it must have been a hot turbine and he was overcome by toxic fumes.

Myhra: What about the possibility of sabotage?

W. Horten: Well, that is a possibility but *Erwin Ziller* had been flying the *Horten Ho 9 V2* for almost an hour. If it were sabotage it would have happened much sooner in the flight. I had told our people at the Oranienburg Air Base that every night two men had to sleep in the *Horten Ho 9 V2's* hangar so if someone entered they'd hear and/or see it. Many, many possibilities. It better to say that one turbine was running hot and it is possible that *Ziller* blacked out because of toxic fumes and this is why he did not appear to make any corrections. It shows that on this flight, that he made no effort to control the aircraft during its final approach...just like the time with the *Hawker Hurricane*...because of a dead pilot. Afterwards I didn't fire again on this *Hawker Hurricane*. He had been a squadron leader of eight *Hawker Hurricane's*. Six fellow pilots had run away when he came down from altitude and only his wing man stayed behind. Then they engaged us. *Adolf Galland* came from behind the squadron leader and the wing man was out here and I came from here and they turned...he would have had *Galland* in his sights. *Galland* shot but he didn't hit the squadron leader...he was only 50 meters (164 feet) behind but in all fairness, *Galland's* gunsight had been moved. So *Galland* didn't hit him and it was later that *Galland* was shot while passing through the *Hawker Hurricane* pilot's gun sights and that is when *Galland* got hit. Apparently *Galland's* control cable running back to the rudder had been severed and he went home without saying anything to me. He just suddenly left for home! As *Galland* was leaving the area the British squadron leader's wing man turned to *Galland's* backside probably expecting an easy kill. But before he could fire, I gave that *Hawker Hurricane* a salvo lasting two seconds from 600 *meters* (1,969 feet) out and with "*Kentucky windage*". Suddenly he took a hit...right in his radiator. After *Galland* was out of sight, I engaged the second *Hawker Hurricane* and fired. But nothing happen to him or his mount. Nothing. I saw that he was not maneuvering as before and thought that he must have mechanical problems. So I turned outside and observed him for a few moments and then he suddenly blew up...due I guess to my fire probably a direct hit into his engine fuel system. I drew up a bit closer and saw, too, that one of his wings was on fire. I didn't fire any more thinking that these two men had just lost their lives and where were the rest of this dead squadron leader's squadron? Run away, I guess, while their squadron leader and his wing man fought and died as heros. Well, I didn't wait around to see what became of these two men in their stricken *Hawker Hurricanes* because I wanted to catch up with *Galland*.

Myhra: After you returned home were you able to report the two kills?

W. Horten: No, they were not official kills because I had nobody to witness what had happened. Only me. Later I told *Adolf Galland* that I had shot down the two offending *Hawker Hurricane's*. He wanted to give them to me and he would have but there had been the order from the Chief of Staff of the *Luftwaffe General Jeschonnek*. Remember, he had ordered all *TOs* like me to stop participating in any air raids over England. Our losses were just too heavy for *JG/26*. So if *Galland* had sent a message back to base saying that he had witnessed *TO Walter Horten* shoot down two *Hawker Hurricane* fighters today, then both of us would have had considerable trouble with *Jeschonnek*. So we never did it. But I had saved *Galland's* life not only once but many times. Let me tell you. *Galland* didn't even want to make a test flight to see if the *Messerschmitt Bf 109T-2* would have been a better fighter than the *Messerschmitt Bf 109E*. He could have simply given the order for ten modified *Messerschmitt Bf 109T-2s* but he wouldn't. He kept telling me that a *Messerschmitt Bf 109T-2* would be too slow. Impossible!

Myhra: Describe *Erwin Ziller*—what sort of pilot was he?

W. Horten: *Erwin Ziller* was a very experienced pilot. He seemed to have good self control and was confident. He did not have a great deal of experience in piloting turbojet-powered aircraft, however. If I had been there, I would have directed *Ziller* to make only short hops until he got a better feel for our *Horten Ho 9 V2*. I had told *Ziller* not to fly the *Horten Ho 9 V2* until I was present. If *Reimar* and I had both been present perhaps we could have maintained more control on his hops that day and would have stopped him long before he reached the end of the runway. But *Ziller* had been very anxious to fly this new machine and I think that he became too aggressive and independent on his own. But at that moment we were too busy back at Göttingen working on the proposed design of the *Horten Ho 18B Amerika Bomber to carry* the atomic anti-population weapon. *Oberst Siegfried Knemeyer* had flown our *Horten Ho 7* in November or December of 1944. First we went up together and he was sitting in the forward seat as we lifted off the ground and gained altitude. "Do you want to fly it," I asked him? He took over the control and flew the *Horten Ho 7* very well. We had designed our *Horten Ho 7* with dual controls. Later he made a flight by himself and when he landed he told me that the all-wing was the perfect and right design for a long-range bomber. I wondered why he was talking about a long range bomber at this late stage of the war. We needed good fighters ever since our Battle for Britain, yet here now was a well-known and well-respected *Oberst* from the *RLM* telling me that an all-wing design along the lines of my *Horten Ho 7* would make an excellent long range bomber. Some weeks later there was a telephone call from *Knemeyer*. He asks me if *I* could design and build him an all-wing long range bomber? "Is it possible?" he asks. "Can you do it?" he wants to know. Well, I told him that my brother and I would have to calculate the performance requirements of such an aircraft and we would project the performance based on several layouts and different combinations of turbojet engines. I told *Knemeyer* that might take us up to eight to ten days to do the calculations. Well, once *Reimar* and I started, we decided that we could, indeed, give *Knemeyer* what he wanted. I telephoned *Knemeyer* and said "Look, my brother and I have finished our calculations and we figure that we can give you an all-wing *Horten* long-range bomber." He told us to standby and he'd be telephoning us back. He did and *Reimar* and I were invited several days later to *DVL-Berlin* to give a presentation. But at the same time at Oranienburg Air Base our people were waiting for *Reimar* and me to come so that we all could get on with the testing of the *Horten Ho 9 V2*. Our people did not understand why we were suddenly unconcerned with the prototype and its initial testing. When they telephoned us from Oranienburg inquiring when we planned to come there, all we could tell them was that we were busy with other matters and that we'd be there as soon as possible. *Knemeyer* had instructed us to tell no one about the long-range bomber project which he referred to as his *Amerika Bomber Projekt*. I instructed both *Ziller* and *Scheidhauer* not to fly the *Horten Ho 9 V2* until I arrived and that *Reimar* and I would be there just as soon as we could. For eight days we were standing by in Göttingen, not knowing what would come next with *Knemeyer*. It was during this time we received news that *Ziller* had crashed and died in the *Horten Ho 9 V2* on February 18th 1945. A few days later we received an order to come and see *Hermann Göring*. He told us that the all-wing design we had presented at *DVL-Berlin* for an *Amerika Bomber* had been selected for immediate construction. *Göring,* my brother and I believed that our *Horten Ho 18B* would be the biggest achievement of this century. "Get together with *Junkers-Dessau* and *Messerschmitt AG* and together build this aircraft as quickly as possible." That is exactly what *Göring* told us. We returned to Göttingen and learned also that another test pilot of ours, *Hermann Strebel,* had died in the crash of our experimental laminar-flow all-wing *Horten Ho 4B*. We had lost two of our three most-experienced test pilots in the closing days of the war...first *Ziller* and then *Strebel*. It was about this time that American Army troops were a mere 100 kilometers (62 miles) from Göttingen and we realized that the *Horten Ho 18B "Amerika Bomber"* would never be. After the crash and death of *Ziller*, I went to Oranienburg to attend to the funeral and burial. A few days later *Reimar* attended *Strebel's* funeral. I told him that I had gone to *Ziller's* funeral and now it was his turn to go to *Strebel's*. (Strebel's crash in the H.IV.b is stated in Reimars book "Nurflugel" as being on the 18TH January 1945 – exactly a month before Zillers crash in the V2 – PW) The whole war situation was now greatly depressing us. The Soviets were surrounding Berlin and the Americans were rapidly closing in on Göttingen. I managed to return to Göttingen. There was nothing more we could do now but wait for the end to come. Both *Scheidhauer* and *Ziller* flew our *Heinkel He 111*, which we used as a tow plane. *Scheidhauer* also flew the *Horten Ho 9 V1*, but did not fly the *Horten Ho 9 V2*. Once the *Horten Ho 9 V2* was ready for flight testing, we took it to Oranienburg via road transport. We took it to Oranienburg because they had a longer runway than we had at Göttingen. Wings for the *Horten Ho 9 V2* were sent there by rail. Our *Horten Ho 7* was flown to Oranienburg about the same time the *Horten Ho 9 V2* arrived there. The *Horten Ho 229* was to be sent to the *1st* squadron of the *JG/400* fighter wing. The *Horten Ho 7* was to be given to them as well for use as a training aircraft prior to their pilots flying the *Horten Ho 229.*

Myhra: You mentioned that a vertical rudder for the *Horten Ho 9 V2* was necessary for it to be an effective gun platform. Can you explain that a little?

W. Horten: As you know our *Horten Ho 9 V2* crashed with *Erwin Ziller* at the controls. He flew this machine without a conventional rudder. But for military use, for the best gunnery conditions, to have good gunnery success, I felt that we had to have a very stable gun platform. We needed to be able to hold the machine quite exactly on the target within the pilot's gun site. We must be able to make small directional corrections quickly when getting ready to shoot the cannon. I was looking for an aircraft which could aim and fire from 1,500 to 2,000 meters (4,921 to 6,562 feet) distance and—based on my experience—develop a stable platform which we could control very finely. Or very exactly. This way one saves ammunition and has more success. This was my point of view and I felt that our *Horten Ho 9* would require a vertical rudder in order to do this. Sure, we could control the *Horten Ho 9* through the use of drag rudders, for the general flying characteristics were reasonably effective. But it wasn't good enough in my opinion as a good and effective gun platform. Therefore I wanted to have better stability. I needed to find a way to dampen the oscillations and the small amount of "*dutch roll*" that we were experiencing in our *Horten Ho 9 V1* during flight. I wanted a more precise line of fire. Without trying a vertical rudder on the *Horten Ho 9 V2,* I felt that it would not be possible to make our *Horten Ho 9* into an effective fighter when shooting from 1,500 to 2,000 meters (4,921 to 6,562 feet). For example, when we experienced what we call "pumping air" (air or wake turbulence), then it is desirable to have precise control for its directional stability. Otherwise, the airplane can 'porpoise' or 'fishtail' a little when one has turbulance then you cannot shoot straight. The *Horten Ho 9*, in my opinion would never have been able to place exact shots into a target during turbulance without the use of a vertical rudder. Therefore, I intended to place a vertical rudder on one of the production *Horten Ho 229's* from *Gothaer Waggonfabrik*. If our *Horten Ho 9 V2* had survived, I would have had a vertical rudder placed on it instead to compare the difference in control it would have made on the same machine without the rudder to see the effect on exact shooting.

Myhra: Well, if this is true, what about the need for the same sort of vertical rudder on the "*Amerika Bomber*" *Horten Ho 18B*?

W. Horten: One did not need a vertical rudder for a bomber aircraft. And in the case of our *Horten Ho 18B,* which was designed from the beginning as a long-range bomber, dropping an atomic or biological device on the United States did not need to be exact, only close. So there was no need for a rudder on most bomber aircraft. Thus one can save weight and you have more room for other things like fuel and weapons.

Myhra: What other proposed aircraft projects were you considering after the *Horten Ho 229?*

W. Horten: Well, they were mostly my ideas which I presented to the *RLM*, so that we might obtain additional work after the completion of our *Horten Ho 9*. During this time, in late 1944 and early 1945, *Reimar* was busy getting the *Horten Ho 9* ready for series production with *Gothaer Waggonfabrik* and he did not have time to apply himself to new projects. Near the end of the war, the *Luftwaffe* requirements were calling for additional "*Volksjäger*" type aircraft. These were single-engine fighters in the simplest form possible suitable for mass production. Most of the designs called for armament using twin 2 centimeter (0.78 inch) cannon. Many aircraft factories submitted proposed aircraft project designs, including us. We didn't get much response back from the *RLM* because I think they were swamped with ideas from so many different aircraft companies. Well, we were looking for more work so that we could keep our workshops and men occupied, but as the American army kept advancing from the west and the Soviet's from the east, the likelihood of building our proposed projects grew dimmer. Even so, I was interested in building a new, smaller turbojet-powered fighter, one that could be built very quickly and mass produced without the use of strategic materials...a sort of "*Volksjäger*." Then in early 1945, we received the order to construct the radiation-spreading device carrier, the *Horten Ho 18B*. After this order came, the *RLM* told me that we would not be allowed to receive any other aircraft orders, so all my project designs were shelved. Then due to all the bombing raids on our aircraft factories all over the *Reich,* aircraft production personnel, design studios, and assembly facilities were moved into caves and tunnels throughout the Harz Mountains in eastern Germany. One day *Reimar* and I drove to the Harz Mountains where the *RLM* wanted us to design and build the *Horten Ho 18B*. We immediately saw that it would be impossible to construct any aircraft, especially our *Horten Ho 18B* in such places. We drove back to Göttingen and pretty much waited for the end.

Myhra: But aren't there several proposed *Horten* designs for fighter aircraft with a vertical fin with an attached hinged rudder?

W. Horten: Yes this is correct. These proposed designs were based on our flight testing results with the *Horten Ho 9 V1*—and the powered *Horten Ho 9 V2* before it crashed. I felt that any of our aircraft which we proposed as fighters had to incorporate vertical stabilizers. For one thing this would provide better handling and aerobatics and second, it would give better control for aiming the cannons. In short, it would create a better gun platform. We needed a vertical rudder in order to control the aircraft around the yaw axis in a precise way. It was important to hold an enemy aircraft very firmly in the gun sight. Also, once in the air and if the pilot experienced turbulance or the propeller wake of the enemy fighter ahead of him, it was important for the pilot to hold the aircraft on course while aiming at an enemy target. Therefore, we had projected a vertical fin or rudder to complete the design and to make it better for dog-fighting. I wanted our all-wing fighters to be able to accurately shoot down enemy aircraft from a long distance, perhaps up to 2,000 meters (6,562 feet); for this reason a very stable gun platform was absolutely necessary. Tests with the *Horten Ho 9 V1* and to a lesser extent with the short-lived *Horten Ho 9 V2* showed us that these two aircraft would swim though the air and although they could be stabilized, very precise directional control about the yaw axis required a great deal of effort and practice on the part of the pilot. But if a target suddenly presented itself, it might well get away while the pilot in the *Horten Ho 229* was struggling to steady the machine in order to have accurate fire. I felt that such effort and work could be reduced, if not eliminated, through the design of a high vertical fin with a hinged rudder. Also, I wanted to have on the *Horten Ho 9* these new *MK 103* cannons, which had a barrel velocity of 1,100 meters (3,609 feet) per second. The *MK 108* cannons had only 420 meters (1,378 feet) per second velocity. So when using the *MK 103* cannon, I would be able to stand back at 2,000 *meters* (6,562 feet) distance—a little over a mile—and completely shoot up a *Boeing B-17* while they could not reach me with their .50 caliber machine guns. But if I had to come within 800 meters (2,625 feet) of a *Boeing B-17*, then they could shoot me down. See what I mean when I talk about a stable gun platform? With the *MK 108* cannon, I needed to get so close as 300 to 400 meters (984 to 1,312 feet) of my target and be able to steer my machine quickly so I would not be shot down. That was much more dangerous for me as a pilot given the fact that your typical *Boeing B-17* had twelve .50 caliber guns and carried a lot of ammunition. Still not safe enough for me. The *Horten Ho 9* did not give me the yaw stability I demanded, so I wanted to try a vertical surface control. That's all. *Reimar* thought that in normal flying, the drag rudders on the wing tips would be enough to give good directional control. But fighters do not fly in normal conditions and I wanted a vertical rudder to be available in those situations when exact directional stability was essential. Our *Horten Ho 9 V1* was stable and it flew very well. But in turbulance it would not have been satisfactory, in my view, as a good gunnery machine. The pilot could hold the aim on his gunnery course, but required too much of his time and effort. Pilots often don't have such time to bring their aircraft into a positive position where they can shoot down an enemy. Aiming and firing has to be accomplished quickly, otherwise the target gets away unharmed. Secondly, the type of pilot we were left with by early 1945 was young, inexperienced, and had very few flight hours of training. I saw that we could not expect them to pilot a very fast turbojet-engined fighter, aim the aircraft, and try to keep the it stable in order to shoot down enemy aircraft from a distance of 2,000 meters (6,562 feet). So for the purpose of fighter aircraft combat, I found that our *Horten Ho 9 V1* and *Ho 9 V2*—the way they were designed and built—would be no good at all as fighters. Vertical fins with hinged rudders were used on all aircraft designs at this time for control about the yaw axis. An all-wing fighter aircraft also needed such a vertical fin to control yaw, I felt. This was based on my experience as a fighter pilot with nine kills after flying only a short time with *Adolf Galland*, and from my many hours of piloting all-wing sailplanes. Most other designers agreed. So we see no all-wing fighter aircraft without some sort of vertical fin, whether it is on the wing tip, bending up or down at the wing tip, or a small vertical fin placed on the wings, and so on. Most of all the designers in Germany at this time, with the possible exception of my brother *Reimar*, saw the need for vertical stabilizers on fighter aircraft, although each favored his own particular solution to solve this problem of yaw control. My own belief was to simply place a high vertical fin on the center section mid line and attach a hinged rudder to its rear. Very simple, very light, and very effective. In soaring and gliding with an all-wing, it was possible to fly well without the use of a vertical fin but for military use as a heavy, multi-engine aircraft, the all-wing design like ours would have required a fin/rudder combination in order to make it an effective fighter.

Myhra: Is this why most of your proposed all-wing designs after the *Horten Ho 9* have vertical tails? Or did the *RLM* request this addition to your all-wings?

W. Horten: Yes, but the *RLM* did not require vertical tails on our proposed designs. It was I who suggested this change, based on our flight tests with the *Horten Ho 9 V1* and *Ho 9 V2*. I truly believed we would require a more stable gun platform than our all-wing *Horten Ho 9* could currently provide. No, the *RLM* did not suggest a vertical surface—although it was certainly discussed. They wanted to know about the results of flight tests of the *Horten Ho 9 V1* and *Ho 9 V2* because our *Horten Ho 229* was going into series production. But all in all, I think that the *RLM* was pleased with the *Horten Ho 9 V2* design just as it was. Naturally I felt stronger about the stable gun platform because I had been a fighter pilot and I knew the importance of a stable machine in order to shoot down enemy fighters and bombers. Then again, the *RLM* was looking at the *Horten Ho 229* as a fast fighter carrying aerial bombs/rockets against *Boeing B-17* formations. For this purpose, an exact gun platform was really not required as it would have been if the aircraft was just intended for dog-fighting as we had in our Battle for Britain in 1940. But for the *RLM*, the *Horten Ho 229* was good the way it was designed, but for me, thinking like I did as a former dog-fighting pilot with nine kills, no the all-wing design was not good enough. Then again, this was my personal opinion and it was not shared by everyone, especially my brother *Reimar*. There was no intention by any one at *Gothaer Waggonfabrik* to place a vertical fin/rudder on our *Horten Ho 229*. If they had had their way they would have scrapped the *Horten Ho 229* in favor of their own proposed *Gothaer Go P. 60B*...tailless fighter design. I certainly would have tried a vertical fin on the *Horten Ho 9 V2* if it had not been destroyed and if we had the time to make the necessary modification. I would still like to know today what the results of a vertical fin with an attached hinged rudder on the *Horten Ho 9 V2* would have been like. But again, *Reimar* did not agree that our *Horten Ho 9* needed any sort of vertical fin. Anyway, by December 1944, *Reimar* was too busy in designing our *Horten Ho 18B* turbine-powered bomber for *Oberst Seigfried Knemeyer* and the others,

The *Messerschmitt Me 163* rocket-powered interceptor by *Alexander Lippisch*...perceived long-time rival of the *Horten* brothers.

including "the fat one" *Hermann Göring*. *Reimar* was not really interested in my ideas on a vertical fin for the *Horten Ho 9,* or my other proposed projects with a vertical fin for that matter. *Reimar* said that our all-wings didn't need a vertical rudder. I said for sport flying certainly not. But for dog-fighting absolutely! For a long-distance bomber flying straight mile after mile, perhaps no!

Myhra: And what of the *RLM* and your proposed fighters with vertical rudders? What were their views on this philosophical change by the "hard line" *Horten* brothers?

W. Horten: The *RLM* was very hopeful and pleased with them especially since all our designs now had the vertical stabilizer. But then it didn't matter because the *RLM* told us that we would not be given any new projects to design because we had been ordered by *Hermann Göring* and *Fritz Sacukel* to concentrate only on the *Horten Ho 18B*.

Myhra: *Fritz Sacukel* was a very powerful, fanatical, heart-less *NAZI*. He was convicted in the Nuremberg Trials for crimes against humanity and hanged in 1946. How did it come to be that *Gothaer Waggonfabrik* was given the job of producing the *Horten Ho 229* in series?

W. Horten: The *RLM* viewed the *Horten Flugzeugbau GmbH* only as a development laboratory for researching the construction of prototypes and not the place for a high volume production line of a series. Also, there were no facilities at the Göttingen Air Station for series production of the *Horten Ho 9 V2*. All we had at Göttingen were small hangars, and so on. *Gothaer Waggonfabrik*, on the other hand, had the capacity—which at that time in mid-to-late 1944 was relatively free. So the *RLM* felt it was better for *Gothaer* to do the work. After the *RLM* saw that the *Horten Ho 9 V2* was ready to go into production, realizing that *Gothaer* had very little work to do, the *RLM* assigned them the job of putting the *Horten Ho 9 V2* into series production as the *Horten Ho 229*.At the same time in Minden, *Peschke* received an order to build three pre-production *Horten Ho 7s*. Once they were completed, *Peschke* was to build between 15 and 20 *Horten Ho 7s* for use as training aircraft for pilots going on to the *Horten Ho 229*. I know that the *Horten Ho 7 V2* was nearly finished when the American army entered Minden, but I don't have any idea of what happened to it, or the two other prototypes under construction there, as well. I believe that all our *Horten Ho 7s* were destroyed by the Allies. It is a pity for the *Horten Ho 7* was a very fine aircraft. I still have all the plans and we could build one right now.

Horten Flugzeugbau test pilot *Heinz Scheidhauer* at the *Rhön/Wasserkuppe* Spring,1943. A *flak* tower stands in the background.

Myhra: Why were there so many fighter designs being proposed?

W. Horten: I don't know. But I imagine that it had to do with the fact that we, like other aircraft manufacturing companies, were always seeking better and more effective fighters for the *Luftwaffe*. The same goes for our all-wing designs. We had to react to America's faster fighters—their long-distance escorts flying along side of the *Boeing B-17s*. We couldn't believe that long-distance escorts were possible. All my discussions with *Reimar* regarding vertical surfaces were based directly on my experience. *Reimar* had not been a fighter pilot like me. He had never chased after and shot at any enemy fighter as I had done. He never had a *Supermarine Spitfire* or a *Hawker Hurricane* on his tail seeking to shoot him down and the only way to avoid being killed was to go into wild aerobatics in order to survive to fight another day. I was the *TO* in *JG/26* and not even a fighter pilot, yet I managed to achieve nine kills before all *TO's* like me in the *JGs* were ordered never again to fly combat sorties. The *RLM* didn't want to lose their valuable *TO's* in silly dog fights. At the time *Reimar* and I were discussing the merits of a vertical surface on our *Horten Ho 9* in late 1944, very few *Luftwaffe* pilots were alive any longer who had participated in our Battle for Britain back in the Summer of 1940 when I did. Only *Adolf Galland* and a probably only a dozen other pilots were still alive. So I knew better in this situation than *Reimar*, in fact better than most people at that time!

Chapter 02

REIMAR HORTEN Interviews

Background:
Reimar Horten was a aircraft design genius — this much is certain. Even his first full sized glider - the *Horten Ho 1*, designed in 1933 and completed in early1934 – was an all-wing design (in German Nurflugel). It won a cash prize for the most innovative design at the 1934 Summer *Rhön/Wasserkuppe* Sailplane Competitions. By the time *Nazi* Germany surrendered unconditionally on May 8th 1945, *Reimar* had designed and constructed several high performance sailplanes, powered aircraft, found time to build one of the first aircraft to use an all composite structure, put the twin turbojet-powered *Horten Ho 9 V2* into the air, and finally collaborated with *Gothaer Waggonfabrik to bring it into production as the Ho.229 jet fighter.* In addition, *Reimar* was making plans to construct the *Horten Ho 18B*, a four turbojet-powered all-wing "*Amerika Bomber*" to carry a "dirty" bomb (radio active material wrapped around a conventional bomb) to the United States. I met with this remarkable man twice in the early 1980s (1982 and 1983) at his ranch at the foothills of the Andes Mountains in Argentina, staying with him for a month on each occassion. Prior to our interview other people had told me that *Reimar* was a difficult person to get along with, unconventional — that is working 24 hours per day interrupted by only short naps, a true believer in the all-wing planform and prone to lie to authorities when asked if his aircraft contained all certified material (often they didn't !), uncommunicative at times, and that if you once angered him then he would never talk with you again. Yes, the story of his life bears this out — these faults and failings. What are we to make of them?

A marriage portrait of *Reimar Horten* and his new bride *Giesla Hiler*. Córdoba, Argentina. 1949.

Reimar Horten aged 71 and his bride *Giesla* at the *Horten* ranch near Villa General Belgrano, Argentina. 1982. Photo by author.

Interview #1

Date: August/September 1983
Location: *Horten Ranch* - 25 miles outside the Villa General Belgrano, Argentina
Language: English

Myhra: When did you start on your *Horten Ho 9* project?

R. Horten: I began the *Horten Ho 9* without permission, none whatsoever. It was not official. *Walter* and I had very many difficulties in building the *Horten Ho 9*. Initially and indeed for the first few months, all we had were old workmen. We had 170 men in our entire organization and all working hard. Our *Reichsmarshall Hermann Göring* told us on August 28th 1943 "This is the plane I want, " he said to me, " I want it to fly in three months." Well, it couldn't be done...that is fly in three months. I told him that we required a minimum time of six months. "I want it in three months for we are at war," *Göring* demanded. We heard more speeches and always he said "in three months." But I told him that I needed six months. "Well, in six months it has to fly," *Göring* said again. *Göring* ordered the *Horten Ho 9* and then the Air Ministry tried to stop the whole idea! The sixth month was February 28th 1944. On

OUTLINE OF THE HORTEN MONOGRAPH

as per Mr. Wilkinson R. A. E.

Give us informations about the following details :

A)

1. Method of computation of the lift distribution along the span (with list of references and an example of calculation). The same method, but for swept back wings.
2. Method of computation of the ~~tail setting~~ Wing Twist for gliders especially with regard to the trim about the ~~longitudinal~~ Rolling and ~~vertical~~ yawing axes in turns.
3. Method of computation of an airfoil so that stalling will be effected at the centre of the semi span..
4. Computation of the choice of the C.G.-location for high speed airplanes as well as for gliders.
5. Computation of the controls
   a) The ailerons, computation of the ailerons for rolling moments, the elimination of opposite yawing moments, and the computation of the desired hinge moments.
   b) Computation of the elevator forces and the produced pitching moments
   c) It shall be demonstrated with respect to the Horten 4 and H 8, how each of the three flaps contributes to the rolling moment and to the pitching moment.
   d) The design of the rudder, its control forces (single engine flight) and the computation of the control forces. Describe the four types of control flaps employed.

I. Leading edge-split flap (H 2 and H 3 type)
II. Vertically retractable spoilers (H 4 and H 7 type)
III. "Direction indicator" (H 7 b and H 8)
IV. Modified spoilers (H 9 type).

6. Design of high lift devices. Method of computation of the pitching moments for extended flaps.
7. How to flatten out the airplane from the dive. Method of computation of the elevator deflection.required with

First page featuring a list of talking points given to the *Horten* brothers as POWs by *R.K.G. Wilkinson* of the RAE-Farnborough. Questions to be answered include the *Horten's* method of calculating wing lift, wing twist, and computation of flight controls.

- 2 -

and without elastic deformation. Why is a larger elevator deflection necessary in the case of the H 7 after the plywood having been strengthened.

8. The method of computation of the airfoil profiles.
9. The method of computation of the aerodynamic centre and the elevator trim angles.
10. Method of computation of the solution for the examples of H 7, 8, and 9.

B) 1) Describe each other point of view for the computation of tailless airplanes you think important.

2) Give a summary of the experiences, you have obtained about the characteristics of tailless airplanes by means of flight tests and include :

a) the influence of the variation of the C.G.-location on the aerodynamic characteristics with regard to the qualities about the longitudinal and lateral axis,
b) the influence of the C.G.-location on the qualities with respect to stalling and spin,
c) the limits of the C.G.-displacement in practice.
d) report on the stability and the aerodynamical characteristics of the H 3, 4, 5, 7, and 9 (single-engine flight),
e) the qualities on the ground with respect to the manoeuvrability,
f) the measured performance as far as available
g) all points of view you regard as worth mentioning.

C) We are especially interested in A) and B). A numerical result (design and flight tests), numerical data shall be given wherever possible. This is of more importance than general theoretical considerations.

Göttingen, 26.9.1945

Second page featuring a list of talking points given to the *Horten* brothers as POWs by *R.K.G. Wilkinson* of the RAE-Farnborough. Questions to be answered include the *Horten's* experiences with all-wing aircraft.

Reimar Horten's long time friend and colleague *Wolf Hirth.*

the last day of the sixth month we sent a telegram to *Hermann Göring* that our *Horten Ho9* had flown and landed successfully. In reality it was the glider version which had flown and he probably didn't know the difference. If the *Horten Ho 9 V1* had not flown, he would have been very angry.

It was necessary that permission to build the *Horten Ho 9* come through *Göring* and not through *Erhard Milch* who was the chief of the Air Ministry. *Walter* had spoken to *Milch* but he carried no authority and he always needed *Göring's permission.* In August 1943, *Göring* had made a speech in front of all the leaders in the German aircraft industry in Berlin. He said that he had 16 types of twin engined aircraft. Their speeds were all in the range of 500, 520, and 550 km/h and so on. "I will not allow any more planes in this category. I will have performance very much different from these," said *Göring*.

Walter was present when *Göring* made this announcement for *Walter* was in the *Inspection of Fighters Command* and he heard *Göring* speak about those "B" engine-powered type of aircraft. As *Göring* continued speaking he said "I want to have a 1,000 kilometers/hour plane, 1,000 kilometers range, and carrying a 1,000 kilograms of bombs." He said that unless new proposals indicated that a new flying machine could achieve this 3x1000 he would not accept them.

Walter came to Minden and he told me about *Göring's* speech the day before and his desire for a 3x1000 fighter/bomber. No one in the German aircraf t industry had this type of aircraft. I told *Walter*, let us see what we can do and we'll build an all-wing airplane. I suggested to *Walter* the *Horten Ho 9* with a 16 meter wing span, powered by twin *Junkers Jumo 004* turbojets. I calculated its performance - we could build such a 3x1000 project in the form of the *Horten Ho 9.* I can do it. Perhaps 950 km/h is the only speed we'll obtain. We'll offer *Göring* 950 kilometers/hour speed, 700 kilometers range, and 2,000 kilograms of bombs.

I immediately sketched some preliminary designs for the *Horten Ho 9. Walter* returned to Minden in about two weeks when I had finished the design proposal. It was approximately 20 pages long. Walter then took it to *General Kurt Diesing*, *Göring's* Chief of Staff who was surprised that we had something to present so fast. Later *Göring* telephoned and wanted us to come and meet with him. It was on this occasion that I told *Göring* in person that he could have an aircraft with this 3x1000 performance and that I had been working with a few men to prepare its drawings and so on. This was August 1943. It was at this meeting that *Göring* told *Walter* and I that he wanted our plane within three months. I said that it would take at least six months. Thus six months from August 1943 to have it flying, was February 1944. We had some bad luck, too, for the *BMW 003* turbojet engines were not ready so we could still work on the *Horten Ho 9 V1* and make it ready. I decided to fly a model of the *Horten Ho 9* without the engine because it would be much easier to build such an aircraft without engines, fuel tanks, wiring, fuel pumps and so on. We simply could not finish the powered model in six months as *Göring* wanted. Therefore the first *Horten Ho 9* was the same as the powered version except it had no engines, fuel tanks, and so on but we made it fly in February 1944. Later on we needed more time to finish the powered version which was known as the *Horten Ho 9 V2.* So, we did not work on the *Horten Ho 9* completely without orders. Nor was our work without authority. At first, yes. But later on it had been authorized by *Göring* himself.

You know that I worked for a long time without authorization on the *Horten Ho 9* project. This project had started with my sailplane work. The Air Ministry, didn't know this. Then came the moment when *Göring* told us to make the *Horten Ho 9* project. The senior officers of the Air Ministry were encouraged and now I could build what I wanted. But later on the Air Ministry informed *Göring* that the *Horten* brothers were working on sailplanes and other type of aircraft. Eventually *Göring* sent a *Luftwaffe* General to see us. All in all we had seven different workshops, and this General was to visit all of our workshops to see what we are doing. He was going to inspect us. *Göring* telephoned me about it. I told him not only do I have to build the *Horten Ho 9* project but I have to make all these investigations and therefore, before I can advance

Heinz Schiedhaur piloting the motorized *Horten Ho 3-D* powered by a single *Walter "Micron"* 65 horsepower engine. This was a flight demonstration for *Professor Ludwig Prandtl* and colleagues in 1942.

in one direction or another, I need to experiment. *Göring* told me to inform the others in the Air Ministry so that they also understand. I told him yes, I shall. Well, *Walter* was angry about the visits. But I told *Walter* that *Göring* already knows that we must build sailplanes in order to carry on the development of the turbojet powered *Horten Ho 9* project. Plus, I told him that this was a cheap way to develop aircraft and to experiment.

Walter, I must tell you, complained about me building sailplanes during the war. I told him "look at what we have." We have a plane with the planform of the *Horten Ho 2* or *Horten Ho 3* , whereas a line joining the quarter cord points of the *Horten Ho 9* had a different shape.. I saw that the center of lift had not been localized at the point where it had to be. It was far away from the wing tip. It should be, for instance, be at one the third of center of lift of the semi-span. This point should be the center of lift of the entire plane. This point also has to be the center of gravity otherwise it creates instability in pitch. We see, therefore, this lift distribution should be like a bell. This should be in 33% in theory and in practice it was 36% to 38% of the semi span. With our *Horten Ho 1* sailplane I had discovered this difference between theory and practice. I thought that flow separation caused by the fuselage of the H.1 had caused this discrepancy. But I still saw this effect in our *Horten Ho 2* despite the fact that I had put the pilot in a prone position . I thought that there was a loss of lift in the center section and I named it the "center effect." The lift distribution should have had a bell shape and this is what we were missing here – in the center. As we wished to have the center of lift half way to the wing tip XXX and to cure the centre effect, I designed the *Horten Ho 4* and the *Horten Ho 5* planforms to have less sweep back in the centre and more outboard. The center of lift should be at the center of gravity. Unfortunately I miscalculated the true centre of gravity for the first Ho.5 creating a and as a result it crashed.

In the *Horten Ho 5B* I kept the same planform but constructed it in wood and in the *Horten Ho 5C* I could see that it was a better layout. Thinking along these lines I felt that we should make an aircraft with a parabolic planform. The aircraft or sailplane would be curved and so we have a different angle of sweepback at each point along the wing.like this, therefore, in each point, we have the same effect but only smaller. We can calculate point by point the variation in lift distribution. In this way we can precisely calculate the situation.. I began to construct this parabola in 1938 but it was not finished. In 1939 I was in Berlin because we had problems building the *Horten Ho 3B*, and then the war began and the parabel was burnt without flying. This was my concept in 1938 and 1939 the parabola seemed to be the best shape in my view. I had worked two or three times more in the workshop than I did on the theory of lift distribution and I had used a lot of paper but there were better ideas. You see, with the parabolal design I was seeking to establish the angle (twist) of each rib station, purely from a mathematical derivation. Determining the lift distribution was very difficult. I began my calculations on the basis of some data I had obtained

Professor Ludwig Prandtl in 1943 (1875-1953).

from *Alexander Lippisch* and changed it point by point at the local angle of sweep. It was complicated but I had moved on to other ideas by then. This pure mathematical form was not however ideal and we did not need the sweepback in this complex parabolic shape. It was better to have a straight sweep with a parabolic line in the centre section. Thus the *Horten Ho 5* was better than the parabola for the mainplane was a straight line and not curved. So the parabolic curve was not aerodynamic but only mathematical.

Then came the start of the war. *Walter* had gone to his troops and I was in the reserves. But I was not called up, I had been forgotten. I was at home and thinking about new projects, new sailplane ideas, of long distance bombers with six engines and so on. I began a design with a straight leading edge sweep, by increasing the cord in the centre section it gave the desired parabolic curve when the quarter cord points were joined and gave the shape of the *Horten Ho 4A* or the *Horten Ho 9*. I needed a large aspect ratio to achieve this and the lift distribution I was seeking. That was the thinking behind the *Horten Ho 4*. So the *Horten Ho 4* sailplane was built in order to build the *Horten Ho 9 – to investigate lift distribution.* Therefore all our sailplanes were in investigate these things. Walter could not understand for he'd ask me why are you building the *Horten Ho 6?* I was now in Nordhausen and had built the *Horten Ho 4* Königsburg and saw that it performed well and that it had the bell lift form because the quarter cord line was good. I later realised that when I pull back on the control stick, and increase the lift coefficient, I proportionally loose lift in the center. If I loose lift, the gradient of lift is small and I have very high stability. This form has great stability. One can move the stick and this aircraft is very stable. But the lift distribution is not as it should be and there is a drag rise in the centre section. I realised I had large stability and a loss of lift.

If I curve the quarter cord line further rearwards, lift will rise in the center . If we get more lift than we need, we have more stability and improve the handling. A plane has good handling characteristics if the neutral point is a few percent rear of the center of gravity. I thought that with this form of the quarter cord line I could put the neutral point in front. For a high-speed plane, we have large stick forces and we can reduce them in this planform. To investigate this, theory considers a hypothetical sailplane with two-di-

Hermann Strebel, January 1945. He died flight testing the experimental *Horten Ho 4-B* with its laminar-flow wing after it came crashing down. March 1945.

The *Horten Ho 4-B* with radio call code *LA+AB*. This is the flying machine *Hermann Strebel* died in March 1945.

mensional flow and an infinite aspect ratio. I decided to investigate this planform and this was the reason for the construction of the *Horten Ho 6* with an aspect ratio of 33 to 1. Two dimensional flow and we'll see what is in the center. (Aerodynamic theory falls short of reality as many calculations pretend that the wingspan is infinite and naturally reality falls rather short of this. The very high aspect ratio of the Horten 6 would come close and allow Reimar to see if flight tests validated his theory.... However, the Ho.6 was also the highest performance salplane in the world, and was almost a revenge for the Ho.4 being outperformed by the Darmstadt D.30 Cirrus in performance tests.... "methinks he does protest too loudly"....PW)

The *Horten Ho 6* was not important to me nor something I wanted, it was merely scientific. The need for this knowledge was in order to build the *Horten Ho 9. Walter* did not want me to build the *Horten Ho 6.* He was telling me that I am playing with this *Horten Ho 6.* "No," he said, "it was not necessary." *Göring* told me that he agreed with the *Horten Ho 6. "Do* what is necessary and what you think is best," he told me. At that moment *Göring* said to me "I know, I see it, I understand it. You will make me a plane of 900 kilometer range from all these investigations."

I wanted to reduce stick forces and by building the *Horten Ho 6*, I was able to discover a better technique. I needed to know the position of the stick for low speed as well as high speed. I needed to know the kinematics of the control flaps and their angle of movement. Not only for this third part of the forces, but also I had to reduce the stability so to have less force. The British said that all my research was a dead loss to Germany's war effort. They said it was like zero value. They simply didn't understand. They thought I was playing...as *Walter* also thought. For example, what use did the construction of the *Horten Ho 6* have? This was needed to determine stick forces on the *Horten Ho 9.*

When we visited with *Dr.-Ing. Anselm Franz* at *Junkers Jumo* in 1943 *Walter* asked him for two *Junkers Jumo 004s* for use in our *Horten Ho 9. Dr. Franz* told us he only had twelve *Junkers Jumo 004s* at that time. Engine numbers seven and eight had burned up in the crash of a *Messerschmitt Me 262.* Engine numbers two and three had also been lost the same way. "Give me," I asked *Franz*, "the empty engine casings so that we can use them as mockups." *Franz* said "yes, I will see." He then asked us if we knew how many men he had working on the *Junkers Jumo 004* turbines? "No we don't" Look here he told us, I have a total of twenty men and

The unique drag rudder belonging to the *Horten Ho 3-H*. It rotated up out of the wing above and below to provide air resistance. Although experimental, this type was not used again in any other *Horten* flying machine.

they include the young men you see here. *Dr. Franz* said that if *Junkers Jumo* engineers came to his shop from the *Junkers* diesel works and wanted to use his equipment, he had to let them. "I must stand back while they use my machines," he said. The diesel people had priority. *Dr. Franz* said that he did not have priority for his turbines over other engine development. *Walter* had arranged to get materials for *Dr. Franz and* also tried to get a priority number so that we *Hortens* could obtain the turbojets. *Walter* was able to get some materials for *Dr. Franz* through the Inspectorate of Fighters. "Can you imagine that! We had to help *Dr. Franz* out with materials so that he could build us turbojet engines in 1943." We got our *Horten Ho 9* a priority number and, thus, gave *Franz* the materials he needed to build our engines. *Walter* told *Dr. Franz* that the *Messerschmitt Me 262* being built at Augsburg by *Messerschmitt AG* would not fly in combat because the *RLM* was not that much interested in it. *Walter* once went to *Messserschmitt AG* in his role as a representative of the Inspectorate of Fighters. He asked why the turbojet powered fighter was not being flown more than it was. *Walter* was told by *Messerschmitt AG* that the *RLM* wasn't really interested. After *Walter* got back to Berlin he spoke to *General Adolf Galland* about the *Messerschmitt Me 262*. *Galland's* reply was that he really know nothing about it.

About four to five weeks later, *Adolf Galland* flew the *Messerschmitt Me 262*. After this flight he used his influence with *Göring* to get more *Messerschmitt Me 262's* built. *Messerschmitt AG* had been short of people working on the *Messerschmitt Me 262* and had only a few people building them. *Dr.-Ing. Franz* at *Junkers Jumo* was working with 15 to 20 men on the *Junkers Jumo 004s* and most of them were young boys. It was the fault of the Air Ministry and I think that their *Mr. Hans Antz* was the most negative thinker in all of Germany. Others, too, were negative thinkers such as *Lucht* and *Reidenbach*. *Reidenbach* was pretty much a zero-zero. Both men were pretty much criminal engineers. *General-Ing. Reidenbach* was an idiot.

We finished our year at the technical university in Berlin which was part of our award for winning the *Lilienthal Prize*. At this time the political situation was changing and I had heard on the radio that war could break out with England at anytime. I had been thinking about an aircraft project called the *Horten Ho.8*. We had many engines from old *Messerschmitt Bf 109B's* and *Junkers 210s* of

Dr.-Ing. Rudolf Göthert, formerly of *Gothaer Waggonfabrik*-Gotha. April 25th 1963. In 1944 and early 1945, *Gothaer* had been ordered to produce in the *Horten Ho 229* in series production. *Göthert* opposed the order and sought very hard to replace the *Horten Ho 229* with a design of his own known as the *Gothaer Go P-60B.*

550 horsepower and water cooled, 12 cylinder inverted V's and. I believed that *Walter* and I could build an aircraft with twice the span of 20 meters. We would then have 150 meters square of wing surface and we could arrange for this aircraft to fly around England and over the ocean. I thought that the aircraft could fly for 24 hours with a crew of three. It could be used as an observation and bomber aircraft. In order to fly this aircraft at 4,000 meters (13,100 feet) we'd have to go a great dimension to achieve this. This is how the twin engined *Horten Ho 5A* and *Horten Ho 5B* came to be built. Then the war started.

The war with England was interrupted. *Walter* had flown for a while in France and was later transferred to the *Inspecorate of Fighters Command* in Berlin. On his way to Berlin he stopped to see me at Braunschweig. We spoke about the flying conditions which he had experienced in the war. We were thinking, too, what we could do to help the *Luftwaffe* in the technical sphere. In Berlin *Walter's* chief was *General von Döring*. He had been in charge of *JG/26* prior to the Battle of Britain.

In Berlin *Walter* frequently heard comments how was *Nazi* Germany going to win the war in the skies? The *Horten Ho 5A* had been destroyed on its maiden flight. The wooden *Horten Ho 5B* had been left out doors over the winter and its wooden covering needed to be replaced. *Walter* got an order to have the *Horten Ho 5B* repaired. We weren't quite sure what we'd do with it after it was repaired. *Walter* thought he'd present it to the Air Ministry as one way to again win the war in the skies. *Walter* and I believed that our *Horten Ho 5* all-wing would provide higher performance better than any other aircraft flying in Germany at this time. Orders to repair the *Horten Ho 5B* came through *Ernst Udet's* office. It came from *Udet's* secretary which *Walter* later married in 1943. She also helped organize the command "*Sonder Kommand 3*" in Minden where *Heinz Scheidhauer* and I were building the *Horten Ho 4A* sailplane. Our *Horten Ho 5B* was going to be repaired by *Pesckhe*. About the same time I was looking for more powerful engines of higher horsepower for the *Horten Ho 5B*. Well, all these plans for improving the *Horten Ho 5B* actually turned out to be the plans for a new plane which we were calling the *Horten Ho 7.*

Walter came and told me about the work being done by *Argus* on their so-called pulsejet or ramjet engine. It would produce a thrust of about 600 kilogram (1,322 pounds). He told me that we should try to place one of these *Argus* ramjets in our proposed *Horten Ho 7.* We agreed that we would have two piston *Argus* engines and later on we would place an *Argus* ramjet under the wing between the two piston engines. But *Walter* had been advised by a man from *Argus* named *Ditrich.* He said that the ramjet's performance would not allow a pilot to fly it due to the tremendous noise levels its operation created. Plus, *Ditrich* said that the ramjet was bad for one's health. *Walter* through *Sabrina* in *Ernst Udet's* office arranged to have the firm of *Peschke* construct the *Horten Ho 7* according to my design plans. All further thoughts about design modifications to the *Horten Ho 5* were halted and I concentrated on the construction of the *Horten Ho 7* in Minden. This was in the winter of 1941-1942.

In the first several months of 1942 *Walter* and *Sabrina* had me transferred a group we called *Sonder Kommando 3* in Göttingen. It meant Special Unit 3. *Walter* had first talked with his superior *General von Döring* about it. *Von Döring* told *Walter* "yes, you can do it."

We also started to get into other things at Göttingen. Walter told me that the *Argus* ramjet engine would be no good for use on the *Horten Ho 7*. "*I* think I can get us a turbojet engine from *Junkers Jumo*," *Walter* told me. "If you will come and fly with me over to Dessau, we'll speak to the man at *Junkers Jumo* about obtaining one of these engines." This may have been about March/April 1942.

My first thought was to place a single *Junkers Jumo 004* turbine on the wing of the *Ho 7*, outside of the arc of its propellers. So we'd have two piston engines as well as one turbine. But then there was this problem about weight. The *Horten Ho 7* was being designed to take-off and land on grass airstrips. If we placed one or more *Junkers Jumo 004s* on the *Horten Ho 7* it would be heavy and it meant that it would only be able to land and/or take-off on concrete runways. I thought that this would be bad because it would limit the use of the turbine powered *Horten Ho 7* to only hard-

The proposed *Gothaer Go P-60B* by *Rudolf Göthert* with its prone piloting position. 1944/1945. This is the machine which *Dr. Göthert* claimed was a better flying machine than the *Horten Ho 229 V3* and so the *RLM* should cancel the *Horten Ho 229* series in favor of his *Gothaer Go P-60*. Water color by *Loretta Duval*.

surfaced runways. I also figured that the *Horten Ho 7's* air intakes for the turbines would have to be fairly high up from the surface of the runway to avoid picking up dirt, rocks, and other debris. So the higher the better, I thought. In the *Horten Ho 9* we had an air intake 1.3 meters or 1.50 meters above the runway.

Myhra: What was your first thinking on a turbine-powered *Horten Ho 7?*

R. Horten: My first thought was to take one of my *Horten Ho 7* designs complete with its piston-engines. I'd place a single turbojet between the two piston-engines. I wanted to do this in order to gain experience with the turbine's performance. But this engine was completely oversized for our *Horten Ho* 7. It's aerodynamic pressure in the center section was 1,000 kilograms. A single turbine was 1,200 kilograms so now its center section should now be stressed for 3,000 kilograms. That meant that the whole covering on the wings instead of being 2.5 mm thick should be 7 to 8 mm thick. The outer wing spars then had to be stronger and as for the glued joints , well, I felt that everything should be 3 times stronger.

Myhra: These pictures show what appears to be an all turbine-powered *Horten Ho 7*.

R. Horten: I told *Walter* that we could not use our *Horten Ho 7* as we had first planned. We'd have to leave the *Horten Ho 7* as it had been designed, without turbines. Instead we needed to design a whole new plane. At this point *Walter* made a wooden scale model of a proposed twin turbojet-powered all-wing. The engines were to be completely buried in the center section. This was our first design concept and we had agreed on a form which the *Horten Ho 9* might take. Later on I calculated that the aerodynamics of this scale model were not good and so we had to give the *Horten Ho 9* another shape. Thus, step-by-step we went through a series of designs to come up with the final *Horten Ho 9* planform. This early model shown here in the photo is the first model which Walter built. It did not have a project number, however, Walter carried this model around the Air Ministry to show how our proposed turbine-powered all-wing would look once it was built. So while he was showing off this model I had already come up with a better one. It didn't matter to the Air Ministry because later *Hermann Göring* would give approval to the concept.

The proposed *Gothaer Go P-60C* two seat night fighter design from 1945. This flying machine would have carried the late war introduced, internal, nose mounted, *FuG 240 "Neptune"*centimetric wavelength interception radar. Scale model and photographed by *Reinhard Roeser*.

Myhra: Yet the Air Ministry never really did warm up to the feasibility of an all-wing fighter/bomber.

R. Horten: Yes, the officials in the Air Ministry were not all that enthusiastic about our all-wing. They saw that there was no tail and that its turbine's exhausts came out of the wing at the trailing edge, and so on. They were really not all that interested.

Myhra: Why?

R. Horten: The thing was, I believe, that the people at the Air Ministry felt that the turbine was not an engine for an all-wing airplane. They felt that this new revolutionary engine should only be installed in conventional aircraft designs such as the *Arado Ar 234B* and *Messerschmitt Me 262* in order to achieve good efficiency (Possibly a reference to early concerns about intake efficiency on engines burried in the wing or fuselage PW). We told these people that we could do more with turbojets than could *Messerschmitt AG* with their *Messerschmitt Me 262*. We told them that our proposed all-wing would outperform the *Messerschmitt Me 262* with the same *Junkers Jumo 004* turbines. The Air Ministry felt that was impossible. This was the entire reason for my constant struggle in Germany. For example, the people in the Air Ministry had the idea that our all-wing aircraft were hard to control. Some even stated that if our all-wing went into an area of critical Mach number then it would go out of control. We told them that the critical number based on our calculations for a conventional tailed aircraft was indeed dangerous and that for an all-wing like ours the critical Mach number would be lower than conventional aircraft. In fact an aircraft with a swept-back wing and without a tail, I told them, was even better in that respect for high speed. The exhaust of the turbojets is free from an portion of the tail, since our planes have no tail therefore no turbulence from turbine exhaust. I said that the logical development of the aircraft was the tailless way. Well, said these people in the Air Ministry "that is only your opinion." In the German Air Ministry, few people believed what we *Horten* brothers said and that they wouldn't believe what we were talking about until they saw it with their own eyes.

The proposed *Gothaer Go P-60A* by *Dr. Rudolf Göthert* of *Gothaer*. Scale model by *Reinhard Roeser*.

Margret & Albert Speer seen on September 30th 1966 when *Albert Speer* was released from Spandau Prison after 20 years behind bars.

Myhra: Who in the Air Ministry didn't believe?

R. Horten: All of them. Engineers and designers working there plus the senior level officials such as *Reidenbach*. I also experienced the same lack of confidence in the all-wing here in Argentina as *Walter* and I experienced in Germany. Actually aviation people throughout the entire world did not particularly like the all-wing. At the end of the war the aviation industry in Germany was looking favorably on the all-wing as a good design concept.

Myhra: How often would you talk to the people at the Air Ministry?

R. Horten: Not very often because one could not talk with these people in the Air Ministry as they were without any knowledge. It was a waste of our time. These Air Ministry engineers and administrative types were not pilots and without any knowledge of aerodynamics. Plus none of them had ever flown an all-wing plane and few of them had ever been to the *Rhön/Wasserkuppe*. Even *Hermann Göring* had never been out there. All these people had learned their flying during World War One and all they could think and talk about

This is the tunnel location in the Harz Mountains where in early 1945, *Siegfried Knemeyer* of the *RLM* wanted the *Horten* brothers to initially construct their *Horten Ho 18B "Amerika Bomber."* Later *Knemeyer* would move the *Horten Ho 18B* operation to the new underground hangar Muhldorf near Landsberg. But in the numerous tunnels/caves in the Harz Mountains where German military production had moved late 1944/1945 the all-wing *Horten Ho 18B "Amerika Bomber"* was to have been constructed with slave labor and POWs provided by the *Speer Armaments Ministry* from surrounding concentration camps.

Siegfried Knemeyer realized that while the underground tunnels in the Harz Mountains might be adequate for mass production of *Wernher von Braun's A-4* (*V2*) bombardment rocket missile launched against London, it would never be suitable place to construct the *Horten* brother's *Horten Ho 18B "Amerika Bomber"* project.

were motorized conventional-tailed aircraft. Many of them were not even pilots especially the younger members of the Air Minis try. Thus, I could start the project of what we were now calling the *Horten Ho 9*.

I believed that I would need about 6 months to construct our *Horten Ho 9*. Later on I expected to have the first drawings of the proposed *Horten Ho 9* within three months. Then later on in the workshop I could continue the drawings whilst we had the *Horten Ho 9* under construction.

Our *Horten Ho 9* was not an aircraft in which I could say to our workers "well, tomorrow we go into the workshop and begin." Therefore, I figured I'd need about 12 months to complete the drawings, start construction, and get the aircraft ready for flight. I thought that the *Horten Ho 9* prototype would be flying by the summer of 1943. We started building several components of the *Horten Ho 9* right away. However, *Walter* kept telling us that all the parts of this aircraft would have to be very strong because this would be a very fast aircraft. I answered that if it is to be fast then I need more men to build it. Shortly afterwards I received more men, draftsmen, engineers, and others to help me. Also these extra men included welders to construct the center section metal frame. Now we had grown to between 80 to 100 men in the workshop at Göttingen. Well, *Walter* was organizing all this at Göttingen from his office in Berlin and the Air Ministry did not know anything about it. Then we started working and we still had no order to build this advanced aircraft. In the spring of 1943 we moved all the people working on the *Horten Ho 9* from the large hanger at Göttingen to the *Autobahn* vehicle maintenance facility at Grone about 4 kilometers away.

I frequently asked *Walter* to get me an order from the Air Ministry so that I might work on the high-speed design which we were calling the *Horten Ho 9*. I feared that without an order the design for the *Horten Ho 9* might not go further than that. If it was discovered it might be cancelled.

In one hangar at Göttingen we had two new wings for an *Horten Ho 3* sailplane. I was wondering how I might use these wings. My idea was still on high-speed flight characteristics, so I decided to place these extra wings on a new center section that had the effect of increasing their sweep back to 60 degrees. All I had to do was to construct a new center section plus a few more alterations. Thus was born the *Horten Ho 13*. I gave this glider the name "*13*" because it had the wings of a *Horten Ho 3*. I also felt, too, that we must have knowledge of the highly swept-back wing, a feature we thought very important during high-speed flight. I also wanted to know what was needed for high-speed flight so I needed an aircraft like the *Horten Ho 13* to investigate these unknown flight characteristics. I also needed to know what characteristics to expect during low-speed flight and during landing conditions. So I brought the two *Horten Ho 3* wings to our workshop in Hersfeld and told the men there "wait a moment because I am interrupting your work for this new project to test high-speed flight characteristics on a swept-back plane." It took about four months to complete the *Horten Ho 13*. We interrupted the construction program of the *Horten Ho 9* in order to build the *Horten Ho 13*. At the same time I continued to carry out the design work on the *Horten Ho 9* for an eventual presentation to *Hermann Göring*. For the way the *Horten Ho 9* was progressing, more work had to be carried out in order to gain his approval. The *Horten Ho 9* was going to be a large aircraft and we also saw in it a means of extending our knowledge about high performance planes. We could not hope to complete the *Horten Ho 9* without the experience gained from the *Horten Ho 13*.

Walter at this time had spoken with *General Diesing*, chief of *Reichmarshall's Göring's* staff. Then we had our meeting with *Göring* and he gave us an order (August 1943) to work on the *Horten Ho 9* and finish it in six months. That was only possible due to our previous preparation and work on the *Horten Ho 9* which had already taken place without any work order. With *Göring*'st orde we were now legal and *Walter* decided to change the name of *Sonder Kommando 3* to *Sonder Kommando #9* in honor of the *Horten Ho 9* project. *Walter*, I have to say, was the leader in all of this and was the one who organized it all. It caused him a great deal of stress. But we were now working on the *Horten Ho 9* and had finished the glider version on February 28th 1944 and it made its first flight. We sent a telegram to *Hermann Göring* that we had completed the work which you had ordered in the six months. We also told him that we were waiting for the turbojet engines from *Junkers Jumo* and once we had them we could complete the *Horten Ho 9 V2*.

One of *Wernher von Braun's A-4* (*V2*)'s being launched from Test Stand #7 at Peenemünde 1942-1943.

Then the men whom had been working on our *Horten 4B* (this must either be the Ho.4a or more likely he means the Ho.13 - *Author*) had finished that project were now available to work on the *Horten Ho 9*. It was about this time that I received some bad news about the turbine from *Junkers Jumo*. In front of the *Junkers Jumo 004* engine was the motor to start the turbojet. To the rear of the turbine were pumps, pipes, and other accessories to complete the engine. We had originally thought that the *Junkers Jumo 004* was only a tube of 60 centimeters in diameter. In its ready to run form, all of its accessories had been placed on the outside and its true diameter was really 80 centimeters! Initially, we had intended that the turbojet air intake be placed under the wing (leading edge PW). Now we realized that its starter motor was directly in the air intake so we had to modify the *Horten Ho 9 V2's* air intakes, too. We now placed them right in the leading edge of the wing. I telephoned *Dr. Franz* and he told me that we could have modified the location of the accessories on the *Junkers Jumo 004*, however, the Air Ministry would not allow it because they wanted a standardized engine package for use in all their turbojet-powered aircraft.

Now I had a major problem. I had designed the main spar for the *Horten Ho 9 V2* to accept a 60 centimeters (19.2 inches) diameter turbojet. No one had told me the number and/or amount of accessories placed on the *Junkers Jumo 004*. I had heard nothing. Nothing from *Junkers Jumo* and nothing from the Air Ministry. During the time we were building the air intakes and putting in the main spar, I had frequently wondered where its starter was located, where its electrical generator was located, its carburetors, and so on. But I never bothered to find out because all the plans we received for the *Junkers Jumo 004* stated that its turbine casting was only 60 centimeters in diameter. *Junkers* Jumo had told the Air Ministry that they would give the aircraft manufacturers all information relating to the *Junkers Jumo 004* to help them install the turbine in an airframe. But we were not included in this flow of instructions because the Air Ministry did not know that we existed

The *Horten* brothers...*Walter* and *Reimar*. Behind them are their *Horten Ho 2* and *Horten Ho 3*.

or that we were planning to build a jet-powered aircraft. Therefore, we did not receive any information.

I was thinking that the (spar PW) thickness we needed in order to accommodate the 60 centimeter *Junkers Jumo 004* turbine would be (proportionate to.... PW) a span of about 20 metres. That could not now be done as we had made a committment in our talk with *Hermann Göring*. I resolved to make the center section wider by the addition of one rib bay per side. I also increased the thickness ratio of the center section from 13% to 15%. With this increase in thickness, I could fit in the 80 centimeter *Junkers Jumo* turbojet. This change cost us one full month. I was happy later because the line of the curve of the quarter line of the wing was the same as for that of the *Horten Ho 4A*. It now increased the chord of the centre section and it took on the shape of the *Horten Ho 6*, where the curve of the quarter cord line pointed rearwards. Therefore, the *Horten Ho 6* and the new *Horten Ho 9* had the same aerodynamic effect on the center section. It was a very good thing that I had made the *Horten Ho 6* so that I could test this aerodynamic effect before I flew the new *Horten Ho 9*. It was about September or October 1944 when one of our *Horten Ho 6's* had come to Göttingen and we could see the effect of the aerodynamics of its center section. Well the turbine powered *Horten Ho 9* was finally ready in December 1944. It was transported to Oranienburg, the *Luftwaffe's* secret Air Base in the suburbs of northwest Berlin, for the airfield there was long and it had concrete runways.

The *Horten Ho 18B* as seen from above. This *Amerika Bomber* would have been powered by four *Heinkel-Hirth HeS 011* turbojet engines and attached to the bomber's fixed landing gear. Digital image by *Mario Merino*.

A side view of the underground aircraft factory/hangar at Muhldorf near Landsberg, showing a finished portion as well as an unfinished portion of its 18 foot thick concrete roof. It would be under this 18 feet of concrete where the *Horten* brothers would construct their *Horten Ho 18B*. May 1945.

A poor quality photo of the flying exit end of the giant Muhldorf underground hangar. The *Horten* brothers were told that their *Horten Ho 18B* could begin its takeoff run inside the hangar and fly right out this exit. *RLM* planners believed that this structure would be completely bomb-proof.

We had great difficulties with the *Horten Ho 9 V2*. In Göttingen, *Walter* had organized a barracks and a kitchen where every hour of the day there was soup and hot coffee available. A man who was hungry could go there and get some hot soup. We were working then about 16 hours per day. If a man was needed for welding he was called. If a man was not needed, then he was sent back to bed and when needed again to make this or that, then the man was recalled and sent back. Therefore, there were people in the workshop 24 hours per day, although not every person worked that many hours. This was our life at the end of the war.

It was not very different with me. I had my own room and men could come and speak with me. I told these men to go to the office and arrange times for me to see them and I would come to the workshop at 9:00 pm or 11:00 pm or 3:00 am. Our *Horten Ho 9* was day and night work. *Walter* kept the same number of hours as me.

In other cases on the *Horten Ho 9* for instance, the Air Ministry in Berlin had certain ideas about stress and aerodynamic pressure to which an aircraft should be built to withstand. Frequently I disagreed because many of these regulations were old fashioned and did not apply to my calculations. So I would lie to them. I would tell them that my structure met all of the design standards they had adopted. I did this so I could build my aircraft to perform better. If I had not, then my aircraft would have been to big and heavy for high performance. People in the Air Ministry, for example, could never understand this if they had not worked in aircraft design.

One day *Walter* came with the drawings of a turbojet. It was the *Junkers Jumo 004*. I saw that it was about 900 kilograms static thrust and the performance curves of the projected speed at thrust had been drawn in by hand. I laughed but it was sufficient information. This was the winter of 1941/1942 when I was still in Minden. *Walter* had found that the thrust would increase with speed. The *Junkers Jumo 004* had about 600 kilograms of thrust at take off and then would increase to around to 900 kilograms during flight. *Walter* had copied the thrust curves of a *Junkers Jumo 004* by placing the original sheets up to a window and made a tracing. But they had been wrong. There were 600 kilograms where I thought that there were 900 kilograms.

I started calculating what was needed for gliding but this was not yet clear. I had thought that the weight of the aircraft would be 3,000 kilograms (6,614 pounds) at first but then its weight grew to 5,000 kilograms (11,023 pounds) and then later on 5,500 kilograms (12,125 pounds) and ultimately 6,000 kilograms (13,228 pounds). An aircraft of this weight was impossible for a wooden wing. I did not know what we were to do? The plywood thickness and calculated strength of fittings or bolts needed in a 5.5-ton was also not possible I thought. This jet-powered *Horten Ho 9* was creating more and more difficulties for me. For example, the aileron surface I had considered was now insufficient. I had to change the design over and over. So thinking of a 5-ton or 6.5-ton fast fighter/bomber was

The size of the Muhldorf underground factory/hangar can be determined by the man standing on the wooden ramp at the bottom of the photograph. The structure exists today and it is being used by NATO forces.

RLM's Siegfried Knemeyer and the man behind the *Horten Ho 18B "Amerika Bomber"* project.

becoming more and more worrisome. Well, I resolved that we would finish the *Horten Ho 7's* design. For the *Horten Ho 9* it was going to be an entirely new design

In getting back to the *Horten Ho 9*, when I started calculating aerodynamic pressures I looked at my drawing board and discovered that the forces were too high and that the wood would not resist such pressure. I had made a test with fittings which we had constructed. We had to change the fittings in order to bring them up to the strength needed. We had come up to within 15 to 20 percent of the design load needed in the *Horten Ho 9 V2*. But we were still short of what was required. But we had to fly with the aircraft because we had no time to repeat the tests.

In finishing the *Horten Ho 9*, its drawings were modified for the higher forces. Therefore, the idea to have the *Horten Ho 7* turbojet-powered like the *Horten Ho 9* was changed in the first months of 1942. This time the thinking, drawing, and dimensioning of parts of the *Horten Ho 9* was also altered. This is something which we could not tell anyone. Today if we say that an aircraft has to have this and that, we would make it that way. But the construction in wood for forces as large as we would encounter on the *Horten Ho 9* had not been done before. Wood is a material which will not permit local forces, high local forces. In wood we were gluing and we were calculating the area of the glued joint. Plus the wood beneath the surface was moulded and this changed the whole design. This was stuff which people in the Air Ministry could not know anything about.

But the *Horten Ho 9's* ribs, its wing spars, and secondary spars which enclosed the torsion tube all had to be within 22 centimeters and for the tension of gluing in the wood the normal factor of security in gluing was 1.8. In Germany, at that time, it was 1.5. Therefore the dimension of the second spar was about 3 centimeters. But the 3 or 4 centimeters was not possible because we needed not 2 centimeters for gluing but 3 centimeters. So on each side the plywood was 3 centimeter's and to close the torsion box we needed 22 centimeters. I needed to discovered how this could be done. It was

Eugen Sänger designer of a piloted suborbital rocket bomber to bomb America from space. About 1945.

Sänger's suborbital rocket bomber project would have been launched via a 2 mile-long monorail track pushed by a multi rocket propulsive sled. Digital image by *Mario Merino*.

appearing that the *Horten Ho 9* would require large, thick wings and how big a problem would this pose for our workers?

Myhra: This problem had happened before. I recall with your *Horten Ho 1* and with your first two *Horten Ho 3's*.

Reimar: Yes. Let me explain further about the two *Horten Ho 3s*. In 1938 we were repairing a *Horten Ho 3* for competition at the *Rhön/Wasserkuppe*. At our workshop I had made an aileron out of plywood. The normal plywood used then was about 12 mm. But for this control surface flap I didn't have the plywood we needed. I called the firm *Gabul* for the correct aircraft standard material . Instead I was sent plywood of another type. I checked it for strength and it seemed superior for our use. So I used it. Before the wood was covered with fabric, inspectors from the *Rhön/Wasserkuppe* committee came to inspect it. One inspector encountered the wood, which in his opinion was not aviation grade. It was correct as far as I was concerned. But they would still not allow me to use plywood which had not been authorized for use in aircraft construction. I spoke with these men. I showed them my calculations and the test with the wood. They agreed with my tests. They told me that they would think about it but it appeared that it would be okay. Later I applied the fabric, painted it, and the *Horten Ho 3* was test flown. I had had a second *Horten Ho 3* ready to be finished, too. In the mean time I and others must have flown our first *Horten Ho 3* for over 100 hours near Bonn. Then two weeks before the *Rhön/Wasserkuppe* competitions were to start, I received a telegram stating that the material which I had used in the construction of the two *Horten Ho 3's* was not authorized for sailplane use. In the telegram they told me that these two sailplanes were no longer authorized to fly. Furthermore they said that I would have to retire these planes. I was not even allowed to fly them back to Bonn but had to trailer them. But I decided to change the material replacing it with authorized aviation-grade plywood. I tore open the fabric on the upper and under sides of the wing and proceeded to take out the unauthorized wood. It took the whole two weeks prior to the *Rhön/*

The *Eugen Sänger* suborbital piloted rocket bomber as seen from its port side. Digital image by *Josha Hildwine*.

Wasserkuppe. I finished the first *Horten Ho 3* and thought that I would not be able to complete the repairs to the second *Horten Ho 3*. But just before the *Rhön/Wasserkuppe* was ready to start, somehow I managed to complete the second *Horten Ho 3*, too. I was angry over this incident which I considered very unimportant for the amount of time which I had lost. So, in the future, I vowed to work more closely with inspectors but not to tell them what type of wood I had used but to keep everything quiet. I also built my aircraft so inspectors would not be able to see my work. I also had my sailplane friends tell inspectors that my work was according to regulations. This way I could get my airworthiness certificates without any trouble.

Myhra: Did you practice the same thing even when you built powered aircraft such as your *Horten Ho 5* and *Horten Ho 7?*

Reimar: Yes. For instance with our *Horten Ho 7*, the Air Ministry in Berlin had certain ideas about the stresses and aerodynamic pressure to which an aircraft should withstand. Frequently I disagreed because many of these regulations were old fashioned and did not apply to my calculations. So I would lie to them. I would tell them that my structures met all the design requirements which they demanded. I did this so I could build my aircraft to perform better. If not then my aircraft would have been to big and heavy for high performance. People in the Air Ministry, for example, could never understand this if they had not worked in aircraft design.

Looking back now over the years I think now that I choose the right path in my professional career. I had made the right choices. It would have been very good for me to have worked for a firm like *Heinkel AG*. But I think that we would not have developed the *Horten Ho 9* and few if any other sailplanes either. Without a career to develop, for example, the *Horten Ho 5*, *Horten Ho 7*, and even the *Horten Ho 9*, all these designs would not have been developed if I had gone to work for *Heinkel AG*. Unless, that is, I was in charge of my own all-wing department. Instead, I would have been just a part of a big *Heinkel AG* team. I wouldn't have been able to experiment on sailplanes nor the *Horten Ho 9*. Frankly, I do not believe that my brother and I would have been able to develop any of these *Horten Flugzeugbau* aircraft which were built.

Myhra: What happen to the *Horten Ho 5* and *Horten Ho 7* after the war?

Reimar: The prototype *Horten Ho 7* was at Göttingen. When the war ended the American troops gathered it up along with other ex *Nazi* German aircraft around there. What they found was brought to the air base, placed in a big pile and burned. Our biplane glider towing aircraft were burned plus our *Heinkel He 111* which we had

The *Eugen Sänger* suborbital bomber project, its bomb bay doors wide open and its radiation- spreading device is away. Digital image by *Joshu Hildwine*.

used to tow the *Horten Ho 9 V1* sailplane. All in all I estimate that perhaps 100 to 150 *Horten* planes, both sailplanes and powered aircraft were destroyed this way through out Germany after our unconditional surrender. They were burned by both American and British troops. (In fact the Hortens had built less than 40 machines in all between 1934-45..PW)

We had six *Horten Ho 7's* under construction by *Peschke* at Minden at war's end. The hangar's roof was blown off by a bomb and the steel rafters had come crashing down on the six unfinished *Horten Ho 7s* in side. Twenty *Horten Ho 7s* had been ordered all together. Two or three new *Horten Ho 7s* were scheduled to fly by March 1945

The only *Horten Ho 5* we had left at war's end was our *Horten Ho 5C* which we had given to *AVA* in Göttingen in late 1943. *Professor Stuper* at *AVA* had hangar space where they kept the *Horten Ho 5C*. He flew it from time to time. On one flight I witnessed he had landed with full flaps about 500 meters in front of the hangar. To avoid hitting the hangar he opened the throttles of both engines while the flaps remained in the down position. He managed to lift off and appeared to be climbing but was flying towards the hangar. He continued, trying to get more height out of the *Horten Ho 5C* but it was impossible due to the flap setting. It's landing gear touched the roof and immediately the aircraft was sliding across the roof for about 50 meters. Then it fell off the other side and on to the ground below. The *Horten Ho 5C* had lost all of its undercarriage, propellers and began burning as it lay on the ground. Firemen immediately came and put out the fire. *Professor Stuper* was not hurt badly. I estimated that the *Horten Ho 5C* was about 30% destroyed. It could not be repaired at that time so we put it out of the way in the hangar at the Air Base with thoughts to repair it later when we had the time. It was never repaired. The first *Horten Ho 5*, the *Horten Ho 5A*, which had been built out of plastic had crashed. The second *Horten Ho 5*, and known as the *Horten Ho 5B*, had been a two seater. Then it was later rebuilt by *Peschke* as a single-

Two top *Nazi* German rocketeers: *Walter* Dornberger and *Wernher von Braun*. Both would wanted a piloted long-range bombardment rocket missile to hit New York City. Their two stage *A- 9/A-10* rocket missile would have had the range to drop a radiation-spreading device on New York City.

Wernher von Braun's piloted two stage bombardment rocket missile *A-9/A-10 "Amerika Rocket Bomber"* seen shortly after launch. Digital image by *Josha Hildwine*.

Wernher von Braun's piloted suborbital rocket bomber has propelled itself out of and away from *it's A-10* booster rocket. Digital image by *Josha Hildwine*.

seater and known as the *Horten Ho 5C*. That it had been lost this way was sad.

Myhra: Why not use metal in the spars instead of wood?

R. Horten: *Walter* wanted to construct his great plane so that it did not reflect radar beams. I had heard as early as 1933 that the length of the Allied radar beam was 9 centimeters (3 ° inches), therefore I looked at all the spars, plywood, and outer plywood skin that had the dimension of less than 9 centimeters. So we had to build it that way so *Walter's* all-wing aircraft would not easily give itself away to the Allied radar. If I had used metal we would not have had these problems. These were the challenges *Walter* set me when he wanted our *Horten Ho 9* to fly through radar undetected. These were the problems I had in working with wood but the *Horten Ho 9* was designed to be built in wood from the outset -we never changed that concept.

Myhra: What were your problems in designing in wood?

R. Horten : We decided that the wooden structure of the *Horten Ho 9* would be entirely glued. Even the fuel would be contained in metal-less outer wing fuel tanks and made leak-proof with glue. Secondly, any metal used in the *Horten Ho 9* had to be covered with wood to make it unresponsive to radar waves. Radar went through the wood without bouncing back. However, if it later hit metal, then the radar wave would bounce back through the wood to be detected by a radar receiver because the beam would be scattered. That was our concept. Therefore, the center section which was made of steel tubing, had to be covered with wood. This wood had glue mixed with coal to absorb the radar waves coming off the metal steel tubing.

Myhra: You could have built the *Horten Ho 9* out of aluminum if you wished?

One of *Wernher von Braun's* piloted *A-9* suborbital rocket bombers on its way around the globe to hit New York City with a radiation-spreading device. Digital image by *Josha Hildwine*.

R. Horten: Yes, in fact it would have been much more easy to build.

Myhra: Why not do it then if time was so short in order to get the *Horten Ho 9* to the Front?

R. Horten: If we had built the *Horten Ho 9* out of metal then it would not have been undetectable by Allied radar.

Myhra: Allied radar as it was used in 1944/1945 was for an early warning that Axis bomber aircraft were approaching. Thus Allied fighters could scramble and go up to fight them. We are talking bombers here, not fighters.

R. Horten: The *Horten Ho 9* was to have been a fast bomber. Remember *Hermann Göring* wanted an honest 3x1000 bomber? Our workmen, too, didn't have the skills needed in metal-working. Metal work requires a great deal more time and skilled manpower to achieve good results. Also, we could not use the aluminum wings for use as fuel tanks. We would have had to build metal fuel tanks inside the wings and we would have lost about one half the volume of sealed wooden wing-tanks. So with wood, one could use less skilled workers. We had to use workmen without training. The time needed to build a metal wing verses a wooden wing in 1944 Germany was about 1 to 10. That is ten hours for a metal wing verses only one hour for a wooden one.

Myhra: Why did *Walter* want his all-wing 3x1000 fighter/bomber turbojet powered?

R. Horten: With conventional aero engines at this time we had a top speed of between 400 to 500 kilometers/hour (249 to 311 miles per hour). When I calculated the speed of our first *Horten Ho 9* design with turbine engines it gave a top speed of about 900 km/h (559 mph) and during the war the fastest fighter or bomber was

Generalmajor Adolf Galland and *Professor Kurt Tank* seen looking over one of *Tank's Focke- Wulf Fw 187* reconnaissance machines.

A Soviet *Polikarpov I-16 "ratta"* or rat. This was a veteran of the Spanish Civil War and was superior in the skies over Spain until the arrival of the *Condor Legion* brought in the brand new *Messeerschmitt Bf 109* in 1937.

The *Focke-Wulf Fw 190* originated in 1939 and it entered *Luftwaffe* in early 1941. Over 20,000 were produced in various versions. *Kurt Tank* had hoped to replace the *Messerschmitt Bf 109*, however, never did.

considered the best and was therefore the one which was built. So we had to raise our sights to 900 km/h. Remember, too, *Walter* was present when *Göring* gave a speech at the Air Ministry in early 1942 that he'd no longer accept any more twin-engined planes flying at 400 to 500 kilometers/hour top speed. The *Dornier Do 17*, *Junkers Ju 88*, and so on,when they needed parts in while located in the USSR, Norway, or Africa then the *Dornier Do 17's* aileron would not fit on the *Junkers Ju 88* and so on. *Göring* said it was all one big mess and that he and his Air Ministry would not tolerate it. Plus, *Walter* said, that *Göring* was angry over the fact that the performance of these twin-engine fighter/bombers was much the same. Thus there was no reason to have so many of the same aircraft. *Göring* said that in the future he'd only accept an aircraft project for development if it promised 1,000 kilometer/hour speed, 1,000 kilometer range, and carrying 1,000 kilogram bomb load. *Göring* wanted a fighter/bomber capable of multi-use. Industry leaders present told *Göring* that it was impossible to make an aircraft capable of the performance he was demanding. This included *Heinkel AG*, *Messerschmitt AG*, *Focke-Wulf* and the others. However, none of them had the performance offered by the turbojet engine and their designers were thinking in terms of piston-engines. With an airscrew, 500 kilometer/hour was about all that was possible. But with a turbine, *Walter* was thinking, it would be possible.

Myhra: No one offered 1,000 kilometer/hour performance through the use of turbines?

R. Horten: Apparently not. Our thinking was different. *Walter* had earlier given me the performance data of the *Junkers Jumo 004*. I wasn't really sure either. I had been calculating that a 3x1000 all wing might not be possible even though it was turbojet powered. I wasn't depressed because I felt that we *Hortens'* could still give *Göring* something close to his 3x1000 flying machine. I was thinking that with turbines I might be able to achieve 850 to 900 km/h (528 to 559 mph). Later on perhaps with more powerful turbines we might be able to raise the maximum speed up to 960 km/h (597 mph). To sweeten the pill, I though that we *Hortens* could offer *Göring* a 2,000 kilogram (4,400 pound) bomb load instead of the 1,000 kilogram bomb load he had demanded. Later, in my calculations about speed I figured we could certainly achieve about 920 km/h (572 mph).

Reimar Horten, Villa General Belgrano, Argentina. 1982. Photo by author.

Myhra: What was *Walter's* thinking about these numbers?

R. Horten: I told *Walter* at that time we should start a project powered by twin turbojets immediately. He agreed. We decided to call the project the *Horten Ho 9*. We felt that we could guarantee *Göring* that this *Horten* brothers fighter/bomber project would almost achieve his 3x1000 performance target. I asked *Walter* to talk to *General Diesing* who was *Göring's* chief of staff. *Walter* wanted to know if *Göring* would be interested in a fighter/bomber with approximate 3x1000 numbers? *Walter* told me that if *Göring* said no then we'll not even start the project.

Myhra: Did *General Diesing* give *Walter* any indications on how *Göring* might feel about a fighter/bomber with a performance close to the 3x1000 he was demanding?

R. Horten: No, but Göring sent us a telegram in August 1943 to come and meet with him. It was one thing to talk with him, but quite another to get money to build a prototype. I was prepared however, as I and members of my group had worked on a turbojet-powered fighter/bomber idea for about nine months. In all this time we were estimating forces, stress, and aerodynamics of the proposed project. I had been doing aerodynamic calculations on the *Horten Ho 9* such as lift-distributions and so on when the order came from *Göring* stating that he wanted a prototype flying within three months. I told him that this was impossible. We are at war was *Göring's* reply. I asked if I might have at least six months? He gave in and granted us six months to have a prototype flying. Well, on the very last day of the sixth month, February 28th 1944, our *Horten Ho 9 V1* made its first flight. We sent him a telegram. With this news *Göring* was satisfied with the *Horten* brothers. You see, most every other aircraft designer gave *Göring* completion dates for their aircraft projects and they seldom, if ever, produced the project on time as we had just done.

Myhra: How many *Horten Ho 9* prototypes did *Göring* want initially built?

R. Horten: We had spoken with *Göring* of the *Horten Ho 9* in terms of only two prototypes: powered and un-powered. With our glider version flying on February 28th 1944, *Göring* wanted our turbine powered prototype flying three months later: May 28th 1944. But we were having exceptional difficulties with the turbine *Horten Ho 9*. I had spoken with *General Diesing* about the turbine shells we'd received from *BMW* and had built the center section to accept them. Then I told him how they *BMW* said they would have them ready anytime soon. But when we received empty turbine shells from *Junkers Jumo 004* they wouldn't fit the openings made for the *BMW* turbines. I told *Diesing* that we had been forced to change our center section frame several times already. Even though all *Horten* workers were working in shifts around the clock to get the

Rudy Kosin, former chief aerodynamiscist at *Arado*. Munich, 1986. Photo by author.

Hermann Göring seen in his *Fokker D7F* in 1918. His love of the bi-plane from World War One never left him and even during World War Two, when times got tough, he longed for those glory days in his *D7F.*

A port side view of *Hermann Göring* in his all white *Fokker D7F*. About August 1918.

Reimar Horten and author *David Myhra*. The *Horten Ranch* outside the Villa General Belgrano, Argentina. 1982.

Horten Ho 9 V2 ready by the end of May, I told *Diesing* that we'd lost 2 to 3 months in building and rebuilding the center section frame. Six months would pass before the *Horten Ho 9 V2* made its first flight at Oranienburg Air Base (November 1944) and not the three months *which Göring* wanted.

Myhra: How did *Walter* go about first getting the *BMW 003* and later the *Junkers Jumo 004s*?

R. Horten: Well, first of all, turbines were top-secret in Germany at that time. *Walter* had his difficulties especially with *Hellmut Schelp*, the *RLM's* director of turbojet development. *Schelp* claimed that turbines were none of his business. But *Walter* was in the Inspectorate of Fighters and he knew about these turbojet engines which were under development. In the course of his work he had been to *BMW* at Spandau, to *Junkers Jumo* at Dessau, and to *Heinkel AG*. *Walter* had managed to obtain documents regarding these top secret power plants but he didn't have everything.

Myhra: When did *Reimar Horten* first learn about the turbojet?

R. Horten: *Walter* had first learned about the revolutionary turbojet engine and he came to see me in Minden in October or November 1941. That is when I first learned of it. At that time, too, *Walter* took me in his *Messerschmitt Bf 108* and we flew to Peenamünde to see the first public flight of *Lippisch's Messerschmitt Me 163* bi-fuel liquid rocket-powered interceptor prototype with H*eini Ditmar* at the controls. I remember one flight. *Ditmar* made a low pass over the spectators and then turned it on its tail and climbed vertically for 3,000 meters in seconds and we couldn't see him anymore. After the flight, speed recording equipment showed that *Ditmar* in one flight of the *Messereschmitt Me 163* had reached 1,000 km/h (621 mph). Later in the afternoon *Walter* and I flew back to Minden and then he flew on to Berlin. The purpose of the trip, said *Walter*, was to show you what *Lippisch* had designed. At this time the *Messerschmitt Me 163* was still pretty much a secret. *Walter* wanted me to see the performance of this *Messerschmitt Me 163* and to offer me some emotional support that the high speed performance figures I was calculating for our turbine-powered *Horten Ho 9* of 950 km/h (590 mph) was not all that unlikely. In fact *Walter* felt that 950 km/h was indeed possible because *Lippisch* was already reaching beyond it everyday of the week. Yes, I agreed but what I was really impressed with, was that *Lippisch's Messerschmitt Me 163* had only 6 mm of plywood covering the wings. This was of considerable interest to me. *Lippisch's Messerschmitt Me 163* had a wing span of 8 meters and I had proposed 16 meters on our *Horten Ho 9*. So I was quite happy to see that the *Messerschmitt Me 163* flew so well and at such a high speed with only a 6 mm thick plywood wing skin. I was now very interested to get on with our turbojet-powered *Horten Ho 9*.

Willy Messerschmitt about 1930.

Two former *Focke-Wulf* aircraft designers postwar: *Martin Winter*, left, and the *Focke-Wulf Fw Ta 183* design genius *Hans Multropp*. Interrogation London, England 1946. Both men would later be hired by the British a later still, immigrated to America and worked for *Martin Aircraft*, Baltimore, Maryland.

A starboard side view of the wind tunnel scale model of the single seat turbojet powered fighter *Focke-Wulf Fw Ta 183* by *Hans Multhopp*. Late in the war it had been selected for series production. Only design drawings were completed by war's end. *Kurt Tank* built a flawed copy in Argentina post war called the "*Pulque Dos*" or arrow two.

Myhra: Did the *Hortens'* ever consider putting a *Walter* bi-fuel liquid rocket drive in one of their all-wing aircraft?

R. Horten: Well, Walter always wished to have a high-speed design. Early on in the design of the *Horten Ho 9* we first considered using a *BMW* turbine with one of *Helmut Walter's HWK 509* bi-fuel liquid rocket drive attached to it. This particular engine arrangement was known as the *BMW 003R*. He was really serious and was pushing ahead in this direction. I asked him to reconsider. We should first obtain experience with turbojet-powered aircraft. I did not wish to have the *BMW 003* and a rocket drive in one airframe. Instead, I wanted an engine that had been tested such as the *Junkers Jumo 004* and *BMW 003* and was more reliable. Actually I really didn't want to get involved in rockets of any kind because *Alexander Lippisch* had already gone in this direction. So I wanted to concentrate entirely an on turbojet-powered all-wing.

Myhra: The *Hortens* were initially given *BMW 003s* for use in the *Horten Ho 9*. Why?

R.Horten: Initially our *Horten Ho 9* was known about to only a handful of people. *Ernst Udet* had committed suicide.. *Walter* had talked with the American college-educated *Hellmut Schelp* in the *RLM* who said that the *Hortens* had to use the *BMW 003* but they were not ready even to be installed in our center section frame at this time. I wasn't pleased by this development but the new turbine was a highly controlled item in Germany at this time and in many ways we were a sort of beggar. *Walter*, in his position with the Inspectorate of Fighters became friends with the engineering people at *BMW* especially the man in charge of *BMW's* turbojet engine department. His name was *Dr.-Ing. Hermann Osterrich*. Walter initially asked *Dr. Osterrich* for a pair of his *BMW 003* turbines. He didn't have any turbines which had been certified as flight ready. So *Dr. Osterrich* gave *Walter* two *BMW 003* empty engine casings. We could use them as mockups in our *Horten Ho 9's* center section frame. This we did. But it wasn't long before *Dr. Osterrich* suggested to *Walter* that the *Hortens* would be better off obtaining a pair of flight-ready *Junkers Jumo 004* turbines.

Focke-Wulf's Kurt Tank shown in Argentina in the late 1940s.

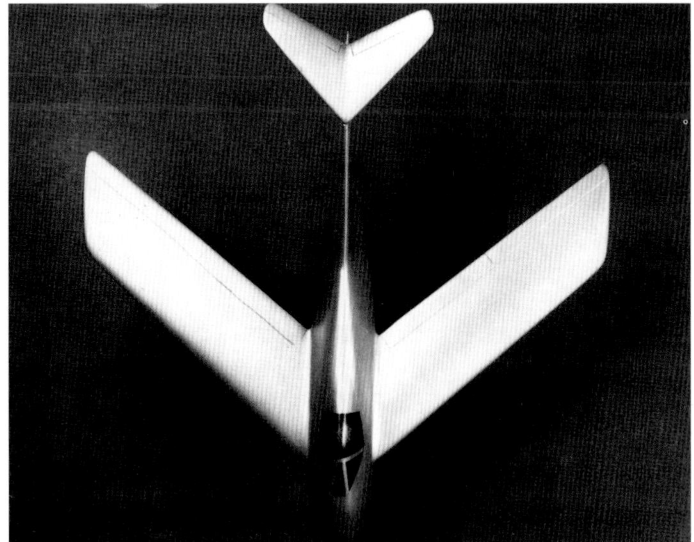
Top view of the wind tunnel scale model of the *Focke-Wulf Fw Ta 183* by *Hans Multhopp*.

Myhra: How did you feel about that?

R. Horten: I wanted this, too. The *Junkers Jumo 004* was at that time being tested in the *Messerschmitt Me 262*. If the *Hortens* took a turbine givimg less thrust and less speed than the *Messerschmitt Me 262, t*hen our critics would say that the *Horten* all-wing is no better than any other aircraft. If we had the same speed or higher than any other turbine-powered aircraft but with only half the take-off distance and half the landing speed of the *Messerschmitt Me 262*, then we were in competition. This is what I thought. Plus our all-wing would have great handling characteristics, no stalling and so on. But it was *Schelp* who wanted us to use the *BMW 003* but they were not ready to be installed. They were in no condition for installation while the *Junkers Jumo 004's* had been under development for probably two years longer. If we had used the *BMW 003* as *Schelp* wanted then we were running a great risk. What if the *BMW 003s* failed in flight? Then they would blame the all-wing as a failure. This was critical to us. I wanted to reduce the competition between our *Horten Ho 9* and the *Messerschmitt Me 262*. I knew

Oberst Siegfried Knemeyer seen entering the cockpit of the motorized *Horten Ho 3-G* at Oranienburg. Spring 1945. The top of *Walter Horten's* head is seen in the background. *Knemeyer* very fond of the *Horten* all-wing flying machines...especially their twin motored *Horten Ho 7*.

Hanna Reitsch (1912-1979) with *Walter Horten* (1913-1999).

Men of the *Horten Flugzeugbau* standing in front of a *Horten Ho 3,* November 1944, Göttingen. Left to right: worker, *Ing. Schmidt* (*RLM*), *Ziller, Scheidhauer, Rösler,* helper, helper, *Strebel,* helper, and helper. The "helpers" were *Luftwaffe* airman assigned to the *Horten Flugzeugbau.*

Left to right: *Reimar Horten*, *Erwin Ziller*, unknown, and unknown.

Erwin Ziller attending to the port side rear fuselage of an *Focke-Wulf Fw 190.*

Reimar Horten. 1982 Argentina. Photo by author.

Left to right: *Udet, Heinkel, General-Ing. Wilhelm Lucht* (*RLM*), *General-Ing. Gottfried Reidenbach (RLM), Robert Lusser,* and *General-Ing. Wolfram Eisenlor (RLM).*

April 5th 1941. Second flight of the *Heinkel He 280. Ernst Udet* in center, clockwise *Ernst Heinkel, Wolfram Eisenlor, Helmut Schelp, Robert Lusser, Dr. Werner Baumann* left of *Lusser. General-Ing. Lucht, Carl Francke* background, *Dr. Lehner, General-Ing. Gottfried Reidenbach, Siegfried Gunter.*

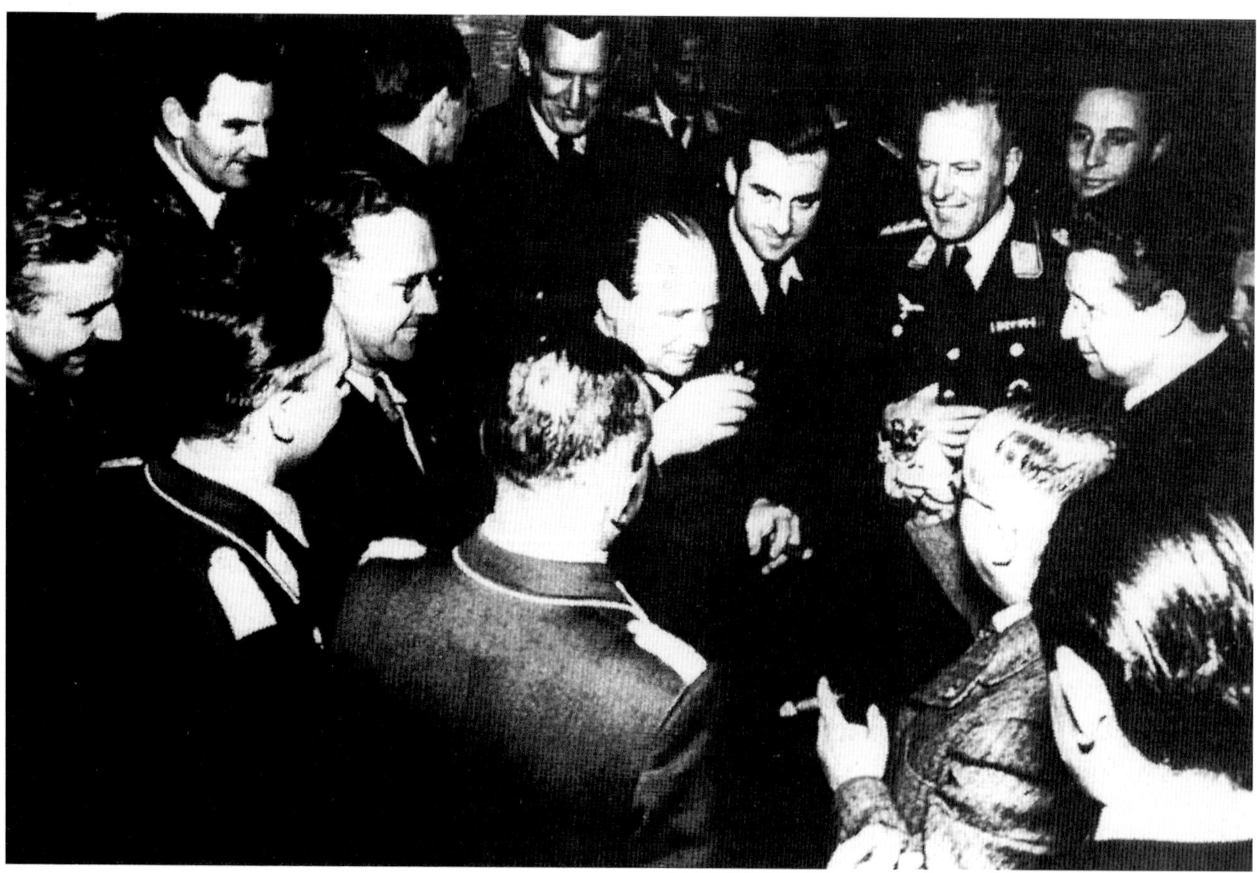

One of *E-stelle*-Rechlin's most gifted test pilots...*Otto Behrens* in white overalls. Shown in Argentina with the *Kurt Tank*-designed "*Pulque Dos*" in the background. This machine later killed *Behrens* during a test flight.

Heinz Scheidhauer in the early 1940s.

Wolfgang Späte Kommander of *1./JG400* seen in early 1945.

Wolfgang Späte at far right.

Coat of arms of *JG/400* with its *Messerschmitt Me 163* but soon to be re-equipped with the *Horten Ho 229.* 1945.

Reimar Horten. About 1944.

our *Horten Ho 9* would out perform the *Messerschmitt Me 262* no matter what turbine we used, however, if we had *BMW 003s* and we did better, then critics would say that the *Horten Ho 9* did a better job because it used different engines. This was not acceptable. Later on the *BMW 003* bug's would be worked out and it would deliver greater thrust. I had nothing against *BMW*. For the *Hortens'* and our purposes the *BMW* simply was not ready and we wanted to compete with the *Messerschmitt Me 262* for speed, handling, and flight characteristics. We needed the *Junkers Jumo 004* to have a level playing field.

Myhra: When did the *Horten* brothers receive their *Junkers Jumo 004s*?

R. Horten: When the *Horten Ho 9* prototypes were ordered by *Göring* we went immediately to *Junkers Jumo* to speak with the director of turbojet development, *Dr. Anselm Franz*. We wanted to know when we might expect the turbines to be delivered to our workshop in Göttingen. No money would be exchanged. *Junkers Jumo* needed our signature on their papers. Later the *RLM* would reimburse *Junkers Jumo*. I don't remember exactly what they cost at that time but I think somewhere in the neighborhood of 50,000 *Reichs Marks* or twice the cost of a large piston engine.

Myhra: Did you receive these turbines immediately or did you have to wait?

R. Horten: No, we had to wait to receive them. *Dr. Franz* told us why. In his department *Dr. Franz's* staff had only built 12 flight-ready turbines. Two of the twelve had been destroyed in the crash of an early *Messerschmitt Me 262*. Several others had been lost, too, in flight-testing. *Franz* was wondering which of the remaining turbines he'd give us. We told him that we were not quite yet ready for them but only wished for a pair of empty turbine casings which we might use as a mockup in the *Horten Ho 9's* center section frame. Later on, we told *Dr. Franz*, he could give us two ready-to-run *Junkers Jumo 004s*. He immediately gave us two used *Junkers Jumo 004* engines. They had no accessories on the outside, no internal components and no starter motors. The were like one long pipe but they would do because we needed to know where the engine attachment points were located before we installed the ready-to-run turbine. We took the two empty *Junkers Jumo 004's* back to Göttingen with us.

Myhra: The complete ready-to-run *Junkers Jumo 004's* diameter was large than the empty turbines you took back to Göttingen with you. When did you find out the *Junkers Jumo 004's* true diameter after all the tubes, pipes, hoses, wires, pumps, and so on where attached?

R. Horten: It was a great surprise to us. The completed ready-to-run *Junkers Jumo 004* would not fit through the spar on the *Horten Ho 9* and there was no way to make it fit unless the center section frame was redesigned and enlarged. I wanted to use *Junkers Jumo'* turbines because they were already powering the *Messerschmitt Me 262*

End of Interview #1

Interview #2

Date: August-September, 1982
Location: *Horten Ranch* - 25 miles outside Villa General Belgrano, Argentina
Language: English

Myhra: Do pilots experienced in flying sailplanes make good test pilots in high performance aircraft?

R. Horten: We found that when a pilot has flown a great deal in a single-seat sailplane, he will often retain the habits and techniques of a glider pilot and indeed these habits will always remain with him. These habits are not appropriate when piloting power aircraft. These are customs which will seldom be corrected by a teacher or an instructor and this what we found with pilots who had flown many hours in sailplanes but with only a few hours with an engine. Well, this skill of flying, that is for pilots accustomed mainly to sailplanes, is not suited for high-speed aircraft. Therefore, for high-speed flight testing, it is not good to have only pilots of sailplanes. For example, my son who flies the *Boeing 757* would not make a good sailplane pilot. A completely different skill is involved.

Myhra: I would think that one's flying skill was easily transferable that is from plane to plane. That if one was a good sailplane pilot, well, you would also be a good power pilot.

R. Horten: No, not from gliding to power. Yes, from power to power. If you have a sailplane, for instance, to land it you have to touch down gently at the point of stalling. If you have a plane, for instance like a *Boeing 737*, you have to touch down with 2 meters (6.6 feet) per second vertical velocity (vertical sink rate). Plus you've got thrust available from the engines. That is to say you have to touch down with a noticable rate of descent but not so with a sailplane. In the example of the jet-powered aircraft, the approach is made with power on, anyway the pilot needs an entirely different skill. You must come with power at the top of the end of the runway and then reduce the power but only a few seconds before touching down. In a sailplane one comes in to land using air breaks and comes down in style completely different from that of a powered aircraft. If you have a good glider pilot it is difficult for him to land large powered aircraft like a *Heinkel He 177* or a *Heinkel He 111*, these aircraft are completely different. Well, take the case of *Leutnant Erwin Ziller*. He had experience piloting a *Heinkel He 111* and he always approached using power to the runway threshold and landed like they do today with large aircraft. This is the way to land large aircraft and it is completely different from how you land a sailplane.

Myhra: Did you always feel that *Heinz Scheidhauer* would not be qualified to pilot your turbojet-powered *Horten Ho 9 V2*?

R. Horten: Yes, always. *Heinz Scheidhauer* was accustomed to landing all aircraft as if they were sailplanes so he was not able to land a large powered plane the way it has to be done. While landing the *Heinkel He 111* for instance, he could carry it off but not the way it should be done. As a pilot *Scheidhauer* always over-estimated himself. He had no theoretical knowledge and you can't easily explain to a man like that how it should be. He had learned his flying skills in sailplanes and always applied this experience to every aircraft he flew no matter if it was powered or a glider. That is not possible.

Myhra: *Erwin Ziller* came to Göttingen, to the *Horten Flugzeugbau* in March, 1944.

R. Horten: This was because *Walter* had told the German Air Ministry that we needed an *Heinkel He 111* and pilot to tow our *Horten Ho 9 V1 glider*. Göttingen had a small airfield and therefore we got the *Heinkel He 111* and its pilot *Erwin Ziller*. Well, our *Horten Ho 9 V1* glider was not yet ready. But *Heinz Scheidhauer* wanted to learn how to fly the *Heinkel He 111*. *Ziller* let him and they flew it together until Ziller let him fly it solo. Once at Guntestburg, the chief of the airfield at Nordhausen told *Scheidhauer* that he could fly the *Focke-Wulf Fw 58*, this was a little B-class aircraft. *Scheidhauer* confided to me that he had never flown the *Focke-Wulf Fw 58* and he wanted me to show him how to fly it. I had flown the *Focke-Wulf Fw 58* before at flying school. So we carried out some familiarization flights to accustom him to the aircraft. Later *Scheidhauer* flew with the airfield chief to an airfield on the Baltic coast, despite the fact that *Scheidhauer* had no formal tuition in powered aircraft. He was piloting sailplanes at the beginning of the war and this is why he was sent to a transport glider flying school. At the time the war began he was transferred to the *Luftwaffe* air base at Köln , to a paratrooper unit, to fly the large troop gliders which could carry ten fully equipped soldiers. By telling you this I am not criticising *Scheidhauer*. It is only to explain why *Scheidhauer* could not fly our *Horten Ho 9 V2*. He was not capable. At this time the *Horten Ho 9 V2* was an aircraft weighing some seven tons even without armament. It was a big machine. *Scheidhauer* had only flown small sailplanes and the *Heinkel He 111* was the biggest thing he had flown.

Myhra: How much did the twin engined *Heinkel He 111* weigh?

R. Horten : Oh, about ten tons with a full bomb load. But *Heinz Scheidhauer* managed to fly it. I will tell you how it was with him. *Scheidhauer* flew the *Heinkel He 111* like a sailplane. He'd want to touch down after a long descent, with engines dead and that is not the way its done with a large aircraft. Large planes have to really touch down and not glide in like sailplanes. *Scheidhauer* could not understand this. He always thought that a landing that was long and soft was the best kind. A gliding-landing is wrong in a large plane. Another thing, *Scheidhauer* wanted to land without the engines running! He'd make his final approach without engines operating. With a large plane one never, never cuts the engine while in the glide path. Instead a landing must be done with at least some power, otherwise if you approach low and need to apply power, youcannot as the engines are stopped – this is a bad situation. *Erwin Ziller* knew how to pilot large aircraft and was always in the habit of approaching with power if he had the undercarriage out and flaps down. The attitude of the aircraft had to bc the same as at take off so that if there was any problem he could to go around and make a new landing attempt. But not *Scheidhauer*. He wanted to kill the engines while landing.

Myhra: I have heard that *Ziller* had been a *Junkers Ju 87 "Stuka"* pilot in Polish Campaign and that he had later flown *Focke-Wulf Fw 190's* in the North Sea against Allied shipping.

R. Horten: I will tell it like it was. *Erwin Ziller* had flown at Nordhausen and not in Poland. He had flown the *Junkers Ju 87 Stuka and* he told me, it was very good in diving. The *Junkers Ju 87 flew so well that* it would fly by itself, said *Ziller*. The other thing he told me was that the *Focke-Wulf Fw 190* was not so good. In Göttingen, there was a *Focke-Wulf Fw 190* which had been in the airfields workshop for repairs and when it was finished it had to be test flown. There were at that time no pilots in the workshop with experience on the *Focke-Wulf Fw 190.* A test flight can be done only by a man who had flown this type of plane on other occasions so that he knows what was good and not so good about the aircraft. The chief engineer of this workshop asked *Heinz Scheidhauer* if he had flown the *Focke-Wulf Fw 190? Scheidhauer* told him that he had. Good, said the chief engineer, then would he like to test fly it? The next day *Scheidhauer* sat in the cockpit and looked around at the controls to see how they were arranged and he made his first flight in the *Focke-Wulf Fw 190* as a test pilot. That was unacceptable for if he had had an accident he would have destroyed all our work at Göttingen on our *Horten Ho 9* project. We wanted to know how was it possible that *Scheidhauer*, knowing that he didn't have any flight training in a *Focke-Wulf Fw 190* could have taken that aircraft up for a test flight? After the flight *Scheidhauer* was boastful. "Now I have flown the *Focke-Wulf Fw 190." But*, he never flew one again, either! *Walter* was so angry that *Scheidhauer* would do such a thing and put the whole *Horten Ho 9* project in danger. At that time we couldn't afford the risk of him flying the *Focke-Wulf Fw 190.* This could not be. This was *Scheidhauer*.

Myhra: Did *Erwin Ziller* ever make an unauthorized flight of the *Horten Ho 9 V2* at the Oranienburg Air Base in mid December 1944? *Walter* told me that *Ziller* was only supposed to make some high-speed "hops" until *Walter* could be present.

R. Horten: Well, for *Walter*, now this event is now more than forty years ago. The *Horten Ho 9 V2* was at the Oranienburg Air Base and ready to start testing. It was on December 18th 1944, I recall. We all were there. *Ewrin Ziller* got into the *Horten Ho 9 V2* and *Walter* and I had gone to the control tower. *Heinz Scheidhauer* followed about 5 meters (16.4 feet)behind us. I was angry that *Scheidhauer* had even come for he was not needed as a pilot for our *Horten Ho 9 V2. Walter* told me "let *Scheidhauer* come anyway because he can learn about the *Horten Ho 9*. Let's not have any bad feelings here now and besides his presence will not disturb us." So I went along with *Scheidhauer*'s presence. I thought that as *Walter* had a rank of *Major* and I was only a *Hauptmann*, with his rank that he should make the decisions on the *Horten Ho 9 V2's* flight testing program. I was surprised when *Walter* gave me the radio microphone and said, "Here, you handle this because you know the technical details of our *Horten Ho 9 V2 better." I* spoke with *Ziller* and we went on to make the flight. I remember all the words because I was asking *Ziller* about the trim, what was his speed? At this time *Ziller* was at about 2,000 meters (6,562 feet) altitude. I had also told him that the colour of the turbine exhaust looked good during his take-off. I spoke with *Ziller* the whole time while he was aloft. Later, after about forty minutes, *Ziller* came around to the airfield. He flew over the control tower and I told him via the radio that his undercarriage was out and everything looked good for his landing. I asked him again his speed? I told him that he should add a little more flap now that he was making his final approach. I suggested that he also reduce his speed by 20 km/h (12.5 mph) down to 150 km/h (93.2 mph) and let out the air brakes and reduce the thrust. *Ziller* them made his final approach and landed. We broke off radio communications. Well, *Scheidhauer* had been standing in the background and he had heard all the radio communications between me, *Ziller*, and *Walter* throughout the forty minute flight. *Scheidhauer*'s only comment I recall was that he said he would have been a little nervous to do what *Ziller* had just done. Well, we all went out to the runway and it was then that I saw that the *Horten Ho 9 V2's* rear undercarriage had suffered some damage. I saw that it had been caused by the recent landing. But *Ziller's* first flight with the *Horten Ho 9 V2*, in all, had been good. But he was also a little nervous. During landing he apparently had both feet pushing on the wheel-brake pedals, therefore the moment the wheels touched the ground, being locked, they bent the center section frame up at the rear wheels due to the brakes being applied. *Walter* noticed it too, and told me that "there's something here that's not good." I said to him "don't say anything about it now." We immediately towed the *Horten Ho 9 V2* to its hangar, to investigate the failure of the rear wheel struts. *Walter* agreed. At the Oranienburg Air Base there were always many people around the runways, hangars and so on. So *Walter*, *Ziller*, and I were alone now in the hangar. *Ziller*, too, was there. I don't remember if *Scheidhauer* was there or not.

Myhra: I don't think that he was there because he now does not remember the *Horten Ho 9* suffering rear wheel strut damage on that December 18th 1944 flight.

R. Horten: Yes, I do not believe that he was there either. I recall asking *Walter* and *Erwin Ziller* if we could go on flying our *Horten Ho 9 V2* even with the rear frame-strut damage? Or would we be forced to rebuild the framework and fittings on the rear wheels? During the design of the rear wheel support, I had not anticipated a landing where the brakes would be applied before touch down. That was the situation which caused the damage because greater forces were placed on the rear wheel framework than I had anticipated. While we were inspecting the *Horten Ho 9 V2* in the afternoon, I called *Rudolf Preussler* into the hangar and told him to bring in the workers and drain all the fuel from the tanks. Then I told him disconnect each wing from the center section. When all this was completed the next day, I told *Preussler* to tow the center section to the central workshop at the airfield. *Walter* and I would drive our car back to Göttingen that night and I told *Preussler* that we'd immediately redesign the rear wheel frame-support. I told him I'd have all the replacement parts sent to Oranienburg in a few days time. *Walter* and I then left Oranienburg by car to Göttingen. It was a long drive. We needed plenty of time to drive to Göttingen for we had to go in darkness because air raids were a constant danger. *Walter* and I left the *Autobahn* at Hannover and then drove on to Göttingen on less-traveled roads which were much safer than the *Autobahn*. We arrived at Göttingen in the early morning about dawn. I went immediately to the design office and called for the design drawings of the rear landing gear. We then looked at the center section frame's trailing edge. We checked to see what steel tubing we had in stock and changed the drawings so that the framework would be able to withstand a landing with the brakes on. This design change occupied the entire day of December 19th 1944. I did manage to get a little sleep and then went right back to the workshop. In spite of the damage to the rear wheel frame support we were still very happy that our *Horten Ho 9 V2* had flown and flown well. We thought that the *Horten Ho 9 V2* would be repaired and ready to fly again around Christmas time 1944. That same evening (December 19th 1944) I went to Hersfeld with one of our workers and with the new drawings. At Hersfeld there was a copy machine and we had to make copies of the drawings and by 12:00 am this worker was on the train to go to Göttingen. So by dawn on December 20th 1944 the modified plans were back in the workshop so the changes could be made in the metal frame tubing. *Hans Wenzel*, who was in Göttingen, made the new, heavier-duty steel tubes to the new dimensions and he was well along in fabricating these new parts for the *Horten Ho 9 V2*. Since all this was underway and it was almost Christmas, I thought I'd have time to go see my father and mother at Rottweil whilst our the people at Oranienburg were carrying out the repairs on the *Horten Ho 9 V2*. I had gone to Rottweil on either the 24th or 25th of Christmas 1944 and on the 26th I was back at Göttingen with my car. My auto had a wood-burning gas generator so we were able to drive. Later we had said good-bye to my parents and returned to Göttingen. This was the last time I saw my Father alive because when I had returned to Dietingen after the war with *Wilkinson* of the RAF-Farnborough, my father had already died. So I know exactly that it was before Christmas that the *Horten Ho 9 V2* had flown. When I returned to Göttingen they had just finished all the new steel tubes for the repairs to the *Horten Ho 9 V2* but they had not been sent on to Oranienburg. I was very angry with *Hans Wenzel*. I asked him why have these parts not been sent to Oranienburg? Well, that very night (December 26th 1944) one of our men was sent to Oranienburg with the parts needed for the repairs. So in the first week of January 1945 the *Horten Ho 9 V2* was still in the base maintenance hangar at Oranienburg Air Base. Also, there had been more problems than we anticipated. These problems were not technical but they were due to the fact that other military aircraft had arrived in the airfield's workshops from the Russian Front and they had been repaired first. Some of these repairs were major ones; therefore, the *Horten Ho 9 V2* was pushed off to the side in the hangar. *Walter* went off to Oranienburg to see if he could get our *Horten Ho 9 V2* repaired more quickly. It worked. Repair work was started on *Horten Ho 9 V2* about January 10th 1945 and it took until the end of January 1945 before it was finished. So work which should have only required three days took us took instead three weeks. Well, this happen to us because at the Oranienburg Air Base we were in a war zone . We could hear the Russians due to their shelling of Berlin when the wind came from that direction. Consequently the *Horten Ho 9 V2* was of no interest to the military people at Oranienburg, given the closeness of the Eastern Front and because it carried no armament

Myhra: Was *Walter* able to get a priority to fix the *Horten Ho 9 V2's* rear wheel struts?

R. Horten: Yes, but we now had lost about a month of testing time due to delays. It was *Franz Berger*, whom you know from your biography, was a draftsmen who lived in our house in Bonn after his house was destroyed. He had his wife and four children in Slaisan, a province in the east of Berlin and he had with *Heinz Simon*, obtained a car with fuel which was not easy to get and had come first to Göttingen. We had no time for this because both *Walter* and I were very busy. They got to the Oranienburg Air Base and there, (*Simon* told me this last year he was here in Argentina), they had seen the *Horten Ho 9 V2* and they had been told that yes, it had flown and yes, next week it will fly again. *Berger* could not wait for the Russian Front was east of Slavian and he needed to pick up his wife and his four children, all less than ten years old. *Berger* was able to get back. But on the highway they were stopped many times and were told that he had stay and fight the Russians. *Berger* was a civil worker and not a soldier and he told them that he had his four children and wife in the car and he could not go. Somehow he was allowed to continue. Now this was the end of January 1945. *Simon* could tell you the date better. Then, later on *Erwin Ziller* was able to resume his flight-testing with the repaired *Horten Ho 9 V2*.

Myhra: Did your associates/workers also install *Fowler* flaps on the *Horten Ho 9 V2* at this time, too, while its landing gear damage was being repaired?

R. Horten: No. No *Fowler* flaps. The *Horten Ho 9 V2* only had flaps in its center section and used as air brakes or landing flaps.

Myhra: I had heard that while the *Horten Ho 9 V2* was being repaired a modified trim control had been installed, too.

R. Horten: Trim taps had been located on the ailerons. It was difficult to access the rear wheel gear mounting points and I wanted that the gear should acessed nicely without bulges in the upper wing. All this would provide a smooth upper wing and that needed a few more hours of work. But all these improvements were difficult to make at this time for the climate for working was poor due to the nearness of the Eastern Front. That was the problem. Also, test flights made in February 1945 meant the possibility of seeing enemy aircraft as the Eastern Front was so near to Berlin. Further flight testing of the *Horten Ho 9 V2* meant we'd have to change locations. The February 18th 1945 crash of the *Horten Ho 9 V2* came about the time we were ready to leave the Oranienburg Air Base. For instance, *Rudolf Preussler* had been at the railway-station at Sachsenhausen concentration camp (*KZ*)in order to get all our tools and equipment back to Göttingen. He was not at the airfield. Also, *Heinz Scheidhauer* had been instructed to be in the control tower, but had been instead on the airfield, getting ready to go back to Göttingen.

Myhra: *Heinz Scheidhauer* says that he was only at Oranienburg just a few times and only when the *Horten Ho 9 V1* was being flight tested there.

R. Horten: No, that is not true.

Myhra: *Heinz Scheidhauer* also told me that he was only at the Oranienburg Air Base once when the *Horten Ho 9 V2* was test flown and that was on December 18th 1944.

R. Horten: Yes, he was at the *Horten Ho 9 V2's* first flight before Christmas 1944.

Myhra: He also told me that he didn't go back to Oranienburg Air Base again after that first test flight of the *Horten Ho 9 V2*.

R. Horten: No. No.

Myhra: *Heinz Scheidhauer* told me that the man who was supposed to be at the control tower during *Erwin Ziller's* fatal crash on February 18th 1945 was an *Arado Flugzeugbau* engineer who had been assigned to *Gothaer Waggonfabrik* for helping them with series production of the *Horten Ho 229*.

R. Horten: I'm sorry that *Heinz Scheidhauer* had to say this for it is wrong.

Myhra: Tell me about *Dr.-Ing. Paul Schmitt* from *Argus* and your thoughts to put a ram-jet engine on your *Horten Ho 7*.

R. Horten: *Dr.-Ing. Paul Schmitt* had been contracted by the German Army and not by the *Luftwaffe* for his design of the intermittent propulsion duct and he had a different design to make it. Later, post war, *Paul Schmitt* came to the Argentine Air Force at Córdoba. There he was designing a five-ton turbojet engine with length of 4.5 meter (14.8 feet) and a diameter of about 1 meter (3.2 feet). He told me that we must make it and with time we can make it better and with automatic controls it will be lighter in weight. I think that *Paul Schmitt* was a man who had good ideas. From Argentine he went to Mexico. One year later he joined General Electric Company and I think he was working in the turbines of GE. I didn't hear from him anymore after he joined the General Electric Company..

Myhra: Do you know if *Paul Schmitt* alive?

R. Horten: I don't know. However, we were of the same age. I think maybe, yes.

Myhra: Tell me about *Dr.-Ing. Franz* of *Junkers Jumo*?

R. Horten: I first visited with *Dr. Franz* in 1943 but he had been speaking with *Walter* previously. *Franz* told us that he couldn't give us a "mockup"of his *Junkers Juno 004* for he had none to give away. So I had asked him how many *Junkers Jumo 004* engine assemblies had he built. He said that they had built twelve. Twelve I said? Yes only twelve, he answered. It appeared that two of the twelve had been destroyed on a *Messerschmitt Me 262* prototype. A few other *Junkers Jumo 004s* were being test flown in other prototype *Messerschmitt Me 262s*. I asked him if he could make at least two more for us? "No;" he told me I have no priority through which to purchase materials such as steel, and so on. *Walter* then said "Oh, we have sufficient metals and we can give you some." We were talking like this. I asked him how many men do you have...200? "Oh no," he said, "counting my apprentices, all together twenty people. In a *Junkers Jumo* factory which had 3,500 men, *Dr. Franz* had only twenty. He told me also that if he had pieces in a turning lathe and *Junkers Motoren* people came, he'd have to remove his piece so that the others could work in their piece. The people at *Junkers Motoren* who built the diesel engines had the priority said *Franz*. Diesel engines were to have been made for *Lufthansa*. See, at this time, they all thought that the war had been won. So they now wanted to think of peace and the most important was the *Junkers Jumo* diesel engines for their huge seaplanes like *Blohm und Voss' Bv 222* and *Bv 238*. *Adolf Hitler* said that he would not have any development continued which would not be ready within six months and then be ready for the Front. At this time, then, all things under development were virtually stopped. When *Hitler* made these remarks *Hermann Göring's* German Air Ministry said that they would not spend the money for those products under development and not ready within the six month time limit stated by *Hitler*. The Air Ministry then began asking how much time was needed for this project and that project? If someone told them that it you require one or two years, well the Air Ministry said no, it is unrelated to the war effort so stop it. This attitude was a complete error of the highest order when during the early months of the war all development was stopped. If *Wilkinson* of RAE-Farnborough is saying that I was only making sailplanes during the war, then he must be thinking that *Nazi* Germany really wasn't at war. So we must have been at peace, allowing me to work on sailplanes. Well, we were at war and sailplane related projects were forbidden! But then, I could not have my workers, ten or twenty men doing nothing in the workshops at Göttingen and elsewhere. I had to give them work to keep them busy. So instead of making just one sailplane, I'd have them make three because the material was very cheap and thus cost almost nothing. So I built these three sailplanes with different washout or with different designs for the wingtip rudders and other details. I could also enter these sailplanes in competitions in order to assess their handling and performance. That was my approach and we had to work on my sailplanes in the back ground. So people like *Wilkinson* of RAE-Farnborough should have known that this was how development was controlled in *Nazi* Germany at that time. On the other hand, aircraft design which didn't lead to completion within six months was not allowed. If I made a sailplane and the German Air Ministry was told that the *Hortens* were doing this or that, they (the German Air Ministry) would likely not care. But if these people said that the *Horten's* are making a jet powered fighter prototype then the Air Ministry would probably have said that building fighters is contrary to *Hitler's* order and we would have been stopped. *Wilkinson*, I guess did not know this. He was fooled.

The *Junkers Juno 004* had only 4.6 atmospheres of pressure increase and I remember that *Prandtl* who was my teacher at the University of Göttingen (he was also the director of the aeronautical center in Göttingen). told me how *Waltz* in the department of compressors at Göttingen was working on improving the *Junkers Jumo 004* turbine. Well, *Junkers Jumo* should have gained one atmosphere of pressure in each of its nine compressor stages. So even with nine such compression stages the *Junkers Jumo 004's* total compression was still only 4.6. *Professor Ludwig Prandtl* was angry that *Waltz* and *Junkers Jumo* could not reach 1 atmosphere in each of the nine compression-stages. Most turbines today have nine stages, by the way. *Prandtl*, too, was working with other people at Göttingen in an effort to rise the *Junkers Jumo 004's* compression to 9.0. *Prandtl* was a great genius. You know also that *von Karman* was at the University of Aachen and he was the first student of *Prandtl*. *Prandtl* died in 1953, by the way.

Myhra: Did *Wilkinson* just not understand that you needed to construct all these sailplanes to gain experience and help your work on the *Horten Ho 9*, for example? Or was there more to *Wilkinson's* opinion? The *Horten Ho 6's* experience was used on the *Horten Ho 9* as with other sailplanes you built in order to collect different data.

R. Horten: Yes. But for a long time we were not officially allowed to carry on this type of research work if it didn't directly lead to completion within six months. *Wilkinson* claimed he didn't understand. The other thing is that I wished to have a wind tunnel and to use this for experimentation. For this reason I had moved from Minden to Göttingen. But, when I visited *Professor Prandtl* at his house in 1942 and we spoke together. I told him that it would be a great help to me if it were possible to place one of my all-wing models in his wind tunnel. *Professor Prandtl* said that "although I'm the director of the Institute, I am sorry that I cannot promise access to the wind-tunnel for these decisions about who or who is not to use the wind tunnel are made in Berlin."

Myhra: Who in Berlin had charge of the Göttingen wind tunnel?

R. Horten: It was a commission of many different men who had defined what would be measured in all the wind tunnels through out *Nazi* Germany then as well as in the future. So, for us *Hortens* the use of the Göttingen wind tunnel was impossible. *Ludwig Prandtl* was only the administrative manager of the tunnels. *Wilkinson* also, did not know this. But this is how it was. The men who were in Berlin were technical rather than scientific people. They were from the aviation industry and they would only measure things which were clear but what they wanted was the security that the aircraft coming out of *Nazi* Germany's aviation manufacturing plants were not flawed. So they didn't want to waste the wind tunnel's time doing basic research but only wanted to do practical investigations. So there was no fundamental research. For example, this commission knew virtually nothing about the sweptback wing. When *Dr.-Ing. Rudolf Göthert* of *Gothaer Waggonfabrik* measured the wing profile on the *Horten Ho 9* in his wind tunnel in Göttingen in 1944, he made great errors. None of his data was useful. In Göttingen *Dr.-Ing. Reganscheid* had also made measurements in 1943 on swept-back wings like on the *Horten Ho 9*. *Professor Prandtl* told me about it and suggestedI speak with *Reganscheid* about his wind tunnel results which showed that the sweptback wing will turn about the wing tip and enter into a spin. I contacted *Reganscheid and* I also said to *Ludwig Prandtl* that if he had the time I'd like him to come to the airfield. I'll come to get you with my car and bring you back to the airfield and give you a demonstration that a sweptback wing will not turn about the wing-tip and stall (tipstall PW). This is not possible said *Professor Prandtl*. but I'd like some of my assistants also to be present. Yes, I said, I agree. They included *Professor Pohl*. Then came the day at the airfield. We showed them the *Horten Ho 4a* and *Heinz Scheidhauer* was also going to give them a demonstration by flying the *Horten Ho 3* fitted with the small engine. Well, *Scheidhauer* came to 50 meters (164 feet) and stalled the *Horten Ho 3* by pulling up vertically. Then came the stall and *Scheidhauer* was able to recover in a few meters. He continued to repeat this maneuver. I told *Professor Prandtl* that this is to demonstrate that it is impossible for the *Horten Ho 3* with its swept back wing to enter into a spin. *Ludwig Prandtl* was at first very much against *Scheidhauer* carrying out this test. He didn't want us to do it because he sincerely believed that *Scheidhauer* would crash. I told *Prandtl* that I couldn't stop the demonstration as the *Horten Ho 3* was not fitted with a radio. Still, *Prandtl* vigorously protested and was very upset. *Prandtl* felt that

Scheidhauer would fall and die, attempting to prove to him that the sweptback wind would not spin. *Professor Prandtl* did not want to be a part of this. But *Scheidhauer* had done this, many time before and now that *Prandtl* was present he did it again and again around the airfield. In this moment *Prandtl*, *Reganscheid*, and *Pohl* changed their minds about the sweptback wing and their belief that such a planform would enter into a spin and stall. *Prandtl* told me that what they had witnessed with the *Horten Ho 3* was completely different from that which they had measured in the wind tunnel in Göttingen. Then I had a conference with the *AVA* and told the people about the sweptback wing. I didn't tell them about my bell wing-lift distribution ideas but I told them that the form of distribution would be the same only where the twist of the wing changed with the movement of the aileron. Therefore, the measurement must be made with zero moments for we have no tail and with the aileron deflected in this form the lift distribution is similar for each value of CL. This was completely new to the people at *AVA* and I remember that *Professor Betz* who was an assistant to *Professor Prandtl* told me that he was angry that his measurements were wrong for this polar was not in equilibrium. I told *Betz* that equilibrium was needed and he told me that we always have a variable center of gravity in the plane. I told him that this was a result of design and not a product of aerodynamics for we have the load distribution of fuel, and so on all around the span and not over the length. If you have a plane with fuselage and tail you have a great variation in the center of gravity. But if you have the load in the wing it is less and it's design could be made so that the center of gravity movement is zero. It had been outside the experience of the aerodynamic institution that one could rely on design and not merely aerodynamics to produce an aircraft which would not stall merely because it had swept back wings. So *Betz* said well, now I can only agree. *Prandtl* was always very interested in our work. *Betz* had sought to show that the Institute was not to blame for their negative findings on the swept-back wing. He could not understand that the Institute had been measuring things in conditions which didn't apply to real-life.

Myhra: Did *Professor Prandtl* felt embarrassed that their calculations were wrong?

R. Horten: The measurement of swept-back wings in wind tunnels was completely different from the data collected during test flying. This was due to the induced angle of attack, one way, and the other way, the boundary layer for lateral pressure/gradient will go spanwise, especially at the trailing edge towards the wing tips and this changes everything. This was not, I will say, considered by the wind tunnel people. Also, *Rudolf Göthert* of *Gothaer Waggonfabrik* had not known much about this phenomenon either when he made his measurements on the center section of the *Horten Ho 9's* wing. Well, the center of lift and center of gravity should coincide.

Myhra: Tell me about *Dr. Kupper* from *Gothaer Waggonfabrik.*

R. Horten: *Dr. Kupper* was also a professor of engineering in an university. He had also been with *Junkers Flugzeugbau* and he was a very good designer and aerodynamasist. In the1930s he went to the *DVL* in Berlin/Adlershof and brought with him a sailplane of 26 meters span(85.3 feet). In 1931 he had designed for *Robert Kronfeld* a sailplane of 30 meters (98.4 feet) span. It was the longest span ever built. (The Austria PW) This sailplane had very high performance and a very low sinking speed. *Kronfeld* crashed it in 1932 at the *Rhön/Wasserkuppe* and then *Dr. Kupper* produced a new design each year and built sailplanes all over Germany. He came to *Gothaer Waggonfabrik* in 1935 and without the knowledge of *Alexander Lippisch* built, the *Gothaer Go 147* a two seat tailless aircraft, powered by a single *Argus As* engine of 140 horsepower. This was the design which the German Air Ministry wanted but *Kupper* died in 1938 in one of his own sailplane designs after it went into a spin at Berlin/Adlershof. He flew these machines himself. This left *Gothaer Waggonfabrik* without a designer. The *Gothaer Go 147* had been finished but nothing came of it. Now *Dr. Rudolf Göthert* came to *Gothaer* in 1943/1944 from the *DVL* where his brother worked and by that time our *Horten Ho 9 V1* had already flown.

Myhra: Why was *Gothaer Waggonfabrik* not very happy with your *Horten Ho 9 V2* and the *Horten Ho 229?*

R. Horten: Well, *Gothaer Waggonfabrik* at this time had their own all-wing project designed by *Dr. Rudolf Göthert* and they wished to build it but they had no experience. *Rudolf Göthert* wanted the pilot to be in the prone position. This was a good idea but we had previously experimented with our *Horten Ho 3F* and *Horten Ho 4A* and thousands of hours of flying in the prone position. *Dr. Göthert* was more of a pilot and less of a designer. *Gothaer Waggonfabrik* had produced a drawing of the prone pilot position in 1944 and we laughed. *Dr. Göthert* did not understand what was the key to all this and I resolved with *Walter* that we will not speak about our bell lift distribution with Gothaer. It was late in the war and we will make our future with the *Horten Ho 9* and its bell lift-distribution. Therefore I didn't talk about it until it was written up in the book Nurflügel by *Peter Selinger*. *Jan Scott* came here to Argentina in 1979 or 1980 after I had retired and was writing the book Nurflügel. I told *Scott* about the bell lift distribution but he didn't understand. Then I wrote him a letter explaining it all and *Scott* published it in a soaring magazine. I think that it was not understood, either, by the readers. Therefore, one year later I wrote another article and sent it to *Scott*, to give more explanation but it was not understood. In 1983 the book Nurflügel came out in Germany and about 10% of the readers probably understood what I was talking about. The other 90% no. I wonder if the lift-distribution is very difficult to understand or what is the reason? Maybe the readers do not have the mathematics needed to understand? In 1918, *Professor Prandtl* had published the elliptical lift-distribution of lift and since that time the best aircraft have this type of, wing form without twist and down wash over the wingspan. This was a mathematical approach from *Prandtl* and it was excellent but *Prandtl* was a theoretical man and not a pilot, nor a designer - a practical man. He had forgotten that often aircraft do not fly in a theoretical manner - straight on but often yaw, right, left, as if it is swimming and if it is approaching a stall, a little yaw will cause it to stall one wing and at the same time the whole of the wing. This its to say it will roll and the ailerons will not help to correct it. It got out of control due to the pilot and this is what the pilot well understands and how it will behave. The pilot cannot fly with the wing generating the maximum lift, as this is dangerous, for the whole wing will then enter into a stall.

Walter had once been sent from Berlin to the Eastern Front to recover a *Siebel* twin-engine transport aircraft after one engine had failed. He brought it to the repair workshop Königsberg, where I was stationed, and they replaced the engine. This took only one day and while he was there we spoke about the *Horten Ho*. *Walter* told me that he could get an order from *Udet* for *Pesckhe* of Minden to repair the *Horten Ho 5*. I told him that it was essential, that I should also be moved to Minden, with some workers so that we had a group of personal there to work for Minden was only a repair depot and had no design capacity. Then *Walter* got order from the Air Ministry and signed by *Ernst Udet,* to repair the *Horten Ho 5* and transferring me, with five others, one engineer and three draftsmen. *Wenzel* and *Scheidhauer* went to Minden, too, and we also took the *Horten Ho 4A* there. There, in the winter of 1941-1942 we produced the necessary drawings for changes to the plane whilst *Scheidhauer* flew the *Horten Ho 4A*. He made an investigation of it in turns and in spins and how he gets in spins, continuous spins from 1,000 meters (3,280 feet) and how it recovered. We altered the center of gravity of the plane and repeated the spin testing. The center of gravity was changed by means of a weight which could be jettisoned in case of an emergency. He flew from Minden over the *Steinrudder Mar*, the large lake there, xso that it would not endanger to people on the ground if he had to throw out the additional weight. I gave *Scheidhauer* the order to fly fifty hours per month, with different programs to test the effectiveness of rudders, ailerons and so on for flutter and to ascertain what should be done in order to perfect future sailplanes. But all this was not sufficient for me to do and I continued my studies at the University of Bonn. I was enrolled there for two days per week for the study of mathematics. I had to go Bonn, for instance on Saturdays and Tuesdays and the other days of the week I was in Minden and worked with *Walter*. To help me out *Walter* had given me an airplane, a *Focke-Wulf Fw 44* which was an old biplane. I used it to go to Bonn Hangalar airfield to avoid the long railroad trip which would otherwise have taken about five to six hours. At the Bonn airdrome was *Franz Berger* who told me that they had the capacity to build one *Horten Ho 3* there. Two of the *Horten Ho 3's* which had been in Kitzengen before the war and had not been finished had been under repair in Minden. Now *Peschke* had finished them and also repaired the *Horten Ho 5B*. Therefore; I told *Berger*, well, we'll take a *Hortren Ho 3's* center section and put a "*Walter Micron*" engine of 45 horsepower in it. *Berger* was enthusiastic. Now I had a workshop in Minden and one in Bonn. Plus I was studying at the University. All this work now was sufficient. To make my life more easy I moved from Minden to Göttingen, not just for the *Horten Ho 3* but at the same time, the workshop from Bonn was also moved to Göttingen. At the University of Göttingen I also had the courses I wanted to take at the University of Bonn. Therefore, I had no longer to make any trips to Bonn or Minden. Later, I visited *Prandtl* and told him of my desire to investigate the swept-back wings in his wind tunnel. He told me that he could not help for he had no authorization.

Myhra: Who was the person in Berlin heading up this committee?

R. Horten: It was the brother of *Dr. Rudolf Göthert* from *Gothaer Waggonfabrik* and his name was *Dr.-Ing. Berhard Göthert*. Therefore the first thing which I wanted to do in Göttingen (wind tunnel research) I had failed to achieve. I thought that what would be the purpose of Göttingen now? I received one or two draftsmen, engineers, and so on and looked at what I could do with the *Horten Ho 5*? With the *Horten Ho 5* in Minden, everything had been clear. I was waiting for them to finish in the workshop and therefore, speaking with *Walter*, I told him about the shortcomings of the *Horten Ho 5*. Its engines were too small. We must have *Argus As10* engines of 240 hp each. Also, we could use the *Horten Ho 5* for investigation into other engines, for instance, the pulse jet engine of *Schmitt* or even turbines. In this way I now had to review the whole construction of the *Horten Ho 5* and we should now make it into a two-seater. Therefore, step-by-step came the design of the *Horten Ho 7*.Then there came the question of its maximum diving speed because I needed to calculate what stiffness it needed in the wing in terms of torsion. The torsion is always a different question and the speed we were thinking of was about 330 km/h (205 mph). With the *Horten Ho 7,* I had gone off with 550 km/h (342 mph) and therefore, it was a new design, instead of thin plywood or fabric covered controls on the *Horten Ho 5*, it was now all, covered with plywood of 2.5 mm and the wing-tips rather thicker. Later in *Peschke's* factory we carried out a test on the stiffness or torsion on the *Horten Ho 7* and a pictures exists of this When I came toI Göttingen there were many carpenters who were building a cottage and I didn't know that this cottage was built without an order beccause these carpenters were without work. In Göttingen, the administration was glad to find work for these people. We received about twenty men I remember form Göttingen and most of them were carpenters. Then I was in some difficulty as to how I was to use them? At *Peschke* there were more metal workers and so *Walter* organized in Berlin, that *Peschke* would receive a new work, order for the prototype of the *Horten Ho 7*, and we in Göttingen would build the wings out of wood as we had sufficient capacity. When Peschke finished the *Horten Ho 5* they could then move directly on to the *Horten Ho 7*. By now we had prepared all the drawings in Göttingen. *Peschke* had a large capacity for metalworking and soon finished the center section of the *Horten Ho 7*. We had made the outer wings of the *Horten Ho 7* in wood at Göttingen, and sent them to Minden. As *Peschke* had the order to build a complete *Horten Ho 7* we had therefore another pair of outer wings. We now had two pairs of outer wings. One built in Göttingen and one built in Minden. The *Horten Ho 7* first flew with the wings built by *Peschke* in Minden. Later on we changed the outer wings after *Scheidhauer* had damaged the *Horten Ho 7* in a landing accident when he didn't lower the undercarriage. We now had many people in Göttingen and I was getting more draftsmen. But we had finished the *Horten Ho 7*. But at this time, too, I was thinking about the *Horten Ho 9* and this was about at the end of 1942. I began thinking of the *Horten Ho 9* with twin turbines and the first draftsmen started work about this time (end of 1942). Generally, work on the *Horten Ho 9* really picked up after the new year (1943). At this time, too, the workshop people were running low on work to do but I could not give them any. I had brought to the workshop at Göttingen, two *Horten Ho 2's and* some five *Horten Ho 3's*, from the aerobatics school. Parts of these aircraft were in bad condition for they had been flown by 100's of pilots in the school there. In addition, maintenance on these *Horten* sailplanes had also been poor.

Myhra: The director from the *Autobahnmeisterreich* who gave the *Hortens* that workshop in Grone near Göttingen was named *Dorch*. Who was this person? How did *Walter* come to know him?

R. Horten: Yes, *Walter* knew him. *Dorch's* office was in Kassel and he was a director of this zone of the *autobahn*. He was involved later in the war with France. *Dorch* was ordered to France to prepare the defenses against the invasion of the Allies. With his workers, he was to make the necessary defences along the Atlantic Coast and this organization was called Organization *Todt* named after the man who ran it. It was *Todt* who originally built the *Autobahn* network in Germany. *Dorch* built the bunkers along the French coast and *Walter* was there in France in *JG/26* and they met. Plus, *Walter* had flown *Dorch* in his *Messerschmitt Bf 108* up and down the French coast showing *Dorch* where his workers were and the projects under construction. Therefore, *Walter* and *Dorch* had become really good friends.

Myhra: Walter made friends very easily.

R. Horten: Yes, he was open, and attracted friends easily without difficulty. Our other brother *Wolfram*, was like *Walter*, too. One of *Walter's* duties was to oversee the officer's mess and he was often there with Dorch. Then, when *Walter* later came to Göttingen, he called *Dorch* who was in Kassel, and the two saw each other often. It was *Walter* who told *Dorch* that he needed a place for his men to convert into a workshop. *Walter* mentioned to *Dorch* that there were vacant buildings at the *Autobahnmeisterreich* near Göttingen. *Dorch* said, "Oh yes you can have them for they are not now needed." Later, we found that the autobahn facilities were too small and we need similar facilities at Hersfeld about 110 kilometers (68 miles) south of Göttingen. *Dorch* said that there was only one man left at his Hersfeld facility and it was his job to answer the telephone and he asked *Walter* if he could stay. *Walter* said yes he could stay. So we put thirty men into the workshop at Hersfeld and this was not only a workshop but it had air pressure, water, electric power and the most important a building which were many rooms for draftsmen, engineering, and so on. Plus in the second story were sleeping rooms and a kitchen. So all these things could very nicely accommodate thirty men. We had to do nothing for this facility. So we were able to begin. It was very easy to start.

When I was speaking with you about Göttingen. I forgot to say that we were beginning to prepare plans for the *Horten Ho 9*. But I was the only person working on the *Horten Ho 9* because *Walter* was in Berlin and our draftsmen were working on the *Horten Ho 7*. Therefore, the workshop in Göttingen simply didn't have sufficient work. I told the workers that we'd repair some of our *Horten Ho 3's* but opening up some of the *Horten Ho 3s* showed that most of the wings were in very bad conditions. In most cases the entire outer wings had to be rebuilt and the center sections, well, some were still good but many were bad. Some we had to construct from new. In this way, I made the first changes. I had three *Horten Ho 3s* from Bonn and I called them the *Horten Ho 3D* and I wished, I told *Walter*, that we should use the *Horten Ho 3B* and change to engine or *Horten Ho 3F* with an *Volkswagen* engine to have a better combination with folding air screw and so on. I put *Berger* on. this job and let him make the drawings and we had one *Horten Ho 3* changed over to the *Volkswagen* engine. Other *Horten* sailplanes were there in poor condition. *Scheidhauer* did not fly them. The workshop called me that they wanted to do something but I told him that I had an insufficient number of draftsman so I couldn't do more. Plus for the *Horten Ho 3* we didn't have sufficient engines either. I asked *Walter* what shall we make here? Well, he said, there are the *Horten Ho 3s* and they are all greatly in need of repair. Well, I thought, one possibility was why not have a *Horten Ho 3* with a pilot in the prone position? We called it the *Horten Ho 3F*. *Walter* told me that if we make one, I will have to prepare drawings and make some modifications to the cockpit and so on. Also two draftsmen were working, including the chief of our workshop (*Seaboata*) well, we have less working hours if we make the *Horten Ho 3s* together. Put away the other, older *Horten Ho 3s* and we'll make three *Horten Ho 3Fs*. Then we had five more *Horten Ho 3s* and we should change them also I told *Walter*, well, make the outer wings all the same and instead of three, now make five. Then all will be new. But they had been old *Horten Ho 3Bs* and *Scheidhauer* told me that they will not be flown if there are *Horten Ho 4As available*, therefore, I told him that we will convert them into two-seaters. We made one of the *Horten Ho 3s* into a two-seater but it was late and we had no capacity to change the steel center-section and so the whole project was placed into the workshops at Hersfeld. It was completed In Hersfeld and it later came back to Göttingen and was flown there. It was now called the *Horten Ho 3G*. In Hersfeld we had made major components for the *Horten Ho 13* and we were making steel fittings for the *Horten Ho 9*, *Horten Ho 10*, and so on at Göttingen. We transported all these steel fittings by car to Göttingen for these components were very small. *Hans Wenzel* was doing all of the metal work at Hersfeld by himself. *Wenzel* was not an organizer but he was a worker. He made all the metal pieces himself. He did all this with the thirty men at Hersfeld. These men did what we at Göttingen could not make and we gave them to *Wenzel* and this workers to make. Hence, all the steel fittings and pieces such as the attachment fittings for the outer wings and the center section was made by *Wenzel* at Hersfeld. Therefore, the two-seater *Horten Ho 3* came to Hersfeld and the thirty men there quickly finished it. Now the second had come and the first which had created a difficulty. The old *Horten Ho 3B* had an airbrake above the center section with four brakes. These were controlled only by the pilot in the rear seat. We could not let the old brake in the center section be left to the second pilot. (Who could not control the landing using the air brakes as he would be unable to see the ground on the final approach due to the enormous wing root chord..PW) What to do? I sent the outer wing to be modified. *Heinz Scheidhauer* had no time to fly it. We gave it to the people at Homburg and there it was flown. Later on when Hersfeld was making the *Horten Ho 4B* and I remembered that there were two new pairs of wings for a *Horten Ho 3B* and an old center section which had been changed over to a two-seater. I thought about the air-brake problem and when they were working on the center section I had to design a new airbrake. I put on each side three brakes in the rear spar, which rotated like a wind mill. This was a new type of airbrake with is not used today. It was easy to make.

This is a picture of the *Autobahnmeisterreich* facility at Grone by Göttingen. This was the principle building here and this is entry. In this part *Walter* lived, this window was mine. This was for the draftsman and the other side also. This here was not a workshop but a kitchen and sleeping rooms. Here was the workshop location. See these large doors which could be opened to admit large trucks.

Myhra: Later on your enlarged these workshops. Why?

R. Horten: Yes, we built on three more garages.

Myhra: You had wooden barracks on the opposite side also?

R. Horten: They were only for sleeping and design rooms. *Walter* had arranged that there was always a large pot of bean soup and every man could come in the kitchen and eat whenever they wanted to and at any hour - in the war this was very important. The kitchen was only for soup.

Myhra: Where did *Walter* live otherwise?

R. Horten: In the same building but it does show on this photo. This picture also shows my bedroom, the other side *Walters* and behind also was *Walters*. The other rooms were used for the draftsmen. The workers slept in a barracks-like building which we had built. In one room there was the heating plant for the whole facility. The kitchen was in the wooden barracks behind. These pictures you have here are probably from the year 1943, when we began working at this facility. We had three entrances into the workshops. These pictures show snow on the ground so it must be winter of 1943/1944.

I have to tell you about Göttingen. We had come there in the Spring of 1943 and I was ready to involve all the laborers in the design of the *Horten Ho 9*. *Walter* had come from Berlin to Göttingen and lived at the *Autobahnmeisterreich*, too. At this point a man called *Schmidt* arrived at our office and gave us a telegram. This telegram told us to stop working and to return the personnel to the units they had come from. We were beaten. I asked *Schmidt* who had seen this telegram? He answered that this telegram was secret and no one else had seen it. I told him that we will talk about this tomorrow and that he was to speak to no one else about it either. This telegram had come from the Air Ministry and I said to *Walter* you have failed because you should have stayed in Berlin to ensure that such a telegram was never sent. What should we do now? We did the following: The airfield at Göttingen had given us a week before an order from another of the Luftgau (the next higher organization) should be implimented so that the air facilities must be dispersed as far as possible so damage from air raids would be minimized. Or if bombed, then the facilities would not be totally destroyed. I told *Walter* that we now had to do the following: First, we cannot fly at Göttingen all year. Tomorrow we will give an answer to the telegram and say that we have sent away all the personnel and stopped the work here.

Myhra: When was this?

R. Horten: In March 1943. The next morning I called *Heinz Scheidhauer* and told him to take his sailplane to the *Rhön/Wasserkuppe*. The same evening, we telephoned our friend *Seff Kunz*, the chief of the *NSFK National Sociaslist Flying Corps*, he was from Bonn and we had known him since 1933. *Walter* and I had been in his sailplane group and I had flown my "C" with *Kunz*. Therefore, I called him by his first name. I asked him if we could go with out sailplanes to the *Rhön/Wasserkuppe* and he said sure. *Scheidhauer* went there. The other men I sent to Bonn. The people who had previously come to Göttingen with the *Horten Ho 3D* , we sent back to Bonn. Instead of the airfield at Bonn, they went to Aegidienburg, a little village, and connected them with the airfield Bonn. In this way, they had another source for obtaining materials and other things and I sent the people from Bonn there so they were at home now with their families. But I had to give these people work, too. Long before the war dragged on I had schemed the *Horten Ho 6. This* had been more of a dream for me and then I had to bring in *Berger*, showing him the drawings of the *Horten Ho 4A* and we'll make it now into a *Horten Ho 6. Berger* began to work in Aegidienburg with twelve men and so we were all gone now from Göttingen. So if an inspector should come to Göttingen from the Air Ministry, we had taken the order and responded. We had not disobeyed the order by keeping all the men at Göttingen. It is called in German "the judge of war." This means the men who say whether you live or die. The highest men in justice were these judges. So if I had an order from the Air Ministry and will not do what it says completely, the judge of war could tell me that you will die. Therefore, I had to send my people to Göttingen to these little villages for my defence so that I can say that I've responded to the order. In this way, the *Horten Ho 6* began to be built. You see it was not because I like sailplanes. I like sailplanes - no question. But during the war I was not only thinking of high performance sailplanes. I would not have built the *Horten Ho 6* were it not for that order from the Air Ministry. I sent thirty men to Hersfeld. *Scheidhauer* with about fifteen to the *Wasserkuppe* and now *Walter* had organized thirty men more in Berlin before the Air Ministry dispersal order had come and they came to Göttingen and I did not know what to do with them. So we had just got rid of thirty workers and now here come another thirty more. It was a difficult time. I sent part of this group to Gut Tierstein near Rottweil and they begin working. A man named *Schmidt* and his brother were glad to work in their own house. So Gut Tierstein got thirty more men. At first it wasn't clear what they could but I told them I can't, give you a draftsmen, so you have to build a series of *Horten Ho 4B* sailplanes but they had not begun by the end of the war. (Not so, it seems that at least one production machine was completed and at least one other was mostly finished, major components for at least two more were well advanced but Reimar was not in touch with his groups in the final weeks of the war..PW) These people were only sent to Tierstein because they couldn't go to Göttingen. In Göttingen I could stay with several people for they were airfield staff. The command *LIN #3*, what it was, had finished and we could send the Air Ministry a telegram; that we have finished *LIM* #3 and sent back all the people. The people who had originally been in Göttingen stayed there and now we were ready to begin anew our *Horten Ho 9*.

Myhra: *Walter* was in the *Inspectorate of Fighters Command* No.3 in Berlin?

R. Horten: Yes. It was called the *Luftwaffe Inspection* No.*3* (*LIN* No.3). and this was the summer of 1942.

Myhra: Here is the only picture I have of *Dr.-Ing. Hermann Oestrich*.

R. Horten: I never learned why *BMW* could never finish their *BWW 003* turbine? It was a very bad thing this changing of the engine's diameter.

Myhra: When did you first learn of *Erwin Ziller's* death in the *Horten Ho 9 V2?*

R. Horten: I think I first heard about it from the crew who had witnessed it. The ground crew told us that *Erwin Ziller* had made his approach normally like the other flights but this time his altitude was a little low however, lower than usual. The ground crew. told us that one of the turbines was responding but the other was not. I believe that today if an engine is throttled back the plugs will be warmed. In all aircraft it is quite normal that as soon as they reduce the throttle they will warm the plugs. However in the days we flew in Oranienburg it was unknown. They would reduce the throttle and not warm the plugs. If the pilot accelerated and the engine was cold, it was possible that it would not respond. Similarly if you reduce the throttles when a piston engine is cold, it also might not accelerate. In this case of the *Horten Ho 9 V2* the two engines were cold, for it was winter time and the temperature was lower than 0°C (32°F) with ice and *Ziller* had descended from high altitude in a normal circuit and then came lower. It appears that when *Ziller* tried accelerating only one turbine responded. *Ziller* could fly normally with one engine but *Ziller* seemed to be surprised, seemed to be not prepared to fly on a single engine because he turned about the vertical axis but had not corrected this with the rudder. *Ziller* throttled back and applied rudder and again accelerated but had then descended even lower and made a mistake. The mistake was to lower the undercarriage too early before he had begun his final approach to the airfield and the flaps were also lowered. In this situation flying with one engine became even more even more difficult but it should still have been possible. What is not clear is whether he had also deployed the airbrake . I cannot say. As we had no radio communication it will never be known. I think that the two engines were ready to run and in good condition. Was there was anything like sabotage? I don't think so. I asked *Rudolf Preussler* when he came back to Göttingen had you run the other engine? He told me that the engine had been fine. That both engines were sound. Today, he and others say that one engine was not running and the other had been cold. Well, they are now saying some different things because after the accident, they told me that both engines had been OK. In this case I think that *Ziller* had landed for he had no radio contact with the control tower and this was not normal. I told you yesterday and if this was really the case, then *Heinz Scheidhauer* was not the man who caused this accident but if *Scheidhauer* had been on the radio we should at least know today what happened up there. If anyone had been killed in such a situation, we had to look for reasons to prevent it in the future and this information had to be passed on to the Air Ministry. That is to say we had to write a report describing the accident as if the Air Ministry knew nothing. But all we wrote at that time was about half a page that the accident was due to pilot error. Well, this report critcised *Ziller* but it saved *Scheidhauer*. If I had said that there was no radio communication there would have been an investigation by the " judge of war" and it would have been very bad for us.

Myhra: Why did *Heinz Scheidhauer* act in a negative way with *Erwin Ziller*?

R. Horten: I will tell you. I think that *Heinz Scheidhauer* had gone to his bedroom room to change his clothes and so that he could go out on the airfield and fly it instead himself. *Scheidhauer* blamed *Ziller* for he was angry that he could not fly the *Horten Ho 9 V2* and that *Ziller* was flying but he was not authorized to fly the *Horten Ho 9 V2* although he wished to do so. There are other also matters. *Walter* had sought permission from Air Ministry, for *Ziller* to fly the *Messerschmitt Me 262* at *E-Stelle* Rechlin. *Ziller* went there but he could not fly due to the weather and enemy aircraft and returned to Oranienburg Air Base. At this time *Ziller* had still not flown the *Messerschmitt Me 262* but still flew the *Horten Ho 9 V2*. Later on, after the *Horten Ho 9 V2* had been repaired, *Ziller* went back to *E-Stelle* Rechlin and made three or four flights in the *Messerschmitt Me 262*. Then he came back. When *Ziller* came back from *E-Stelle* Rechlin, *Scheidhauer* went to Rechlin from Göttingen. *Walter* and I had to go to Kahla on the orders of *Karl-Otto Saur*, from the Ministry of Supply. We were to transfer the workshop from Göttingen to Kahla. They had given us two days to do this. We had to go to Berlin to talk with *Saur* and could not go to Oranienburg Air Base because *Saur* was a man who had above him civillian workers and had many "judges of war" . It was he, *Saur, rather than the SS* who could kill and towards the end of the war it became very dangerous for all soldiers. Therefore, we had other things to do for *Saur* and could not go to the *Horten Ho 9 V2*. It was not just that I was designing the *Horten Ho 18*, I was completely occupied with our organization and we had to travel to Kahla and speak. A *Gaulieter*, a *NAZI* named *Fritz Saukel* had organized Kahla. We didn't wish to go there, for there were 10,000 men and other factories like *Messerschmitt AG*. Above the mountain there was an aircraft assembly facility where *Messerschmitt AG* was preparing to build the *Messerschmitt Me 262. Gaulieter Saukel* told us that they were making two hangars with a cement roof 5 meters(16.4 feet) thick as protection against bombers. We'll make provision for you and you office on the other side of the hangars and in the forest a wooden house to sleep and where you can design. When there are air raids you can find safety in the forest. The workers at Kahla were French, Polish, Russian, Jews, and other nationalities from the concentation camp *(KZ)*. There were many people there.

I had asked *Saukel* what were they eating? We walked around a very large barracks 50 by 100 meters (164 by 328 feet) and there was a huge kitchen with many tables and benches to sit on and some people were making soap and The men came, got their food and could sit down and eat up to 200 to 300 at a time. This kitchen was always serving people. They'd eat, and go back to work. Additionally, other workers were constructing bathrooms which were needed as the smell there was bad. In total, the whole working atmosphere was not what I liked. The other thing was that the first twenty workers from Göttingen were now living with their families in Göttingen. How was I supposed to bring them to Kahla when it looked like a prisoner of war camp? It would have been bad for them. *Saur* wanted it this way. He demanded we do it this way. This is why we could not be in Oranienburg and protect *Ziller* at that time. Therefore I told *Ziller* that I could not come. That was the reality. *Scheidhauer* was there too. Prior to that, through the entire month of January 1945, I had to go to *Junkers*-Dessau, to Kahla, to Berlin and so on and only spent a few days in Göttingen. It was also the same for *Walter* . We said that it was a good thing that *Scheidhauer* was in Göttingen, at least we have one *Horten* official in Göttingen. But we came to Göttingen and *Scheidhauer* was not there. "Where is *Scheidhauer*?" Our workers didn't know. Is he in his home? I went to his house which was only 5 kilometers (3 miles) away and his wife said that he was in Rechlin. We didn't know this. He had gone off to *E-Stelle* Rechlin without permission and without saying anything to us. He had his duties in Göttingen where we had one hundred people or more and he wasn't suppose to go away. Well, two days later *Major Otto Behrens* who was the Chief of Testing at *E-Stelle* Rechlin called *Walter* by telephone. I was present. *Behrens* said that *Scheidhauer* is here at Rechlin. He informs me that he has to fly the *Messerschmitt Me 262*. He can't just come at any time to fly it. *Walter* replied that he didn't know anything about it. Send him back. *Behrens* said that he'd send him back but if things were good maybe tomorrow he could fly the *Messerschmitt Me 262*, but that today, he *Behrens*, had other tasks to do. No, thanks *Otto*, said *Walter*. Well, *Scheidhauer* did not fly the *Messerschmitt Me 262. Behrens* sent him back instead. *Scheidhauer* didn't come directly to Göttingen but he went to Oranienburg instead. He wanted to fly the *Horten Ho 9 V2* and was angry that he was unable to fly either the *Messerschmitt Me 262* or our *Horten Ho 9 V2*.

So it was that while *Ziller* took the *Horten Ho 9 V2* up, *Scheidhauer* was in the dressing room preparing to pilot the *Horten Ho 9 V2* himself. *Scheidhauer* was planning to fly the *Horten Ho 9 V2* right after *Ziller* landed. *Scheidhauer* was undisciplined. We had had problems. *Scheidhauer* first came to Minden and worked for me in 1937,and in 1938 when he was in the hospital, I told him that we'd be friends and that you can call me *Reimar*. I shall call you *Heinz*. Later on in 1943, when *Walter* came to Göttingen, *Scheidhauer* asked me if it would be all right if *Walter* called him "*Heinz*" and he "*Walter*."

I spoke with *Walter* and he said, yes, we'll do it. *Walter*, said look *Heinz*, we have spent much time together and we'll call each other *Walter* and *Heinz*. Well, the next Saturday, when all our workers were assembled, *Scheidhauer* said right in front of them "*Walter*, what would you do instead of so on?" *Walter* went white. He could not say this in front of the soldiers. He could not allow *Scheidhauer* to call *Walter* by his first name. *Scheidhauer* would have to say *Hauptmann Horten*. *Walter* later told me to instruct *Scheidhauer* never to call him "*Walter*" again. I later spoke to *Scheidhauer*. I told him that between the two of us we'll be *Walter*, *Reimar*, and *Heinz* but not in front of other people, no. *Scheidhauer* did not understand why it had to be like this. On one occassion he came to me and said that all the pilots who had flown gliders onto the Belgium *Fort Eban Emael* were now all officers but I am only still a *Feldwebel*. I said that I'd speak with *Walter* and see what his thoughts were. I spoke with *Walter* but he did not wish to support the idea. I said that all Scheidhauer's comrades were officers and he is not because of his posting here. This is not good for either him or us. Well, *Walter* said he'd forward the recommendation to the Air Ministry personnel office. Three months later, *Scheidhauer* was a *Leutnant*. So what did he do when he became an officer? Well, once I entered the barracks and because *Scheidhauer* wore the uniform of an *Leutnant* his enlisted comrades had to clean his room and clothes. *Nichol* and even *Simon*, who had been my friend since 1928 and who was only a solider , was cleaning *Scheidhauer*'s boots. I mentioned this to *Walter* and he said that this was unacceptable.

I called *Scheidhauer* in and told him. His response was that he had the right to have the enlisted people clean up his room and clothes because of his rank. *Walter*, replied that we had personnel to help the officers and that if he liked, that he was free to transfer to some other *Luftwaffe* flying group. *Walter* later told me that he didn't want to send *Scheidhauer* away. That he couldn't bring himself to do it but, if he wishes to leave, I will help him. I told *Walter* that I'd not tell *Scheidhauer* about this for we were now at war with the USSR and anyone going to the Russian Front was half condemned to death. I didn't do it. I told *Walter* that *Scheidhauer* had made his flying reputation in 1938 at the *Rhön/Wasserkuppe*. He had flown into *Fort Eban Emael*. He has done his duty. We will protect him. He has not committed a breach of discipline. He was, as I have recounted, in Rechlin without authorization. He'd also gone to Oranienburg Air Base without authorization and we had more work in Göttingen than we could cope with and no help from *Scheidhauer* and when he was in Oranienburg he gave no help to *Ziller*. I very often talked to *Walter* and told him that I was very sorry that we didn't have *Hanna Reitsch*. She was a very good pilot, better than *Scheidhauer* and of very good character. That is what we needed. About *Scheidhauer*'s character, well, I will tell you one more thing. He didn't graduate from college. He had left. A person, who has not finished their education, will have an inferiority complex and this complex makes him like an actor. Before entering the aircraft and starting he'd look to see how many people were looking at him. That is not the spirit of a test pilot. A test pilot had to work and had to enter into danger and avoid danger. He had to investigate and not to look for people to impress. We were very angry when *Scheidhauer* made the first flight with the *Horten Ho 6* at Göttingen airfield which lasted about one hour. I was busy and later I called from my office and I went to the University. It is then that I learned that he had taken off and was flying it. I got on my motor bicycle and went back to see him landing. The take-off is very important but I had no opportunity to observe it but was important to *Scheidhauer* that the whole airfield witnessed his first, flight in the *Horten Ho 6*. This was an inferiority complex. I must also talk of his character. If you had anything which was against him, he would begin to lie. To lie, to lie. If you asked him, for example if he had spun in the *Horten Ho 4A*, *Scheidhauer* would say:"I've never have had a spin with the *Horten Ho 4A." He* had had to. For example, throughout the winter *Scheidhauer* flew the *Horten Ho 4A* for six months and approximately 50 hours per month for a total flight time of 300 hours. He must have entered into a spin with our *Horten Ho 4A* a hundred times. Then he told me that he had never had a spin in the *Horten Ho 4A!* He told this directly to me. I was there. That is a form of mental illness and consequently I did not previously talk to you about it.

Myhra: How did the repairs on the *Horten Ho 9 V2* work out?

R. Horten: Well, the trailing edge of the frame had been bent upwards 10 to 15 mm (4 to 6 inches). That was a repair which we made after Christmas 1944. This part was not strong enough especially when *Ziller* touched down with his feet on the wheel-brake pedals. When he applied the wheel brakes then this caused a rearward load and deflected the frame. It produced a great deal of force. Because of the distortion, the rear wheels could not now be retracted into the wheel wells. Therefore, we had to make it stronger.

Myhra: Who was the man from *Arado* representing *Gothaer Waggonfabrik* during these test flights at Oranienburg Air Base?

R. Horten: I do not recall having anyone from *Arado* in Oranienburg representing *Gothaer Waggonfabrik*.

Myhra: Here is a photo showing the *Horten Ho 9 V2's* turbine air-intakes under the center section's leading edge.

R. Horten: Yes, this photo was taken long before the test of the *Horten Ho 9 V2*. If the *BMW 003* turbine engines were ready in 1943 I thought that they could go to the upper side but then we changed to the *Junkers Jumo 004s*.

Myhra: Why was *Klemm Flugzeugbau* told not to build any *Horten Ho 9s*? At one time *Klemm* was to have built twenty *Horten Ho 229 V3s* and *Gothaer Waggonfabrik* to build twenty *Horten Ho 229s*.

R. Horten: Yes, at first but later *Gothaer Waggonfabrik* received the whole order to build forty and *Klemm* to build fifty *Horten Ho 3d's*. The reason why *Klemm Leichtflugzeugbau GmbH* was denied was a political decision . *Dr.Ing. Hans Klemm* had his own factory at Böblingen near Stuttgart and had made very good light airplanes. Well, the Air Ministry decided to have "B" planes (biplanes) and the *Klemm's* were not invited. Well, *Klemm* had good designers and had build a good plane called the *Klemm Kl 35D*. This was a two-seater with a 105 horsepower *Hirth* engine and a very good plane. About 100 of these *Klemm Kl 35D's* had been built for the *Luftwaffe* pilot-training schools. But *Klemm Leichtflugzeugbau* was considered only a secondary factory and he had become very angry and now hated the *NAZI's*. This was either in 1939 or 1940. Now came the political element. *Klemm* had been a member of the *NAZI Party* for a long time, going back to the mid 1930s. Out of protest, he took his *NAZI Party* uniform, packed it a box, and sent it all back to the *Party* via the mail. Then the *NAZI Party* became angry, too. *Hans Klemm* was almost sent to a *KZ*. His factory was taken over by the *Party* and all the leading personnel removed. But *Klemm* had run a good workshop for wooden aircraft construction and at the end of the war the *Party* said that this factory should not go without work. Consequently, *Siegfried Knemeyer* told the *Klemm* factory to build fifty *Horten Ho 3d's*. I don't know how many they finished by May 1945 because *Klemm* had several workshops surrounding Stuttgart and these individual shops specialized: some in wing ribs, some in wing spars, and so on. *Klemm* even had a workshop for fabricating steel parts such as our center section frame work. All this would have been a good job for the *Klemm* factory to do and they were well organized. I had never spoken with *Dr. Klemm*. He had been removed from his own factory about 1939-1940 and so I never met him. (H.3d centre sections were being assembled at Tubingen where 12 incomplete units were found in June 1945. The wooden wing panls were assembled at Dornsdorf where 12 complete pairs of wings had been burnt on April 15th 1945..PW)

Myhra: When *Knemeyer* and *Eschenauer* assigned the *Horten Ho 229* for production why did they not give *Klemm* an order for twenty machines?

R. Horten: The production order came from the Air Ministry to give twenty *Horten Ho 229 V3s*, say, to *Gothaer*. Someone said that twenty *Horten Ho 229 V3s* were not enough so give twenty also to *Klemm*. This is how work was politically distributed at that time. Later it was changed and *Gothaer* received the whole order of forty *Horten Ho 229s*. I think that it was *Eschenauer* who gave the entire order to *Gothaer*. I think that it was *Knemeyer* who had given the twenty *Horten Ho 229 V3s* to *Klemm*. I don't know the reasons surrounding this decision.(It is interesting that although

Reimar claims to have been working closely with Gotha to turn the Ho.9 into a design suitable for series production,he does not seem to be aware that the production version was to have been based on the as yet unbuilt Ho.229 V6 which had many modifications not incorporated in the V3, V5 and V5 prototypes which were under construction, especially a substantially deeper underside to the centre section. Note that all previous illustrations and model aircraft kits which are labelled Ho.229 A-0 or A-1 , represent the V3-5 and not the V6 pre-production aircraft...PW)

Myhra: The firm *Peschke* was to build twenty *Horten Ho 7s*?

R. Horten: Well *Peschke* of Minden had initially repaired the *Horten Ho 5.* The *Horten Ho 7* was next. It was to be a trainer for pilots going on to the *Horten Ho 229. Peschke* had had good experience in woodworking, making ribs, spars, wing assemblies, steel fabrication, too. So *Peschke* had a good deal of experience in terms of *Horten* construction. Since 1929 *Peschke* had run a pilot-training school in Bonn. I believe that one *Peschke*-built *Horten Ho 7* had been finished by the end of the war. Perhaps a second *Peschke Horten Ho 7* was nearing completion. All our *Horten Ho 7s* were lost at war's end.

Myhra: What did the *Gothaer Waggonfabrik* people mean when they said that the *Horten Ho 9* suffered from "*dutch roll*?"

R. Horten: The so-called "*dutch roll*" tendency of the *Horten Ho 9* was a foolish thing. Dutch roll, named for a Hollander (Dutch) technical high school teacher who investigated this phenomena, is a combined oscillation over the longdituinal axis and also the vertical axis. We had a swept-back wing planform. The slip recovering moment of a swept back planform is proportionally dependant on the CL. That is to say that the combining of these two moments differs with different CL. If we came to land or take off with a large angle of attack, the moment of recovery over the longitudinal axis is large. In this scenario we have the possibility of *dutch roll* but I think it happened only in very few cases. It was really a technical situation. *Walter* made it sound serious, that's the problem. We had *dutch roll* creating an oscillation only in the near stalled position. Never in horizontal flight. Therefore, it is not problem when shooting To say that our *Horten Ho 229* would not be effective gun platform is not so. It is without merit. If we had *dutch roll*, a vertical fin would not reduce it. The fin can only compensate for the swept-back and dihedral. It is bad that the Air Ministry wanted to add a vertical fin. Additionally, if we had oscillation, it only had a period of about 5 or 10 seconds. The pilot could control it and the *Horten Ho 229* would continue flying straight ahead. The *dutch roll* is a combined movement from side to side and up and down. So if you damped out one of them you couldn't reduce the other for they could not be combined. The damping moment is large with an all-wing. There were other effects, movement in another direction. We had it in all aircraft and we called it the natural form of flying. One was in straight flight in the form of lateral oscillation. This moment is about one second in a sailplane, or 2 seconds in a large aircraft. In a fast fighter if it is about 10 seconds, the pilot can damp it and it will be eliminated. For us and the *Horten Ho 229* the *dutch roll* was unimportant. What is interesting was that the pilot could control it. If the pilot was experiencing a combined oscillation then he could interrupt the connection or coupling. That is to say if we have movement around the vertical axis, which in English is called,"*weathercock stability*" we have no *dutch roll.* If the plane is flying along and then sideslips, if we have weathercock stability it then yaws toward the sideslip. In turbulance it my then slip and turn the other way. If we have zero weathercock stability it will create only an oscillation about the longitudinal axis. That is to say ;that we do not have *dutch roll.* The whole *dutch roll* criticism of our *Horten Ho 9* came from the *DVL* at Berlin/Adlershof who did not understand. If I had given the *Horten Ho 9* a vertical fin the *dutch roll* probably would have been greater. It would have been worse. Anyway, I agreed to go along with *Walter* with this vertical fin proposal but told him it will still have an adverse effect. I believed that a vertical fin would make the likelihood of a *dutch roll* even greater. (This was a genuine concern as too large a fin can create spiral instability...PW)Well, all this talk of a vertical fin came from the Air Ministry who had no previous involvement in the design of the *Horten Ho 9.* Now they wanted to get involved and there were many people in the Air Ministry who had their own ideas. Well, the *Horten Ho 9* had 'been designed and completely accepted by *Göring* without any input from the Air Ministry but now they wished to make changes. *Walter* had to struggle with these people. He heard them talk about the need for a vertical fin at every meeting. These people in the Air Ministry had no worth-while ideas of their own at all.

Myhra: Do you remember *Oberst Artur Eschenauer*?

R. Horten: No, not very well. I never met or even saw him. We had much trouble with the Air Ministry and their biplane mentality. For example, they had even developed biplane in 1941. This was the German Air Ministry. Look, *Fieseler* made a biplane in 1941. This planform was completely out of date but the Air Ministry had given the order just the same..

The men of the Air Ministry told people that an all-wing plane could not safely enter into a turn because while in the turn it would enter a downward side-slip. These people also said that since it did not have a fuselage, it could not fly well. Well, we had proof that what the Air Ministry said was wrong. In fact, our all-wings had better flying characteristics than their old tailed-aircraft. This is why we had to produce different types to show them that the flying wing design was a safe plane. The people in the Air Ministry did not believe that we had developed a safe, aircraft which performed well. *Knemeyer* came and flew the *Horten Ho 3.* He flew low, over and around the airdrome, made circles, and so on. Well, he was really enthusiastic. He told us that he hadn't believed that the all-wing could fly like that. Regarding the *Horten Ho 3* and the order to build fifty for pilot-training schools, well people at the Air Ministry said that building many *Horten Ho 3s* was unnecessary. So after *Knemeyer* flew the *Horten Ho 7,* his opinion was contrary to the general opinion of his own Air Ministry. (Rather than a compliment this could be taken that Knemeyer considered that pilots did need some transitional training from conventional types before they flew the Ho.7 – i.e. that tailless types did have some non standard characteristics...PW)

In total, we spent three years at Göttingen from March 1942 to March 1945 in which we made the *Horten Ho 7* and the *Horten Ho 9*. We designed the *Horten Ho 8*, *Horten Ho 12*, and conducted studies of super-sonic flight with the *Horten Ho 13*. We were working with what we had available. Each aircraft or sailplane addressed a question. That is, it had a task to do and this task was to provide the security of knowing that the next plane would be very flyable. We had an plane, for instance the *Horten Ho 3*, with a wing washout designed to have a bell distribution CL of 0.6. This was at about the best gliding angle. During landings or circling flight we would reach a CL of 1.2. This difference was 0.6 with washout plus the deflection of ailerons/elevons. We had to test to see if the elevon could actually do this and we found that it would. The nose of the aileron and many other things had to be investigated, in particular we had to determine the airflow over the underside of the aileron's nose. (Perfecting the shape of a "Friese nose" aileron, which when the aileron is deflected upwards, the nose protrudes below the undersurface of the wing. This causes drag which counteracts adverse yaw which would otherwise swing the nose of the aircraft away from the direction of the turn. It can reduce or eliminate the amount of rudder required to fly an accurate turn. In Horten designs this was an important consideration as the drag rudders were mounted in the wing and particularly in sailplanes would cause a considerable amount of drag when used...PW) Now we had the *Horten Ho 9*. Bell distribution was 0.3. We had to go to 1.2 and the difference was now three times greater. The aileron had to be larger, the nose profiles had to be different and we had to look to see if all this was possible. If it was not possible we will go to 0.3 and with a rudder position of zero. The rudder was bad and the aileron in position zero. This aileron deflected 7 or 8, for instance above and we had 0.6. If it was forty degrees we had 0.9. Now, if we had 21° it should go to 1.2 and if not it will bring down the nose and the plane has inversion of movement with stick force behind to go lower the nose. That is the thing which could not be and we had to investigate all this with sailplanes. And we did! This proves that these experiments were necessary for the *Horten Ho 9* and had a direct relation to the *Horten Ho 3*. This is why we had tried so many different types of ailerons/elevons in the *Horten Ho 3* for the sole purpose of investigating. So these *Horten Ho 3* were not built merely to play and to develop sailplanes. I don't understand how *Franz Burger* could say these things about us. He understood nothing I guess.

Myhra: I do not believe that *Franz Burger* understood the whole picture but only a small portion of it. It was just unfortunate that the US Army intelligence talked so much to him about the *Horten* brothers activities.

R. Horten: Yes it was. I believed that *Franz Burger* died in 1963 or 1964. I recall that when I was at the Royal Air Force Establishment (RAE) from August 1945 through December 1946, my tasks with five other men was to design a passenger aircraft plans for *deHavilland*. I asked them for permission to finish the *Horten Ho 8 as we could* do it with only a few men but they didn't agree. Therefore, I thought that it would not be possible to work with them there because we were like prisoners of war. Then in the spring of 1946 I visited *Prandtl* with *Wilkinson* at the University of Göttingen where he was also a prisoner of war. I told *Prandtl* that I'd finish my studies at the University if he'd help me. He told me "yes, but without aerodynamics." Later on I went back to him and gave him my plan of work for the determination of aircraft wing profile camber lines with a fixed center of pressure. After this he said to me "that it couldn't be, it couldn't be." He said that he'd speak about it to a mathematics professor and perhaps he can work with you on this." Well he spoke to the professor and then told me to go to him. This was in March 1946. I got permission to go out from the soldiers and went to the professor and showed him my work of some twenty pages and gave him a copy of it. He asked me is it for the *Dipl.-Math* or is it for the Doctorate? I told him that it was for the *Dipl.-Math* and he said that it was acceptable as it was. A fortnight later I had an exam and then I had finished my studies for a *Dipl.Math*. This professor said that if I were to extend this paper to some fifty pages it would be sufficient for my Doctorate. He said to ask *Prandtl which* I did. *Prandtl* said that this would be okay but it must have nothing to do with aerodynamics. Later my work was presented to the American military government officials in Göttingen and it was judged to be acceptable and they found nothing relating to aerodynamics it in. At the end of 1946 I had finished my studies and earned my *PhD*. Then *Wilkinson* heard that I had finished my studies at the University of Göttingen. He had not known that I had been working on my *PhD* and he was not very happy about it either. In fact he was very cold with me, very cold. About one month later I had finished my work at Göttingen and returned to Bonn. I think that my working on my *PhD* without *Wilkinson's* knowledge made him very angry towards me and this may have been one reason why he wrote such a negative report on our aircraft activities.

Myhra: I wrote to *Wilkinson*. I had some questions about this time but he did not respond to my letter.

R. Horten: You have to present my apologies to *Wilkinson* that I had done this when he was my chief at Göttingen but I had no work to do and this plane had already been designed. They were drawing it during that year. One hour per day was sufficient and the other seven hours I was unemployed and I used that time to finish my studies at the University. I had not told this to *Wilkinson. I* did not want to offend him. I wanted only to finish my studies and therefore, *Wilikinson* according to my thinking, was not hurt in anyway. It was not good for me that I had surprised *Wilkinson* about my *PhD* studies of which he knew nothing. If you will write him another time, give him my greetings. Ha Ha.

Myhra: No, I have no further plans to contact him. Perhaps my letters reminded him of what happened between the two of you forty years ago. I believe that he was wrong in criticizing your all-wing aircraft like he did. Perhaps today, he too realizes his mistake and does not wish to be reminded and therefore will not correspond with me. Maybe he's still angry and therefore will not cooperate.

R. Horten: In England during the war there was much anti-German propaganda. However in Germany we did not have the propaganda against England. Propaganda against Russia, yes. But not against France - no. We were in France as soldiers and seen how it was. They were good and we could work together as equals. We had the opinion that the English race of people were the same as us. We were brothers. Even the speech is not so different. We had seen Denmark, Sweden, and Norway and we viewed these people as equals. Then we lost the war. The English came and we were ready to work with them, all together. But the English didn't want to take our hand because they said that it was bloody and so on. This was one approach and no other way was possible at that time. *Wilkinson* was a part of this propaganda.

Myhra: But this wasn't because of you but of *Adolf Hitler* and his associates.

R. Horten: Yes, but we were told do nothing after the war and *Wilkinson* called us "tinkerers." See, if we didn't use a wind tunnel then we were not considered scientific men. We used sailplanes in place of wind tunnels. I would have liked to have had the use of a wind tunnel. I had a great program for the wind tunnel here at the *IAe*, Córdoba. I went there sometimes to the director asking his permission because the wind tunnel was not often used. He agreed and told me to make some models and I made six and tested them in the tunnel. Then one day he came and told me that now the wind tunnel is just for you and do with it what you want. So I installed different models of all- wings, and it is best to design large aircraft from small prototypes and not full scale.

Myhra: Why?

R. Horten: For the cost is minimal and the other thing is that if I'm a small factory and make a new plane, I will have to change some things, for in all new aircraft one has to make some changes before it is ready for serial production. A large factory might be able to use their name to pay for these changes. But if I'm a small factory, and have no reputation, I might not be able to afford the necessary changes. Any new useful developments usually come from small factories and not the large ones. For instance *Focke-Wulf Flugzeugbau* would tend to copy old designs which have worked well. This is so that the plane will perform well during its initial testing and quickly enter into production. In the *Horten Flugzeugbau* we didn't have that type of thinking. We thought always "what is the best solution?" Thus we made and we tested it. If it didn't work out as anticipated then we changed it and tested it again. We looked for other solutions. If I made the *Horten Ho 13* with a sweep-back of 60° and think well, the angle of deflection of the ailerons had to be twice the normal. Well, air which passed there needed more deflection. Well, for me that was nothing, I will do it that way. If this were in a large factory, it would be asked why was it not known before that the boundary layer needed more deflection and so on? The directors would not approve this and say that person who made these calculations is no good. Therefore no really new aircraft would be produced. They would continue to copy the old ones and with only minor changes. We had the twin-engine fighter bombers in World War Two in Germany and they were all similar. If they were all similar then they were not really needed. All that was needed were one or two types not ten. The *Luftwaffe* was flying in Norway the *Heinkel He 111*, in Italy the *Dornier Do 217* then the chain of supply is very, very long and covering the whole of Europe. We had too many planes of equal power, loading, range and speed. The same characteristics. This was a bad thing. The Air Ministry stopped the *Messerschmitt Me 262* due to the fact that many people in the Air Ministry did not want to take the responsibility for this new aircraft. That was not *Walter's way*. He came to Augsburg *LIN* No.3 and saw the *Messerschmitt Me 262* there and asked them what was it? Has it flown? Yes, they told him 800 km/h and more but few people in the Air Ministry were interested in it. *Walter* asked further questions and later he told *Adolf Galland* that at Augsburg there was a new fighter which had flown and no one in the Air Ministry was interested. Yet we needed that fighter each minute the war continued on. *Walter* told *Galland* that he had to fly it. *Galland* was silent and was a further 2 or 3 months before he went to Augsburg and flew it. (Galland however stated that we flew the Me.262 on the instruction of Milch..PW) When he flew the *Messerschmitt Me 262* he liked it but wanted some modifications made to it which took up to half a year. We lost one year in wartime with the *Messerschmitt Me 262* due to the Air Ministry. (In fact the main delay was in the engine development programme…PW)
I sought to finish my *PhD* because I didn't want anyone to say that I hadn't completed what I had started. At that time I suggested to my long-time friend *Hans Multhopp* that we finish our *PhD's* together. But he declined saying that the name "*Multhopp*" was sufficient and that he had no need for the *PhD*. If I had gone on to *Northrop Corporation* or a similar factory in the USA I don't know if it would have been necessary to have a *PhD*. *Hermann Göring* had given us 500,000 *Reich Marks* and told us "this is for the development of the *Horten Ho 3*" and give it to *DVL*-Adlershof and we did. We gave them a copy.

Myhra: It was not for the *Horten Ho 9?*

R. Horten: No for our *Horten Ho 9* design had been completed and given to *Gothaer Waggonfabrik*. But this is only an organizational matter. *Hermann Göring* had given also *Alexander Lippisch* 500,000 *Reich Marks* for his work on the *Messerschmitt Me 163*. A set of plans, too, had been give to *DVL-Adlershof*. He also asked me what I'd do after the war and I told him I will go to Freiburg for that is the best part of Germany and work there at the University and have my factory at the aerodrome in Freiburg. "Well," *Göring* said "one hangar shall be for me." He also asked me what I'd do with the 500,000 *Reich Marks* and I told him that I'd buy tools. *Göring* said to *Ulrich Deising* "that there was a *Reich* center for repairing aircraft for the Eastern Front and that they could buy their tools and materials at this center." That is to say that we had 500,000 *Reichs Marks* and could buy with it about five or seven houses but we told him that we'd buy tools. When the order to construct the *Horten Ho 9* arrived from the Air Ministry's Department *F* (Finance) a minister named *Mr. A. Moore* had to give us this money (300,000 *Reich Marks*) for the *Horten Ho 9*. Once *Walter* and I flew to *Junkers* in Dessau where he had his offices. We showed him photographs of the *Horten Ho 9* under construction in the work shop and he asked how much money would we need now and we told him 300,000 *Reich Marks*. He then sent it to the Bank of Göttingen. This was a part payment. This 500,000 *Reich Marks* had nothing to due with sailplanes and was not part of the 500,000 *Reich Markss* but quite separate. We had to buy materials plus there was to be a third *Horten Ho 9* aircraft with a vertical fin. No, we did not make sailplanes for our own use but only for investigations. When I made the six-engined *Horten Ho 8* as a flying wind tunnel, I designed it firstly to have a large aircraft especially to experience all the problems one would encounter with a big wing span and so on, so that we might learn from it for the *Horten Ho 18* both in design and in work shop practise. Secondly, we needed a wind tunnel and if they would not give us one and the ability to use it at the University of Göttingen, we would make one by ourselves. This wind tunnel had two new ideas: first, we would fly in the open atmosphere, to experience the turbulence which the other ground operated wind tunnels didn't have thus we could investigate laminar profiles/designs in what is really the natural environment. Second, we would fly with a speed of about 300 km/h (186 mph) but inside the venturi of the tunnel the speed would be 2.5 or 3 times greater. We would have a high-speed wind tunnel with low energy and could fly at different altitudes, too, with a sub-sonic speed. We did not have a supersonic tunnel but only for subsonic Mach numbers. For our work we had no access to the wind tunnels in Göttingen although they were very powerful and of great energy. We had an aircraft which had to be flown and we needed the experience which could only be obtained with a wind tunnel so with the *Horten Ho 8* we'd have our own tunnel - just for us. That was the idea and it was no plaything. Not everyone has always understood my views on these things which I've been talking about, and that includes *Walter*. Reimars internal motivation. This internal drive did not mean that I was playing with aircraft and that I didn't want to do things but it was a necessity. No, *Franz Burger* did not understand. He was only a workman, and not educated in aerodynamics. He was the only person. US military intelligence people questioned at length about *Horten* aircraft. Why didn't the intelligence people talk to us at length?

Myhra: It would have been better if the US intelligence people had never talked with *Franz Burger*. *Wilkinson* had also talked with *Burger*.

R. Horten: Yes. *Franz Burger* had never been one of our so-called insiders. We did not talk to all the men about our ideas, what was between *Walter* and me, was really a secret. Our discussions and ideas were not for the workmen. I had talked with *Alexander Lippisch* on the *Wasserkuppe* and I asked him why and how he had the ability to go to the wind tunnel at Göttingen? He said to me."Don't even think about it because it is very expensive." The use of the wind tunnels for his *Storch*-series of aircraft had cost over 100,000 *Reich Marks*. Well, I could not think of using a wind tunnel for 100,000 *Reich Marks* so I would design and build sailplanes for the same purpose. The use of our sailplanes was a net loss of nothing to Germany during World War Two. The cost of material to build these sailplanes? There was plenty wood available and plywood and so on and we wasted nothing compared to the wood wasted by other military activities. If the men in the *Wehrmacht* spent over half of their time waiting for military action, well, why not take this time and devote it to aeronautical research. Thus, we wasted nothing with our men who were waiting. It was better for these men to be working rather than doing nothing with their free time.

All new things have to be developed with risk. The net effect of our aircraft was that by the end of the war most of the new aircraft projects on the drawing boards were were tailless, with the exception of *Focke-Wulf Flugzeugbau* and their night-fighters. This includes *Arado*, *Blohm und Voss*, *Heinkel AG*, *Junkers*, *Messerschmitt AG*, and so on, the whole aircraft industry was going tailless for their projects. Why? They had learned something of this planform and that its layout was excellent. But not for World War Two but for future wars! I thought that if the war had only lasted one year longer, we would have achieved ten years worth of development or more. The USA fought in Korea and Viet Nam to see how their new planes, arms, and organizations perform.. We in Germany had fought the first war in Spain in 1936 to see how it was to fight a modern war against the USSR. It was not Spain we were fighting but rather the USSR in Spain and what if the USSR were to win. But then the *Messerschmitt Bf 109* arrived and things changed, for the Soviet *Ratta* had been better than the biplane *Heinkel He 51*. *Walter* first flew the *Heinkel He 51*in Koln and told me that he reached 350 km/h (217 mph) and the *Messerschmitt Bf 109* achieved about 400 km/h (249 mph) and later on with other engines it reached 500 km/h (311 mph). This promised a competition as to which was better, the Spitfire or the *Messerschmitt Bf 109*, well sometimes one and sometimes the other. The good things which *Walter* said about the *Spitfire*; well, I'm not of the same opinion.

Myhra: He talks about its higher ceiling, greater wing span, and so on.

R. Horten: He had to know about these differences. If the Air Ministry was calling for 70 to 90 kilograms (155 to 200 pounds) of steel plates for pilot protection, this weight reduces the ceiling by 200 to 300 meters (656 to 985 feet) and when they were flying at their ceiling and making a turn they would loose 200 or 300 meters in height or more and if the *Messerschmitt Bf 109* was above the *Supermarine Spitfire*, well the *Supermarne Spitfire* still had some reserve and was lighter in weight. If this weight had been taken out, the *Messerschmitt Bf 109* could reach the same height and make the same maneuvers as the *Supermarine Spitfire* without losing altitude. I am not of the opinion that the *Supermarine Spitfire* was better than the *Messerschmitt Bf 109*. In the condition they flew the *Messerschmitt Bf 109*, the *Supermarine Spitfire* was better. But the engineers in the Air Ministry were not good. They were always giving orders to add more those instruments, equipment, and so on like the armour plate and that is why its ceiling and speed suffered against the *Supermarine Spitfire*. We had had the same thing in the year 1955 or 1960 when Germany was constructing the *Lockheed F-104*. The *F-104* without sweepback was a very good aircraft for Mach 2.0 but it had to pass Mach 1.0 and when doing so it was out of control like all aircraft. If now, the wing loading was too high at Mach 0.8 or 0.9 in this configuration it looses control and it would crash and 150 German pilots died out of 600 such aircraft. The Air Ministry of the *Bundes Luftwaffe* they wanted to have all the instruments which would enable the pilot to fly low with an auto-pilot and it cost about 300 kilograms (661 pounds) of weight. It made supersonic flying at low altitude very dangerous. It increased the wing-loading which contributed to high-speed stalling at 0.8 and 0.9 Mach. Hence the accidents and it was not because of *Lockheed* but more due to the Air Ministry. We had the same thing with the *Messerschmitt Bf 109*. It was a light, good aircraft but with all the additional things that they wanted on the aircraft, it gradually deteriorated, too. At the end of the war a group of *Focke-Wulf Fw 190s* came to Göttingen. These aircraft were to be used in the Ardennes offense of December 1944. This group was on their way to Frankfurt but had landed to refuel. Thirty-six aircraft took off and were circling around the airfield at about 500 meters (1,640 feet) and then came two *North American P-51* fighters which began shooting. I saw several parachutes and in five minutes there were only two *Focke-Wulf Fw 190s* left. The *North American P-51* then left returning home. They had shot down 34 *Focke-Wulf Fw 190s*. One of the two surviving *Focke-Wulf Fw 190s* had been in a spin and had recovered and was then able to land. That is the point. The *Focke-Wulf Fw 190* was not worse than the *North American P-51* and in five minutes 34 were lost. How was this possible? The *Focke-Wulf Fw 190* was covered with steel plates and this cost 500 kilograms (1,102 pounds) and they could not climb and the pilots were young and with little training. This is not a criticism of the *Focke-Wulf Fw 190* but of the organization, yes, it was. If a group of 36 *Focke-Wulf Fw 190s* were flying, they should have been protected by fighters above. The *Focke-Wulf Fw 190* was not a fighter but a ground attack machine. So when the German offensive began in December 1944, there were no German aircraft in the sky. They had all been lost earlier.

Myhra: Was it a mistake to build the *Focke-Wulf Fw 190?*

R. Horten: I think that about 5,000 had been built. It was a totally bad aircraft. Firstly, it was a low wing. *Messerschmitt* used the *Handley-Page* slots so that it could not enter into a spin but in the *Focke-Wulf Fw 190* when you were pulling the control stick back, you'd enter into a spin accidentally. The *Messerschmitt Bf 109* would not act this way. Secondly, the traditional German engine design employed a low mounted propeller crankshaft and an inverted "V"bank of cylinders. The pilot had a clear view here and here. The radial engine blocked the forward view over the front fuselage so that you could not see. This is to say that the view of the *Focke-Wulf Fw 190* was worse than that of the *Messerschmitt Bf 109*. Thirdly, the design. If we have high loads we use the surface of the wing for compression and tension. We call it monocoque design. The monocoque design was used in the *Focke-Wulf Fw 190* but we do not have large loads in the wing tips. If I have a main spar in the wing and its is interrupted by the undercarriage, why continue it to the wingtip where it is not needed as the loads at that point are low - it was not a good engineering concept. Fourthly, *Willy Messerschmitt* had made his design so that the retraction unit was close to the fuselage. That was desireable but this could not be done on the *Focke-Wulf Fw 190* and the undercarriage was set way out in the wing. The fuselage and engine mounted above the wing could only removed with a wrench. The *Focke-Wulf Fw 190* had to go into a hanger to have the engine removed and re-installed. The wing, too, was built in one piece and could not be dismantled. The fifth thing is that we must know what we want. Do we want to shoot one projectile into the enemy bombers or do we wish to fire several projectiles? In the *Focke-Wulf Fw 190* these projectiles were of low caliber. The *Supermarine Spitfire* had eight guns and the *Focke-Wulf Fw 190* could not have a center gun like the *Messerschmitt Bf 109* due to the axis of its propellor. Plus the *Focke-Wulf Fw 190's* two guns were in line with the air screw and thus, their effectiveness was reduced. *Focke-Wulf Flugzeugbau* used the radial engine and it was not possible to have a center-mounted cannon of 20 mm which the *Messeerschmitt Bf 109* had. The guns on the *Focke-Wulf Fw 190* were also interrupted by the rotation of the propeller blades. So not a great number of projectiles were going out. *Kurt Tank* had put two additional guns outside the propellor arc but they had to converge at 200 meters (656 feet) before the aircraft and this was not satisfactory. It would have been better to have one good cannon in the center of the aircraft. Thus, the *Messerschmitt Bf 109* was again better. Many facets of the *Messerschmitt Bf 109* were well designed but they changed considerably during its career to become more like the *Focke-Wulf Fw 190* and I didn't understand this. The *Focke-Wulf Fw 190's* required double the man-hours of the *Messerschmitt Bf 109* to construct. I believe that it would have been better to have two *Messerschmitt Bf 109s* than one *Focke-Wulf Fw 190*. What does *Walter* say about the *Messerschmitt Bf 109* vs the *Focke-Wulf Fw 190?*

Myhra: He was telling me about the differences in the two aircraft while we were talking about *Ernst Udet*. *Walter* said to me that *Udet* had been blamed for several aircraft failures such as the *Heinkel He 177*, *Messerschmitt Me 210*, and the *Focke-Wulf Fw 190*.

R.Horten: Yes, the *Messerschmitt Me 210* was a very bad plane.

Myhra: Why did *Adolf Galland* want a new aircraft like the *Focke-Wulf Fw 190?*

R.Horten: That is a good question. I don't know. Along with *Kurt Tank* here in Argentina there had been *Peter Riedel* and others. We wanted to speak about these things but we agreed not to talk about things that happened during the war. *Riedel* thought of *Tank* as a pig. Few people even in Argentina wanted to talk about what might have been or what things went wrong and why. Things went wrong as early in 1941 with *Tank* and the *Focke-Wulf Fw 190*. So it was a long time ago and we didn't want to talk about it anymore. We were not friendly with *Tank* during the war. I think that he may have tried to stop our early work in Göttingen by going to the Air Ministry. *Tank* was an opportunist. If there was anything good for him he'd do it. I'm not clear even today, why he asked me to join him in Argentina for many of his people had been working in France for a jet engine manufacturer in the Pyranees. These people only joined *Tank* in Argentina when they had run out of work. I didn't come to Argentina as a member of *Tank's* group. I came on my own. I was surprised to find *Tank* in Córdoba. *Tank* had been to Berlin to speak with the Soviets as had *Siegfried Gunter* from *Heinkel AG* . Most of the people associated with *Tank* said that they would not go to the USSR with him, but if he told them instead he was going to Argentina, then it was a different story. *Tank* and I talked but I told him that I must first go to England and see if I could obtain a job there. So I went. When I returned to Germany without a job I didn't know if *Tank* had gone to the USSR or not. This is when I traveled to Rome, to the Argentinian Embassy to get in contact with *Perón*, I did not know if *Tank* was in Argentina, either. It was my plan not to become part of his group but only to help him because I went to Argentina to continue with my all wing aircraft. That was my goal. If it was good or bad well maybe *Tank* thought that I had come only to work for him. No, my plans were only to help the people in *Tank's* group. I did not speak to *Walter* about *Tank* for *Walter* thought badly of him for what he did during the war. Really, very few people wished to accompany *Tank* to Argentina only his own engineers and the best like *Hans Multhopp* didn't come.

Myhra: I don't think that *Hans Multhopp* and *Kurt Tank* got along very well together.

R. Horten: They were two completely different people and could not get on together. *Hans Multhopp* was a scientific man and *Kurt Tank* was an organizer. *Tank* was a busimessman and as such he was not wanted in Argentina. Now *Tank* as a pilot had done very well. He was a good pilot. But intellectually, *Multhopp* was far superior to *Tank* and also in his character . I remember *Multhopp* in Göttingen. He liked to tell jokes all day and would laugh like a school boy. It was good to talk to him and we had some very good discussions. *Multhopp* was a man of deep knowledge. *Tank* was about third in the industry. Next was *Ernst Heinkel* and the best was *Willy Messerschmitt*. With *Messerschmitt* I had had the best relationship. When we were POWs in London in May 1945, there was *Tank*, *Messerschmitt*, *Walter*, and I in one prison block. We played bridge together. *Tank* and *Messerschmitt* didn't want to play with their former workers, so the four of us played together with *Tank* and *Messerschmitt* against the *Horten's*.

You know the *Messerschmitt Me 163* was needed, not as an interceptor but it opened the door for high-speed aerodynamics. For this reason it was neessary. We certainly didn't need 279 of them produced but 10 to 12 were needed. *Alexander Lippisch* had made a great step forward with his *Messerschmitt Me 163*.

Myhra: How many workers were there in total in the *Horten Flugzeugbau* at its peak?

R. Horten: We had a total number of about 170 workers. Hersfeld with 30, Rottweil with 12, Ageidneburg with 12, Göttingen with...

Our concept and what there is to say, is like this. If we have a development of anything I can put it into an animal analogy. Think of a simple moth. The life of this insect may only be one day. We will study the life experiences of this insect and can see the life experiences - as it will multiply frequently -of maybe 100 generations. That is in 100 days. If we have an insect which lives one or five years - a dog for example and if we change it and observe a hundred generations, then we must wait for a total of 500 years. This is 500 years compared to 100 days . In fact, our thinking is if we have an aircraft which is a sailplane and we have some problems we can develop it by redesigning or modifying it to create a new aircraft in a short time. In other words, you have to build a new aircraft each year to gain experience. If you have one large aircraft like the *Northrop XB-49* with eight turbines the life of this aircraft should be ten years and to make a better one, the next generation of development is about another 10 years instead of 1 year. The development for this will be ten steps or ten generations greater. For example, ten generations of sailplanes will take ten years but ten generations in great aircraft will require 100 years. The cost of the little plane is small while the cost of the large plane is great. Therefore, we have to develop little planes and make them perfect. Then when the flying characteristics are satisfactory we can progress to a larger scale. I think that it was a mistake for *Jack Northrop* to go from a small plane to a large plane without the experience of developing the handling characteristics with smaller planes. If there is a negative feature in the design of a great plane then it is very bad for the hopes of the whole factory has been staked on it. If there is a small plane which does not work out we put it aside and go on to the next small plane. Also the cost is minimal. This is another reason to work with sailplanes without engines. The engine is not needed for the aerodynamic investigation and indeed the propwash will normally disrupt the aerodynamics. It is therefore better to investigate aerodynamics in a sailplane after being towed aloft. Its cost is less than any other method. That is my response to *Wilkinson's* report. He said that we were only interested in sailplanes. I had to build sailplanes and if the sailplanes were good I had to build powered aircraft too. I began with the *Horten Ho 1* and then immediately with the *Horten Ho 2*, and as the *Horten Ho 2* was successful, I progressed not to the *Horten Ho 4* but went on to the twin engined *Horten Ho 5*. I had made a great step to the twin engined aitcraft but at that time it was too much of a step. I needed two more years to successfully develop this plane. Later on the *Horten Ho 7* flew like a normal aircraft. But in all the tests we asked something of each aircraft. We made tests. Then we waited to see if what we put into the sailplane will give us the response, the answer. This answer had to come quickly, within three or five months and not in years. Therefore, it is better to build more sailplanes, frequently, as opposed to one large plane. During this time we had no answers to our questions and if we had no answers then we could not develop other aircraft. That is to say that the development of an aircraft is not a one-way street. It is a cone. We have here a question and have here a test, in both sailplanes and powered planes, and so on. One cannot only go in one direction. The idea was that each sailplane was to provide an answer, to a question, which we called the "test" . We needed the results and we needed them frequently. This work of ours is not considered in *Wilkinson's* report. Thus he turned the report into a criticism. We needed the sailplanes.

Myhra: I spoke with *Dipl-Ing. Felix Kracht* formerly of the *DFS*, in Toulouse, France and he is still angry over Germany's loss in World War Two. He was one of those men who was a *Flugbaumeister*. Those people, whenever I've spoken to person who was a *Flugzeugbaumeister* seem to believe that they were superior to all other people.

R. Horten: *Felix Kracht* is negative. The thing is that you can't turn back the clock. It is running on and not running back. And each thing has its own time. Now a new world war is impossible.

Myhra: I have had many good talks with *Rudolf Preussler*.

R. Horten: He was one of the best middle men I had. It was his job to look after the aircraft to inspect it in all respects. He was also interested in the production of the aircraft and how the prototype might be made better.

Myhra: *Heinz Scheidhauer* told me some very negative things about *Erwin Ziller*. He said that *Ziller* was arrogant and that he had a dark side. That *Ziller* claimed to be the best pilot in the *Horten Flugzeugbau* and so on.

R. Horten: No, *Erwin Ziller* was not arrogant. He was a very modest person and in fact he did not talk much about himself. He was a good comrade.

Myhra: That's what *Rudolf Preussler* said, too, but *Heinz Scheidhauer* gave me an opposite view of the man. He said that *Ziller* was not well liked by his comrades, that he boasted a lot. *Scheidhauer* told me that *Ziller* had been released from his old squadron because they did not like him. *Ziller* was supposed to be a loner, didn't have any close friends and so on. He stated that *Ziller* was undisciplined,.that is he'd do whatever he felt like doing. *Scheidhauer* told me that *Ziller* had been in a nursing home recuperating from hepatitis and his old squadron in Norway told *Ziller* that they didn't want him back anymore and to find some other squadron to work in. *Scheidhauer* said that *Ziller* was in the nursing home and had no work to do or no job because no one wanted him. *Scheidhauer* said that he had known *Ziller* from the days of their successful attack on the French Fort Eban Emael and that the felt sorry for him. *Ziller* was feeling low, rejected, and unwanted. *Scheidhauer* said that he talked to you about having *Ziller* join the *Horten* team at Oranienburg.

R.Horten: No. My experience with *Erwin Ziller* was that he was a quiet and modest man. We were like brothers. Instead, *Heinz Scheidhauer* was not wanted by his comrades for he was not arrogant but boastful. Oh, *Ziller* had many friends, in fact more than *Scheidhauer*. *Ziller* was a very good man. I don't understand why *Scheidhauer* is speaking against *Ziller*. *Ziller* didn't do anything bad to *Scheidhauer*.

Myhra: How was it that *Erwin Ziller* came to work in the *Horten* organization?

R. Horten: *Walter* had asked for him. We had called for a pilot. Well, I'll explain it. One day *Walter* was ordered to come in and see the area commander of Göttingen. He was an *Oberst* and he told *Walter* that we needed a man in our workshop to give political or *NAZI Party* philosophy speeches to the men of the work shop. This was in early 1943 when we had only been in Göttingen a month or two. I told *Walter*, well, if there must be someone he cannot stay here without doing anything. He must be a pilot that could aero-tow *Heinz Scheidhauer* and who also could fly the *Horten* sailplanes. Some days later, the chief of the Göttingen airfield, an *Oberst Shamm*, and the area *Gaulieter* came to visit us and asked *Walter* and I if they could send us an official to conduct political meetings each week in our work shop. I said, sure if he is a pilot who also can help us in our work we have nothing against this. The *Gaulieter* was pleased and he said he'd see if they had a person who also was a pilot. Then came this political person. He gave some speeches to our workers on Sunday mornings for one hour. He also talked about the news of the week. This *NAZI Party* person stayed with us for about one year but eventually told *Walter* that he couldn't stay any longer. *Walter* acted surprised and asked him why not? "It is no longer the time for talking anymore but it is time to fight. I have flown the *Junkers Ju 87* (*Stuka* dive bomber) and I will go to my old squadron to fly again." *Walter* said he understood and he was free to go back to his old unit. Then this person flew, was decorated three times, and then was shot down and killed. To replace this person, we had to quickly look for another pilot to aero-tow the *Horten Ho 9 V1* and we needed an aircraft like the *Heinkel He 111* because the runway at Göttingen was only 1,000 meters (6,214 feet) in length. There were hangars all around the airfield so it was a very bad place to fly out of. We could not start towing the *Horten Ho 9 V1* because it was very difficult and we had to offload much of the fuel. For the first take off towing the *Horten Ho 9 V1* we had to attach two booster rockets to the *Heinkel He 111* of 5 to 6 seconds burn duration and 1,000 kilograms (2,205 pounds) of thrust each. In this way we were able to get airbourn and the pilot who came with this *Heinkel He 111* was *Erwin Ziller*.

Myhra: From what airbase did *Erwin Ziller* come to you?

R. Horten: *Erwin Ziller* and the *Heinkel He 111* was lent to us. *Walter* had spoken to someone in the Inspectorate of Fighters command and we were able to obtain the *Heinkel He 111* with pilot. We then kept *Ziller* because the *Horten Ho 9 V1* was ready to fly. *Ziller* was a good pilot and had flown a great deal and *Walter* came to the realization that *Ziller* might also be a good pilot for the *Horten Ho 9 V2* because we didn't have anyone then. That was the point. But for *Heinz Scheidhauer*, this was a knock back for he mentioned that he'd fly the *Horten Ho 9 V2*. But *Scheidhauer* was not able to do this. *Walter* and I had not agreed to let *Scheidhauer* do this. *Ziller* was with us for about six months-and no more. But I was very impressed. I told *Ziller* when he joined us that he could speak with me in the evenings anytime after 10 pm because any earlier than that I was busy with my workers. He'd come often and we'd speak from 10 to 11 pm and then when he had gone I'd continue on with my calculations until 2 or 3 am. Sometimes my friend *Heinz Simon* would come over at 2 am and we'd talk for an hour. Then I'd tell him that we had to sleep for a while. At 7 am I would go to the drawing office with all the designs I had worked on during the night, for them to be entered into the master drawings. Many times I worked the whole night through. This was a time of very hard work but it was normal. *Scheidhauer* had it very easy. He came at 7 am to the airfield and looked at the weather, made a flight or two, and then went home to his wife. If I told him to fly a particular test, well he always wanted me to be present. But I didn't have time to be with him. So, if there were any difficulties I spoke to *Ziller* and told him of the things which needed to be done. *Ziller* was more understanding than *Scheidhauer* and more into engineering matters. If I had told him the kind of landing I wished to be tested, *Ziller* understood it easily. We could communicate together but not with *Scheidhauer*. The takeoff, how it is handled, when we had critical speed, and so on, well *Scheidhauer* didn't understand. He was absolutely not a test pilot.

Myhra: Well it seems the negative things *Heinz Scheidhauer* was telling me about *Erwin Ziller* he was really telling me about himself.

R. Horten: I can say this in one word. *Erwin Ziller* was the test pilot and *Heinz Scheidhauer* was a sport flier. You cannot put a sport flier in a new aircraft.

Myhra: You are saying that a sport flier is not a good test pilot?

R. Horten: A test pilot is a pilot who hasa technical interest like an engineer. He should be able to think in technical terms. *Erwin Ziller* could do this.

Myhra: *Heinz Scheidhauer* also told me that he had only been at Oranienburg Air Base once and that was for the first flight of the *Horten Ho 9 V2*. I also asked him about the crash of the *Horten Ho 9 V2* and how it might have happened. He said that he was not there when it happened. He claimed that this man from *Arado Flugzeugbau* named *Burne* was supposed to go to the control tower and talk to *Ziller* during the flight. *Scheidhauer* said that *Ziller* was a very impatient person and had become frustrated due to the bad weather and the fact that he had been unable to fly the *Horten Ho 9 V2* for so many days, that *Burne* from Arado and *Ziller* walked together across. the field heading for the *Horten Ho 9 V2. Burne* went to the control tower and *Ziller* to the *Horten Ho 9 V2. Scheidhauer* said that the plan was that *Ziller* would wait with engines running until *Burne* arrived at the control tower and they made radio contact. Then during the flight they would talk to each other. But what happened, says *Scheidhauer*, *Ziller* had the engines-running and then took off before *Burne* established radio contact. All during the flight *Ziller* made no radio contact with anyone.

R.Horten: Look, I had asked *Heinz Scheidhauer* several times who was in the control tower and who was on the radio with *Erwin Ziller* during this flight? He always answered that he didn't know. *Scheidhauer* came to Göttingen later after *Ziller*'s death and I asked him "what was the cause of *Ziller's* death?" He told me "it was *Ziller's* fault." He said that "*Ziller* always came in too low to the airfield."

Myhra: *Heinz Scheidhauer* said that he had not been in Oranienburg the day *Erwin Ziller* died on February 18th 1945. He said that he was back at Göttingen.

R. Horten: This is a thing which I don't understand. It was the crash of *Erwin Ziller* and *Walter* had gone there to represent us at the funeral and when *Walter* came back I got a call on the telephone that *Hermann Strebel* had died at the Hornberg and *Walter* told me "now you have to go and I will stay here." I had previously made him go to Oranienburg as I had to stay in Göttingen and work on the *Horten Ho 18*. We could not go together the way we had gone so often. Then *Walter* told me that I should go to the Hornberg. Now in the book <u>Nurflügel</u> by *Peter Selinger* it is reversed (Stated as 18th January 1945..PW). *Hermann Strebel* died before *Erwin Ziller*. I remember that it was the other way around.

Myhra: When *Heinz Scheidhauer* was relating. this story to me, I told him that this isn't the same story I have heard from other people. I've heard, I told him, that *Ziller* was suppose to be a very nice, friendly and easy going person. Then *Scheidhauer* said to me "you can write whatever you want to write because in five years we'll all be dead and it won't make any difference any more."

R.Horten: *Heinz Scheidhauer* has no sense of what is true. He speaks something else. Perhaps the death of his wife has disturbed him, I will have to excuse him.

Myhra: I have no further interest in going back to *Heinz Scheidhauer*.

R.Horten: I'll tell you something else. The book *Selinger* wrote, well he had asked *Scheidhauer* to look for photographs for the book. There is a picture in the book of my son *Dieter* as a boy playing with a model airplane and it has nothing to do with our work. It was a family photograph and it does the book no good to have this photograph in what is a technical book. "What could I do?" Another thing, Göttingen was a grass airfield and when it grass grew high, it was cut by a machine and was picked up by a man on a trailer pulled by two cows or oxen. It was then taken to this man's barn. *Scheidhauer* spoke to this man and then hitched the two cows up to the *Horten Ho 12*. The *Horten Ho 12* had a tricycle landing gear and you could move it by hand without difficulty, it was that easy. Now he has these two cows before the *Horten Ho 12* and took a photograph of it being pulled by them! This was to be a joke saying "look here we don't have fuel so we must use these two cows to tow." We had plenty fuel up until the end of the war. Then *Selinger* put the picture in our book! That was a lie. That could not be and it was bad. Why did they do this ? (In fact this was almost the only picture of the completed Ho.12, no other was available. There was some friction with Selinger over information from Karl Nickel which Reimar disputed – the two men had feuded for many years..PW)The same with the text. *Selinger* had spoken with *Karl Nickel* and he gave *Scheidhauer* a report on our testing with a delta wing model the *IAe 37* and *IAe 48*. Whilst *Nickel* and *Scheidhauer* were here in Argentina there was nothing done on the *IAe 48*. I had begun the *IAe 48* in secret only two months earlier and didn't reveal it to either one of them because both were returning to Germany. I had done all the calculations in my house and didn't discuss it with them. They didn't know anything about the *IAe 48*. In the book it is written that all three of us were united in making the *IAe 48*. *"Lies*, lies in all these things." *Nickel* had nothing to do with aerodynamics. He is only a mathematician. He didn't understand lift distribution. Nothing. First *Selinger* asked me "May I give you manuscript to another person and I said yes, he can read it." Later *Selinger* asked me if *Nickel* could read it and I told him no. For *Nickel* is a man who'd look at everything and if he didn't understand anything, he will write an article and forget where he got all the information. He would steal ideas and the writing of other people and make appear as his own. *Nickel* was only introduced to lift distribution in 1942 by myself and soon there after he was publishing articles about it in his name as the *Nickel* lift distribution and so on. In addition, *Selinger* had gone to *Scheidhauer* with the manuscript and things were changed by both *Nickel* and *Scheidhauer*.(Nickel is a talented mathematition with many works to his credit and continues to champion the cause of tailless and all wing aircraft. However he believes today that Reimars bell-lift distribution theory is flawed and the two men were never reconcilled..PW)

Myhra: I continue to gather material on the *Horten Ho 9* book which *Walter* wants me to write.

R.Horten: It will be difficult to write because *Walter* was not in Oranienburg very much plus it was more than forty years ago. He has heard about the details from all these people like *Scheidhauer*, *Rosler*, *Preussler*, *Wenzel*, and so on and they all tell different stories. *Walter* cannot say which is true and which is not.

Myhra: *Walter* wants to talk about his tactics in fighting other aircraft...stories from the Battle of Britain.

R. Horten: That is his interest and I can't help out in that matter. I did not fly in the Eastern Front and I did not shoot down any enemy aircraft. All I did was some practice gunnery in an *Messerschmitt Bf 109*, a *Focke Wulf Fw56 "Stosser"* and with a Czech aircraft. I've flown some of the fighter types but never in combat so I can't participate in any discussion.

Myhra: The *Horten Ho 9 V2* book will start out with *Walter* in France and go on comparing the *Messerschmitt Bf 109* with the *Supermarine Spitfire* and how things began to go bad for the *Luftwaffe*. Then *Walter* starts talking about an all-wing fighter which would be a superior aircraft to the *Supermarine Spitfire*. *Walter* then brings up this idea to *Adolf Galland* and he says no to it due to a lack of interest, time, and so on.

R. Horten: It was not the time to develop the all-wing fighter for the war had passed.

Myhra: Actually *Reimar*, Germany had already lost the war with the Battle of Britain.

R. Horten: The old pilots who were experienced had already lost their lives over England and many others were prisoners there, too. There was not another generation of pilots to take their place and continue. *Walter's* three groups in *JG/26* or a total of about 110 pilots had been reduced to 10 or 11 pilots. About 100 pilots had died or become POWs over England. Then about four weeks later *JG/26* again had 110 pilots. A week or two later this number had been reduced to 59 pilots. Therefore, it is not correct that *Adolf Galland* needed a new fighter better than the *Spitfire*. The war was already at that time finished for us.

Myhra: The *Luftwaffe* had been almost destroyed in the Battle of Britain. They were virtually wiped out during the several months that the battle lasted.

R. Horten: It was not only caused by the *Supermarine Spitfire*. For instance if the *Messerschmitt Bf 109* was over England and was under attack and a bullet entered the engine then its cooling water came out. Ten minutes later the engine would seize and the pilot had to bail out and then became a POW. Or, if he landed in the English Channel in the water, he usually lost his life. Nevertheless, these pilots never came back. If a *Messerschmitt Bf 109* shot up three or four *Supermarine Spitfires* in their engines and they went down, well they would land, got into the next *Supermarine Spitfire* and began fighting again. Thus, in one or two hours the same pilot was back in combat again. Although the English lost many aircraft they lost very few pilots. We lost an equal number of fighters and pilots.

Myhra: *Walter* seems to think that the reason for *Nazi* Germany's defeat in the Battle of Britain was due to the *Messerschmitt Bf 109*. He believes that if he had had an aircraft like the *Horten Ho 9 V2* that the situation would have been different for *Nazi* Germany.

R. Horten: A twin engine aircraft would have been better for this task. There had been the *Focke-Wulf Fw 187* a twin engine single seat fighter which could fly for four hours. The *Messerschmitt Bf 109* had a duration of only one hour and 15 minutes. It arrived over England and had a combat duration of about 15 minutes and then it had to go home.

Myhra: In talking with *Walter* it seems as if he went on a kind of crusade in order to get his all-wing *Horten Ho 9* fighter built. Then *Walter* wanted to go back and re-fight the Battle of Britain all over again but only this time with his all-wing fighter instead of the *Messerschmitt Bf 109*. It also seems to me that *Walter* just couldn't take the loss of all his friends and colleagues over England in 1940 and not do something about it. Perhaps the *Horten Ho 9* to *Walter* was his kind of revenge...to do justice to the *Supermarine Spitfires*. That the *Supermarine Spitfire* was the cause of all those deaths. All his friends and colleagues who died. Whenever I talk with *Walter*, he always goes back to the Battle of Britain. Always.

R. Horten: Speaking about the *Supermarine Spitfire*, they had a great failure and this was that the engine until the end of the war was carbureted. The *Messerschmitt Bf 109* was injected. That is to say if you are flying with positive G, the carburetor is okay but with injectors who can take it in any position. Thus the injector is a very good feature to have in combat. There had been in Africa the fighter ace *Hans-Joachim Marseille*. Who knows what he did? The English made a circle of fighters and he entered into the circle, made half a turn and was flying inverted and could see very well and shot as he turned within the circle. In two minutes he had shot down nine *Supermarine Spitfires*. This was in a circle! Thanks to the injected engine.

Myhra: The control stick in the *Horten Ho 9* could be moved to give fine control at high speed and a more course control at low speed?

R. Horten: Yes. There was a button to pull out and you were able to bring the control stick up about 30 mm from a normal height of 16 mm. As a result the relation of control was changed. In the down position the control stick. was used for take-off and landing. We made it so that the stick itself could not move up or down unless activated by he pilot. It was an all mechanical system and very useful for high-speed flight. The skin of the *Horten Ho 9* was first calculated at 6 mm which we thought would be sufficient for all around torsional stiffness. I would have liked to have few ribs based on the experience of the *Horten Ho 4B*. I wanted to have 3 to 4 mm exterior and put 2 mm of plastic in the interior. In total, 6 mm of plywood.

Myhra: How were the wing leading edges made?

R.Horten: The leading edge of the *Horten Ho 9's* wing was to be produced in Slavian, but it was not delivered.

Instead of two plywood caps of 1 mm, that is 3 mm for the outside gave us 3 times 11 or 4 mm and 2 mm in the interior gave us 6 to 7.5 mm. That was the normal which we wanted to do. But they had not come.

Therefore, we laminated ten sheets of 1.5 mm plywood to give a thickness of 15 mm and moulded on a former in order to make our leading edge, so that we would have a plane to fly. *Gothaer Waggonfabrik* was also waiting for these but they could not be delivered because the Russian troops were coming. That was the reason that the wing leading edges had not been installed at *Gothaer*.

When the war began in September 1939 I was ordered to go to a flying school and there I obtained my military pilot license. When I completed it I was ordered to fighter training school. Three months later, an order arrived, transferring me to the air transport school at Braunschweig. There I was to modify a *Horten Ho 3* sailplane into an ammunition-carrying glider. When this was done, the Battle of England had been finnished and *Walter* visited me enroute from France to Braunschweig, before going on to Berlin to have his conference about the *Messerschmitt Bf 109* and other combat aircraft such as the *Messerschmitt Bf 110*. When *Walter* came to visit me at Braunschweig we arranged for him to stay the night. We talked about the problems encountered during the Battle of Britain and of the *Spitfire* versus the *Messerschmitt Bf 109*. I told him that we must go on to repair the *Horten Ho 5* which was now outside the hangar at Potsdam. They were using the hangar now for other aircraft in the school and had pushed the *Horten Ho 5* outside and due to the wind and weather it was getting damaged. I told *Walter* the only way to progress was with this plane, the *Horten Ho 5*. When he was in Berlin, he should speak to the authorities for permission to repair the *Horten Ho 5*. At the same time I had finished all the modifications on the *Horten Ho 3s*. In Munich there were two more *Horten Ho 3s* under construction when the war started and they had not been finished. I proposed that these two *Horten Ho 3s* should also be completed and added to the fleet of the *Horten Ho 3s* modified to carry ammunition. The commander asked where I could do all this because he said, we have no facilities to build new aircraft. I told him that we could do it in the *Peschke* repair work in Minden. Because *Peschke* had no work, I gave them the two *Horten Ho 3s* to complete as well. This was in the winter of 1940.. The two *Horten Ho 3s* were transported from Kitzingen to Minden and I assessed what it would take to complete the two *Horten Ho 3s*. About this time *Walter* came to visit meand I told him that the *Ho 5* at *Werde* in Potsdam was out in the open air, but that it could also be repaired by *Peschke* in Minden. *Walter* went on to Berlin and it was not until the summer of 1941 that *Peschke* got the order to repair the *Horten Ho 5* and by that time it had suffered even more damage. *Peschke* didn't care if it took many, many hours to repair the *Horten Ho 5* for they were enthusiastic about working on it. In this way the *Horten Ho 5* was repaired but it took nine months time to do it. That is more that it took to build it originally in *Köln*.

Myhra: Last night you were talking about the number of people lost in *JG/26*.

R. Horten: *Walter* was in Köln and had flown from the *Auskirchen* near Bonn to over the Western Front in France but in winter 1939-40 there was no contact with the French. Later he had his first combat and had been promoted to technical officer (TO) and also as a fighter pilot. Then they changed the engines in the *Messerschmitt Bf 109*. There came from *Daimler-Benz* their new *601* engine which produced 1,400 horsepower instead of 1,100. They installed one engine in *Walter's Messerschmitt Bf 109* and during a visit of the *Reichsmarshall* to Koln *Walter* demonstrated the first(re-engined..PW)*Messerschmitt Bf 109* in Germany. He showed *Hermann Göring* the *Messerschmitt Bf 109's* climbing speed. *Walter* told *Göring* that "this is the *Messerschmitt* fighting machine we've been dreaming of." But then before more engines were delivered, war with France came in May 1940. So in six weeks of war, it was not possible to make any changes and the new *Daimler Benz 601's* were not widely used in the Western Front. It was too late for them. Then came the war against England. They had to use their old 1,100 horsepower engines and not the 1,400 horsepower. Therefore, the *Messerschmitt Bf 109* was a step behind the *Supermarine Spitfire* in performance. *Walter* flew twice before the losses of *JG/26* were very great. He frequently came to me at Braunschweig. First *Walter* told me of how *JG/26* had begun flying to London with 110 pilots lead by *Adolf Galland*, and six weeks later *Walter* came back and told me that only 10 or 11 pilots remained in *JG/26*. *Walter* was ordered to obtain new pilots and new *Messerschmitt Bf 109s* to be trained for combat over England. Four weeks later a new group of *JG/26* were formed. Four to six weeks later *Walter* returned again to me and told me that we had again lost the whole of *JG/26 squadron* and only nine now remained. *Walter* was on his way to Berlin and was getting ready to organize a third group for *JG/26*. At the same time, the order to stop Battle of Britain was given. Therefore, *Walter* had time to speak to me. He said "the war is not over and it will take much longer. How can we fight against the *Supermarine Spitfire* and more importantly, fight over the sea to go to England and return?" I told him that the only way forward was to have a twin engined aircraft with long endurance and that it should be an all-wing. This all-wing must be similar to the *Horten Ho 5*. So we must rebuild the *Horten Ho 5*. This is what I told him frequently. *Walter* was angry for he had talked with various authorities including *Ernst Udet*. A new aircraft design would require a year although we had plenty of time during the war. The order to rebuild the *Horten Ho 5* came in the summer of 1941. At this time I was without any work although I was an instructor for night fighting or transport-type aircraft there and although I was flying at night, during the day I was free.

Myhra: You say that the basic *Horten Ho 5* would have been developed into a fighter against the *Supermarine Spitfire*. What kind of competition would that have been?

R. Horten: I do not say that the *Horten Ho 5* could struggle against the *Supermarine Spitfire*. I would say that the basis of the *Horten Ho 5* must be developed as a powered aircraft with greater horsepower or even a turbojet engine: first as the *Horten Ho 7* and then later on the *Horten Ho 9*.

Myhra: Yes, but then you were talking about a twin-engined *Horten Ho 5?*

R. Horten: Yes; I thought that it must be an aircraft with two engines because the single engined aircraft would always be in danger if one of its engines were lost. If it was a twin-engined aircraft then the pilot and the aircraft are not likely to be lost. The most important thing is to save the pilot. In the case of the *Supermarine Spitfire*, our *Luftwaffe* shot them down but many pilots would parachute to the ground and the next day he would be back up in the air with a new *Supermarine Spitfire*. Our losses came when the coolant in the engine was lost and then the engine would seize. Usually the pilot was okay but he'd become a POW and didn't return to Germany until after the surrender. Therefore, the fighting conditions of the battle were bad for us when the pilot had to bail out over England or the English Channel. Plus the *Messerschmitt Bf 109* had only a total endurance of 75 minutes! Round trip flying from France to England took 60 minutes and then the pilot had about 15 minutes of combat time. It was far too little. Plus, if the *Luftwaffe* pilot spent 15 to 20 minutes in combat and even though he may have been successful and won the match, chances are that he'd never make it back to France. Thus, we lost pilots if we won the fight or if we lost the fight. They didn't have sufficient fuel and would ditch into the water on their way home.

Myhra: Was *Walter* talking at that time about a twin-engined fighter?

R. Horten: I told *Walter* that it was necessary to rebuild the *Horten Ho 5* and then go forward from the *Horten Ho 5* to the next stage - an all-wing with bigger engines. It was most important that the aircraft be a good fighter. We could not turn the *Horten Ho 5* directly into a fighter. We could only use it as basis of improvement, to go on to the next aircraft, increasing speed, ceiling, maneuverability and so on. In addition we'd have to discuss armament and later a fighter would evolve out of all this testing. We are talking here about developing normal aircraft and during peace-time this takes about five years. In wartime this development could be shortened to two years.

Myhra: What were *Walter's* thoughts about the war at this time?

R. Horten: *Walter* and I agreed completely in this concept of a twin engined all-wing fighter. *Walter* was very angry that the best men of the *Luftwaffe* were being lost and that the *Focke-Wulf Fw 187* was not being produced. This was a twin-engine single-seat fighter. It was abandoned in about 1938. This *Focke-Wulf Fw 187* was capable of about 500 km/h (311 mph). But we could do better with the all-wing. *Walter* had seen the struggle to maintain a performance advantage. The thing is that the better aircraft - even if its only a nose-length ahead of the other - will be able to shoot down the other. That is to say a little better performance means a great deal in a dogfight. If you have a fighter which does 550 km/h (342 mph) and the other only 517 km/h (322 mph) that is only not merely 5% or 10% more. It is 100% more! For the faster one will shoot down the other. That is the point. Therefore, everything possible must be done to have an edge in fighter aircraft performance.

Myhra: What did *Walter* think of Germany's future after the Battle of Britain?

R. Horten: At that time we didn't have the *Focke-Wulf Fw 190.* It came later. *Walter* was thinking only in terms of the *Messerschmitt Bf 109* then and wishing to have more powerful engines. The 1,400 horsepower *Messerschmitt Bf 109* and later on with the supercharger, were able to produce more power. The maximum power of the engine could be increased to 1,800 horsepower. Even at this rate, the *Daimler-Benz* engine was rapidly damaged and had a short life. *Walter* was very active in seeking ways to improve the performance of the *Messerschmitt Bf 109.* He talked frequently with the engineers at *Daimler-Benz*. The *Luftwaffe's Inspectorate of Fighters Command* No.3 - Berlin, was interested in finding a man who had flown in combat and who had a knowledge of engineering. The Chief of *Inspection of Fighters Command* No.3 was *General von Döring*. He asked for *Walter*. Before *Walter* gave an answer he came to see me at Braunschweig and we talked about it. I said to him that it was a good idea for us. You have to go to Berlin and organise it so that I can repair the *Horten Ho 5.* At this time I was still an instructor at the glider pilot training school at Königsberg/ Nordhausen and I didn't need *Walter's* help for at least 6 months. At the school each new group of trainees had to make 10 night towed flights with a *Junkers Ju 52/3m.* So I was kept busy during the day and at night when I wasn't doing night-training I was designing the *Horten Ho 4A*. Plus around the base were more workmen than the base workshops required. Groups of these workers were mine for the asking, provided I had work for them to do. Many of these workers were people I knew from the *Wasserkuppe*. One day I met *Wolf Hirth*. *Major Reeps* was the commander of the base and he told me that *Hirth* had graduated from the pilot-training school with the lowest rank possible. Yet he was a famous pilot. *Reeps* said to me that I was charged with watching over *Hirth* so the other pilots would not give him any trouble. I told *Hirth* about it and invited him to join me in our barracks. "No, I'll stay here with *Knopher* and the others," he told me. "No, you will come with me," I told him. He did and then I also had to fly with *Hirth* because I was ordered to do so. Actually *Hirth* was a much better pilot than I was but I had to treat him as a student. During one flight in the night, from take off to landing, *Hirth* was telling me jokes. *Hirth* had a good sense of humor.

Wolf Hirth knew that I was constructing the *Horten Ho 4A*. Well, we had men at the base doing nothing, we had the wood, material, and so on. The *Horten Ho 4A* cost me absolutely nothing to construct! When the *Horten Ho 4A* was finished and *Heinz Scheidhauer* had flown it, the orders came to transfer the whole glider transport activity to Frankfurt on the Order. I was told by *Major Reeps* to stay in Königsberg/Nordhausen until everybody, all equipment, and aircraft had been transported. We had two groups of 30 men each, plus instructors, and two *Junkers Ju 52/3m's*, I stayed another two months in Königsberg. At this time the telegram came from *Walter* stating that he had arranged for the *Horten Ho 5* to go to *Peschke* and also assigning me to the *Luftwaffe* repair workshop in Minden. Before the telegram was received, *Walter* had come to Königsberg from Berlin to review his fighter groups because the war with the USSR had now began. He met me and together we drafted a telegram ordering my reassignment. We also saw to it that *Scheidhauer*, *Wenzel*, and other good draftsmen, engineers, and so on came with me to Minden. All in all I brought five other men with me to *Peschke's*. I thought that the drawings of the *Horten Ho 5* would have to be redone because I was planning on changing the *Horten Ho 5B* to a single-seater which we were calling the *Horten Ho 5C*. Therefore I needed two draftsmen and one engineer.

As soon as the war with the USSR began, Air Ministry officials in Berlin saw that this war would not end within a few months. Then *Ernst Udet*, whom *Walter* had visited many times, ordered that the *Horten Ho 5* should be repaired. If it was to be repaired, then I'd have to go to *Peschke*, too. So began the designing of our all-wing fighter during the war.

Myhra: The *Horten Ho 5* was to be the basis for a potential new fighter? It would be your research base?

R. Horten: Yes. What I had to do was to design a stronger center section for the new all-wing because I was planning on installing the new *Argus As 10* with 240 horsepower. Then, I thought of also installing, a *Schmidt-Argus* ram-jet tube above the wing on the center section. But it was too noisy. The noise was terrific. It was not therefore possible to carry on with this ram-jet. Then *Walter* came to me with some information about the secret new turbojet and he said that we should instead consider the *BMW* 003 turbine engine. At this time the *BMW 003* had a factory rating of 600 kilograms (1,323 pounds) thrust. I thought that we might put one above and one below the center section. I was thinking, too, of maybe taking off without the turbines running and then start them later. Thus we'd have a "flying test bed" as we called it. But before we could get the flight ready *BMW 003* the *Junkers Jumo 004* became available. They had initially been used in the *Messerschmitt Me 262* prototype.

Myhra: Why not two *Daimler-Benz 601s* from a *Messerschmitt Bf 109* and place them in the *Horten Ho 5* or a *Horten Ho 7*?

R.Horten: The *Daimler-Benz 601* from the *Messerschmitt Bf 109* would have been difficult to use because its 1,000 horsepower required a propeller with a diameter of 3.5 to 4.0 meters (11.5 to 13 feet) and this propeller needed its blade tips to be at least 1.5 meters (4.9 feet) above the runway so that it wouldn't touch the ground during takeoff or landing. Thus, we needed to have the propeller shaft up to 3.5 meters (11.5 feet) above the ground. This meant a tremendously tall aircraft. To use the engine from a *Messerschmitt Bf 109* would have required a large aircraft to give the height we needed. Therefore, I couldn't use the *Messerschmitt Bf 109's DB 601* engine and this is why I was very much interested in the new turbines. But I wasn't very knowledgeable about these new turbines. I remember asking *Dr. Franz* from *Junkers Jumo* "how many horsepower do these turbines produce?" He told me that "they didn't calculate turbines in horsepower any more but its power was measured in terms of thrust." I said, "but if its rotating then you have horsepower." He replied "yes, I produce 4,000 horsepower for my charger." So I thought that the turbines provide more horsepower than we needed. The diameter of turbine was 60 centimeter (23.6 inches) and I thought that we could bring the turbine exhaust right through the wing's trailing edge and thus reduce the size of the aircraft and have a fighter. That was the idea.

Myhra: So there were no piston engines suitable for a *Horten* all-wing fighter?

R.Horten: Piston engines were very good but they were difficult to install in our all-wings. During this time the *Messerschmitt Bf 109's Daimler-Benz 601* engine had given way to their *801* radial for the *Focke-Wulf Fw 190* which produced 2,500 horsepower. Therefore, the Air Ministry agreed to produce the *Focke-Wulf Fw 190* but later on this engine when installed gave only 1,400 horsepower and by the end of the war only 1,800 horsepower. The engine installed in a *Focke-Wulf Fw 190* suffered from overheating and poor materials and so on. But the *BMW* 003 had 900 kilograms of (1,984 pounds) thrust and I told *Dr. Hermann Oestrich* that when I made my next visit that you'd tell me that the turbine had passed a 1,000 kilograms (2,205 pounds) thrust mark. "No," he said, "we cannot promise anything more than 900 kilograms and this is certain so you much calculate your performance based on 900 kilograms of thrust."

Myhra: What would you have done for engine power if the turbine had not been available? What engine would you have used on your *Horten Ho 9* fighter?

R.Horten: I had an idea to use the *Daimler-Benz 601* from the *Messerschmitt Bf 109.*

Myhra: Well, then, how would you have mounted these engines given their large diameter propellers?

R. Horten: There had been the twin-engined *Dornier Do 24* sea-plane in which its two engines were mounted back to back. The aft engine was a pusher while the forward engine was a tractor. Both engines were installed above the wing. On the *Horten Ho 9*, for example this arrangement would have been 50 centimeters (19.7 inches) high and I thought I'd have sufficient height for the propeller. But this type of engine arrangement complicated things although it was still possible. I believed that I needed a water-cooled engine and with the use of such large diameter propellers the *Horten Ho 9* would have needed a strong center section. I thought at this time if we have no alternatives we shall build the *Horten Ho 7* with a 1,000 or 1,500 horsepower and would go to *Dornier* and find out how they had designed the engine mounting for the *Dornier Do 24.*

Myhra: Would the engines on the *Horten Ho 7* then have been mounted atop the wing like in the *Dornier Do 24?*

R. Horten: No, I would have still buried them inside the wing with drive shafts of 1 to 1.5 meters (3.2 to 4.9 feet) out to the propeller and this would be built in one piece. That was my idea when I was building the *Horten Ho 5*. But then *Walter* obtained information on the *BMW 003* turbine and more and more I forgot about 1,000 to 1,500 horsepower piston engines and all the difficulties their installation would mean.

Myhra: This would have been a pusher-type propeller?

R. Horten: Only a pusher. The thing is that the pusher propeller makes the aircraft stable, whereas a propeller in front the aircraft makes unstable.

Myhra: A pusher propeller would have required a taller landing gear.

R. Horten: It would not have been possible to make the landing gear longer for we also would have had greater weight. The center of gravity is high and when it is high, one must have the wheels widely spaced. So in terms of design, we were very limited, we had to look at all possibilities. *Alexander Lippisch* built an aircraft he had designed later in Vienna. I often told others that *Lippisch* was lucky that Vienna was bombed because that aircraft would not have been good. *Lippisch* in this design had gone a step too far. So it was with our piston-powered twin engined *Horten Ho 9* - I saw that the turbine would come and thus the piston *Horten Ho 9* would have been out of date.

Myhra: It must have been very frustrating trying to locate a motor of the proper horsepower and overall size to fit into the wing on the *Horten Ho 7?*

R. Horten: When I told you about the *Horten Ho 5,* to have it a prototype fighter, you must understand that I took a *Horten Ho 5* and made a fighter out of it. What I wanted to work on in this problem was if the *Horten Ho 5* had 16 meter (52.5 feet) of span and the *Horten Ho 7* had also 16 meters of span, then the layout should work in any other similar aircraft. I thought if I have about 40 to 50 square meters of wing area and 60 meters span, that the dimensions for a fighter would scale up to a good dimension for a light bomber. We could not develop the two things at the same time. I had to finish the fighter and then progress to the bomber. This was my problem.

Myhra: Were you more interested in a fighter or bomber or a combination of both?

R. Horten: In an all-wing aircraft the basic design makes it light and we have more room as a result. In a small aircraft it is very difficult to find the space that exists in an all-wing. If you have sphere, say 10 centimeters diameter and you make it twice the size or 20 centimeters diameter, the larger one will have four times more surface and 8 times more volume. Increasing it from 10 to 20is not proportional. So in an all-wing you need volume for fuel, for all other mechanical equipment and so on. Take for example the *Horten Ho 3* of 20 meters span and make an *Horten Ho 8* of 40 meters span and multiply. The first has 37.1 square meters wing area but the second has 150 or four times more but the volume is 8 times more and I have, therefore in relation to the area, double the volume - this is achieved using the same configuration. Therefore, I was planning a large plane for not only was it easier to design but as I said before , if I have a small plane I could change the design year by year, and development is faster. If I have a large plane like *Jack Northrop's XB*-49 I cannot make significant changes year after year. I can modify it maybe only every five years. That is to say, one first has to make a small plane, to perfect it. Then I keep improving on the design until I can make a large plane. So in this respect I agreed with *Walter* when he said that we had to make a fighter. The fighter with the all-wing planform is a very difficult thing. It is not good to make it too small for it is better to have a larger machine.

Myhra: Why do you say that it is difficult to make an all-wing fighter?

R. Horten: The difficulty is that when you are in a war you have to design and look for things which could be used immediately for the Front. Therefore whilst a fighter was greatly needed in World War Two *Nazi* Germany, when *Hermann Göring* told us to design the bomber I was surprised. I was happy because it was technically possible and a large aircraft such as this was in fact something which I was thinking about already. I wanted to build such a large plane. But to make the *Horten Ho 18* successful I would have required two years and the war was clearly finished in May 1945, so I could not understand why the order was given. With the *Horten Ho 9* fighter, when I started it in 1943 I had hoped that it could be ready for release to the Front within one year. In Brandis/Liepzig, they were waiting to fly the *Horten Ho 9*. If *Erwin Ziller* had flown the *Horten Ho 9,* for another 10 or 20 flights more and the Russians had not advanced, *Ziller* would have taken the *Horten Ho 9* to Brandis/Leipzig and other pilots would have had the opportunity to fly it too and soon afterward *Horten Ho 229s* from *Gothaer Waggonfabrik* would have arrived, equipped with cannon for fighting in the Front. (This reveals that Reimar was completely out of touch with the poor rate of progress at Gothaer…PW) We could not wait much longer because *Göring* told us when he ordered the *Horten Ho 9* that the *Horten Ho 9* had to be ready for its maiden flight within three months of his order. I told him that this was impossible. I was angry for we had been forbidden by the Air Ministry to work on the *Horten Ho 9* and now *Göring* tells me that he wants it within three months! I had already done three months work on the *Horten Ho 9* before *Göring's* order. I told him that it was possible that the *Horten Ho 9 V1* glider might fly within six months. "No, have you forgotten *Horten* that we are at war," he told me. I told him that we had no prospect of doing this. "Make it possible, it must be for we are at war," *Göring* replied. Then we spoke about other things. The before we left *Göring* said "Then in six months it will fly?" And I said "yes, in six months." *Göring* was good to do this. *Alexander Lippisch* was told by *Göring* that his plane (probably the P11…PW)was to be flyable in three months, too. It was impossible and *Lippisch* told *Göring* that he had been bombed and could not produce any more aircraft. But we finished the *Horten Ho 9 V1* within six months, on the February 28th 1944 and on that day it was aero-towed with *Heinz Scheidhauer* piloting. Right afterward we went to the communications board and sent a telegram to *Göring* saying "First flight of *Horten Ho 9 V1* successfully completed." At that moment, we could have had anything we wanted. We were friends. *Göring* had given us six months and the first flight of the *Horten Ho 9 V1* took place exactly six months later and *Göring* was pleased. In German industry, *Göring* was thought of as a fool for the manner in which he carried on his role as the *Reichsmarshall*, for example asking for new aircraft within three months . But, today, I think that he was not a fool. Germany was in a struggle so we had to have superior aircraft within a short period of time. I was able to produce the *Horten Ho 9 V1* within six months. Others should have been able to do it also.

Myhra: *Hermann Göring* wanted the *Horten Ho 9 V1* within six months but you said that the Air Ministry didn't want the all-wing at all?

R. Horten: In January 1943 I began work on the *Horten Ho 9* but then in March 1943 came the directive from the Air Ministry that our activity in the workshop at Göttingen had to cease. I had already put in three months work on the *Horten Ho 9.* My principal work in Göttingen at that time had been on the *Horten Ho 7* while *Peschke* was finishing the *Horten Ho 5* . The Ho.7 drawings had to be completed by us because *Peschke* had only three draftsmen there. A plane like the *Horten Ho 7* required about 500 drawings. The *Horten Ho 4A*, which was smaller, had about 200.But a hundred were sufficient for the *Horten Ho 7* because we were always to hand. Once *Peschke's* people started working on the *Horten Ho 7*, I took one of my engineers and the two of us started working on the *Horten Ho 9* for I needed project drawings in order to perform calculations. At this time I thought I could finish the *Horten Ho 9* in April-May 1943 but for some two months I had to work again on the *Horten Ho 7* so I couldn't work at this time on the *Horten Ho 9.* That was one of the problems. I had to organise things so that I had prepared drawings for the section at *Peschke* where they were working on the *Horten Ho 7.* Little by little as the *Horten Ho 7* was nearing completion the men could start working on the *Horten Ho 9.That* was my idea. However, my plans had been interrupted for we had lost time, I think six months or more because of the extra work required on the *Horten Ho 7.* Then, when our workshops were dispersed to different locations I wrote a telegram to the Air Ministry that the Göttingen workshop no longer existed and therefore nothing came of it. But now all the men were at various locations and I had to continue with the plans for the *Horten Ho 4A*, *Horten Ho 6*, and so on. I could not be at each location every moment of the day as I had previously at Göttingen. I was angry so I continued on with the *Horten Ho 9* without the permission of the Air Ministry. So this is what I mean when I say that the Air Ministry didn't want the *Horten Ho 9* when they told us to stop work at Göttingen. There then came another opportunity. *Hermann Göring* arranged a conference in the Air Ministry for the whole aircraft industry, which *Walter* attended. *Walter* was spending half his time between Göttingen and Berlin at this point. *Göring* told the conference that the aircraft industry was too expensive and he didn't want any more new airplanes with the exception of a 1000/1000/1000 aircraft. *Göring* was very angry and pounded the table "I won't accept any new designs unless they have 3x1000 performance. I will not have 500 km/h, 550 km/h or 600 km/h that is not the difference what I want." I think that *Göring* was right. Therefore this meant 1,000 km/h of speed, 1,000 kilograms bombs, and that means a fighter-bomber, and 1,000 kilometers of range reserve at the end of the flight or 3,000 kilometers total range.

Myhra: Why did *Hermann Göring* need 3x1000 aircraft? For what purpose?

R.Horten: Many uses. For use in the North Sea area, for example, it was about 1,000 kilometers to Norway. *Göring* was thinking of a twin engined aircraft to fly over the Alps to the Mediterranean area. So coupled with the distance and over water, *Göring* needed an all around aircraft capable of 3xl000. The people in the Air Ministry thought that *Göring* was a fool to think of a 3xl000 aircraft. His own Air Ministry thought such an aircraft was .impossible so their attitude was to let *Göring* speak about whatever he wanted. *Walter* came to Göttingen and told me about *Göring's* request. *Walter* thought that *Göring* was foolish, too, that no one in the industry could produce a 3xl000 aircraft at that time. I told *Walter* that *Göring* was right and that he was not a fool. We could do it! I said that the others in the industry could think what they wanted but we *Hortens'* could do it with one of our all-wing designs. *Walter* told me that it was not possible. Shortly after this conversation I began thinking seriously about the *Horten Ho 9* but when I made my calculations I could not achieve 3xl000. Instead I was getting 900 kilometers, 920 kilograms and so on. With bombs I had difficulties. If he wanted two bombs of 1,000 kilograms well that would have been good for lift compensation. Then when I figured 1,000 range out, 1,000 return, and 1,000 reserve, well I thought that couldn't be. The best at that time I could come up with was 700 kilometer range because of the limitations of fuel-capacity. I went to speak with the people at *BMW* and *Junkers Jumo* about the specific consumption of the turbines and so on. I made an outline sketch of the proposed *Horten Ho 9*, calculated its performance and gave this data to *Walter*. He in turn took it to *Göring's* office. *Göring's* technical officer was *General Diesing* and *Walter* showed our twenty page report to him. *Diesing* told *Walter* that he'd be getting back in touch with him. But *Diesing* was not a man who had confidence in us for he told others that the young *Horten* brothers couldn't build such an aircraft. That it was impossible for us to even think of such a project. However *Diesing* made copies of our proposal and sent them out to the industry, *DVL*, and so on. They had our report and we in turn waited for a reply from *Diesing*. We went about three or four months without an answer from *Diesing*. From time to time *Walter* would call *Diesing* saying that "we are waiting for your response. to our proposal." *Diesing* finally spoke to *Göring* about our proposal and the Reichsmarhall liked it.

Myhra: What kind of man was *General Diesing*?

R.Horten: *Kurt Diesing* was a good organiser for *Reichsmarshall Göring* and I don't believe that he had any opinion on our all-wing designs.

Myhra: Why did *Diesing* send out your proposal to people in the industry, *DVL* and so on?

R. Horten: Because he had no opinion of his own and the Air Ministry general engineers like *Lucht* and *Reidenbach* were absolutely slow. I think that *Diesing* knew that he couldn't get much help on the merits of our proposal from his own staff. The only one who could tell him, before he took it to *Göring*, were the comments from *DVL* and the industry. For example *Kurt Tank* read our proposal and had given the Air Ministry a negative response. *Tank* didn't like the idea that the *Luftwaffe* was thinking about manufacturing their own aircraft. You see, we were in the *Luftwaffe* and *Tank* said that designing and manufacturing aircraft should be left to the industry. *Tank* said that the *Luftwaffe's* job was flying. He didn't want the *Luftwaffe* to build aircraft. *Kurt Diesing* said that he didn't get a critical response from *Tank* only an angry argument that the *Luftwaffe* had no business in aircraft manufacturing. So *Diesing* said that he couldn't use *Tank's* response. *Diesing* wanted to know from *Tank* if our *Horten Ho 9* proposal was even possible and *Tank* didn't give him that information. Really, people like *Kurt Tank* or *Willy Messerschmitt* or *Blohm und Voss didn't* know anything about the all-wing and were not of much use to *Diesing*. Few people in the industry which the exception of *Lippisch* knew anything about the prospect of an all-wing delivering a 3x1000 aircraft.

Myhra: What did the people at *DVL* think about it?

R Horten: At *DVL* our proposal. was read by *Professor Bock*. He told *Diesing* that the proposal looked very interesting but they had no experience with all-wing aircraft and that he couldn't respond one way or the other.

Myhra: So *Kurt Diesing* wasn't able to get a good critical opinion of your *Horten Ho 9* as a 3xl000 fighter/bomber? *Diesing* still didn't know if the *Horten Brother's* proposal was a good idea or a bad idea?

R. Horten: Yes. *Walter* called *Kurt Diesing* asking him "When can I hope to have a conversation with you on the *Horten Ho 9?" Diesing* kept asking *Walter* to be patient for a few more days. I remember that I was at the airfield in Göttingen getting the *Horten Ho 3F* ready for a flight in the prone position. During the time we had been waiting for *Diesing*, I had also been working on and flying the *Horten Ho 4A*. From time to time I'd fly the *Horten Ho 3F* and the *Horten Ho 4A* for we had no order to continue on with the *Horten Ho 9*. At this time the drawings *of the Horten Ho 7* had been finished too. I had also directed 10 to 15 men to begin work on the *Horten Ho 9*, still without any authority. When I was about to enter the *Horten Ho 3F* to fly it, one of my men came running over and told me that I'd received a telegram from Berlin. I thought now what can this telegram be all about? The last time I had received a telegram from Berlin it said to close down the activities at Göttingen. I went inside the hangar and saw that the telegram was not from the Air Ministry but from the office of the *Reichsmarshall* and looking further it was from *General Diesing*. It read:"Come immediately to Berlin-Königsberg to see the *Reichsmarshall*." At this moment I could not fly the *Horten Ho 3F* because I was so excited that we were going to see *Hermann Göring* in one or two days. I went right away to *Walter* and told him that I needed to make copies of some drawings, I needed to clean my uniform, and then we took the night train to Berlin. One or two days later *Walter* and I arrived in Berlin at 8:00 pm and then took the train to Königsberg arriving in the morning.

Myhra: Exactly what was at Königsberg?

R. Horten: *Hermann Göring* has his office for the Russian Front at Königsberg. We were met at the train station by one of *Göring's* aides and then drove about 20 kilometers to his office. En-route whilst on the train we once heard the warning of an air-raid and at then the train stopped and everyone got out and ran into the nearby fields. *Alexander Lippisch* was also on this train was for he too had been invited to Königsberg. *Walter* and I had a sleeping car because we had left Berlin at night. *Lippisch* didn't have a sleeping car but I invited him to join us which he did. That night *Lippisch* and I talked about lift distribution and so on for hours. I was not afraid to talk to *Lippisch* about my theories and ideas for we now were at war and things were different. I told *Lippisch* about my bell lift distribution ideas and *Lippisch* wanted to know why I didn't publish this information? I told him that I would do so when I had the time. I wanted to describe my bell lift distribution and other ideas in my book which I started I writing in the mid 1970s. Later *Peter Selinger* changed much of it in the <u>*Nurflügel*</u> book.

The next morning we arrived at 7:00 am in Königsberg. Once we got to *Reichsmarshall Göring's* office which was about 30 kilometers (19 miles to the south) *Walter, Lippisch* and myself were told to wait. At 12:00 noon we were invited into lunch and at the great table was *Hermann Göring*. All he was eating was an apple and we were being served soup. In total there was about twenty men at *Göring's* table. I remember that *Göring* sat on one side of the table in the middle and the three of us were sitting directly across from him.

Myhra: Who were the other people at the table?

R.Horten: Oh, generals and officers of *Reichsmarshall Göring's* staff. We ate for about hour and then *Göring* said that he wished to speak privately with me and *Walter*. But first the *Reichsmarshall* wanted to speak alone with *Alexander Lippisch* and then we'd be next. *Göring* asked us to wait for about an hour. But before this, the whole time we were all eating *Göring* was speaking and from time to time my face must have turned red. *Göring* said that "he viewed his German people in three categories: First, were the workers...the general mass of people; Second, were the scientific people who were the creators of scientific ideas; and the Third were the politicians. "I'm in the third group," *Göring* said. "The politicians have the task," *Göring* continued, "that the mass of workers will go and give the money and the material for the investigation of science. But to organize all this is the job of the politicians. We must look to see that the mass of the people do not know this." For example this was the way *Göring* spoke "I see three types of young men. We can look at their childhood years and if these boys somedays play football, well, this is good because this is where the mass of people spend their time. If they go on Sunday to church this is also good for as employers of the state they will fill their place in administration. The third class is the group: who go on Sunday to fly sailplanes. This is the class which I need not only for the *Luftwaffe* but this is the class who are thinking about building and designing. In these type of people I see the scientific class." *Göring* was looking right at us...*Walter* and me. All those present, indeed the whole table heard it. I did not expect that *Göring* would be talking about us *Hortens'* in this manner. It was too much for me. Then *Göring* finished the lunch and he went into a private meeting with *Lippisch*. About hour later *Lippisch* came out of *Göring's* office. *Göring* had given him an order to began work on his twin engine fighter prototype to be built in Vienna, Austria.

Göring had given *Lippisch* three months in which to finish his prototype and *Lippisch* was depressed. He knew that he couldn't finish the aircraft given the 3 month deadline and the state of the German aircraft industry at the time (1944). I believe that it would have been better for *Lippisch* if he had stayed with *Willy Messerschmitt* because he could then have produced the prototypes and used *Messerschmitt's* technical staff and production facilities. Then it was our turn to talk privately with *Göring*. Our meeting with *Göring* lasted more than one hour and it was a very good humoured meeting. We laughed together. We spoke about our *Horten Ho 4A* sailplane and its pilot's prone-position flying. *Göring* wanted to know how can a pilot could fly an aircraft while laying on his stomach? *Walter* kneeled down laying himself over a chair and showed the *Reichsmarshall* the prone position. "And you have flown the *Horten Ho 4A* this way," *Göring* asked *Walter*? "Yes many times *Herr Reichsmarshall*," said *Walter*. *Göring* was astonished and wanted to know how all this was possible? We told him and then *Göring* said that he wanted to know all about our *Horten Ho 9* fighter. *Göring* was open and both *Walter* and I, could speak with him as we did with our own father.

Myhra: How many people were present when you and *Walter* were speaking with *Reichsmarshall Göring*?

R.Horten: Just me, *Walter*, and his aide *General Kurt Diesing*, but no one from the aviation industry for most people like *Kurt Tank*, *Ernst Heinkel*, and *Willy Messerschmitt* were frightened of *Hermann Göring* because he shouted at them. However, with us he was very nice.

Myhra: He seemed to be happy whenever he was with you or *Walter*. I have a photograph showing *Walter* walking with *Göring* and a few steps behind are *Udet*, *Milch*, and *Kesselring*. Anyway, *Göring* and *Walter* are talking and *Göring* is smiling.

R. Horten: *Hermann Göring* was captivated by the all wing concept. During our meeting *Göring* said to us "If I think that you'll fly 960 km/h well, this is what I need for the Front. I flew the *Fokker D-7* of World War One and if I wanted a plane just for me I'd still want that old *D-7*!" *Göring* said that his dream for years had been to have an 3xl000 aircraft. I believed what he told us and that it was his true thoughts. *Göring* didn't really relate to a turbine powered fighter yet he knew that his *Luftwaffe* couldn't compete in the skies without this technology, however, his mind was still thinking of that *Fokker D-7!*

Myhra: *Hermann Göring's* intelligence level was around 140...much higher than most of the population whose average IQ is around 100.

R. Horten: Well, I saw that he was very bright in just speaking with him. If he asked me "what will you do with the 500,000 *Reichs Marks?* I told him that we'd buy tools and machines to perfect the all-wing *Horten Ho 9*. *Göring* said to *Diesing* send a telegram to *ESWEGA* (the *Luftwaffe* central distribution center at Munich) so that they can obtain the tools and machinery they need." Well, that was wonderful because the prices I was charged for tools and equipment at *ESWEGA* was only half of what these same items would have cost me on the open market. So with 500,000 *Reichs Marks* we actually had one million in real terms. Later, when I told *Göring* that the *Horten Ho 9 V1* had flown, he mentioned that I was only an *Oberleutnant* and without decoration. He called in *Diesing* and told him that he was promoting me to *Hauptmann* (Captain) and was giving me the class one *Kriegsritterkrauz* with sabers for distinguished service.

Myhra: And *Walter*?

R. Horten: *Walter* was to be promoted to the rank of *Major*. When we first talked to *Hermann Göring, Walter* was a *Hauptmann* and I was an *Oberleutnant*. Plus *Walter* had already received his *Kriegsritterkrauz* for combat in the Battle of Britain.

Myhra: What did the leaders in the industry such as *Kurt Tank* think of your personal contract with *Göring* over the *Horten Ho 9?* He must not have been too happy with the *Luftwaffe* now starting to build their own fighters?

R. Horten: I had had differences with *Kurt Tank* before over tailless aircraft. *Tank* told me that he had not thought about the all-wing. But his aide *Hans Multhopp* was against the all-wing. *Tank* gave me a 3 or 4 page report written by *Multhopp*. He was an aerodynamicist and not a designer and he made great errors for this reason.

Myhra: What is the difference between an aerodynamicist and a designer?

R. Horten: An aerodynamicist looks at how the aircraft will behave in the air. A designer is an architect of the aircraft and where all its systems must fit inside a given volume. An aerodynamicist is a part of this and has to look for the "air loads" in the plane. The designer has to consider not only air loads, but also the static forces in the plane. He has to determine the aircraft's oscillations problems and has the problems of volume and performance of the aircraft. I think that *Hans Multhopp* was the best aerodynamicist we had in Germany but as a designer he did not have experience.

Myhra: You said that the Air Ministry wanted to investigate your building of sailplanes while you were working on the *Horten Ho 9*. What was this all about?

R. Horten: The Air Ministry didn't know anything about aerodynamics for they wanted to say that the money we *Horten's* received was to build the *Horten Ho 9* as *Hermann Göring* had instructed. This is for that task and they didn't like the idea that I was building sailplanes with money to be used for the *Horten Ho 9*. I needed to test my ideas for the *Horten Ho 9* with sailplanes and it was hard to explain this to administrative types in the Air Ministry.

Myhra: But how did this all start and how did it come about? Did they send some staff people to *Göttingen* and there they saw you building sailplanes and then when they returned to Berlin these people told their superiors?

R. Horten: The *Reichsmarshall* sent *General Werner Junck*, a general from his staff, who in June 1932, as a *Flugkapitan* made the maiden flight of the *Heinkel He 70*. It was this same *Junck* whom *Göring* had now sent to Göttingen to report to him about our workshop activities all over Germany; because he was assigned to flying matters whereas *General Diesing* was more for administration.. *General Junck* probably didn't have much to do and *Göring* sent him so he came to us and began asking us about what we were doing?

Myhra: About what month and year was *General Junck's* visit?

R. Horten: It was near the end of the war. *General Junck* was supposed to have come shortly after we received the *Horten Ho 9* contract from *Hermann Göring* but he didn't arrive. *Junck* came much later about March 1945 and he came first to Göttingen and then went on to our other workshop locations. In his report to *Göring* he noted how many men we had, what work they were doing, what aircraft they were working on, and so on. We met *Junck* again after the surrender. We all were POW's in England and he told me that he had visited all of our workshop facilities. *General Junck* was a man whom we could speak to because he was a pilot and a practical man. If I had said to *Junck*, look all you want, but please do not speak to *Göring* about this or that sailplane, then *Junck* would have done what I asked him. He would not have been against me. My work on sailplanes was difficult to explain to other people, to *Kurt Diesing* never. He would have done only what *Göring* asked and no more.

Myhra: Well somebody must have complained to *Reichsmarshall Göring* about all the *Horten Flugzeugbau* workshops. They must have gone to *Göring* for some personal or other reason to complain.

R. Horten: If a plane was flying then you could see it and we had flown the *Horten Ho 13* in Göttingen. Someone might ask "What are you doing there," and I'd would reply "I'm making a study of a supersonic wing." This person might ask me "how many men are working there?" He might not say more about it. *Göring* was not a small man. and I doubt if he'd be concerned. But if I had 1,000 men working on it then it might be different. *Göring* might say "that cannot be." But 10 or 15 men is nothing.

Myhra: Did someone suggest to *Hermann Göring* that the *Horten brother's* were somehow doing something illegal in their workshop when you should only have been working on the *Horten Ho 9?*

R. Horten: I think that *Walter* or I had spoke to *Hermann Göring* about the supersonic wing and how it was a new style of wing. The whole aviation industry and the *DVL* in Berlin were astonished that a sailplane with this type of wing was actually flying! They were surprised, too, that we *Hortens* were making these investigations without their knowledge. At the *DVL* in Berlin, one of their people said that we should take this aircraft and demonstrate it right over the heads of people from the aviation industry. That was to say why didn't the industry make this type of investigation years before? They were flying test aircraft and the industry wasn't aware of the aerodynamics of our Ho 13 and its supersonic wing. The person who said this was the chief of the *DVL Professor Günter Bock.*

Myhra: *Geneal Junck* then returned to *Reichsmarshall Göring* and told him what the *Horten's* were doing?

R. Horten: Somehow *Hermann Göring* had heard about our sailplane building activities especially the *Horten Ho 13* with the swept-back wing. Somebody also asked us about the reason for the *Horten Ho 13* and we told them and showed them photographs, too. So *Göring* wanted more information and thus sent *General Junck* to investigate.

Myhra: Someone at the Air Ministry probably thought that you were wasting their money on sailplane construction?

R. Horten: The amount of money we spent on our *Horten Ho 13* sailplane was very small. The questions which we wanted answers to were in -flight aerodynamics. That we might be able to one day fly the *Horten Ho 13* was not the reason nor was it important that we had 10 to 15 men assigned to its construction.

Myhra: What did *Generals Reidenbach* and *Lucht* and others at the Air Ministry say when *Göring* gave you the contract for the *Horten Ho 9?*

R. Horten: Both of these men were general engineers and they were nothing.

Myhra: Yes, but *General Reidenbach* gave you a lot of difficulty.

R. Horten: *General Reidenbach* was a man who was against everyman. He was a negative man always. It was because of people like *Reidenbach* in the Air Ministry that *Walter* and I had to camouflage our work so that they would not disturb us. If these men went from general to general and told each one that our *Horten Ho 9* is bad, we would have had many problems. Therefore, *Walter* and I believed that it would be better if people at the Air Ministry like *Reidenbach* knew nothing of our all-wing activities. This was our view. The *Heinkel He 70* was requested by the Ministry of Transport in 1928 and they asked the industry for a single-engine plane of high-speed. At this time the Ministry was asking for 360 km/h (224 mph) and room to hold four passengers. *Junkers Flugzeugbau* had come out with the *Junkers Ju 60* and later with the *Junkers Ju 160* but it was not as good as the *Heinkel He 70.* I think that *Messerschmitt AG* had built a prototype aircraft called the *Messerschmitt Me 18* for the competition but it was not successful.

Myhra: How was it that you took the *Horten Ho 9 V2* to the Oranienburg Air Base for its flight testing program?

R. Horten: We had at Göttingen a grass airfield of about 1,100 meters (73,609 feet) and very many hangars. Oranienburg Air Base had a concrete runway maybe of 2,000 meters (6,562 feet) and for the first flight of the *Horten Ho 9 V2* we thought that it would be better if we had a large airfield. That was one reason. Another reason was that we wished to have our *Horten Ho 9 V2* close to *Göring's* office at *Karenhall* which was about 5 to 10 kilometers (3 to 6 miles) away. *Göring* went to the Oranienburg Air Base from time to time to see new aircraft and *Willy Messerschmitt* had sent his *Messerschmitt Me 262* to Oranienburg. *Arado Flugzeugbau* had also sent their *Arado Ar 234C* there. This is why we wanted to have our *Horten Ho 9 V2* at Oranienburg. Once, when *Kurt Tank* came to Oranienburg with *Oberst Siegfried Knemeyer*, who was the chief of aircraft development within the *RLM* near the end of the war. When they went into *Arado Flugzeugbau's* hangar to see the four turbojet-powered *Arado Ar 234C* they also visited other hangars to see new aircraft. *Knemeyer* and *Tank* also came and looked at our *Horten Ho 9 V2* standing there. *Tank* had been working with *Hans Multhopp on* a proposed turbojet-powered fighter known as the *Focke-Wulf Ta 183* and this was to have had a single *Heinkel-Hirth HeS 011* turbine in the fuselage with the exhaust under the rear fuselage. When *Tank* saw our *Horten Ho 9 V2* he realized, too, that his factory was behind in turbine-powered aircraft. Other aircraft builders, like us, were far out in front of him.

Kurt Tank walked into our hangar with *Siegfried Knemeyer* and saw the twin turbines and turned to *Knemeyer* and said that the propeller could still propel an aircraft to supersonic speeds. "The propeller,"said *Tank*, "has not been eliminated, instead it is really a matter of better fuselage design."*Tank* may have said this because he knew that his turbine-powered *Focke-Wulf Fw 190* idea had been a failure and probably wanted more time from the Air Ministry to develop a new turbine powered design such as their *Focke-Wulf Ta 183. Tank* also suggested to *Knemeyer* that he should not put our *Horten Ho 9 V2* into serial production until his *Focke-Wulf Ta 183* had flown.

Myhra: That proposed turbine-powered *Focke-Wulf Fw 190* was a silly idea. *Kurt Tank* had the notion back in 1942/1943 to install a turbojet unit in the nose of one of his standard *Focke-Wulf Fw 190's*. The *BMW 801* radial engine would have been replaced by one of *Focke-Wulf's* own turbojet engines known as the *Focke-Wulf Fw T1*. However, *Focke-Wulf Fw's* turbine engine project was stopped by *Schelp* at the Air Ministry around 1943. Very little is known of *Focke-Wulf Fw's* turbojet engine ideas such as its *T1*. It appears that the *T1* was to have consisted of a two-stage radial compressor and a single-stage turbine with an annular combustion chamber, the fuel being injected downstream. The *T1's* exhaust outlet was unusual, too, the gases being ejected from openings circling the fuselage.

R.Horten: *Kurt Tank* had problems with his *Ta 183* because the *Heinkel-Hirth HeS 011* turbine had to be installed in the front of the fuselage and then there was the question of what to do with the exhaust? It required a long tail pipe. Conventional thinking on turbine-powered fighters and bombers was changing late in the war and the best configuration which worked as a turbine powered aircraft was a tailless. In those days it was thought that a tailed turbine aircraft should have twin engines like the *Messerschmitt Me 262* and the *Arado Ar 234B* and *Ar 234C*. Later the *Heinkel He 162* showed the difficulty of installing a single turbine. The turbine on the *Heinkel He 162* was mounted above the fuselage and with two vertical surfaces on the horizontal stabilizer The *Heinkel He 162* was first flown on December 6th 1944 by *Dipl.Ing. Gotthold Peter*. He was a civilian from *DVL* and had been one of our four pilots at the 1939 *Rhön/Wasserkuppe* competitions. *Peter* flew a *Horten Ho 3B* and he didn't do well in the competition. *Peter* died on December 10th 1944 during a low level high-speed demonstration about 700 km/h or 435 mph flight when his *Heinkel He 162* crashed after the starboard wing disintegrated due to flutter.

Myhra: How was the *Horten Ho 9 V2* taken to the Oranienburg Air Base?

R. Horten: I think that the *Horten Ho 9 V2's* center section was towed to Oranienburg on its own undercarriage. The wings were taken to Oranienburg Air Base by a trailer behind an automobile. We had flown the *Horten Ho 7* to Oranienburg and back.

Myhra: Was the *Horten Ho 9 V2* ever flown to Neubrandenburg? The reason I ask this is that *Mr. Kaufmann* from *Gothaer Waggonfabrik* told the *CIC* people that the *Horten Ho 9 V2* had been once flown in and out of Neubrandenburg.

R. Horten: I know of that village but I don't know if our *Horten Ho 9 V2* was ever taken there. Now the *Horten Ho 9 V1* might have landed up there one time but I doubt if the *Horten Ho 9 V2* was ever flown there.

Myhra: Tell me about this man from *Gothaer Waggonfabrik* named *Dr.-Ing. Rudolf Göthert* and why he didn't like the *Horten Ho 9 V3?*

R. Horten: He wrote an article about swept-back wings. He said that the sweep-back was not practical for use in tailless aircraft because they had a natural condition of equilibrium, therefore, it was not good for us. So this article was put aside for future use and study. Overall the investigation of the swept-back wing concept in Germany had been very poor. This was the reason that *Professor Ludwig Prandtl* had not published his data because he saw in our sailplanes that his data was contrary to actual experience. I had spoken to *Professor Prandtl* about this and how the bell lift distribution allowed the swept-back wing to fly well but it was not clear to *Prandtl*. This was a very new idea for him plus he was getting old. Here was *Prandtl* with twenty years of data on swept-back wings and why it wouldn't work and then I come along with the bell lift distribution idea. *Prandtl* could not believe it although he was very interested, he was a gentlemen but he didn't accept the fact even through *Heinz Scheidhauer* demonstrated it to him.

When the Air Ministry began inquiring into the reasons for us building our *Horten Ho 13 Walter* thought that maybe we should talk about it with *Prandtl*. One day I went to speak with *Professor Prandtl* after one of his classes. I told him that we have problems with the Air Ministry and was it is possible for him to write a postcard on our behalf to "whom it may concern" that the research work of *Horten brother's* was in the general interest of aviation research. "Oh, I'll do it," said *Professor Prandtl*. A few days later *Prandtl* sent us a letter which he had written to the Air Ministry and it was very supportive towards us. *Walter* took the letter to Berlin to show to the people in *Reidenbach* and *Lucht's* Air Ministry department (perhaps the scientific group known as *LM amt B* because the technical group was known as *LM amt C* and personnel was known as *LM amt P*, and *LM amt R* was the Command group for the *Luftwaffe* generals) that the *Horten's* were noted and recognized in their work as performing scientific research basic to the industry. So I believe that the scientific department Air Ministry *LM amt C* was where *Walter* took *Prandtl*'s letter because *Prandtl* worked with these people and not the *LM amt* C. The *LM amt C* had been *Ernst Udet's* old department. I don't recall who was in charge of *LM amt C*, either a general or a professor. Well, *Prandtl*'s letter helped us greatly in changing the Air Ministry's opinion of us in favour of all-wing aircraft.

Myhra: What about *Dr. Rudolf Göthert*?

R. Horten: The only thing I know about him is that he originally had been in Berlin at the *LFA* and had a great involvement with the wind tunnel there. He investigated high lift profiles and flaps and so on. *Dr. Rudolf Göthert* did investigations into the swept-back wing and later, I recall, published it, but it was nothing important for us with the all wing. They were really investigating particular aspects of aerodynamics without looking at the whole problem. I told you the other day that development cannot be on a narrow front. It must be over an extended field for if you have a wing profile you cannot develop only one, you must develop a family or various families and examine which is the best. This was not being done by *LFA/DVL* or other researchers in *Nazi* Germany during the 1940s. They made only one study but we didn't know the alternatives. These might have been completely different, either good or bad, we wouldn't know. This is why the work of the *LFA* and *Rudolf Göthert* as well as his twin brother *Dr.-Ing. Berhard Göthert* from *DVL* and their colleagues elsewhere, was not useful for us in general. It was only useful in certain applications and special aircraft. So we had, for instance, in Göttingen, investigations into a four-engined transport aircraft which was to be built by *Arado Flugzeugbau* with two complete undercarriage units made up of ten or twelve wheels plus a system of skids so that it could land anywhere, a wide fuselage, and *Fowler* flaps for high lift configurations. It was all good and interesting but *DVL* and Göttingen tended to specialize in investigations which were directly applicable to only certain types of specialized aircraft. *DVL* might spend half a year or more doing wind-tunnel studies on this huge transport. I knew this because *Walter* would occassionally give me copies of these secret reports and most of the time I'd return them to him for they had absolutely no application to our work in the all-wing fighter program.

Dr. Rudolf Göthert later left *LFA* and joined *Gothaer Waggonfabrik* and had to design an all-wing fighter for *Gothaer* but he was not up the task of designing such a planform. Consequently when he completed the design and showed it to us, one could readily tell that it was his first project and that he wasn't a pilot either. *Walter* and I laughed at it.

Myhra: *Dr. Rudolf Göthert* had an all-wing design called the *Gother Go P-60* and he wanted the Air Ministry to take it and cancel the *Horten Ho 229 V3.*

R. Horten: Yes, I recall that *Rudolf Göthert* had worked against us on our *Horten Ho 229.* This is the strange thing. If we had given the idea like the all-wing *Horten Ho 9* to other competitors, they would make some modifications and tell the Air Ministry that the all-wing was their design, their plane. It was embarrassing for *Gothaer* to build our all-wing and really, it would have been better for us had the *Horten Ho 229* stayed with *Klemm* and never gone to *Gothaer Waggonfabrik.*

Myhra: Did you have many difficulties with *Gothaer Waggonfabrik* over the *Horten Ho 229?*

R. *Horten*: Yes. But the difficulties had come after the war. During the war they said nothing negative about us for they knew that we could speak with *Reichsmarshall Göring* and then *Gothaer Waggonfabrik* would be overruled. So the *Gothaer* people appeared friendly to us and our friends at the Air Ministry. I could not understand why there were bad feelings at *Gothaer* toward us. Later on, after the war, I saw the *Gothaer* name given to our *Horten Ho 229* and this report had come from the Americans. It seemed to me that the Gothaer staff preferred the name *Horten Ho 229.* If I had been employed by *Gothaer* then the all-wing fighter would have been a *Gothaer* and not a *Horten*, that is sure. But it was not so. I was not employed by *GothaerWaggonfabrik* We had set up our own company and we made the prototypes of the *Horten Ho 9* and given only to *Gothaer* to be build in series.

Myhra: What month was the *Horten Ho 9* given to *Gothaer Waggonfabrik* to produce in series?

R. Horten: It was the autumn of 1944. The *Gothaer Waggonfabrik* people came to Göttingen and I had to send our engineer *Hans Brune* to *Gothaer* in the city of Gotha where he then lived. He came back to Göttingen twice a week with all the problems he had identified and we then had to try and resolve them. So for me, it was completely clear that we owned all the designs and if there were any changes in the design by *Gothaer*, I was the one who had to authorise them and say yes or no. I had the last word in these things. So I was astonished to see and hear postwar that our all-wing flying machine was being called *Gothaer*. It could not be.

Myhra: Who was this man *Hans Brune*?

R. Horten: *Hans Brune* lives today in the town of Duisburg and should be about 70 years now.

Myhra: Why was *Hans Brune* sent to *Gothaer Waggonfabrik*?

R. Horten: He was the best man we had and as our head draftsmen, he had worked on all the drawings of the *Horten Ho 9. Hans Brune* was my principle assistant in preparing the drawings so he knew the whole aircraft. After we sent *Brune* to *Gothaer Waggonfabrik*, we replaced him with a man from *Fieseler* named *Herr. Knowl* and he worked along with the rest of the office on the *Horten Ho 8.*

Myhra: Who picked *Gothaer Waggonfabrik* to build the *Horten Ho 9* in series? Was this person *Oberst Artur Eschenauer*?

R.Horten: That I cannot say. It is possible that *Oberst Eschenauer* had asked *Walter* "would you be pleased if *Gothaer Waggonfabrik* built the *Horten Ho 9* in series?" It was not clear who would build the *Horten Ho 9* in the beginning but it was to be decided between *Klemm* and *Gothaer*. Initially each firm received an order for twenty aircraft to be built. Later, they had decided it would be better if only *Gothaer* built the *Horten Ho 9* while *Klemm* built the *Horten Ho 3.* I think that was *Siegfried Knemeyer* who decided Klemm should build the *Horten Ho 3* because he had flown the *Horten Ho 3E* with the *Volkswagen* engine at Oranienburg. X. For us it was easier to have *Gothaer* built all the *Horten Ho 9's* because we couldn't send two men away to assist with the *Horten Ho 9's* construction, one to *Gothaer* and then one to *Klemm*. Also the two facilities were widely separated: *Klemm* in the far south of Germany and *Gothaer Waggonfabrik* in the east.

Myhra: If *Gothaer Waggonfabrik* received the work order in the fall of 1944, well by May 1945 the *Horten Ho 229 V3* was only—80% ready for flight.

R.Horten: I am also astonished that it was not more advanced. I think that *Gothaer Waggonfabrik* had some difficulties in *Friedrichsroda* with hangar and workshop space. I don't know the situation there. I had visited Friedrichsroda and saw two or three houses for draftsmen but no hangars, and I didn't know where the airfield was located or if they even had one. In the city of Gotha they had an airfield and it hadn't been bombed either. Therefore, I didn't know where the *Horten Ho 229*' s were being constructed in Friedrickroda The leading edge sections of the *Horten Ho 229's* wing built by Slavian had not arrived and later we had to send our tools and jigs to *Gothaer* so that they could construct them for the first few *Horten Ho 229s* until the production items were delivered by Slavian .I think that *Gothaer'sr* higher management and organization had many shortcomings and maybe their slowness was also caused by the war at this stage. By late 1944 and certainly into 1945 there was no longer communication by telephone, limited travel by rail road, by auto, and so on. Materials were not available to the general aviation industry. But for us *Horten's,* well, we had material and whatever we wanted because of *Eschenauer*, We were able to obtain all we needed much better that the civil aviation industry. I thought that it would have been better to make ten or more *Horten Ho 9s* in Göttingen rather than at *Gothaer* for we had all the material plus we had all the personnel we needed. If our people had built one *Horten Ho 9* it would have been easy to build ten. But because *Gothaer*, was building it from scratch, the first *Horten Ho 229* needed six months, while the second *Horten Ho 229* required three months. Finally the tenth *Horten Ho 229* would have only taken one month.

Myhra: Why then did you not build more *Horten Ho 9s* at Göttingen?

R. Horten: The Air Ministry ordered us to have the *Horten Ho 229* built in one factory which was located in the center of Germany and in a factory which had spare capacity. *Gothaer Waggonfabrik* had built the *Gothaer Go 244*, a powered version of a transport glider which had capacity of 20 men and this aircraft had been canceled. Therefore, *Gothaer* was without work at this point in the war, plus their facilities were located in the center of Germany. *Gothaer* had apparently asked the Air Ministry what they should do now, as the *Gothaer Go 242* had been canceled? It just so happen that the *Horten Ho 9* was ready for serial production about the same time and *Gothaer* being free, received the entire order. We *Hortens* had nothing to say in this matter. We had only to be ready to help *Gothaer* and nothing more.

Myhra: At *Gothaer Waggonfabrik* they made many design changes on the *Horten Ho 9*. They changed the nose wheel gear for example.

R. Horten: The nose wheel on the *Horten Ho 9* had come from a *Heinkel He 177's* tail wheel and *Gothaer* produced a new design. This undercarriage was not built by *Gothaer*. The undercarriage nose wheel strut for the *Horten Ho 229* was to made by two firms, one was called *Foudy* in Frankfurt and the other firm was *RhineMetal* in Dusseldorf. All other undercarriage parts, switches, cables, and so on for the *Horten Ho 7*, *Horten Ho 9*, and *Horten Ho 229* were made by *ElectroMetal* of Comstat near Stuttgart. *Foudy* had also built the nose wheel strut for the *Horten Ho 3* and the *Horten Ho 7*. The man we worked with at *ElectroMetal* was named *Dr. Eisenbein* and he had really worked fast. I recall that he had come to Göttingen and looked over our *Horten Ho 9*, for example, what the gear looked like, how it should retract into the center section, the room available, and so on. Then he came back a few days later and had many, many suggestions and ideas on making the undercarriage retract. After we settled on a solution he left and about two weeks later he delivered the complete undercarriage for our *Horten Ho 9*.

We also had an aircraft junk-yard at the Göttingen airfield. They had numerous *Messerschmitt Me 210s*, other *Luftwaffe* and American and British aircraft which had crashed. I recall that there were also *Heinkel He 177s* plus some new aircraft types as well. Some of our workers went there from time to time and once they returned with the tail-wheel assembly from a *Heinkel He 177* and they believed that we might use it on our *Horten Ho 9*. I told them that we'd look at its weight, size, and so on and we installed it. For the *Horten Ho 9* w e used the main strut a wheel assembly from a *Messerschmitt Bf 109*. We had to look considerations such as movement, load capacity, the overall weight, and. the gear's retraction and extension conditions in general. Also, how is the opening for the gear set in the wing. The *Messerschmitt Bf 109* had an undercarriage of a type which it appeared might meet our requirements for the *Horten Ho 9*. We got two *Messerschmitt Bf 109* undercarriages from a depot in Frankfurt. I recall telephoning the repair facility at Göttingen and asking them if they had a tail wheel assembly from a *Heinkel He 177*. We were told that "yes, we have ten units and others which are partially damaged." We sent a man to the repair facility and he returned with the tail-wheel assembly.

Myhra: But the *Heinkel He 177* tail-wheel assembly carried a massive rubber tire.

R.Horten: It could be that *Gothaer Waggonfabrik* had made a bad error and were thinking of the *Horten Ho 229* like a fighter and had not considered it that it was also supposed to transport 2,000 kilograms (4,409 pounds) of bombs and the undercarriage must also support this. I don't know even today what the thinking of *Gothaer* had been when they changed the undercarriage on the *Horten Ho 229?* I think that the load capacity of the *Heinkel He 177* tail-wheel was adequate but not with a great margin. I don't know why that *Gothaer* considered the air pressure in the wheel was too high, and given the late hour of the war, it was looking for a low pressure tire so that the aircraft could take off from a grass field? A small wheel with high pressure and a large amount of fabric in its construction, is heavier than a large wheel with only three or four layers of fabric in it and a lower pressure. If there is sufficient room for the gear to retract behind the main spar and they can use the large tire they would use it. I think that it could be the reason for the change.

Myhra: Did anyone provide design help you when you decided to place the *Heinkel He 177* wheel in the *Horten Ho 9?*

R.Horten: At *RhineMetal*, Dusseldorf its director was named *Brune von Tettlebach*. His son was a fighter pilot in Köln with *Walter*. I visited *RhineMetal* and they had everything needed to operate the undercarriage.

Myhra: The nose wheel gear in the *Horten Ho 229* was very different from the *Horten Ho 9 V2*. *Gothaer* did not use the *Heinkel He 177* tail wheel gear.

R. Horten: The issue of the wheel was caused more by the industry and what we had available such as *Continental Tires* and some others. We had to check and to see what factory made a wheel of the dimension we could use but I don't recall now anymore what was the best at that time.

Myhra: Tell me about the wood glue you used for the *Horten Ho 9*.

R. Horten: We had in Germany different glues and when we were building the plastic *Horten Ho 5* the normal glues for wood didn't work out. There was a man called *Dr. Pinton* and he specialized in glues. He asked me what I needed and I told him that I needed a glue which would be resistant to fuel because I wanted to build a fuel tank inside the wing and that I wanted to "paint" the inside of this tank with fuel resistant glue. *Pinton* experimented and developed a glue he called "*601*" which we used to make internal fuel tanks and also to paint the other interior sections of the wing. Thus we had, double the space and volume in the wing to use it for fuel. On the *Horten Ho 9* we used metal tanks.

Myhra: By adding coal to the glue you made it radar resistant. Who requested that your all-wing fighter be radar-resistant?

R. Horten: It was not a request, it was our own decision. We thought that if we had a metal aircraft then radar would detect it so we must camouflage it and wood was the best solution. The radar waves would pass right through wood as far as the metal center section frame. Coal in the glue would absorb radar waves from bouncing back from the metal center section frame. Then came the question "what were the length of these radar waves?" Because if we had less than half the length of these waves we have no need to put coal in the wood which was covering the metal components. That is to say if we had a metal bolt or fitting on the wing or ailerons attachment points which were of 3 centimeters length and the wave the radar wave frequency was 9 centimeters, the critical length is 4.5 centimeters, half the length of the wave. If it was less, then the metal would not be detected. Therefore, it was very important to learn all about radar and as a result I think that we were able to camouflage 90% of the *Horten Ho 9's* radar signature. Thus, if the *Horten Ho 9* was on the Eastern Front, it would probably be entirely invisible to radar.

Myhra: Where would this "radar front" have been and in what type of air operations would the *Horten Ho 9* been involved in to need a 100% undetection?

R. Horten: If the *Horten Ho 9* had been ready for use in Norway, for instance, or in areas where shipping used radar directed guns, if there had been anything like this, the *Horten Ho 9* could have been detected. Aircraft carriers could then launch a defensive strike of aircraft to defended their fleet. The other thing is that if the *Horten Ho 9* had been flown to England as a bomber and detected was detected en-route, then, a defense could have been established long before it reached its target. Thus *Walter* and I wanted the *Horten Ho 9* to be undetectable by radar waves.

Myhra: Did you know for sure that all your efforts with putting coal in the glue, for example, resisted radar detection? Had you done any testing?

R.Horten: This was clear through tests conducted by *Telefunken Company*. They had obtained Allied radar equipment which had been found in an aircraft in Amsterdam, Holland. *Telefunken* then investigated the length of its radar wave, how they were absorbed, and so on. *Telefunken's* test results were immediately published and sent out to the German aviation industry. These reports were secret. So we knew about the nature of these radar waves and how they could be absorbed through different use of wood, coal and other material.

Myhra: What was the maximum operating ceiling of the *Junker Jumo 004?*

R. Horten: The *Junkers Jumo 004* could safely run up to 17,000 meters (55,774 feet) height and at the end of the war we were told that it could run up to 20,000 meters (65,616 feet). But the pilot had to watch the fuel flow of the *Junkers Jumo 004* because this became very critical at high altitude. Later the *Junkers Jumo 004* had flown 14,000 meters (45,931 feet) with the *Ar 234B* without difficulties and our *Horten Ho 9* having less wing loading than the *Ar 234B*, we thought we'd have a higher ceiling if the *Junkers Jumo 004* would permit it.

Myhra: When I talked to *Horst Gotz* in May 1986 at Flensburg he told me that the *Ar 234B* he flew in 1943 and 1944 allowed him to reach only 10,000 meters altitude and that was pretty much its limit through the end of the war. *Gotz* said at that altitude the *Junkers Jumo 004* would tend to flame out if you were not careful.

R. Horten: At this time the *Junkers Jumo 004* and its fuel were not in good condition. The fuel was not yet mixed to give greater exhaust velocity and if it had been *Horst Gotz* could have reached higher-altitudes. I think that with this new fuel mixture *Dr. Franz* at *Junkers Jumo* was far out in front. He told, us late in 1944 that his *Junkers Jumo 004's* could reach 17,000 meters (55,774 feet) altitude. I remember calculating for the *Horten Ho 18 "Amerika Bomber"* that we would have had to climb for an hour X, at climb rate of XXX meters (1.6 feet) per second X, so that we could reach *Amerika* arriving at 12,000 meters (39,370 feet) height. At this height we'd release the "atomic bomb" and then immediately go up to 16,000 meters (52,493 feet) and up to a maximum height of 18,000 meters (59,055 feet). At this height we'd then go into a long gliding angle returning to Europe. This was our calculation to give us 13,000 kilometers (8,078 miles) range. I still doubt that given the rate of fuel consumption that the *Horten Ho 18* would have achieved this range, nevertheless, we had to begin our development, make a *Horten Ho 18* and see what was possible. Perhaps the first *Horten Ho 18* might have made 10,000 kilometers (6,214 miles), while the second would have had a better greater range and so on due to aerodynamic improvements, better engine operating efficiencies, and better fuel efficiency.

When I made the first calculations based on what I was told at the Air Ministry this plane had to fly up to optimum range at its ceiling height. That was wrong. I saw from my calculations that it had to fly 370 meters (1,214 feet) lower than the stated ceiling at each point because its ceiling changed with weight and the weight changed due to the consumption of fuel. Therefore to have maximum range, it had not to fly at absolute ceiling but permanently climbing. These had been things which no one noted at this time, therefore the calculations from *Junkers Jumo* and *Messerschmitt AG* had not been correct. As a result, I could tell that they had made a poor calculation. They had regarded one factor as a constant while it wasn't constant, it was a varaible, therefore the optimum ceiling to fly was different. This idea had been proposed in a formula by a French aerodynamicist called *Brigget*. But apparently many of us in Germany didn't know about it at that time.

Myhra: What relationship did the *Hortens* have to *Karl-Otto Saur*?

R.Horten: *Karl-Otto Saur* was the chief of the Ministry of Supply and he was also interested in the "*Amerika Bomber*." He wanted a range of 13,000 kilometers (8,078 miles) but at the time in early 1945 we had only 10,000 to 11,000 kilometers (6,214 to 6,835 miles) and not 13,000 kilometers. I told *Saur* that we should go on and build the *Horten Ho 18* with its projected range of 10,000 to 11,000 kilometers and seek to get 13,000 kilometers out of it later. No, *Saur* wanted assurance that we got 13,000 kilometers before we even started and from the first plane. That type of talk is only possible from a person who has no knowledge.

Myhra: What was *Saur's* specific role in the *Horten Ho 18* project?

R. Horten: *Karl-Otto Saur* was the man who practically took over the running of the Air Ministry in the last months of 1944 and the remaining time in 1945. He was from the Supply Ministry and picked up the Air Ministry after it had about failed. In late 1944 *Saur* took charge of all aircraft production in *Nazi* Germany and he ordered, for instance, the *Fieseler Fi 103 "V1 flying bomb"* and other things. Later, I think it was the last month of the war, *Saur* ordered prototypes. *Göring* told *Saur* that he'd have them ready in three months, but *Saur* told *Göring* to have it ready in two months. *Saur* told *Göring* two months but that he'd have all the workers and facilities needed to have the "*flying bomb*" ready in two months. Therefore, with our work on the *Horten Ho 18*, *Walter* and I had to go Kahla from Berlin to meet *Saur* and tell him about the workshop facilities, workers, and hangars being readied to build the *Horten Ho 18*. When we met with *Saur*, he was nervous and talked a great deal. *Saur* thought that everything was ready to start on the *Horten Ho 18* and he wanted to know why the facilities were still unready?

Myhra: Was *Albert Speer* involved, too, with the planning for the *Horten Ho 18?*

R. Horten: *Karl-Otto Saur* was in *Speer's* Ministry and so it was all the same. *Saur* was *Speer's* right hand man and we *Horten's* never did talk or see *Speer*. But *Saur* was a fanatic but had no knowledge of aircraft. In April 1945 *Saur* still believed that huge hangars, thousands of aircraft workers, supplies, materials, and so on could be gathered together for work on the *Horten Ho 18* without difficulty. However, the moment *Saur* started planning the facilities required for the construction of the *Horten Ho 18*, he was completely up in the air. He didn't know how to set about it. I could not work with *Saur*. *Walter* and I had spoken with *Saur* several times and later I'd let *Walter* go and talk to him by himself for *Walter* would say to *Saur's* demands and treats "I have to ask my brother about these things." If I had been there I would have had no reason to deny *Saur's* demands. That was the reason that *Walter* went to see *Saur* alone. *Saur* was bad and I could not communicate with him. *Göring* was different and with him I could talk. I could explain things to *Göring* and he'd understand. He would say "yes." For instance, *Göring* wanted the *Horten Ho 9* to fly within three months of the contract date. I told *Göring* that it would take more nearly six months and *Göring* didn't answer. But at the end of our conversation, *Göring* said "I'll see it fly then in six months." So we agreed and at the end of six months the *Horten Ho 9 V1* flew only because I had been working on the project the three previous months. With *Saur* this would have been impossible.

Myhra: The *Horten Ho 18* would have been built at Kahla within six months?

R. Horten: Oh no. The *Horten Ho 18* would have taken us two years. This talk of six months was nonsense. But how do you explain the time needed to construct an aircraft like the *Horten Ho 18* to someone who knows nothing of aircraft construction and above all who is an fanatic? I still told *Karl-Otto Saur* that six months was impossible. By that time the Russians were coming over the Oder River and when we were talking to *Saur* in Berlin and when we came out of his bunker after the meetings we could hear the artillery from the Western Front. That was something which we didn't want to see.

Myhra: Thus, you knew that the *Horten Ho 18* would never be built before the war ended.

R. Horten: That is the point. We had worked day and night and if such a man came, we had to go and we had to speak with him. Days were lost for work. The worse thing was that *Walter* and I were nervous speaking to a man such as *Karl-Otto Saur*. With *Reichsmarshall Göring* we didn't feel that nervous.

Myhra: What did *Karl-Otto Saur* think of the war effort and at this time hearing the Russian artillery outside his bunker?

R. Horten: It didn't seem to bother him in respect of the need to build the *Horten Ho 18*. But it was clear to us that even if the *Horten Ho 18* was ready it still couldn't fly to America and back some 16,000 kilometers (9,942 miles) because at this time flight mechanics on the *Messerschmitt Me 262* were putting crude oil in the tanks of the *Messerschmitt Me 262* and this was the fuel it was burning. Our *Horten Ho 18* would never have been able to carry enough fuel to reach America had our engines burned crude oil. The reason is that we needed a lighter weight fuel similar to diesel oil.

Myhra: *Nazi* Germany did not have an atomic bomb. What they did have was a conventional high explosive bomb wrapped in blankets of radioactive silica to be carried to America on the *Horten Ho 18* but it had never been tested so the nuclear people didn't even know if it would explode?

R. Horten: No, it had never been tested. Besides, the German atomic bomb was not finished either. Even so where would they have tested it in Germany? That is another thing, even if some one could make the atomic bomb, there had to be something to transport it. So us *Horten's* were called in only to build the transport and not the bomb.

Myhra: So it was their problem to make the atomic bomb ready? Then again, they may have been able to create a radiation-spreading device which would have needed the *Horten Ho 18B*.

R. Horten: I have here a *Dr. Schnurr* who was later the director the atomic center in Karlsruhe and is now retired. During the war he worked at *I.B. Farbin* in Trosdorf and also with *Noble-Dynamit AG*. At this factory they had some 8,000 workers half of them POWs. *Schnurr* once told us that he'd just finished a new explosive which had 60% more explosive force that dynamite. He went and told an admiral of the Navy that we can fill your torpedo's with this new high explosive. The admiral told him "Look here *Dr. Schnurr*, this is not interesting to us. We are now thinking in terms of 1,000 times more explosive force." *Schnurr* said to him that "speaking as a chemist, this is not possible but only as a physicist is this possible." Apparently the admiral was thinking in terms of the atomic bomb as early as 1944.

Myhra: Was *Dr. Schnurr* involved in any way with Germany's radiation-spreading bomb program?

R. Horten: He told me that he knew about work on a radiation-spreading device. He knew about the heavy-water facility and he believes that several such devices were under construction. He told me of no difficulties in building the bombs. The problem was not in getting one of these devices to London in *Wernher von Braun's A-4 (V2)*, for example, but the problem was in getting one to North America. It was not possible, therefore, *Göring* had given the order near the end of the war for the "*Amerika Bomber*" or the *Horten Ho 18*. I don't know if we would have achieved the range. Perhaps our first effort would have given us 10,000 kilometers (6,214 miles) or range, better still if it was 11,000 or 12,000 kilometers. Today we have the *Boeing 747* with a range of 11,000 to 12,000 kilometers perhaps even with overloading up to 13,000 kilometers and with 350 people, well that is a load of about 40 ton. Nothing is impossible. Only the time and technical advancements are what is required and these come through effort spent.

Myhra: What were the difficulties to obtain 12,000 kilometers? Was simply a matter of carrying sufficient fuel?

R. Horten: I had spoken with *Professor Prandtl* and with *Dr. Franz* of *Junkers Jumo*. *Franz* had some curves going from 1.4 to 1.8, that is the specific fuel consumption at low altitudes was 1.4 and at high altitudes 1.8. I told him that these numbers are such that you cannot publish them. They should be 1.2 and he was laughing at me because he thought that I understood nothing of his turbines. Then I went to *Professor Prandtl*. I was his pupil at that time and I told him the difficulties we were having with the turbine's fuel consumption. The previous week in a class he had lectured that one row of blades in the turbine had to give a pressure of 1.0 atmosphere but today Professor *Waltz*, who was working at the University of Göttingen on supercharger research, had managed only , 0.5 atmospheres with only one row of blades in the turbine. Therefore, with nine rows of blades we have 4.5 atmospheres and we should have nine with the same arrangement. Aerodynamically speaking, *Prandtl* said that the efficiency of the turbine was bad. With nine rows of blades the fuel consumption should go lower and up to 1.0. Now we have 0.5 atmospheres and at this time 1.4 specific consumption. The British "*Durwent*" engines specific fuel consumption was about 1.3 and it had about 4 or 5 atmospheres. The engine had too low a pressure and they had even to go higher. That was the principle failure in our turbine work in *Nazi* Germany for a long time facing long-distance flight...specific fuel consumption was high given the low pressure of the turbine.

Myhra: Could *Dr. Franz* have improved the low fuel consumption numbers on their *Junkers Jumo 004B* in time for the *Horten Ho 18B?*

R. Horten: No, however, *Dr. Franz* was very serious about improving the *Jumo 004B's* fuel economy. He said that he'd work to change the numbers by improving the pressure of the turbine and he said to me that he "hoped" to go higher. I think that *Professor Waltz* and the University of *Göttingen* had gotten up to 1.0 atmosphere per row in some of his research superchargers by the time of the war's end in 1945. But trying to do this in production turbines like the *Junkers Jumo 004*, well *Professor Waltz* and the others didn't have the answers yet.

Myhra: Well, they just didn't have the knowledge yet but may have if their time hadn't run out. But it appears that there were many people working on the problem at that time.

R.Horten: Yes, there was much research going on at Göttingen in trying to increase the pressure of the turbine engine in the so-called Institute of Supercharging and *Professor Waltz* was its director.

Myhra: Did *Dr. Franz* believe that his *Junkers Jumo 004s* would be able to operate continuously during a 12,000 kilometer nonstop flight?

R. Horten: *Dr.Franz* had said yes many times regarding the reliability of his *Jumo 004s* to run continuously for 12,000 kilometers in our about the *Horten Ho 18* but how could he have known this for he was not into airplanes but only into turbines.

Myhra: Did *Dr. Franz* know that you were attempting to build the *Horten Ho 18* as a radiation spreading device carrier? Did *Professor Prandtl* know this also?

R.Horten: Yes, *Dr. Franz* knew this but not *Professor Prandtl.* Neither did *Professor Waltz* who was working to increase the pressure in each stage of the compressors. *Professor Prandtl* was the chief of us all and was a theoretician while *Waltz* was a practical type of person. *Prandtl* kept hearing from *Junkers Jumo* and the Air Ministry "why can't we obtain more pressure in the turbines?" *Prandtl* in turn put pressure on *Waltz* and kept asking "why not, why not?"

Myhra: When the idea was made to go to America with the all-wing *Horten Ho 18B* did *Karl-Otto Saur* go to *Dr. Franz* saying that the project required more reliable and fuel efficienct engines? Or did you go to *Dr. Franz* with the same demand?

R. Horten: *Dr. Franz* had been in the discussion on the "*Amerika Bomber*" project before we *Hortens'* were brought in, in desperation by *Siegfried Knemeyer*. I was a young man at that time as was *Dr. Franz*, but he'd tell me "wait, wait, we'll make all possible." The requirement for lower specific fuel consumption was a high priority.

I'll tell you when the first discussions took place. It was in the Autumn of 1944 and maybe around September or October. I took my drawings of the *Horten Ho 18A* to *Knemeyer*. He liked it and then arranged that we *Hortens* get together with designers from *Junkers* Flugzeugbau and *Messerschmitt AG*. The design which came out of this *Junkers-Messerschmitt AG* and *Horten* committee was our *Horten Ho 18A* with a huge vertical tail with an attached rudder. Plus, the turbojet engines were all located under the wing. *Hans Brune* who had gone to *Gothaer Waggonfabrik* on the *Horten Ho 229* but also came with us to Dessau (*Junkers Jumo*) to work on the *Horten Ho 18*. This was because if we had to change some things in the *Horten Ho 18*, pertaining to calculations or performance then *Brune* could help make the changes. Before we became involved, say two months before like July 1944, the first questions came "could you make an all-wing of exceptionally long range?" I had begun to think about it and I had also started working on the *Horten Ho 8*. I had to start the *Horten Ho 8* while working on the *Horten Ho 9* for it was the larger airplane. I had to prepare myself before answering these questions especially on a long-range version of the all-wing bomber. After *Junkers Flugzeugbau/ Messerschmitt AG* made all these unnecessary modifications to my *Horten Ho 18A*, I went immediately to *Reichsmarshall Göring* and complained strongly.

Myhra: Who initially asked you these questions about enlarging your *Horten Ho 9* into the all-wing *Horten Ho 18A "Amerika Bomber"*?

R. Horten: *Walter* had been talking to *Oberst Eschenauer*. But I was working, too, on the *Horten Ho 9*. Then came the invitation to go to Dessau to speak about the all-wing as an long-range bomber. Five or ten men were there each from *Junkers* and *Messerschmitt AG* to defend their project ideas. So we all presented ideas and then questions would come regarding maximum lift, cruising speed, what is your ceiling, what is that and that. We gave our presentation. They had aircraft ideas with about 50 square meters of wing area while we had 150 square meters of wing area plus different *Reynolds* numbers, different this and that. Overall, the discussion lasted about three days and idea then had to conform to the others. (The extremely broad wing chord has a beneficial effect of reducing the Reynolds number and therefore drag – the large aircraft is always more efficient than an identical one of a smaller size – this is a particular advantage for long range designs ... PW)

Myhra: Let's get back to the *Horten Ho 9*, although the *Horten Ho 18A* is extremely exciting, too. How do you feel about the *Horten Ho 9* as a fighter say compared to the *Messerschmitt Me 262?*

R. Horten: Our *Horten Ho 9* had the speed of the *Messerschmitt Me 262* or more and less speed and landing and take off distance as the *Messerschmitt Me 262*. However, the *Messerschmitt Me 262* could not carry a 1,000 kilogram (2,205 pounds) bomb as a fighter-bomber must do. But the *Messerschmitt Me 262* was the only turbine-powered aircraft ready for series production. I think that some 400 had been built by the time of the surrender. They could not be defended during landing which was clear and if a *North American P-51* was nearby during this time, the *Messerschmitt Me 262* was shot down. For the *Messerschmitt Me 262* needed about 5 seconds or more to accelerate. The *Messerschmitt Me 262* was hard to defend. This was an organizational problem. The airfields originally had a flak group to shoot down enemy fighters and to defend the *Messerschmitt Me 262.* But they no longer had these because they had been taken away for use on the Russian Front. So how could the *Messerschmitt Me 262's* fly if they were not protected? The same was true for the *Messerschmitt Me 163* when coming in for a landing. It was easy to shoot it down at this time but in flight enemy planes could not touch it.

It was a point that *Heinz Scheidhauer* had criticized *Erwin Ziller* about, that is *Ziller* in the *Horten Ho 9* came in fast and with high turbine power and then only reduced once at the airfield boundary. But we know now that all large aircraft must be landed this way. One had to come in with power on, approaching the field with flaps down and the undercarriage out and the moment when *Ziller* was sure that he could land, reduced the throttle. *Scheidhauer* flew his aircraft like a sailplane pilot. He liked to approach the airfield without power coming in like a glider and then land. With the turbine-powered *Horten Ho 9* this could not be. This was the very reason why *Walter* would not let *Scheidhauer* fly the *Horten Ho 9. Scheidhauer* would have made trouble for us in that aircraft. Also, *Lufthansa* with their *Junkers Ju 52/3m*, entered the airdrome with power and reduced it only at the last moment like 5 seconds before touchdown. The *Messerschmitt Me 262* and also the *Horten Ho 9* had to be landed with at least some power.

Myhra: When *Erwin Ziller* flew against the *Messerschmitt Me 262* in the *Horten Ho 9* at Oranienburg, he was able to out fly the *Messerschmit Me 262?*

R.Horten: *Erwin Ziller* was accustomed to piloting the *Heinkel He 111* and always entered the airfield with high power. That is the normal practice with powered aircraft. At my flying school at Halberstadt, with the *Junkers Ju 33* and *Ju 34* and also the *Focke-Wulf Fw 58*, we approached the base with some throttle and reduced it when we landed. That is the opposite type of landing compared to sailplanes. In sailplanes you have the air brake to control the descent. In the case of a powered aircraft you enter the airfield with a negative air brake due to the propeller's thrust. At the moment of landing you reduce this thrust to zero. With an aircraft like the *Boeing 747* you have to land with the throttle and upon touchdown they have automatic thrust reversers which then give power. It is just the same in reverse for the *Boeing 747* cannot reduce the power totally for this would result in longer stopping distances and they don't want that. From touchdown to stopping they may have 1,500 meters (4,921 feet) and therefore, the engine must be accelerated quickly for the reverse thrust. Touchdown comes 3 seconds later and then there must be full thrust in order to brake. On the other hand if you land with the throttles at idle, you have to use your wheel brakes a great deal. This is not acceptable. So piloting sailplanes is quite different from piloting powered aircraft .

Myhra: Tell me about the difference between the *Horten Ho 9* and the *Messerschmitt Me 262.*

R. Horten: Suppose, we had about the same wetted surface and the *Messerschmitt Me 262* had half of that on account of its fuselage and tail. The other half was in its wing. The *Horten Ho 9* had all its wetted surface in the wing so we had about same the wing loading as the *Messerschmitt Me 262.* The wing loading is important for take-off and landing, for dogfighting, for ceiling, for climbing and all these things. I would say that the *Horten Ho 9* would have had a better performance due to its reduced wing loading. I think that wing loading was a very important thing and the *Horten Ho 9* should have been better in dogfighting than the *Messerschmitt Me 262* and would have the airspeed necessary for intercepting the *Boeing B-17* bombers. Therefore, *Walter* always pressed that we should install in the *Horten Ho 9* the *MK 103* cannon. That is a cannon of 3 centimeter with 1,100 meter per second muzzle velocity. This was in comparison to the *MK 108* cannon with its 3 centimeter projectile, but a shorter barrel, and only 450 meter per second velocity. If you are shooting against the wind, higher resistance for example, say at 500 meters against the wind, I suppose the trajectory of the *MK 108* will drop 20 to 30 meters. On the other hand the *MK 103* cannon will fall down 2 or 3 meters. Therefore, for a fast plane like the *Horten Ho 9* it must also have high-speed cannon with high-speed projectiles like the *MK 103.* The *MK 108* cannon which had been proposed by *Gothaer Waggonfabrik* should not have been installed due to its low velocity. Instead any cannon in the *Horten Ho 9* had to be one of high-speed like the *MK 103* that they could shoot long-range. *Walter* told me that the *Horten Ho 9* should be able to shoot at enemy planes 1 kilometer (3,281 feet) away. In this case all the guns on the *Boeing B-17* bomber were of lower caliber (50 caliber) and of lower velocity. They were not effective if the fighter was shooting from a distance of 1 kilometer. One or two projectiles from a *MK 103* could enter the *Boeing B-17* and thus would bring it down. Therefore, the *Messerschmitt Me 262* with its four *MK 108* cannons were not effective against the *Boeing B-17.* I agree with *Rudy Kosin* that a fighter had to keep his distance from the *Boeing B-17* and should not have had four cannon of *MK 108* installed but two *MK 103* cannon. I believe that would have been sufficient against the *Boeing B-17s* and more effective than the slow speed *MK 108* projectiles.

Myhra; What would have been the flight characteristics of the *Horten Ho 9* verses the *Messerschmitt Me 262?*

R. Horten: That is another question. The *Messerschmitt Me 262's* wing had been built without slots and was like the *Focke-Wulf Fw 190.* This characteristic was that if you were in a dogfight, one wing will enter and stall and the other time the other wing and the plane will move over its longitudinal axis and could enter and spin. This spin could be to save the plane and pilot while in the dogfight but normally the other fighter will go behind the spinning aircraft which is out of control and shoot it down.(The Me.262 was fitted with automatic slats..PW)

Myhra: *Erwin Ziller* flew against the *Messerschmitt Me 262* at Oranienburg on several occasions with the *Horten Ho 9.*

R. Horten: Yes, *Erwin Ziller* was able to verify climbing, take-off, landing, and flew turns against the *Messerschmitt Me 262. Ziller* was not a fighter pilot but we found that the *Horten Ho 9* was better at these maneuvers than the *Messerschmitt Me 262. Ziller* in the *Horten Ho 9* was able to get behind the *Messerschmitt Me 262* and this was due to the *Horten Ho 9's* lower wing loading. It was not due to *Ziller's* piloting skills but wing loading. The *Horten Ho 9* was better than the *Messerschmitt Me 262* in a tight circle.

Myhra: I would imagine then that if the *Horten Ho 9* was in the hands of a skilled fighter pilot like *Walter*, that the *Horten Ho 9* could quickly out maneuver a *Messerschmitt Me 262?*

R. Horten: I believe there would have been no competition between these two aircraft and within a few seconds *Walter* would have been behind the *Messerschmitt Me 262* with the *Horten Ho 9*. This is not to say that *Heinz Scheidhauer* was a bad pilot. He was a good soaring pilot but he was not a powered pilot. *Erwin Ziller* was a good power pilot and had the skill needed to operate a turbine-powered aircraft. *Walter* had flown bombers and later fighters and was very good in aerobatics and combat. Whether he was good in takeoffs and landings I will not say, maybe that others were better in various types of aircraft for different aircraft types are all different. I think that *Ziller* was the best man we had for the *Horten Ho 9* for our first flights because his take off and landing characteristics were good. For the first time these abilities were what we were looking for. Later, other pilots should have flown the *Horten Ho 9* like *Walter* and try combat maneuvers. *Scheidhauer* should not have test-flown the *Horten Ho 9* because it was his custom, to fly in the style of a glider pilot. This type of flying is very different for a turbine-powered aircraft. It is a completely different type of flying. Therefore, we didn't want *Scheidhauer* to fly the *Horten Ho 9* but he thought he could fly it as well as others such as *Ziller*. He could not. He wanted to fly it but it was against our opinion and against*Walter's* .order. .

Myhra: Had *Walter* ordered *Heinz Scheidhauer* not to fly the *Horten Ho 9 V2?*

R. Horten: Yes, we didn't want to him to fly it. We told him this even before in Göttingen that the *Horten Ho 9 V2* was for *Ziller* and he'd make all the test flights. I told *Heinz Scheidhauer* that maybe later on we'd see if he could still fly the *Horten Ho 9 V2. Walter* flew with *Scheidhauer* in the twin seat "*Kranich*" sailplane and he saw that *Scheidhauer* was not up to flying the *Horten Ho 9 V2*, that he was not able to fly it for he lacked the necessary skills to pilot powered aircraft. *Scheidhauer*'s flying skills acquired over the previous ten years were not those required to fly a turbine-powered aircraft. Today a soaring pilot is not able to fly a *Boeing 747* he but if he insisted such a man must forget all his soaring habits. Flying powered aircraft is quite different from soaring aircraft. But this is not a criticism of *Scheidhauer*.

Myhra: It would have been good if *Walter*, too, could have flown the *Horten Ho 9 V2* and then he could have compared its performance and handling to that of the *Messerschmitt Bf 109*, *Focke-Wulf Fw 190*, and the *Supermarine Spitfire*.

R. Horten: Yes, *Walter* was a good fighter pilot and had flown all Germany's fighters. Also, he had flown earlier the *Junkers Ju 52/3m*, *Dornier Do 23*, *Junkers Ju 86*, and so on, therefore he'd much experience. He never did fly the *Horten Ho 9 V2* although he had flown the *Horten Ho 9 V1*.

Myhra: *Erwin Ziller* had flown the *Focke-Wulf Fw 190* many times. What did *Ziller* say about the differences between the *Horten Ho 9 V2* and the *Focke-Wulf Fw 190?*

R. Horten: Yes, *Erwin Ziller* had flown the *Focke-Wulf Fw 190* many times. We never spoke about the differences between the two aircraft. I spoke with *Ziller* after his first flight in the *Horten Ho 9 V2* of December 18th 1944. But our pilots at the Western Front were not happy with the *Focke-Wulf Fw 190* and everyone had hoped that it would have been a better aircraft than the *Messerschmitt Bf 109* and it was not. In fact it may have been worse. When the *Focke-Wulf Fw 190* entered into a dogfight, it tended to go into spins.

Myhra: Did *Erwin Ziller* not talk to you in the evenings about the test flights earlier in the day?

R. Horten: Yes, but *Erwin Ziller* usually spoke to *Walter* and I'm sure they compared the two aircraft. They both were in agreement that *Focke-Wulf Fw 190* was not good. In fact many people did not like it. For the fighter pilot who normally only few fighter aircraft, the *Messerschmitt Me 262* was not good during landing and starting. For the turbine-powered aircraft, the best fliers were the bomber pilots.

Myhra: Why was that?

R. Horten: Because they had to approach the airfield with more power and if they were short or low and they had to accelerate and if they were piloting a turbine-powered aircraft like the *Arado Ar 234B*, it needed more time. This was a cause of *Erwin Ziller's* accident that he was flying with one engine and he was too low. I think that what he was doing would have been OK with two engines but with one engine, he had to fly the *Horten Ho 9* at full power and I think that since *Ziller* had become accustomed to approach the airfield with only half the power, a single engine flight gave him only one half the power he normally had. He needed full power on the good engine.

Myhra: Yes, but *Erwin Ziller* should have known this because he flew the *Heinkel He 111* many, many times and probably some of these times one of its two engines might have been shut down.

R. Horten: *Erwin Ziller* flew the *Heinkel He 111* and if he was able to fly this aircraft on one engine he'd have to give the *Heinkel He 111's* good engine full throttle.

Myhra: Did *Erwin Ziller* ever fly the *Horten Ho 7* with only one engine operating?

R. Horten: *Walter* and I did. *Heinz Scheidhauer* also did. I think *Erwin Ziller* also. Once at Göttingen *Scheidhauer* flew the *Horten Ho 7* and with him was a representative from the firm *Argus*. The air screw came also from the firm *Argus*. These two men had flown up to 2,000 meters (6,562 feet) and suddenly the plane turned and reduced the throttle and when the *Horten Ho 7* was again horizontal found that one of the engines was oscillating while the other was still good. *Scheidhauer* stopped the bad engine and landed with one engine. Afterward we found that in the propeller hub a pinion had been broken and one of the blades had gone into a reverse thrust. The man from Argus tried to fix it but took the reversing mechanism with him back to the factory by train. Several days he returned with a new reversing mechanism. Nevertheless, the twin engine all-wings could be landed on one engine. There is a third type of pilot I want to tell you about and I call him the engineer-pilot. He is a man who flies with each plane which according to the theory behind the design and uses the plane in place of the theoretical values we have. That is what we needed for an aircraft's first flight in general.

Myhra: *Kurt Tank* was that sort of person.

R. Horten: Yes, *Kurt Tank* was of this type. He knew when one of his new designs was good, what it could do and what it could not do. That is a type of a pilot engineer. Many of these types were "*Flugzeugbauführer*" people that know what a plane theoretically can give to them. Another type of flier is the aerobatic type who usually knows nothing of theory but who has trained and uses the aircraft to the strength of their body that is the forces they can personally resist while flying. This type of flying is dangerous for the plane can easily be destroyed. For instance in Köln there was a soldier who flew the *Messeerschmitt Bf 109* and before had flown the *Heinkel He 41*. With the *Messerschmitt Bf 109* he had 50 to 80 km/h more speed and he was happy. He made a loop and any loop is difficult. He made a second loop and a third but during the third the wing began coming apart, made a few rolls and then landed. If the wings are damaged and one continues on with aerobatics that shows that the pilot knows nothing. These type of pilots work only with the forces in their hands. This type of flying couldn't be used on new aircraft only planes already found to be good for aerobatics. Men who were good at aerobatics were needed in the *Luftwaffe* because they were good shooters.

Thus, *Erwin Ziller* had to fly the *Horten Ho 9 V2* and not *Heinz Scheidhauer*. If *Ziller* had flown the *Horten Ho 9 V2* twenty or more flights and then brought it to Göttingen, then perhaps *Scheidhauer* could have flown it then. *Scheidhauer* is of the opinion that his flying skill is pretty good and *Ziller* had flown badly when he approached with low power into the airfield at Oranienburg. I told *Ziller* that the *Horten 9 V2* had to be flown with half power right down to ground. On the other hand *Scheidhauer* liked to come down and land with the engines only idling.

Myhra: When all the flight testing had finished at Oranienburg where would the *Horten Ho 9 V2* been taken next? Back to Göttingen, to Brandis/Leipzig, or where?

R. Horten: If it had not crashed, the *Horten Ho 9 V2* would have been flown to Brandis/Leipzig. In Göttingen we had no prospect of flying the *Horten Ho 9 V2* because its airfield was very small about 1,100 meters (3,609 feet) long and around the entire airfield were hangars. It was a very bad place to fly a turbine-powered aircraft in and out of Göttingen. Brandis/Leipzig, on the other hand, was where the *Horten Ho 9 V2* should be. We only went to Oranienburg account of its long runway, good hangar facilities, and to be close to the *Hermann Göring* and the Air Ministry. Later, I think in January 1945, *JG/400* was ordered to accept the *Horten Ho 229* and they were flying out of Brandis/Leipzig. I thought we'd fly the *Horten Ho 9 V2* a few flights more at Oranienburg and then take it to Brandis/Leipzig along with some of our personnel. We even had gone to Brandis to look over the facilities and to see what was good there and what was bad and how we might make things better there for operating the *Horten Ho 9 V2*.

Myhra: *Wolfgang Späte* didn't want the *Horten Ho 229* for his *JG/400*.

R. Horten: Well the *Horten Ho 229* had been assigned to *JG/400* by *Oberst Artur Eschenauer* and/or *Oberst Siegfried Knemeyer*, I don't know who *Walter* had been involved with in all of this at the Air Ministry.

Myhra: Had you personally talked with *Späte* about the *Horten Ho 229?*

R. Horten: No. *Wolfgang Späte* was not in Brandis/Leipzig; the day *Walter* and I had gone there.

Myhra: I've heard that *Wolfgang Späte* was unhappy over having to accept the *Horten Ho 229* for his *JG/400*.

R. Horten: I didn't know this.

Myhra: He said that the all-wing of the *Horten's* still had problems with directional stability and in turbulant air the all-wing suffered from a *dutch roll*. *Artur Eschenauer* had ordered *Wolfgang Späte* to use the *Horten Ho229* in *JG/400*.

R. Horten: *Wolfgang Späte* was a product of the *DFS* and their sailplane activities. We had seen *Späte* at the *Rhön/Wasserkuppe* but when war broke out he went instead to the fighters and not to the transport gliders like *Heinz Scheidhauer*. With the fighters he had great success, I think about 18 victories and he reached a high military rank. Then *Späte* became involved with the *Messerschmitt Me 163* but this *JG* had not enough aircraft for a whole fighter group. Therefore one *Staffle* was to be given the *Horten Ho 229* and I don't know why *Späte* was unhappy with the order to fly the *Horten Ho 229*.

Myhra: *Wolfgang Späte* didn't want the *Horten Ho 299*, he said, because he felt that it was directionally unstable.

R.Horten: *Wolfgang Späte* flew his *Messserschmitt Me 163* and this little aircraft also experienced *dutch roll* with its 8 or 9 meters of span. Even the *Northrop XB-49* didn't experience the *dutch roll* much with its very great swept-back wing while the *Messerschmitt Me 163* with its short span would. The *Horten Ho 9* had about twice the wing span of the *Messerschmitt Me 163* and this was better. The *Horten Ho 9 V2* experienced less *dutch roll* than the *Messerschmitt Me 163* so I can't understand why *Späte* didn't want the *Horten Ho 9* for this reason alone. *Späte* must have had other reasons. *Späte* wrote a book on his *JG/400* but I have not read it but maybe he talks about his objection to using the *Horten Ho 229.*

Myhra: In his book *Wolfgang Späte* talks about a conference held by the Air Ministry on tail-less and all-wing aircraft. At this conference, he writes, were *Alexander Lippisch*, the *Horten* brothers and many others. I didn't realize that *Späte* had such close ties to *DFS* and their sailplanes. This, too, might be a reason why he preferred *DFS* aircraft to those built by the *Horten* brothers?

R.Horten: If *Wolfgang Späte* liked the *Messerschmitt Me 163*, well, it had been the old *DFS 194. Walter* and I had been POWs and were in London on April 7th 1945. *Walter* and I had become POWs on March 31st 1945 so we didn't hear any more about the assignment of the *Horten Ho 229* to *JG/400*. I know that the *Horten Ho 7* and *Horten Ho 9 V1* had been transferred to Brandis/Leipzig. But I wasn't present in Germany to know about the objections/discussions of *Späte* over allocating the *Horten Ho 229* to *JG/400*. Really the *dutch roll* characteristics were secondary. The most important thing was that the aircraft was comfortable and responsive to handle. But dynamic and static stability, I believe, was of minor importance. What is important is that the pilot can control the aircraft and that it has good equilibrium, that the trim is good. These are the important things. *Dutch roll* is a form of dynamic stability and to me it is of secondary importance. Plus we have dynamic stability in different forms. If we have large static stability we have no dynamic stability. If we have less static stability we have more dynamic stability and this is over the three axis and when we have static and dynamic stability we have another type of stability. Periods of oscillation is what should be controlled. We have the stability without oscillation and that is fluid dynamics stability and we have a point where we have dynamic stability in what we call critical stability without movement. So all these things are very complicated and we cannot easily say that this aircraft is good and that aircraft is bad because it depends very much on whether we have a tailed plane and how we position the center of gravity. Stability also depends of the center of gravity and how it changes during flight. For instance, the *Messerschmitt Me 262* or the *Horten Ho 9*, the condition to fly makes it necessary that the center of gravity was fixed in one point and didn't move.

This matter of stability, well, we could talk about it for hours. It has much to do with the aircraft's vertical axis, of its longitudinal axis, and of its horizontal, that is its elevator. All these different axis need to be considered and instability comes from the combined movement of these axis and if one of the two have no stability, we called it "*weather cock stability*" and if we have this in small or zero form, we have no *dutch roll* for *dutch roll* is the combination of these axis working together. Therefore all this talk about the all-wing having *dutch roll* is from men who know little about the theoretical combinations of it. I told *Walter* in 1944 to speak to the men of the Air Ministry but he could not for these people were unable to understand him and was unable to identify what difficulties or questions these people were having over the *Horten Ho 9*. The Air Ministry was asking *Walter* for a large rudder or fin on the *Horten Ho 9* and I considered these ideas to be very bad and I believed that *dutch roll* would increase if a rudder was placed on the *Horten Ho 9*. It was less without the fin. Without the fin only periodic movements of oscillation we needed to have stability in the longitudinal form and so the oscillation tends to be dampened out and then we'd have what we called "dynamic stability." So we

The *Horten* brothers own *Heinkel He 111* medium bomber which was used to tow sailplanes to altitude including the *Horten Ho 9 V1* sailplane.

had difficult times with the people in the Air Ministry over what they called *dutch roll* because they themselves had made no calculations to understand. I would have liked to have held a class with these people to explain it to them and give them the mathematics needed to help them understand.

Myhra: Some of your proposed shorter span all-wing fighters appear with a vertical fin.

R. Horten: We proposed a vertical fin only because of the reduced wingspan when the half span is say only 4 meters (13 feet 1 inch) plus the Air Ministry wanted them but I still believed that a vertical fin would contribute to oscillation. *Alexander Lippisch* in his *Messerschmitt Me 163*, had there a good design because he had his vertical fin behind in the fuselage, had slots in the wings which helped the *Messerschmitt Me 163* to resist entering into spins. The *Messerschmitt Me 163* as a result, had good flying characteristics. The negative part of the *Messerschmitt Me 163* was that it had more resistance more drag. So with the *Messerschmitt Me 163's* aspect ratio of about 4 then washout is more difficult. In the *Horten Ho 9* we had an aspect ration of between 7 and 8 like the *Northrop XB-49* so I was able to eliminate the *Handley-Page* slots plus give it a little twist. But below an aspect ratio of 5, you have to go to slots or go to more swept-back and get into a different means of lift and you need no washout. My Argentine *IAe 37* delta had been designed without washout.

Myhra: Was *Wolfgang Späte* any kind of an aircraft designer?

R. Horten: I don't know. I never met him. He was born around 1912...about the same time as *Walter*.

End of Interview

Chapter 03

HANS WENZEL Interview

Date: October, 1985
Location: Ettenheim, West Germany
Language: German.
Commentary: *Gerhard Hopf*

Background:
Hans Wenzel was a highly skilled aviation welder...perhaps one of the most valuable workers in the entire *Horten Flugzeugbau. Wenzel's* work became indispensable. His speciality was the ability to take the complex engineering drawings created by *Reimar Horten* for the center section's steel tube framework and tuen them into reality. *Wenzel* produced everything from framework of the *Horten Ho 3* to the highly complex structure of the *Horten Ho 6*. He stood by *Reimar Horten* uncomplainingly building and modifying one center section frame after another, for the *Horten Ho 9* each time the dimensions of the turbojet engine were altered or when the *RLM* told them to substitute a different engine. Once the final version of the Ho.9 center section was completed in 1944, *Reimar* put *Wenzel* to work building the framework for the *Horten Ho 8* all-wing transport, a task which occupied him right up to Germany's unconditional surrender May 8th 1945. Had the engineering drawings for the H.18b been prepared, *Hans Wenzel* and his assistants would have begin building the centre section for the "*Amerkia Bomber Project*."

Reimar Horten had first met *Wenzel* in 1941 while they served together in a transport glider unit. When *Walter Horten* set up his Sonder *Kommando* 3, *partly* to avoid *Reimar* being posted to the Russian Front with his unit; *Reimar* told *Walter* to take *Hans Wenzel*, too and he moved with him at each different posting. *Wenzel* was always there to turn Reimar's concepts into metal, fabric and wood. If the idea didn't work out as *Reimar* had originally hoped, *Wenzel* patiently worked with him, making change after change. *Hans Wenzel* probably knew *Reimar* better than any one else in the *Horten Flugzeugbau*. "Although I worked hand in hand with him everyday and frequently ate lunch with him" *Wenzel* told me, "I really never got to know the man himself." Completely trustworthy, *Wenzel* was a quiet, soft spoken person who followed directions without criticisms without complaining. A man of apparently unlimited patience, *Hans Wenzel* said that any proposal to change and/or improveme *Reimar's* engineering designs had to be handled delicately so not to offend or criticize him.

Hans Wenzel. Göttingen, 1944.

Interview

Hans Wenzel (*Wenzel*): I enjoyed working for the *Horten* brothers in the 1940s. *Reimar* was a very nice person. We called him the "living slide rule," because he could do mathematical calculations in his head. Have you talked to his sister and brother-in-law?

David Myhra (*Myhra*): No. *Reimar* does not wish me to talk to either of them.

Gerhard Hopf (*Hopf*): Well do the *Hortens* have something to hide?

Myhra: No. I believe that *Reimar*, at least, does not want any second opinions. *Reimar* and his sister and brother-in-law are not on speaking terms and have not been so for many years.

Hopf: Well going back to all the other stuff, one gets the opinion that the *Horten* brothers never wanted a second opinion from anybody. The end result was a 100% *Horten* product.

Myhra: It appears that the people the *Horten* brothers sought out were ones not likely to give them "second opinions," but more like "yes" people.

Hopf: You had to agree with them 100% or you were out. That is not a very good attitude, especially if you want to do something new.

Hans Wenzel, the *Horten* center section frame-maker. Ettenheim, West Germany. 1985. Photo by author.

Myhra: Well, it seems that the *Horten* brothers didn't allow a great deal of freedom of speech concerning their aircraft theories, or designs, in their office and workshops.

Hopf: Well, if you want to do something new, one should never get too bound-up by your own personality. The best improvements in aircraft, as in other fields, usually come out of knowledge from a multitude of sources. An idea may have come from one person, but then it's the community of other people who pick up on the idea and then help turn it into something great. Sooner or later, if the *Horten Ho 9 V2* project had progressed, the *Horten* brothers would have had to admit to some of their errors and design flaws if that *Horten Ho 9 V2* was ever to be useful. Even now, I'm not convinced that *Horten Ho 9 V2* would have had any military value as a carrier of weapons. It was not a gun platform, not an ordinance carrier, not a cargo carrier, it was just there and managed to fly...and some say not well. This was a design which did not need to go into mass production.

Myhra: When did you start work on the center section framework of the *Horten Ho 9 V2?*

Wenzel: I was assigned to the transport glider school in Königsberg/ Neuhausen in 1939, after completing basic training. I met *Reimar Horten* shortly afterwards. *Reimar* was a technical officer at Königsberg and I was given the opportunity to work on the light transport *Focke-Wulf Fw 58*, a twin engine aircraft of welded steel tube construction. *Rudolf Opitz* was also at the transport glider school. It was my experience with steel tube fuselages which apparently interested *Reimar*. I was transferred from to Königsberg to the *Horten Flugzeugbau* at Bonn. After the transfer to the *Horten* workshop My first work was on *Horten Ho 3s* located at Bonn *Hangelar*. This was in June, 1941. Later I was relocated to Göttingen along with *Reimar* and several other workers. I think that I may have started work on the *Horten Ho 9* project in early 1943.

Hopf: Isn't it unusual that all these people were connected in some way to sailplanes? The same is true for the pilots. There really wasn't anyone there in that glider transport group with any high-speed powered flight experience.

Myhra: Seems like anyone who had experience with sailplanes before the war was placed in the transport glider group at Königsberg. I guess this was because the *Luftwaffe* had a keen interest in using gliders for troop invasion.

A new *Horten Ho 3A* center section frame welded up by *Hans Wenzel*.

A *Horten Ho 4B* center section frame freshly welded up by *Hans Wenzel*. Later *Strebel* would lose his life when his parachute failed to open following the failure of one of the laminar-flow wings at altitude.

Hopf: This appears to be how *Reimar* recruited people for the *Horten* brother's own operation. The transfer procedure was a difficult one. A person had to have a reason to be transferred. What reason could you have to be transferred to a different squadron or weapons group? It wasn't only up to you to decide. If a person was worth his salt, then the squadron wanted to keep him. They would do everything so that he would not be transferred...so the other group couldn't get him. In spite of that situation, the *Horten* brothers must of had a way to "untie" and move people where they wanted them.

Myhra: Would you have to be a pretty high-ranking officer to manage transfer requests?

Hopf: If you requested somebody, or something on your own, you made waves. Now the less significant rank you have, the bigger the waves are going to be. If you criticize your superiors, you were in deep trouble. So, a soldier who individually requested a transfer was in the "dog house."

Myhra: But in the case of people like *Hans Wenzel*, whom the *Horten* brothers wanted badly, how far would a request have to go for a guy like *Wenzel* to be suddenly transferred?

Hopf His flying mates were probably very surprised when he got transferred, as were his superiors. Or, it may have gone this way: In advance, one of the *Horten* brothers would talk to a person about *Hans Wenzel* coming to Göttingen and then ask them for permission to transfer them there. Now that would have been a different situation, because a small guy like *Wenzel* would not have been involved in the process. However, if the transfer goes clear through,

A close-up of the port-side looking aft from the nose of the *Horten Ho 9 V2* modified 3rd center section frame. Primer-colored tubing is from the old 3rd center section while the black pipe sections represents a modification. A factory-fresh *Junkers Jumo 004B* is mounted, however, this *Junkers Jumo 004B's* accessory island is visible forward of the cross-center section upper boom. Several historians believe that the accessary islands on the two *Junkers Jumo 004Bs* were removed and their functions provided for somewhere else inside the center section. This is not a certainty because no photos exist known to this author proving that the accessory islands were moved.

Horten Flugzeugbau Horten Ho 9 V2's center-section outfitters group photo. Behind them is the modified 3rd center section frame cut and rewelded, cut and rewelded, again, and again. Second from left is *Walter Rösler*. Sixth from right peering out between two fellow *Horten* workers is *Hans Wenzel*.

the man would finally end up in Göttingen. If it didn't go clear through, then the people at the unit would insist that he stay there; that wouldn't look so good. His officers would have thought that he wanted to get out of there and go someplace else. So it never looked good when a person wanted to get a transfer.

Hans Wenzel and his wife. Ettenheim, West Germany. October, 1985. Photo by author.

Myhra: What if a transfer did come down from the *Luftwaffe Quartier Meister's Office*?

Hopf: Well then, that was a different story because that made you "untouchable." Anything which came from Berlin was *never* questioned. Here again, once you start questioning things you make waves! If the transfer request came from the *Quartier Meister's Office*, the best thing to do was to leave it alone, because one would never know what kind of can of beans you'd open up if you questioned the order. No person was irreplaceable. Berlin could do anything they pleased, and it wasn't up to you to decide.

Wenzel: Five other men and I were transferred to Hannover/Minden, where the *Hortens* were flying their *Horten Ho 4A* sailplane.

Hopf: Where was that *Horten Ho 4A* built?

Wenzel: In Königsberg at the glider school.

Hopf: Then they must have transported the *Ho 4A* to Minden, too. This was the time when the base commander was interested in the *Horten* sailplanes. *Hans Wenzel* said that he repaired the *Focke-Wulf Fw 58* belonging to *Hanna Reitsch* at Königsberg, so they must have had material at the glider school to repair aircraft fuselages. When they were transferred to Minden, the transfer orders not only involved men, but must have included also the transport

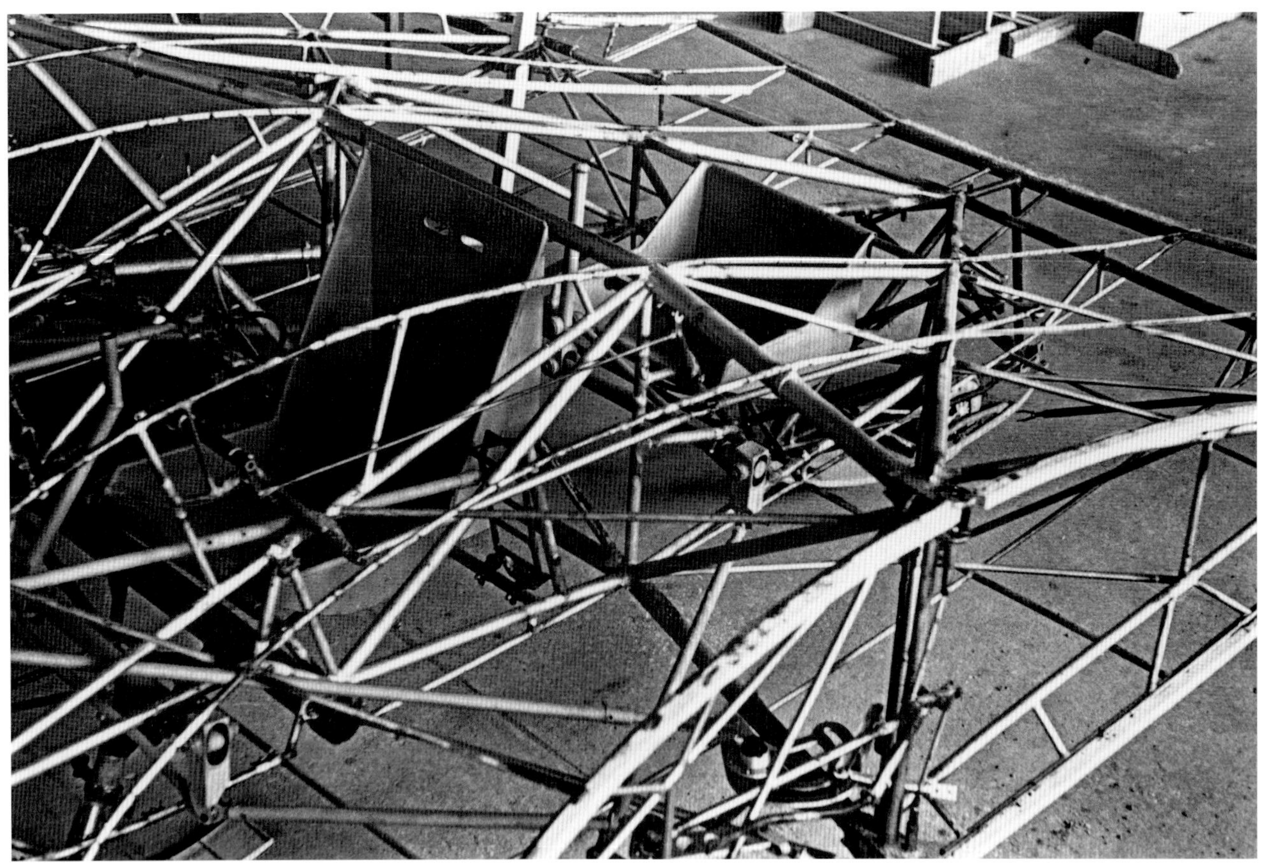

What appears to be the *Horten Ho 3H* center section frame under fabrication by *Hans Wenzel*. This flying machine was to be used in test involving a moving center of gravity. Several historians claim that this frame was a tandem seater. Yet *Reimar Horten*, during interviews by this author said that he was not aware that the *Horten Flugzeugbau* had ever built a two seat sailplane. *Reimar Horten* had total recall. Even though he did not recall this two seater, one was built.

of the *Horten Ho 4A*, too I wonder how they pulled this off within the *RLM*?

Myhra: By that time, *Walter Horten* and *Artur Eschenauer* had gotten together. They found the Göttingen facility, as well as several other empty and unused hangers which the *Hortens* could use to construct their all-wing aircraft. *Walter* says they frequently signed *Ernst Udet's* name on transfer documents. *Udet* committed suicide in November, 1941.

Hopf: But *Reimar* also went with *Hans Wenzel* to Minden.

Myhra: Yes, but Minden was only a temporary place before they all went to Göttingen. This took place in June, 1941, several weeks before *Adolf Hitler* announced his "*Operation Barbarossa,*" or the invasion of the USSR.

Hopf: *Hans Wenzel* says that the *Horten Ho 9 V2* was flight ready in November, 1944. If the modifications required two years, this would not fit the available time to build the aircraft. But then, when these people say nearly two years, maybe it was only one year.

What appears to be the *Horten Ho 229 V5* bare center section frame. The frame would have been similar to the modified *3rd Horten Ho 9 V2* by *Hans Wenzel*.

The 3rd center section frame for the *Horten Ho 9 V2* prior to modifications by *Hans Wenzel*. Shown to the left of the photo is the *Junkers Jumo 004B* and poorly visible to the right is the port *Junkers Jumo 004B*, however, an aluminum tube covers its air intake leading to the air intake opening in the wing's leading edge. In appears that both *Junkers Jumo 004s* have their accessory islands installed. But it is not known if these accessory islands were removed during the modifications of the 3rd center section frame.

Above: the "*orican*" *R4-M* ("*M*" for explosive head) air to air rocket wood launcher rack mounted on the port wing of a *Messerschmitt Me 262*. Below the *R4-M* rocket with its eight long thin stabilizing fins full open after release. *Wenzel* said that *Reimar* had told him the *Horten Ho 229* would carry a rack of 12 *R4-M* air to air rockets under each outer wing.

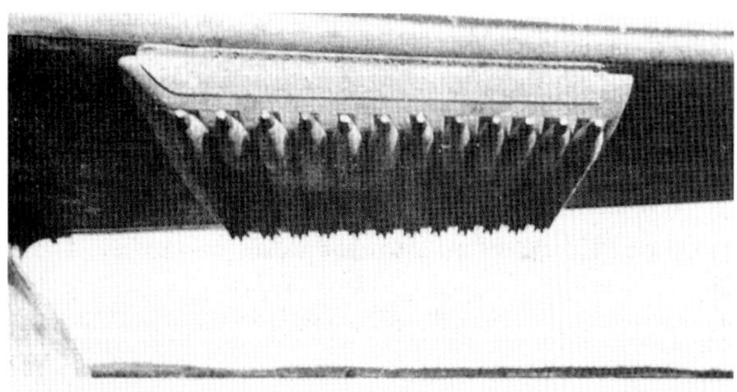

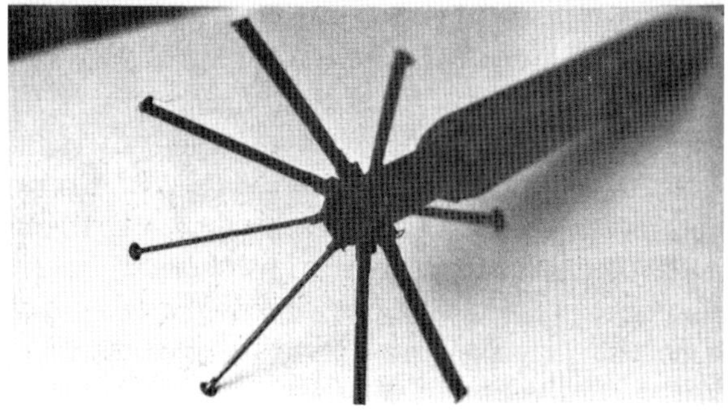

Myhra: I don't believe it took *Hans Wenzel* two years to built one frame, make a new one, and then make modifications. Maybe six months to a year, but not two years. How did *Wenzel* and *Reimar* come to choose the tail wheel from the *Heinkel He 177* and main wheels from an *Messerschmitt Bf 109?*

Wenzel: The *Heinkel He 177's* tail wheel was 1.5 meters (4.9 feet) in diameter. *Reimar* felt it would be suitable as the *Horten Ho 9's* nose wheel. We didn't look at any other wheels for use as a nose wheels because we didn't have much to choose from.

Hopf: Think of the fork that a wheel this size required. Why did they need to use such a big wheel forward and such small wheels in the rear? Think of the strut shaft diameter for that nose wheel! (The large nosewheel was necessary as unlike other aircraft with tricycle undercarriages, the H.9 carried well over half its weight on the nosewheel....PW)

Myhra: *Reimar* said they needed this height in order to give them a correct angle of attack on the wing's leading edge. I've been told that as the *Horten Ho 9* rolled down the runway, the aircraft gently lifted off, unlike a conventional aircraft with a tail.

Hopf: So the *Horten Ho 9* took off in almost a three-point situation. In a *Messerschmitt Bf 109*, for example, we rolled down three-point and then at 90 km/h (56 mph) the tail went up... and then a

A *WG. 21 centimeter* rocket launcher tube mount on the port wing of a *Messerschmitt Bf 109. Wenzel* recalled that *Reimar* also mentioned that the series production *Horten Ho 229* would carry a single launch or double *WG.21* launcher tube per outer wing.

little over 100 km/h (62 mph) you and the *Messerschmitt Bf 109* became airborne. Then you still kept on going for a few hundred yards and then you had enough air speed to go into a shallow climb. The *Horten 9 V2* could not do that because it didn't have a tail.

Myhra: Unlike the people from *Messerschmitt AG*, the *Horten* brothers did not have time to completely design new landing wheels and struts, nor was there any time to test them. So they went looking to see what could be adapted to fit their *Horten Ho 9* design.

Hopf: But just think of the space needed in the cockpit to fit in that 1.5 meter (4.9 feet) diameter wheel! If the nose wheel had been smaller, the remaining space could have been used for something else. Then again, to retract that large wheel, think of the hydraulic pistons required, perhaps two of them. So on and on. That wheel looks stupid on an aircraft which looks so exotic. The *Horten Ho 9* is a remarkable looking airplane. But that nose wheel underneath makes the whole aircraft look ugly. Think of the drag it created when it was lowered...perhaps draining off 50 kilometers per hour right there due to its 50 kilograms per square inch air pressure on it. To merely say that it was a wheel sized to carry the weight of the aircraft is the worst argument anybody could make.

Wenzel: The same tail wheel from a *Heinkel He 177* was also used on the *Horten Ho 9 V1* sailplane.

Hopf: With all of the "reach" the *Horten* brothers had for obtaining supplies and material, you would think that they could have come up with a nose wheel more suitable. For example, in the space required for that tire, one could have put in a lot of ammunition for a 37 mm cannon. I suppose that the width of the tire was almost 0.61 meters (24 inches). Plus you have to figure that the landing gear fork was even wider than the wheel, plus the mounting for the fork, and so on.

Myhra: How much did that tire, wheel, and strut assembly weigh?

Hopf: A lot more that one good man could lift...probably 68 kikograms (150 pounds) just for the tire and wheel rim alone.

Myhra: Did the *Horten* brothers experience any problems with the center of gravity on the *Horten Ho 9 V2* as they kept changing the models of the turbine engines?

Wenzel: I can no longer remember if there were center of gravity problems or not.

Myhra: Wouldn't the center of gravity have to change?
Hopf: Yes, it had to. For one thing, not only did the *Junkers Jumo 004B* engines weighed more (1,582 pounds for the *Junkers Jumo 004B* vs 1,252 pounds for the *BMW 003*), but they were pushed aft to make them fit under the wing covering. As both engines were shifted toward the trailing edge of the wing, the *Horten* brothers were adding more weight and changing the center of gravity of the *Horten Ho 9 V2*. The *Horten* brothers might have done better to move the engines more to the center, or to the leading edge of the wing, as *Gothaer Waggonfabrik* did on the *Horten Ho 229 V3*. The intake area of the turbine is not quite as critical as the discharge of the turbojet. I'd rather have a clean trailing edge.

Myhra: Thinking about the changes in the center of gravity, I can't help but wonder what *Erwin Ziller* thought the first time he took the *Horten Ho 9 V2* into the air. I wonder what he thought about its flying characteristics, center of gravity, and so on because there had been no wind tunnel tests conducted on the aircraft before it actually flew.

Hopf: That is the sad thing about it. The only thing I would complain about *Erwin Ziller* is that he deprived us of practical knowledge. Maybe he died for entirely different reasons than we think. Maybe the aircraft blew his mind? Anybody who flies gliders know that sailplanes are a gentle business. Soaring is perfect balance. But now *Ziller* gets a thing like the *Horten Ho 9 V2,* which prob-

The first design concept for the "*Amerika Bomber*," the *Horten Ho 18A*, of November 1944. *Hermann Göring* requested that *Reimar* bring in *Junkers Flugzeugbau* and *Messerschmitt AG* in building this transcontinental bomber. What a marriage that would have been especially since the others wanted to add a vertical stabilizer with a hinged rudder. *Reimar* went to see *Göring*. He told *Reimar* to forget about *Junkers* and *Messerschmitt* and give him an "*Amerika Bomber*" design without the vertical stabilizer and hinged rudder. *Reimar* did and it is called the *Horten Ho 18B*.

ably is tail heavy, and perhaps he is uncertain about the center of gravity, and so on. But let me say this: That one man (*Erwin Ziller*) had the audacity to deprive all these people of knowledge about what finally happened on that test flight...the final conclusion...well that's sad. And he died for it, too. That makes it even worse. But then again during the war, many other people died, millions of them...one pilot was expendable just like his machine was. Because we got no flight data means that he managed to kill himself absolutely for nothing...that is the sad part about it. He left us nothing. He left nothing for the designers to whom he was obligated, the *Horten* brothers. He didn't do the *Horten* brothers any favors whatsoever. He deprived the *Horten* brothers, too. No matter how one feels about the *Horten* brothers, that's a private thought...but to end their work in failure with not a sliver of paper there to tell what happened...that is sad. I don't understand why he did it. From the whole flight testing program...we have nothing...no data. The blame, if there is any to place, is not only on *Ziller*, it is also due to the commanding officers in charge of the operation. They didn't carry out their supervisory duties properly.

Myhra: At the time, the *Horten* brothers were off working on their *Horten Ho 18B "Amerkia Bomber"* and *Karl-Otto Saur* was keeping them pretty heavily occupied over where the *Ho 18*B was to be built. They were not that free any more, because both *Reichsmarshall Göring* and *Saur* were controlling their daily lives.

Junkers Flugzeugbau told the *Hortens* that they knew how to build large, multi-motored aircraft and that the so-called *Horten Ho 18A* would have a large vertical fin with a attached, hinged rudder. This is a rear view of the proposed *Junkers*-modified the *Horten Ho 18A*. *Reimar* walked right out and over to to *Göring*. *Reimar* got his way, always with *Göring*, and *Junkers* and *Messerschmitt's* participation was canceled. Later *Junkers* called this proposed multi-motored aircraft the *Junkers Ju EF 140.* Water color by *Loetta Dovell.*

A pen and ink illustration of the *Horten Ho 18B* authorized by *Hermann Göring* at *Reimar's* request. About December, 1944. *Wenzel* said that design drawings were being worked on by January, 1945 with a prototype expected by mid 1946.

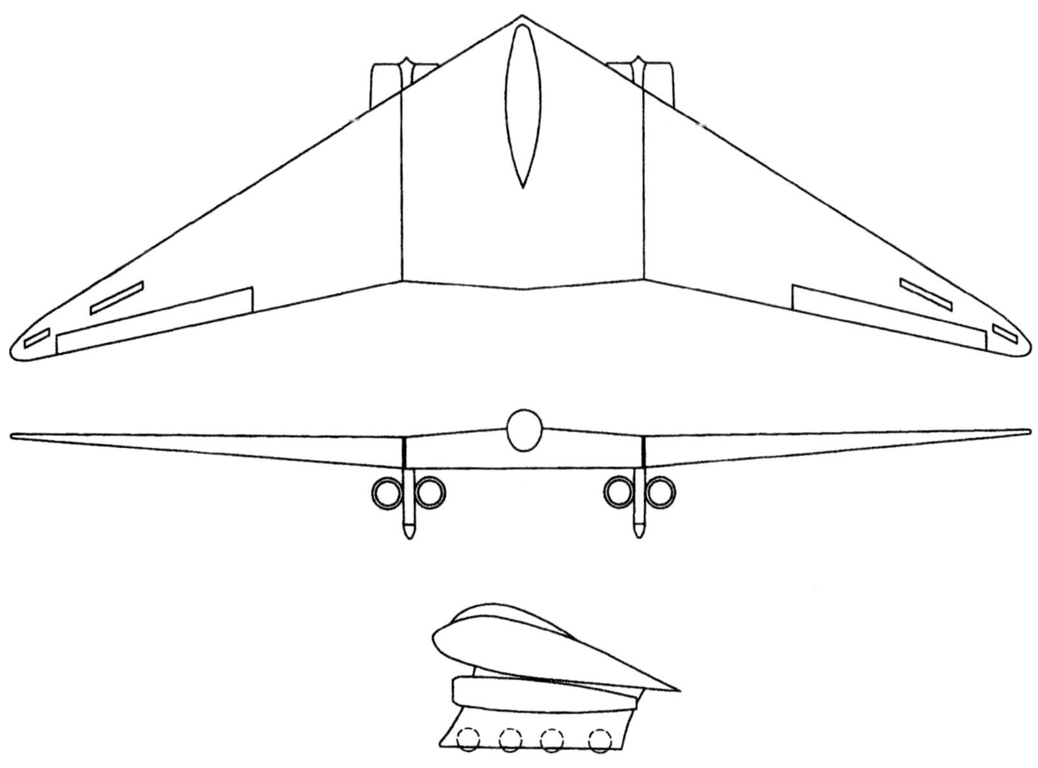

The *Horten* intercontinental bomber design authorized by *Hermann Göring*: the *Horten Ho 18B* as recalled by *Wenzel*. Digital image by *Mario Merino*.

Hopf: But that is no excuse. When the *Horten Ho 9 V2* took off , the *Horten* brothers should have been there directing the proceedings. If a *Messerschmitt Bf 109* took off on that field, well that was different, because thousands and thousands of *Messerschmitt Bf 109s* took off. The *Messerschmitt Bf 109* was a "known" aircraft. There was no novelty in it anymore, because the person in the cockpit knew what he was doing. But in the case of *Erwin Ziller*, he would not have been in the cockpit unless he knew what he was doing. He was a well-qualified man and well aware of all the discipline involved in flight testing. So did the ground crew and the others around them. There should have been three people in the tower listening to the test flight.

Myhra: Well the *Horten* brothers didn't really run a typical *flugzeugbau* operation. It was a garage-type of aircraft building activity.

Hopf: Yes, and look at the results. I don't know much about the civil regulations concerning the construction and flying of glider aircraft. These planes are generally built by young college men, sometimes school boys. There were detail inspections, aircraft inspections, and so on...everything was inspected. The idea was that things which go up in the air can also come down and if so could fall on somebody's head. That was their main concern and obviously of concern to the guy flying the airplane, too. We were not the kind of people who sacrificed young men. Things had to be very accurate. I remember that they had these little metal hardware pieces which were screwed onto the wood work as reinforcement in corners, etc. These pieces had to be welded by a man who was a welder, a certified welder. Now, if one of those little pieces broke,

Wenzel recalled that *Reimar* wanted him to weld-up the center section frame for the *Horten Ho 8* flying wing tunnel. *Wenzel* had been working on the landing gear for the *Horten Ho 8* up until the close of the war...May, 1945. Shown is *Hermann Göring*.

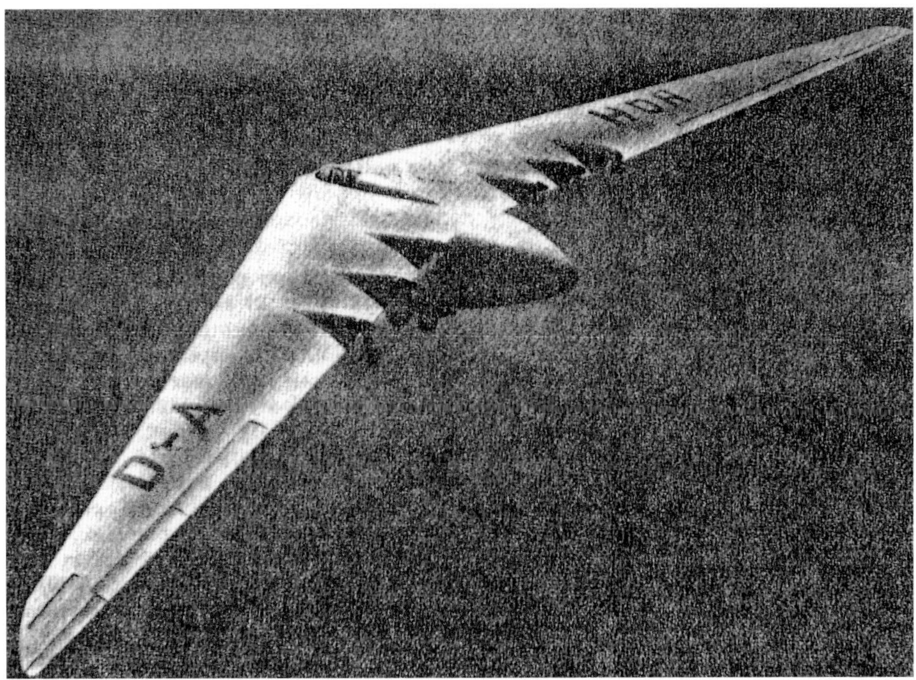

Reimar Horten's six piston-engined Ho 8 transport.

According to *Wenzel, Reimar's* design work on the *Horten Ho 8* was well enough along by January, 1945, that he and his helpers were able to start metal work. Shown in this photo is the *Horten Ho 8's* main gear undercarriage with its four individual wheels. The British was very interested in this transport all-wing and fo r several months post-war, *Reimar* continued to complete all the design drawings for the *Horten Ho 8*. With sadness, the project was ended because the British government canceled the project for lack of monies.

Wenzel recalled that *Reimar* was known within the *Horten Flugzeugbau* as "the living slide rule." Where ever *Reimar* went he brought his slide rule and was constantly doing calculations for the next all-wing project. We wonder how prodigious *Reimar's* output would have been with a laptop computer?

it could not be re-welded. Welding was only a one-time shot. If you had a tubular fuselage and one tube broke out of the corner or something, one could not re-weld it. The whole section had to be changed for the simple reason that by heating the material twice, it produced heat tensions and it might break somewhere else. What the *Horten* brothers did with their *Horten Ho 9 V2's* center section frame...the changing of engines and fixing the damage caused by the hard landing; they welded and re-welded, bent and changed on this frame and I do not believe that this was really proper. However, to the *Hortens* brothers it was common practice. For instance, our fuselages were made from duralumin, which is a harder aluminum. We would get the aluminum from the factory and each sheet was numbered, all accurate and recorded. Then the aluminum was going to be heated...the piece you cut and want to put on. Then it is going to be riveted and hour later...its self-hardening and becoming just as hard as the fuselage. You could not just go over to the junk bin...say you had a 7.5 mm bullet hole in the fuselage and you go to the junk bin and say to some worker...drill three or four holes in this piece of scrap sheet and rivet it on and assume the airplane was all fixed. That is not the way it was. If it couldn't be done right...immediately...even then such a little hole wouldn't make any difference....it could be fixed temporarily just as easily by putting "duct" tape over the hole.

Myhra: Was it done any different in late *1944?*

Hopf: Of course, yes, things were different then. But the *Horten* brothers working as they did on the *Horten Ho 9 V2's* center section frame, would still have been anomolous, because these people believed that almost by themselves, they had a real chance to change the war effort.

Reimar at work at his ranch in Argentina in the mid 1980s. *Wenzel* recalled that *Reimar* was called "*the shek*" by the workers...certainly not to his face, however. Photo by author.

Wenzel recalled that *Walter* was different from them. *Walter* walked and talked with the highest of the high in the *Third Reich*. In this photo from 1939/1940 we see *Walter* dressed in flight gear chatting with *Hermann Göring* as they all are about to board a *Junkers 52/3m* at Berlin. To *Göring's* left is *Albert Kesselring*. Directly behind *Göring* is *Erhard Milch* and to the left of *Milch* is *Ernst Udet*.

Reimar, too, knew a lot of important people. Here *Reimar* is shown sitting next to *Ernst Udet* at a formal *Lilienthal Society* award presentation in Berlin. At the far right is *Ernst Heinkel*. At the far left is *Erhard Milch*. The Italian *General Porro*, Deputy Chief of the General Staff, is to *Milch's* left.

Myhra: I'm not sure of that... I believe that by the time *Reimar* was building his *Horten Ho 9 V2,* he was already building for after the war use. I believe that *Reimar* wanted to fly it, then after the war, when he was talking to the Allied air force experts, he could tell them that he had built and flown a turbojet-powered aircraft. Then he might be offered a job in England, the United States, or France. I believe this is what the driving force was on finishing and flying the *Horten Ho 9 V2.* (This is the inevitable conclusion we must draw from Reimars works in 1944/45…PW)

Hopf: That could be possible. But this would still put *Reimar* in a bad light. Would his workshop staff also get jobs in England or America? Would they, too, be recruited? The aftermath of the whole *Horten Ho 9 V2* project shows that practically no one in the world was interested in the aircraft. For the simple reason that *Jack Northrop* had already made experiments with an all-wing. These experiments were not all that impressive either, I might add. The *Horten* brothers were backing the wrong horse.

Myhra: The all-wing design has been around for years... long before *Walter* and *Reimar Horten* picked up on it. Designers in England, the Soviet Union, even *Hugo Junkers* in Germany had experimented on the all-wing in the 1920s and 1930s. Nevertheless, designers who have shown an active interest in all-wing aircraft have been looked upon as eccentrics by the rest of the aircraft community. These designers have not been the kind of employees an aircraft company would activity seek out. *Reimar Horten* may have been a genius, but the type of aircraft design he lived and breathed was not wanted by the rest of the aircraft industry.(There is circumstantial evidence to suggest that Northrop wished to supress the Hortens achievements postwar – they were after all rivals…PW)

Hopf: That is why they were not too much in demand on the *Rhön/ Wasserkuppe* either. Other glider builders didn't care for that type of aircraft.

Wenzel: We had to put extra weight (ballast) in the *Horten Ho 9 V2* to trim it out.

Hopf: Yes, but that was only a temporary solution until the design was fully tested and finalized. You told me that the *Horten Ho 9 V2* required 800 kilograms (1,764 pounds) of lead. Many planes, especially gliders, had to be flown with lead weights to adjust the center of gravity forward or aft, depending on the weight of the pilot. This was a normal procedure, because flight performance is the only reason why you are flying, besides your own enjoyment. But the *Horten Ho 9 V2* was not an aircraft made for the private pleasure of some individual who wanted to amuse himself. The *Horten Ho 9 V2* was a plane which was supposed to have some tactical value for the *Luftwaffe*. I think its real value in the war effort would have been lousy and that is an understatement. At the same time, while the *Horten* brothers said that they had important things to do...designing the *Horten Ho 18B "Amerika Bomber,"* they should have concentrated on the Allied bombing of Augsburg or any other Germany city. The *Horten* brothers didn't have to go to America. Why go to America when the small version of your all-wing hasn't even been finalized? I guess the *Horten Ho 18*B could have waited eight hours more so the *Horten* brothers could have been in Oranienburg watching the operation and protecting their baby, to see that no harm comes to it. But to even talk about an *"Amerkia Bomber,"* when there wasn't the slightest possible way that late in the war to build it, was ridiculous. If there had been a way to bomb America, the result to Germany would have been even more disaster. If we could have bombed America in 1941, that would have been different. If we could have bombed Pearl Harbor, the Pacific, and then have Manhattan all radiated, well, maybe things would have been different. But in 1945, we could have bombed the Empire State Building and the Americans would have said "Give'm Hell." Then we might have been the recipient of an atomic bomb. It was just too late for the *Horten Ho 18B.*

Myhra: How many other men worked on the center-section frame with you?

Wenzel: Two other men...all three of us worked nearly two years making and remaking the center section frame. We also worked a night shift, for a total of sixteen hours per day. In addition, there were air raids going on all the time which slowed down production.

Hopf: When *Hans Wenzel* says two years, well, that would put the starting time around 1942. There weren't too many air raids yet at that time.

Myhra: I think he means that the complete *Horten Ho 9 V2* took two years to build. Say from November, 1944 when it rolled out...we go back to November of 1942 as the starting time. Thus two years.

Hopf: Air raids would obviously have some effect on the construction schedule.

Wenzel: The *Horten Ho 9 V2* was designed for two hours flight duration with a flying radius of roughly 1,400 kilometers on internal fuel tanks or up to 3,170 kilometers with external drop tanks.

Hopf: That's about 860 miles total range. Easy for *Hans Wenzel* to say today, for we don't know. Let's see. If the *Horten Ho 9 V2's* cruise speed was estimated to be 429 mph (690 km/h) and a duration of two hours' flying time, that would make it's total range on the order of 429 miles (690 kilometers) out plus 429 miles (690 kilometers) back for a total operating range of 858 miles (1,380 kilometers).

Myhra: Did you work on the *Horten Ho 9 V2* after it suffered landing damage by *Erwin Ziller* at the Oranienburg Air Base?

Wenzel: It wasn't *Erwin Ziller* who was flying the *Horten Ho 9 V2* aircraft then. It was *Heinz Scheidhauer*. The reason for the flight was a flight demonstration for *Reichsmarshall Hermann Göring*, *Reichsführer SS Heinrich Himmler*, and others. There was some kind of demonstration and the damage to the *Horten Ho 9 V2* occurred during this demonstration flight. It was a landing accident.

Myhra: Well, this is a new version which we have not heard about before. I don't recall any previous mention of a demonstration flight of the *Horten Ho 9 V2* with *Heinz Scheidhauer* flying it. *Heinz Scheidhauer* did fly a *Horten Ho 7* once for the benefit of *Hermann Göring*.

Hopf: I don't know either what *Heinrich Himmler* would have been doing there.

Wenzel: The *Horten Ho 9 V2* was assembled in Oranienburg and was there for considerable time.

Hopf: We know that *Erwin Ziller* was supposed to be making taxi runs. When an aircraft is making taxi runs, it is to test its ground handling capabilities. You do this before the aircraft ever becomes airborne. Even before it flies in the air for the first time, you want to see how it performs on the runway. This is *very* important. Ninety percent of the aircraft's life is going to be spent on the ground. They were doing this with the *Horten Ho 9 V2*. Doesn't this prove that the *Horten Ho 9 V2* had never flown before? Because if it had flown before, they would have been beyond the high-speed taxi stage.

Myhra: This taxi stage is thought to have been carried out in November, 1944.

Hopf: Well, anyway the *Horten Ho 9 V2* may have inadvertently become airborne and the pilot flew it partially around the field. He did not take it all around but only half-way and touched down in the grass. Apparently by taxiing to the runway, *Erwin Ziller* ran over the runway's concrete lip, or damaged the struts upon landing on the snow-covered frozen grass. Nonetheless, the *Horten Ho 9 V2* had to be repaired. Then the *Horten Ho 9 V2* was repaired and also was modified to have the so-called *Flettner* trim tabs installed. Repair of the damaged landing struts wasn't all that difficult, but installation of the new flaps took most of the time in the shop. Anyway-the *Horten Ho 9 V2* was in the hanger for a considerable time. How many flights did the *Horten Ho 9 V2* make? We know of a flight in which it was damaged. Was there a demonstration flight also?

Myhra: After the *Horten Ho 9 V2* was repaired, *Erwin Ziller* made a second flight for a duration of thirty minutes. This is considered the *Horten Ho 9 V2's* first actual 'official' flight.

Hopf: So there was no harm done. *Erwin Ziller* came back and everything was fine. Except we know there was no data collected. Then there was this third flight, which was the end of the program. Now, what *Hans Wenzel* says is that the whole brass of Germany, such as *Reichsmarhall Göring*, *Reichsführer SS Himmler*, and so on were present to see a flight demonstration of the *Horten Ho 9 V2*. When and where did this flight take place? *Wenzel* seems to think that it took place at the Oranienburg Air Base. But *Hans Wenzel* also implies that it wasn't *Ziller* who was flying the *Horten Ho 9 V2*. *Heinz Scheidhauer* could not have been flying the *Horten Ho 9 V2*, because he wasn't briefed, or experienced on flying twin-turbojet powered aircraft. He only had certificate "*A*" and "*B*." That means he was only a single-engine aircraft pilot. The reason why they put *Ziller* on the *Horten Ho 9 V2* was that he had been briefed and had flown the *Messerschmitt Me 262* at *E-Stelle* Rechlin.

Myhra: *Heinz Scheidhauer* had been to *E-Stelle* Rechlin, too, but he had not been able to pilot a *Messerschmitt Me 262* due to the constant Allied fighter presence over the airfield. This may be the major reason why *Erwin Ziller* was used over *Scheidhauer*. It is probably true that *Scheidhauer* would have been capable of flying a high-speed plane like the *Horten Ho 9 V2*. There has never been any mention before of this demonstration flight with the *Horten Ho 9 V2*.

Hopf: Plus there had not even been a real test flight of the *Horten Ho 9 V2* so that you could feel confident to demonstrate the aircraft to people like *Hermann Göring*. So far, we know that there was only high-speed taxiing, takeoffs, and landings. But neither of the two pilots ever had any experience in demonstration flying with the *Horten Ho 9 V2*. To demonstrate an aircraft before all the brass of *Nazi* Germany, well, one would have to do a little better than merely some high-speed taxi runs. *Reichsmarshall Göring* would want to see the aircraft perform some rolls, banks, and turns — in short, exercise the aircraft and show him what its capabilities are. But no one yet has told us that the aircraft had advanced to the flight demonstration stage. We have not heard that either *Erwin Ziller* or *Heinz Scheidhauer* had done this yet.

Myhra: Then again, this *Mr. Kaufman*, of *Gotha*er *Waggonfabrik* says (See *Horten Ho 229* - US Army Technical Intelligence [ATI] Report) that the *Horten Ho 9 V2* had been flown at Neu Brandenburg.

Hopf: Well, when was that? It couldn't have been after Oranienburg, because the *Horten Ho 9 V2* didn't exist in a flyable state anymore. So it must have been before the crash. We know that the *Horten Ho 9 V2* (after completion) was dismantled in Göttingen and taken by railway flat waggon to Oranienburg. We also know that it was taken there by rail because it was unloaded at the nearby Oranienburg Sachsenhausen *Konzentrationstager* depot. It was then taken to a hangar at the Oranienburg airfield and reassembled. The *Horten Ho 9 V2* then began its first stage of testing (high-speed taxiing) and was supposedly damaged as a result of an inadvertent short flight. After repairs and modifications were completed, *Erwin Ziller* made one successful flight and apparently all went well, but no data was collected...at least any that we know of. But we know, too, that *Ziller* had flown it, according an entry in his *Flugbuch*.

Myhra: We know for sure that *Erwin Ziller* flew it twice afterward — after the inadvertent flight. We also know that there is no record of this so-called first flight, nor the alleged demonstration flight.

Hopf: Well, that really wasn't considered a flight, but an accident.

Myhra: Could that mean that someone else perhaps flew it somewhere else and it was damaged upon landing?

Hopf: Well, considering the strange circumstances under which the *Horten* brothers operated, it is possible that takeoff was not considered 'airborne,' because it happened inadvertently.

Myhra: But wouldn't *Erwin Ziller* list all his high-speed taxi runs in the *Horten Ho 9 V2* in his flight book as well?

Hopf: That is the question which I miss. He definitely should have listed high-speed taxi runs, because they are of great importance. I would assume that he would want everyone to know that he had done that. In addition, the *Horten Ho 9 V2* became airborne. According to flight operations in "normal" circumstances, anything which goes off the ground is 'airborne' and it doesn't matter if its only three inches! *Erwin Ziller* was airborne. He had to use his flight controls. When you taxi, too, you have to use your controls, because of the need to keep the aircraft in the middle of the runway. But you are not flying. You are on three points on the ground. Now the moment you are airborne, you are an aircraft doing what the aircraft is built for. Now he had to make at least one turn and he came down hard on the ground (frozen grass) and that was the end of that. Afterward, *Ziller* made two more flights. The fact that he didn't log the first inadvertent flight...maybe he had reasons. Maybe someone didn't want him to log it because it wouldn't look so nice. In the first place, there would have to be a crash report, an inquiry why there was a crash and resulting damage. Any damage would have to be put in the aircraft's log...date, place, time, and reasons. But the moment the aircraft flies, then this is a different story. It is possible that someone wanted to suppress this event. It would be easy just to ignore that the *Horten Ho 9 V2* was airborne and just a little damaged. Perhaps the damage was ignored also because not only was there minor damage repair, but also major modifications to the control surfaces. After the repair and modifications, there followed what the *Horten* brothers considered to be the *Horten Ho 9 V2's* first flight...which we consider now the second flight. Was all this done in Oranienburg? Not in *Neu* Brandenburg? Are some of these people mistaken today about all the "burgs" at the end of these cities? Could it have been at Oranienburg, because in all the discussions, the name Neu Brandenburg has never once been mentioned. Also never mentioned before was the fact that there was a demonstration flight with the *Horten Ho 9 V2*.

Hopf: There is another thing which seems strange. The *Horten Ho 9 V2* was to be transferred to Brandis/Leipzig after its final test flight. It was eventually to be incorporated into the operations of *1.JG/400*. How could this aircraft be placed in a brand new *JG*.... a plane no one knows anything about? It doesn't make sense, especially when you have twenty other aircraft in *JG/400* which can still fly and fly well?

Myhra: Especially such an unorthodox aircraft like the *Horten* all-wings.

Hopf: I bet there were still 300 *Henschels* around and flyable, which could be used for strafing and ground support work. Any pilot even with a small amount of flight training could fly one of these *Henschels*. So it appears that there are some strange things happening here. The question, were the *Luftwaffe* brass, such as *Hermann Göring* and others such as *Heinrich Himmler* really ever present for a demonstration flight of the *Horten Ho 9 V2?* It becomes especially interesting to hear that *Himmler* was present. In the last days in Brandis/Leipzig, for example, the *SS* gradually took over the forces. Maybe not officially, but they ran a great many things.

Myhra: *Preussler* mentioned that there were *SS* people watching the *Horten* activities in the hangar at Oranienburg. Perhaps, when the *Horten* group was ready to fly the *Horten Ho 9 V2,* these *SS* staffers notified *Heinrich Himmler* and he came over from Berlin to watch.

Hopf: Another interesting item is that they mention *Hermann Göring* and *Heinrich Himmler*. It is possible that *Göring* assumed command himself over Germany at the very end of the war, according to his beliefs that *Adolf Hitler* was incapacitated in the bunker in Berlin and could not act any more.

Myhra: But the first flight of the *Horten Ho 9 V2* was in November, 1944.

Hopf: But maybe there were already plans made between *Göring* and *Himmler*...that they kind of agreed to do something.

Myhra: *Reichsführer SS Heinrich Himmler* was interested in exotic aircraft. He wanted to find that "miracle" aircraft which would save Germany from defeat. This is an area which we should look more into.
Wenzel: I believe that when the *Horten Ho 9 V2* flew for the first time that *Erwin Ziller* was not its pilot. I think that *Ziller* had not arrived there yet.

Hopf: What is the time frame *Hans Wenzel* is talking about? How could *Heinz Scheidhauer* fly the *Horten Ho 9 V2* when the *Horten brothers* objected to his flying it in the first place? He was not qualified, based on *Luftwaffe* regulations. Then this means if the pilot of the *Horten Ho 9 V2* was in fact *Scheidhauer*, then he must have flown the demonstration flight as an unqualified pilot. It wouldn't be surprising, but someone should have at least mentioned this before.

Wenzel: I remember that some British Army soldiers blew up the *Horten Ho 7* at Minden after the surrender. The *Horten Ho 7* had been flown there mainly by *Heinz Scheidhauer*.

Myhra: The *Horten Ho 7* was a twin-engine, piston-powered all-wing which was to be taken to Brandis/Leipzig for use in training pilots to fly the *Horten Ho 9 V2*.

Wenzel: I am not aware of how extensive the damage that was done to the *Horten Ho 9 V2* from a hard landing. But I did forge the landing gear strut mounts. There was a small blacksmith shop near the workshop in Göttingen and I forged some steel pieces in the blacksmith shop where the struts were to be attached to the frame.

Hopf: Since *Hans Wenzel* was the man who built this stuff and he was quite capable of doing it, doesn't it seem kind of strange that if the *Horten Ho 9 V2* suffered structural damage due to a hard landing, he wasn't called to Oranienburg to fix it, or to at least supervise its repair? But *Wenzel* does not appear to be aware of the hard landing incident.

Myhra: But he has mentioned that he was aware of the landing gear damage which occurred on one flight of the *Horten Ho 9 V2*.

Hopf: Yes, but he didn't have anything to do with its repair.

Myhra: Could it be that he is not aware that the damage came from a high-speed taxi run? But he says that the damage occurred during a demonstration flight in front of *Göring*, *Himmler* and others. Could the *Horten Ho 9 V2* been damaged upon landing after the demonstration flight, as opposed to a high-speed taxi run?

Hopf: But if there are the top brass in the *Luftwaffe* standing there with binoculars and watching the *Horten Ho 9 V2* do its thing, they wouldn't come to Oranienburg just to watch a high-speed taxi run. I doubt this very much. I'm sure that they all had seen high-speed taxi runs before. This wouldn't interest them. I think that they wanted to see a very unusual aircraft fly.

Myhra: *Hermann Göring* appeared for a demonstration flight of the *Horten Ho 7* by *Heinz Scheidhauer* in the Fall of 1943 at Oranienburg. Could this be the flight that *Hans Wenzel* is talking about?

Hopf: I sincerely doubt that *Hermann Göring* would have merely showed up one day unannounced, either. When *Göring* went anywhere, it was a real circus. The *Horten Ho 9 V2* would have had to be flown at Oranienburg. Because where else could it have flown? Otherwise they would have had to dismantle the aircraft, place it on rail cars and transport it. Oranienburg was a good place to demonstrate new aircraft.

Myhra: Once the *Horten Ho 9 V2* became airborne, the pilot would most likely fly it around the airfield and bring it in for a landing, wouldn't you think? Wouldn't the pilot try to get the aircraft down right away and wouldn't he have to make one full circuit of the airfield to land into the wind?

Hopf: Normally, a pilot faced with this situation would fly around twice to get his composure back. If you are airborne with the *Horten Ho 9 V2*, well that is probably the safest place to be for the moment. It is very dangerous on the ground with something new, or at least something which is very unfamiliar. There probably wasn't much fuel in the tanks either, and not enough to be airborne for a long time. But I would assume there would be enough fuel to fly two times around the airfield in order to get a little altitude and to get the feel of the aircraft in flight before attempting a landing. *Erwin Ziller*'s problem didn't really come from taxiing on an icy runway. The ice has very little bearing on the situation here. He was taxiing and all of a sudden the runway was at its end, or near the end and he felt like he couldn't stop. Thus he accelerated, pulled the aircraft up and he was airborne. The *Horten Ho 9 V2* did not become airborne by itself. It became a necessity to get airborne in order to avoid a crash at the end of the runway. If this is so, then why he didn't make a decent approach at the end of the flight? It is a mystery to me. He should have completed the inadvertent flight in a normal manner and then the aircraft might not have been damaged. Plus there is no reason why it should have been damaged on the frozen grass strip. Other aircraft in the *Luftwaffe* took off and landed on grass in winter as well as summer. The aircraft could have gotten damaged because *Hans Ziller* was not accustomed to handling the *Horten Ho 9 V2* aircraft at slow speed. Maybe he wasn't aware of its stall characteristics either. *Rudolf Preussler* said that the *Horten Ho 9 V2* made a nice, slow, smooth landing. That is probably not quite an accurate statement. The *Ho 9 V2* could not make that kind of landing. The *Horten Ho 9 V2* was a heavy aircraft with a high wing-loading. It would have to come in fairly fast and it would have a high stall speed as well.

Myhra: There is something here that we do not know.

Hopf: I sense from all these interviews a sort of "I was there" attitude...."I saw," and so on. These people have a sense of pride that they were with the *Horten Flugzeugbau* flight operation. Even after forty years, we still don't really know what all these people were really doing. Now the only one who doesn't show this attitude is *Hans Wenzel*. But he is not very helpful either, because he has thrown in some things which don't match the other people's comments. Could these people be talking about another aircraft? None of the *Gothaer Waggonfabrik*-built *Horten Ho 229s* was completed or ready to fly.

Myhra: No, none was finished. Maybe they could be talking about the demonstration flight of the *Horten Ho 7* for *Hermann Göring* in the Fall of 1943? On the other hand, *Mr. Kaufmann* says in the ATI report that the first flight of the *Horten Ho 9 V2* "flew well, but the landing gear was damaged upon landing." If the *Horten Ho 9 V2* "flew well," it certainly doesn't mean that it flew just far enough to make a 180 degree turn and return to the middle of the landing strip and land on the frozen grass.

Hopf: I agree.

Myhra: It also means, too, that maybe the first flight of the *Horten Ho 9 V2* was attended by a larger group?

Hopf: It sounds like it was a planned demonstration flight, then. Therefore it has nothing to do with this taxiing thing and then getting airborne. No way could one then make a statement that the *Horten Ho 9 V2* "flew well." If *Kaufmann* says that was the "first flight," then the accident must have happened after the taxi tests were completed. But *Kaufmann* does not say who flew the *Horten Ho 9 V2*, does he?

Myhra: No. Just that the aircraft "flew well."

Hopf: If the aircraft was said to have "flown well," well, what does that tell you, what does that mean? One can stretch it. It flew well because it didn't crash! Who was this man *Kaufmann*?

Myhra: He is listed as the supervisor of construction for *Gothaer Waggonfabrik*-Gotha. If the aircraft is recorded as "flying well," then we assume that there was nothing unusual about its flight. Even still, the *Horten Ho 9 V2* could have come down a little hard and damaged its landing gear. Maybe the *Horten Ho 9 V2* wasn't damaged during its high-speed taxi tests, but damaged later in a flight?

Hopf: It could be. But could it also mean that the *Horten Ho 9 V2* was taken back into the hangar after the high-speed taxi tests and then modified with the *Flettner* tabs? Maybe *Hans Wenzel* is confused about the damage/modification?

Myhra: He could be. The *Horten Ho 9 V2* was damaged twice. The first time, it was repaired, but the second time — after the crash — it wasn't worth it. But I see from the *ATI* report that the *Horten Ho 9 V1's* flight test program included quantitative measurements of stability and control using instruments provided by *DVL*. But no report of that flight test was written. The flight test pilot was *Heinz Scheidhauer*. What does this mean — that *Scheidhauer* was listed as the test pilot? How many total flights were made? It says here, too, that the *Jack Northrop* all-wing aircraft was used as an example to show that the Americans were thinking of building all-wing aircraft for use in the war effort. Certainly *Northrop* was having his troubles, too. He was working on his all-wings in his shop in California from the money he was getting from his USAF contracts to built the *Northrop P-61 "Black Widow*." For example, *Jack Northrop* had one section of his hanger set aside for all his all-wing stuff. When he got contracts, he took a piece of the money to pay for his all-wing research and staff. *Jack Northrop* was taking funds, too, just like the *Horten* brothers were, and diverting them for other uses.

Hopf: That *Northrop P-61* was all that *Nazi* Germany would have needed in 1944. We could call it the "*Super Lighting*." I see from the (*ATI*) report that the *Horten* brothers stated that there was no directional instability in their all-wing aircraft. It also says that maximum control moment must be used in slow speed landings.

Myhra: What does that mean?

Hopf: I guess that to keep your flight level, or to control your rate of sink, which you do by means of the elevators, sometimes you had to use 100 percent of the elevator movement to achieve the correction. That would mean that the effectiveness of the elevator at slow speed was marginal and that you are at the limit with no reserve. Actually you have to wait until the plane responds to control movements at slow speeds and that could be difficult, especially when you are talking about flying a few feet above ground. That could be the difference between a bounce and a neat roll out. What was the *Horten Ho 229's* landing speed?

Myhra: It's in the *ATI* report. It was 145 km/h (90 mph). Is this relatively fast for 1945? How fast, for example, was the landing speed of a *Messerschmitt Bf 109?*

Hopf: Somewhere in the mid 60s...65 to 70 mph. I read in the *ATI* report that the *Horten Ho 9 V2* was supposed to be able to make a 360 degree roll in 4 seconds at 600 km/h (375 mph). But the *Horten* brothers said they could do it only in 5.2 seconds. I wonder how the *Horten* brothers knew that...by theoretical calculation, or actual flight test.

Myhra: Is that roll rate good, average or poor?

Hopf: That is a pretty rapid roll rate for that speed.

Myhra: How much time would it take a *Messerschmitt Bf 109* to complete a 360 degree roll?

Hopf: About the same amount of time...about 5.2 seconds. I read, too, that someone wanted to fit four 37 mm cannons in the *Horten Ho 229*. Sure, 90 mph landing speed is quite high in 1945...that was pretty fast. The *Messerschmitt Me 163* had a landing speed in excess of 160 km/h (100 mph), but that was entirely a different ball game. It says in this *ATI* report that measurements of stability cannot be carried out.

Myhra: What does that mean?

Hopf: Why can't you make measurements of stability on aircraft with heavy control surfaces like the *Horten Ho 9 V2?*

Myhra: Was the *Horten Ho 9 V2* a kind of aircraft in which the pilot needed to use both hands in order to control it?

Hopf: Yes, I would say so. You either have stability, or you don't. What the *ATI* report probably means is that you could not stabilize the *Horten Ho 9 V2* because it was hard to steer. I find it hard to believe that the *Horten* brothers could not have made the *Horten Ho 9 V2's* controls easy to move and work. If they could get a hold of two jet engines, they certainly could have gotten a hold of ball bearings. No, I would say that this is the way the *Horten* brothers built their aircraft...this is the way they were accustomed to building their gliders. In those early days, one didn't waste money on ball-bearings in gliders, for they were a luxury. The pilot could just pull a little harder, as long as the aircraft performed. All a glider pilot wanted to do anyway was to gain altitude and find a thermal updraft and go on sailing. This didn't require much effort on the part of the pilot. But it's a bit different in a fighter-type aircraft where light controls are a necessity.

Myhra: The takeoff run with a full load was estimated to be 3,000 feet...is that a fairly long takeoff run?

Hopf: That seems normal and is not unusual. Then again, how would these people know how much runway it would take to takeoff if no one had ever done it? The *Messerschmitt Bf 109* with a 250 kilograms (551 pounds) bomb load took twice as long a takeoff run compared to a *Messerschmitt Bf 109* not carrying the bombs.

Myhra: Could they have fit four 37 mm cannons in the *Horten Ho 229?*

Hopf: I think this was wishful thinking.

Myhra: What about the *Horten Ho 9 V2's* wing loading of 40 pounds per square foot? How would that affect performance?

Hopf: I don't know...we would have to have something to compare it to.

Wenzel: The *Horten* brothers became quite frustrated over all the delays with the engines. There was nothing that they could do about it, but wait.

Myhra: But while the *Horten* brothers were waiting on the *Junkers Jumo 004Bs, Reimar* built other aircraft, such as the high-performance *Horten Ho 6* sailplane. The *Horten Ho 6* was to be used for competition against the *D-30 "Cirrus"* sailplane – which at that time had the best glide angle in the world. The *D-30* held numerous sailplane records in Germany at that time and *Reimar* built the *Horten Ho 6* to challenge the *D-30*...and win! Risking construction of the *Horten Ho 6* made *Walter* very angry with *Reimar*, because he was afraid that *Luftwaffe* internal inspectors might find out about their secret *Sonder Kommando. Reimar* said they could claim that the *Horten Ho 6* was necessary as a research effort to test wing profiles...but in reality, he wanted to build it for strictly personal reasons...to compete against the *D-30.*(Reimar had been greatly dissapointed when performance tests did not show the Ho.4a to be superior to the D.30....PW)

Wenzel: I was in Oranienburg with the *Horten Ho 9 V1* glider and *Heinz Scheidhauer* was its test pilot. They had built the *Horten Ho 9 V1* without engines and *Scheidhauer* had flown it and damaged it in Göttingen. In the meantime, they had already started the *Horten Ho 9 V2* back at Göttingen , which was being laid out for *BMW 003* turbojet engines.

Hopf: Does this mean that the *Hortens* already had space in Oranienburg when they were testing the *Horten Ho 9 V1?*

Myhra: It is my understanding that the *Horten Ho 9 V1* never got to Oranienburg. It was only test flown at Göttingen by *Heinz Scheidhauer* and it was never taken to Oranienburg. It finally ended up in Brandis/Leipzig and was burned by American troops after the surrender, during a base-wide cleanup operation.

Hopf: That was my feeling, too. The *Sonder Kommando* X9 - Göttingen *Horten Ho 9 V2* group was shipped out to Oranienburg after the aircraft was finished. All the alterations to the center section frame, to change it from the *BMW* to *Junkers Jumo* engines, were done in Göttingen. Then they dismantled the plane, because they couldn't fly there — the field at Göttingen was not long enough. It was put on a flatcar and delivered to the Sachsenhausen *KZ* depot. There the *Horten Ho 9 V2* was off-loaded and reassembled in a hanger at Oranienburg. All this took place in November, 1944, and the *Horten Flugzeugbau* personnel present there were the general maintenance and flight support attendants. There was no manufacturing, or construction done by the *Horten* brothers in Oranienburg. There they made high-speed taxi runs with the *Horten Ho 9 V2,* it became airborne, was damaged and then was repaired. When *Hans Wenzel* talks about that blacksmith shop, where he forged the landing gear mounts, where was that located?

Myhra: I believe in the village of Grone by Göttingen, in the same building where the *Horten Flugzeugbau* was located.

Wenzel: It appears that the *Horten Flugzeugbau* workers at Göttingen were not well informed about the engineering details on *Horten Ho 9 V2*. I don't know the full reasons, but the changes were needed on the center frame in order to carry bigger engines. I made a new second frame, then modified that frame as well; I don't know why all these modifications were needed, or required. In all, three entirely new center sections were built. Let me list the changes made:

01. The 1st center frame built was designed to carry *BMW 003s*;
02. This frame was discarded after *BMWs* couldn't be delivered;
03. It is decided that *Junkers Jumo 004Bs* are to replace the *BMW 003s*;
04. A 2nd frame is built to carry *Junkers Jumo 004Bs*;
05. The promised *Junkers Jumo 004Bs* are canceled;
06. The *Hortens* are told they'll receive *BMW 003s* instead;
07. A 3rd center frame is built to carry *BMW 003s*,
08. The promised *Junkers Jumo 003s* are canceled;
09. The *Horten* brothers are told they'll receive *Junkers Jumo 004Bs*; and
10. No new frame is built, however the existing frame (3rd one to be built) is modified to carry *Junkers Jumo 004Bs*.

Hopf: This is confusing. All the people so far have stated that the *Horten* brothers received engine casing 'shells' for two *BMW 003* turbojets. Then the *BMW 003s* didn't come and the whole frame was modified for two *Junkers Jumo 004Bs*. The *Junkers Jumo 004Bs* were larger, so massive modifications to the fuselage were required. Now *Hans Wenzel* says that a modification was not made. The first center section was discarded and a new one was made to accommodate the larger *Juinkers Juimo 004Bs*. Then the *Junkers Jumo 004Bs* were put in and the aircraft finished up. In addition, *Wenzel* says that the *Horten Ho 9 V2*:

01. Underwent taxi tests;
02. Flew a demonstration flight with *Nazi* brass present; and
03. Suffered landing gear damage after completing this demonstration flight.

Myhra: *Hans Wenzel*, it appears, also depicts the *Horten Ho 9 V2* as having one more flight, maybe even two more that we known about. This a greater number than the others have recalled.

Hopf: Where was *Adolf Galland* all this time?

Myhra: He was already sacked.

Hopf: Maybe that is why *Reichsführer SS Heinrich Himmler* was there. The *Luftwaffe's* situation had deteriorated so badly that *Himmler* and the *SS* were starting to run the situation. That is possible. It also seems strange that these events have not been mentioned before by the others. Some of these other people must have been there! *Hans Wenzel* is the only one to say this and he is probably the least informed, because he left the *Horten Ho 9 V2* project before it was finished, to start work on the *Horten Ho 12*.

Myhra: Well, when you look at *Erwin Ziller*'s *Flugbuch,* there is no reference to any earlier flights with the *Horten Ho 9 V2.*

Hopf: But still doesn't mean that there wasn't a previous flight with the *Horten Ho 9 V2.* Maybe somebody else flew the *Horten Ho 9 V2* and that, then, would only appear in that particular pilot's *Flugbuch*! The *Flugbuch* is for the man and not the aircraft, though there may have been an aircraft *Flugbuch* as well.

Hopf: Strange. It appears that these men were building an aircraft. Then this man *Willi Radinger* laughs when you mention that the *Horten Ho 9 V2* was to be a fighter aircraft. This is strange! Plus no one has mentioned that a flight demonstration was made for *Reichsmarshall Hermann Göring*. Where were the *Horten* brothers at this time?

Myhra: I need to find out what happened after the *Horten Ho 9 V2* left Göttingen. Was it taken directly to Oranienburg Air Base, or did it make a stop someplace else? Perhaps was it flown to Oranienburg from some other airport?

Hopf: We heard that the *Horten Ho 9 V2* could not be flown to Oranienburg, because the Göttingen landing strip was not long enough for a take-off run. Besides, one does not fly a prototype plane fresh out of the workshop to a place like Oranienburg without knowing anything about what the plane will do. All the testing had to be done first before you could make a transfer. But the test program could not be done in Göttingen; it had to be done in Oranienburg. That is why the *Horten Ho 9 V2* went there. Now, when the *Horten Ho 9 V2* was in Oranienburg, when did it fly, who was there and who flew it?

Myhra: *Walter Horten* obtained some data on the *BMW 003s*. *Reimar* then built an aircraft around this data. About all they had were some specifications of the engine, such as thrust, weight, diameter, fuel consumption, and so on. It is my understanding that when the empty engine casings arrived, they were bigger than what the data said. I've heard, too, that this is the first time center-frame modifications began.

Hopf: I think this was mentioned before, when the *BMW 003* shells came. They had already built the center section fuselage according to the engine blueprints on hand. When the *BMW 003s* came, they didn't fit. Yes, they made alterations to fit the engine casings into the center frame. As time passed, they learned that there would be no *BMW 003s*. There was instead going to be the *Junkers Jumo 004Bs* and they were bigger still.

Myhra: This is when they scrapped the first center frame and turned it into the *Horten Ho 9 V1* glider. According to *Hans Wenzel,* he built a whole new center section for the *Junkes Jumo 004Bs*. Then, the *Hortens* were told again that *BMW 003s* would be ready first...plan to install the *BMW 003s* they were told. They had not yet received the *Junkers Jumo 004Bs*.

Hopf: The *Junkers Jumo 004Bs* were obviously in great demand. There were several squadrons flying *Messerschmitt Me 262s* already and they were probably burning out engines like hot cakes.

Myhra: These engines were only good for about 25 hours of operation...usually even less. Look, the *Horten Ho 9 V2's Junkers Jumo 004Bs* were new. Did the engine which quit...stop because of mechanical problems, did *Erwin Ziller*'s lack of experience cause it to flame out, and so on?

Hopf: Yes, then some of the major components had to be replaced and the engine rebuilt. It is possible that somebody found two *BMW 003s* which were not used any more, or which were not used at all. At this time, there was not one lousy plane which used *BMW 003* turbojets. Everyone was using the *Junkers Jumo 004Bs*, so they were in short supply. May be some prototypes were standing around using the *BMW 003s*.

Myhra: I don't know of any.

Wenzel: The *Horten* brothers were hoping to have the *Horten Ho 9 V2* flight-ready one year after starting construction. But due to all the delays, which were not their fault, it took us one additional year. I believe that the effectiveness of the *Horten Ho 229* would have been great, due to the proposed four cannons it would have carried. Two were 37 mm and two were 13 mm or 18 mm rapid-firing cannons. These cannons could be reloaded in flight. I also believe that the so-called "stove-pipe" rockets, the type used on the *Focke-Wulf Fw 190* against *Boeing B-17* bomber formations, would have been mounted on the *Horten Ho 229*, too.

Hopf: *Hans Wenzel* doesn't know much about armament. For example, one cannot reload the cannons in flight! There is just no way the pilot can go out on to the wing and reload. Some of the *Messerschmitt Bf 109s* carried two so-called "*Dinort*" stove-pipe rockets. If this is what *Wenzel* is referring to, it was known as the *WG.21* rocket tubes firing 21 centimeters projectiles. That was a remarkable piece of artillery. That thing was more valuable than all the cannons together. With the cannons, the pilot would have to make careful aim with the cross-hairs. But with the *Dinort* rockets, you just aimed in the general direction of the bomber pack and by doing so, you could expect to damage three or four bombers. A pilot could not reload in flight. That projectile is that long and about this thick. Where would one store the others? The rockets were placed in from the rear and there was a little device which kept them from falling out of the front of the tube. Then there was a little wire connected to the rockets coming out of the wing. From there it was routed into the cockpit and connected to the batteries. There was a push-button on the stick. It was a rather primitive arrangement. Then again, the *WG.21* were used on *Messerschmitt Bf 109s* and were intended for infantry support duties.

Myhra: I just wonder if *Hans Wenzel* is thinking of the 55 *mm R4M* unguided high explosive air-to-air rocket instead? Twelve of these rockets could be carried on a wooden rack mounted beneath each wing. *Wenzel* says that all these different types of armaments were to be carried by the *Horten Ho 229.*

Hopf: Well, I doubt if it could have been done. Those *R4M* rockets were simple to operate as well. They had approximately the same trajectory as the rounds the *MK 108* cannon, so both weapons could be aimed using the normal *Revi* gunsight without adjustment. On the tail of the *R4M* were eight cute little fins which extended after launch. *Hans Wenzel* also says that after Stalingrad, the war was practically lost for all practical purposes because the *Wehrmacht* could no longer advance and the Front began to go backwards toward the *Reich*. I don't know why he and others place so much emphasis on the war with Russia as being the 'turning point.' In reality, the war began to go against us already in 1940. That is because we could not invade and defeat England. It was almost impossible. We only got as far as Coventry with our *Messerschmitt* and *Junkers* twin-engine bombers. That left about 75% of England beyond the range of our bombers.

Myhra: Are you saying that *Nazi* Germany had already lost the war based on the results of the Battle of Britain?

Hopf: Yes. We had no way of penetrating any farther into England than Coventry.

Myhra: Tell me about the canopy on the *Horten Ho 229*. Compared to other German aircraft designs, it seemed quite advanced and more like those found on the Allied *North Amereican P-51* and *Republic P-47* fighters.

Wenzel: The cockpit canopy on both the *Horten Ho 9 V1* and *Horten Ho 9 V2* were made from plexiglass sheet 20 mm thick.

Hopf: Why did they have to make it 20 mm thick? Now it wasn't a combat aircraft, yet. Plexiglass wouldn't offer the pilot any protection anyway because it would break in a thousand pieces if hit by a bullet.

Myhra: Is 20 mm relatively thick for a cockpit canopy?

Hopf: Yes, and 20 mm is extremely heavy plexiglass. Now if you blow a bubble for a canopy...I would say that even 10 mm would be heavy. We had a conical-like canopy on the *Messerschmitt Bf 109* with aluminum framing and the glass was probably one inch thick...maybe not even that. The Me.163 canopy was relatively light, anyway, it was less than one inch and more like 8 to 10 mm.

Myhra: Let's see...what fraction of an inch is 20 mm? One inch is 24.5 mm...and *19.5* mm is ∫ inch, so this would have made the *Horten Ho 9 V1* and *Horten Ho 9 V2* canopies almost an inch thick! I wonder where they got the plexiglass sheet 20 mm thick at this stage of the war?

Hopf: Plexiglass is made from hydro-carbon, like oil — and oil was considered a rare item. Even small pieces from broken canopies had to be returned to the factory. The reason for this is that the factory could possibly put the small piece to use somewhere else. Well, the *Horten* brothers apparently were able to obtain two 20 mm sheets of plexiglass. I bet any supply officer who got that requisition order pulled his hair out! It wasn't *Hans Wenzel* who decided on a canopy 20 mm thick. Somebody had to decide on 20 mm! Plus that plexiglass had to be a lot larger than you really needed, because after you blow the bubble, one had to trim off the excess. Then again, perhaps that thickness was the only type available to them?

Myhra: I was told by *Willi Radinger* that the *Horten* brothers put those sheets in a large oven and when it became soft they took it out and laid it over a wooden form they had built. They sort of draped the soft plexiglass sheet over the mold.

Hopf: You can tell that *Hans Wenzel* is a fuselage man and probably never even bothered with other things by the way he talks. He was a sheet metal person...a man who built fuselages.

Wenzel: The control column in the *Horten Ho 9 V2* could be moved in all directions. The control surfaces could be moved differentially and together— they could move in an upward and downward motion simultaneously, yet they also had the motion that when one goes up the other goes down. They were intergeared, it was quite a complicated arrangement.

Hopf: If you moved the control stick left or right, one wingtip elevon goes up and on the other wing goes down. This makes the aircraft go into a bank or a roll. Anyway it changes the lateral direction of the aircraft. When you pulled the stick to your belly, or pushed it forward...both wingtip elevons would go up or down together and that would make the aircraft would go up or go down, changing the motion on the pitch axis. Actually you could have the elevons up to climb and also do banking at the same time. This is a very complicated combination of motions. Two motions...you do two motions in the same time...at the same instant.

Wenzel: The *Horten Ho 9 V2* had a lifting "eye" in each wing so that the aircraft could be lifted off the ground by a crane. This could be used to change a tire or work on the landing gear struts. Most aircraft had such lifting "eyes" built into the upper wing.

Hopf: Now that is just not so. Our *Luftwaffe* airplanes never got "lifted" period. You could raise them by "jack screws" and why would you want, or have to lift a plane in the first place?

Myhra: What if the landing gear had collapsed?

Hopf: Then you would use "jack screws," or maybe an inflatable rubber bladder.

Myhra: You mean that the *Messerschmitt Bf 109* didn't have "lifting eyes?" American military aircraft had lifting eyes. They could lift them onto aircraft carriers, for example.

Hopf: Yes but that was a different situation. You needed lifting eyes. If we couldn't get a jackscrew under them, we would put a rubber bag under the wing and inflate it until the aircraft rose high enough to work on it. Now I do remember that our flying boats had lifting provisions on them.

Myhra: How long could the *Horten Ho 229 V2* fly without refueling at normal cruise speed?

Wenzel: The *Horten Ho 9 V2* had about two hours flying time.

Hopf: That would have required a considerable amount of fuel. Now the *Horten Ho 9 V2* only had fuel tanks in the wings...right?

Myhra: Yes, that's my understanding...apparently four fuel tanks in each wing. In one report I have, it also says that the *Horten Ho 9 V2* required 800 kilograms (1,764 pounds) of ballast in the nose of the center section due the center of gravity shifting caused by the *Junkers Jumo 004Bs*.

Hopf: That is stupid. What about the weapons? If each weapon weighs 91 kilograms (200 pounds), then you should have at least four cannons in it. So it doesn't make much sense to carry ballast. It appears that the *Horten* brothers didn't give much thought to the weapons locations. First you had the wing root, where the engines were located. You then had a space for the fuel tanks and the plywood spars. Where are you going to put the weapons? In the plywood wings? Well, if so they wouldn't last very long because of the wear and tear of combat flying.

Myhra: Maybe the ballast was used earlier in the project, in place of the cannons, until flight testing was completed. Then the equivalent weight in cannons and ammunition would be installed later.

Wenzel: The *Horten Ho 9 V2* carried a total of 2,000 liters of fuel in its eight outer wing tanks. This would give it two hours flying time. Each fuel tank could be filled separately.

Myhra: How much fuel would an *Messerschmitt Bf 109* with its *Daimler-Benz 601-E* inverted 12-cylinder inverted vee of 60degrees with supercharger burn at full-speed?

Hopf: It would be producing about 1,395 horsepower at 2,600 rpm and consuming about 0.44 pounds of 92 octane per horsepower per hour.

Myhra: Well, the *Junkers Jumo 004Bs* were much thirstier. A *Junkers Jumo 004B* consumed 1.40 to 1.48 pounds of diesel fuel per pound of thrust per hour.

Hopf: The *Horten Ho 9 V2* would burn about 1,000 liters per hour. If you divide 1,000 liters by 60 seconds, that is not quite 17 liters per minute. Now, we don't know if that was cruising speed, or top speed. One 50-gallon drum is about 200 liters.

Myhra: So the *Horten Ho 9 V2* had the equivalent of five 50 gallon drums in each wing. There was about ten 50 gallon drums of fuel (total) carried in the aircraft. I'm not certain of the aircraft's fuel economy.

Hopf: Well the *Messerschmitt Me 262* couldn't even make a one hour flight duration. We could fly a *Messerschmitt Bf 109* about one hour...if there was nothing happening. This would be just plain cruising. In high-performance flying, that fuel would shrink down to ∫ of an hour. I would assume that a turbojet's fuel use would be in a similar configuration. Consider the *Lockheed U2*. If you are not doing anything, just cruising along it idle speed, think of how light it was and how far one could travel on very little fuel.

Wenzel: In looking at your pictures of the *Horten Ho 9 V2* cockpit, well, one of the levers on the left side of the cockpit released the brake parachute.

Hopf: If you remember when one of the gentlemen described the landing of the so-called "non-flight," well he said that *Erwin Ziller* came in so nice and slow. Well, if the *Horten Ho 9 V2* would have been capable of doing that, why would it need the brake parachute on it?

Myhra: Didn't the *Horten Ho 9 V2* come in fast due to its high wing loading?

Hopf: Well, the time of the "non-flight," *Erwin Ziller* didn't use his brake parachute. But he wasn't flying either. On this so-called "non-flight," well, one could basically call it a crash.

Wenzel: When the pilot comes in for a landing and realizes that the runway is too short, then he could release the brake chute and the plane is slowed down.

Hopf: But the brake chute is supposed to come out only when the aircraft is already on the ground. It is a ground affair. Because if you would release the brake chute while you were still airborne, you wouldn't need a runway. You would crash.

Wenzel: There was a provision on the *Horten Ho 9 V2* that when you pulled the stick up, you shortened the lever arm. A smaller movement of the stick gives a greater response because of the different pivot and the control response was therefore more precise.

Myhra: So, does that mean in high-speed flight, one would pull the steering column up, ecause all one needed was fine flight control?

Hopf: I really don't see the merit in it, but the steering forces at high-speed would be greater, as opposed to slow speed conditions. Well, you wouldn't need as much movement at high speed as one would require at slow speed. So one would only need a tiny bit of adjustment and correction. Then, too, there were no servo units or hydraulics in most aircraft at that time. The pilot had to work the control system completely with his own muscle strength.

Wenzel: In the old *Horten Ho 4A,* they had three tennis balls in the wheel strut for shock-absorbing. The *Horten* brothers used a composition magnesium/metal tube in the *Horten Ho 9 V2. Gothaer Waggonfabric*, on the other hand, used a welded-up 60 kilogram (132 pound) chrome steel tube (probably of a tensile strength of 60 kilograms per square meter). This was light-weight and strong. However, the stuff the *Horten* brothers used in their center-section frame was more similar to electrical conduit. It was very light. When one heated it too much, it would burn, or melt, so I had to be very careful in making all the changes on the framework.

Myhra: Do you remember if the accessory equipment for the engines (pumps and so on) protruded up above the wings? Did they move some of these accessories off the engines and place them elsewhere in the framework? Were the *Junkes Jumo 004Bs* rotated so that the accessory equipment cleared the wing surface?

Wenzel: First, *Walter* obtained empty turbine motor shells from *BMW 003*. I built a center section frame for these. Then the *RLM* said that they would not be getting the *BMW 003s,* but *Junkers Jumo 004s* instead. So I built a second new center section frame. Next, the *RLM* said the *Horten* brothers were to receive *BMW 003s* after all.

Hopf: The first center-section frame was made for the *BMW 003* engines. Then the *RLM* told the *Horten* brothers that there were not going to get the *BMW 003s*, but *Junkers Jumo 004s*. Then *Hans Wenzel* had to make a whole new center-section frame for the *Junkers Jumo*. Then the *RLM* told them that they were getting *BMW 003s* instead, but they never received them. So they finally received the *Junkers Jumo 004Bs* after all.

Myhra: First they were promised *BMW 003s*. Second, *Junkers Jumo 004Bs*. Third *BMW 003s* again and fourth and last...*Junkers Jumo 004Bs*. You mean the center section was changed three times after the first center-section was built? *Hans Wenzel* first built the frame to accept the *BMW 003s*. Then the *RLM* said no, you'll be receiving *Jumos* after all. *Wenzel* then built a new bigger frame. Then the *RLM* said no to the *Junkers Jumo 004Bs*...the *Horten* brothers are to receive the *BMW 003s*. So *Wenzel* had to modify the second frame's mounting points to accept the *BMW 003s*. Then the *RLM* said the *BMW 003s* were canceled and the *Horten* brothers would receive *Junkers Jumo 004Bs. Hans Wenzel* then had to rework the second frame back to accept the *Junkers Jumo 004Bs*. All in all *Wenzel* built three complete center-section frames and modified the third frame once?

Hopf: First *Hans Wenzel* had to make it smaller, then larger. Then they had to make it smaller then larger. Thus the center-section frame was being continually altered. This was not good for its structural strength.

Wenzel: I spent two years working on the center-section frame of the *Horten Ho 9 V2*, making changes required by the *RLM* switching engines between the *BMW 003s* and the *Junkers Jumo 004s*. After I completed the final modification on the *Horten Ho 9 V2's* center-section, I was transferred and assigned to make the frame for the *Horten Ho 12*. This *Horten Flugzeugbau* workshop was near the town of Kirtorf . The *Horten Ho 229's* wing covering was flush, except the hole in the top surface for the cockpit canopy. No accessories from the engines stuck out above or through the covering. The wing surface was completely smooth.

Myhra: The reasons why the *RLM* kept making changes on which engine the *Horten* brothers would receive was because the new turbojet engines still were experimental and *Junkers Jumo* didn't begin serial production on the *Junkers Jumo 004Bs* until mid-1944. *BMW* started production later in 1944 with their *BMW 003*.

Hopf: Did the *Horten* brothers obtain one right-hand and one left-hand rotating turbojet, or were they both right-hand or left-handed?

Myhra: I don't know. Were both right-hand and left-hand rotating engines built?

Hopf: It would be interesting to know, because the turbojets had to be tilted (rotated) to lower the accessory drives, otherwise they would have been sticking up above the wing. If they had only asymmetrical engines, then one engine would have the accessory 'island' on the inside and the other would have on the outside. If they made engines with both directional rotations, then the *Junkers Jumo*

004B's accessory island could both be on the outside, or on inside...depending which way you put them in.

Myhra: I wonder if rotating the engines 15 degrees would have caused any problems with operational performance?

Hopf: No, I don't think it would have created any problem with engine performance. It would have created problems in fitting the engine inside the center section. Perhaps it might have affected engine operation because of the oil sump...one could only tilt the engine so many degrees. If you did more, then it could be possible that the oil sump runs dry, then that is the end of the compressor shaft bearings. This is critical because sometimes an aircraft flies inverted, in a steep bank, or dive. This problem was handled on the *Messerschmitt Bf 109* with a rotating oil pickup. So when the aircraft turned over in a roll, the oil pickup revolved, too. Thus while the aircraft was upside down, what was the bottom of the oil slump was now at the top. With the rotating pickup it didn't matter.

Myhra: Did the *RLM* supervise the building of the *Horten Ho 229*, since they were paying for its construction?

Wenzel: There were no regular *RLM* inspectors on the *Horten Ho 9 V2* project. However, a district inspector would come by Göttingen from time to time.

Hopf: This district inspector probably had several small aircraft companies like *Gothaer Waggonfabrik* to visit. So he could only be at one at a time. Ordinarily the *RLM* would have an office in the *Flugzeugbau* and there were permanent people checking on the construction production all the time. The *RLM* didn't do that with the *Horten* project. There are several reasons. One, it may have been too late in the war effort (mid 1944) for them to have enough manpower. Then, again, maybe the priority of the *Horten Ho 9 V2* wasn't as high as some people thought it was, or should be. Let's face it...anybody with a sense of reason must have realized that you couldn't come up with any new, or better aircraft in large enough numbers to change the war effort by mid 1944. It was a lack of recognition of the problems at hand...in a time of the war, you're 'reacting' and often you cannot foresee all the problems in the war effort that may affect you. We only knew about our own little world. Factories didn't talk about their production problems and of course nothing was written about them. When the war was over for us, everybody just dropped their stuff and surrendered to the British, or the Americans. We just stood there, wondering what we were going to do now? No one asked those questions during the war...questions that should have been asked...are we going stop this before we go down into ashes, or should we stop while there is still something left of the cities, the country, of our civilization?

Myhra: Here is some data on production of the *Horten Ho 229* (see "*Horten Ho 229* - US Army Technical Intelligence [*ATI*] Report").

Hopf: Hmmm, it looks like *Gothaer Waggonfabrik* required static testing on their *Horten Ho 229s* while they were under construction. This static testing lab carried out a different type of stressing testing...they would put weights on the wings, and so on. It is just unbelievable that *Gothaer* could begin mass production of the *Horten Ho 229* without any reliable data from the *Horten* brothers. Not even *Willy Messerschmitt* would do that. Who would you trust more...the *Messerschmitt AG* people, or the *Horten* brothers? I would definitely think that *Messerschmitt AG's* engineers would know more. They couldn't get away with building a prototype aircraft without data and then have a small shop attempt to build an airplane for mass production. It says here in this document (*ATI*) that the prototype of the *Horten Ho 229* first flew at Neu Brandenburg and was damaged during a landing accident. How can this be? I wonder if this could be the inadvertent flight and the frozen grass landing when the landing gear was damaged? I read here, too, that the *Horten Ho 229s* were to get self-sealing fuel tanks. Well, by early 1945, the self-sealing tank was already established. It didn't always work 100 percent, but it helped. The *Horten Ho 229* also was to get armor plating. This didn't always work 100 percent either, but it helped. In some situations, it helped like a steel helmet does. But the helmet doesn't protect someone completely — only under certain circumstances. If some aircraft were hit, pieces of armor plating could be ripped out of their aluminum mounting points. Sometimes these plates would be dislocated and strike the pilot in the face, or in the back of the head. I read here that aft of the turbojet exhaust nozzles, there was a thin steel flashing. This is like tin covering the woodwork beneath the engines' exhaust, to protect the wing covering against heat and flame. Covering the wing with plywood, for example 6 mm, 12 mm, and 16 mm like the *Horten* brothers did on the *Horten Ho 9 V2* — well, one is getting pretty close to point where using aluminum might have been a better choice, weight-wise. Aircraft plywood is not exactly light, especially when it comes to heavy laminations, such as 16 mm.

Myhra: Armament was supposed to be four *MK 108's*, or two *MK 103* 18 mm cannons. Oh my gosh, look here, it says that the *Horten Ho 9 V2* was tail heavy. Some 800 kilograms (1,764 pounds) ballast forward was required! *Gothaer Waggonfabrik* hoped that the installation of cannons would replace some of the ballast. But the weapons were located in the wing root area. So the cannons would not be in the wing, but in the center section, outboard of the turbojets?

Hopf: This means that the heavy part of the cannon, the breach at the rear of the gun, is housed inside the wing, and only the thin barrel sticks out in front. So the heavy part of the weight of the cannon is spread over the whole length of the wing root. Amazing! It wouldn't do much for eliminating the 800 kilograms (1,764 pounds) of ballast, would it?

Hopf: It says here in the *Luftwaffe Quartier Meister's Report* on assigning the *Horten Ho 229* to *1.JG/400*. They are talking about "*Auffrischungs*" which means aircraft lost by attrition. Then they mention "*Neuaufstelleungs*" means a completely new squadron. "*Umrustverbunde*" is mentioned which means already established squadrons which have been re-designated. Apparently, the 9th *Korps* and the General of Fighters were making changes in aircraft assigned to various squadrons. *I.JG/400* was a new squadron and it was going to receive the *Horten Ho 226* (*Horten Ho 7*) as a trainer and the *Horten Ho 229* as a new fighter aircraft to replace their *Messerschmitt Me 163s*. *JG/400* was located around several cities such as Brandis, Venlo, Wiesbaden, and others. Late in the war, *JG/400's* airfields were overrun by the Allies and the only one left was Brandis/Leipzig, which really became overcrowded. There were no other airfields left to which remaining units could retreat. Notice that the number of planes available in the Order of Battle have increased above the number of losses from attrition. That looks pretty good for the industry...considering they were still able to produce aircraft at all. But this is misleading here, because the number of individual aircraft sorties were more numerous than they were before. If the numbers of actual aircraft had increased, that is, twice or four times — like it appears here from the number of sorties flown, it would have been a lot better. In spite of the fact that the industry produced more aircraft, we still didn't hold our own. The number of our pilots was being increased by lowering the age limits. Of course training standards almost completely disappeared...you could fly an *Messerschmitt Me 163* without ever being in the cockpit of an *Messerschmitt Bf 109*. It never actually came to this, but it was anticipated. It was the same thing with the "*Volksjäger*" — the *Heinkel He 162*. The pilot was supposed to go to glider school and learn to fly. This was good and there is nothing wrong with that. But you have no fighter experience as a glider pilot, because all you do is take off and go home. In 1945, the *Luftwaffe* finally got the idea what the whole training thing should be about.

Myhra: You mean that in April, 1945, there were people in the *RLM* still seriously working on these "Order of Battle reports?"

Hopf: Well, high echelon people still kept accurate tabs on what was going on as long as they could. It was their job...their duty. I would guess that there must have been 3,000 people working in the *RLM* alone during its peak. Even in April, 1945, Berlin was still functioning. It continued to function until the Russians broke through the East/West access. Even if each time we took off we were able to shoot down one *Boeing B-17*, well it would have made no difference whatsoever anymore. You had to have situations like that one in *Nazi* Germany when you talk about thirty aircraft shot down per hour. Well if you shoot down 30 *Boeing B-17s* an hour, but the Americans are manufacturing 60 per hour, then sooner or later all of *Nazi* Germany is destroyed by the bombers which get through.

Myhra: *Hans Wenzel* did you ever heard of a man by the name of *Oberst Artur Eschenauer* from the *Luftwaffe Quartier Meisters Office*, Berlin?

Wenzel: No.

Myhra: Why did it take so long earlier in the war, when materials were still available, to build the *Horten Ho 9 V2's* center section?

Wenzel: I'll tell you about the center section mess. First I laid out the *Horten Ho 9*'s center section fuselage to carry *Bramo/BMW 002s*. Then, the *Hortens* obtained two *BMW 003s*. The *Hortens* were not aware that dimensional changes had been made between the *Bramo/BMW 002s, BMW 003s,* and *Junkers Jumo 004s*. Consequently, when we found out, we did not modify the first center section, but set it aside entirely to become the *Horten Ho 9 V1*. So we made a whole new one to carry the larger diameter *BMW 003s*. It would have been impossible to modify the center section built for smaller diameter *Bramo/BMW 002s* to hold these larger *BMW 003s*. Then, with the new center section designed to hold the *BMW 003s*, orders came from the *RLM* that the *Horten* brothers were to get *Junkers Jumo 004Bs* instead. I then modified the third center section to hold the smaller diameter *BMW 003s*. When the *RLM* finally shipped the turbine engines, they sent *Junkers Jumo 004Bs* to the *Horten* brothers. Now I had to re-modify the third center section back to its original configuration to house the *Junkers Jumo 004Bs*. This is the reason why it took so long for the *Horten Ho 9 V2's* center section to be finalized.

Hopf: Did the *Horten* brothers ever have a complete, ready-to-run *BMW* turbine at all? Or did they only have the two empty *BMW 003* outer casings?

Myhra: They had the 6-stage compressor *BMW 003* empty shells. Then again, I've heard that these *BMW 003s* were built out of wood by the *Horten Flugzeugbau* and these were placed in the 1st center section constructed. Then they were told to forget about 6-stage compressor *BMW 003* engines because the program was canceled. That frame was saved and called the *Horten Ho 9 V1*. *BMW* promised them the new 7-stage compressor *BMW*. So 2nd new frame was welded up containing the canceled 6-stage compressor *BMW* but really it would house the 7-stage compressor *BMW*. It appears then the *RLM* told the *Horten* brothers to forget the *BMW 003s* and plan on getting two *Junkers Jumo 004Bs* instead. This is when they built a new 3rd center section frame. Some workers suggested that the *Horten* brothers were told to forget the *Junkers Jumo 004Bs* because they would get the *BMW 003s* after all. Now there is a lot discrepancy here. *Walter* thought that a 3rd frame was welded up after the *Horten* brothers were told that they would be given *BMW 003s* after all. But when the turbojet engines arrived...the *RLM* sent them *Junkers Jumo 004B* turbines instead. This was when the *Horten* workshop went literally crazy. They went and installed the *Junkers Jumo 004Bs* for fit in the nearly completed center section and found the accessory islands protruded up above the center section plywood covering. So it appears that *Reimar* removed the *Riedel* starter unit, the *Riedel* gasoline tank surrounding the air intake...everything back to the accessory island. Still not good enough. *Reimar* wanted to push the *Junkers Jumo 004Bs* as far back in the center section frame as far as he could. The center of gravity was completely changed by this move. In order to discover how the aircraft would perform with air intakes in the leading edge and the change in the center of gravity, *Reimar* took the old *Horten Ho 2* and modified it to represent the changes he'd need to make on the 3rd center section frame. The *Horten Ho 2* was modified and testing conducted. In addition, *Reimar* took an old *Horten Ho 3* and turned it into a test bed, too, to measure changes in the center of gravity. With the results of these hurried tests, the *Horten Flugzeugbau* workers, under the direction of *Hans Wenzel* removed the *Junkers Jumo 004Bs*, removed all the center section plywood, modified the cockpit to hold the turbine instruments in a rectangular bank of instruments. The *Junkers Jumo 004Bs* were placed well aft. Now we know that the *Riedel* starter units were installed but we don't know if the circular fuel tank surrounding the air-intake was installed. No photographs exist showing the completed *Horten Ho 9 V2*. Regardless, the *Junkers Jumo 004B's* were so far aft just so *Reimar* could get his completely smooth upper surface that the center section required 1,764 pounds of lead ballast in the nose area. The *Horten Ho 9 V2* with its *Junkers Jumo004Bs* installed was finished in November, 1944. The center section went by road on a truck used to transport tanks. The outer wings were transported to Oranienburg Air Base on a flat bed railroad car. Arriving at the Sachsenhausen *KZ* rail depot, the wings were off-loaded and transported to the *Heinkel AG* hangar at Oranienburg Air Base and assembled.

Hopf: No, I believe that only two complete center section frames were constructed, because *Hans Wenzel* keeps repeating that he had to do a lot of cutting on the frames after the second new frame was built. He believes that the 2nd and 3rd center frame were each modified twice after they were built. From the time of the 1st frame to the modified 3rd took the entire *Horten Flugzeugbau* two whole years.

Myhra: So, *Hans*, you built two *Horten Ho 9 V2* center section frames, not counting the frame for the *Horten Ho 9 V1?*

Wenzel: Yes.

Myhra: And the second one, which was really the 3rd was modified twice?

Wenzel: Yes.

Myhra: Okay, okay now it appears that we are getting somewhere on all this but no matter what *Hans Wenzel* recalls now whether it was two frames and two modifications each or a total of three frames with the last modified after it was built it doesn't matter because I have photos showing all this center frame dance going on. Plus, I remember that both *Walter Rösler* and *Rudolf Preussler* said that the center section was considered weak due to all the cutting and re-welding.

Hopf: Nobody has mentioned that *BMW 003* engines were being reconsidered after having first dismissed them in favor of *Junkers Jumo 004s*. Is *Hans Wenzel* is the only man to have said this? Why was there such a confusion in the *RLM* between which engine would be used, the *BMW* or *Junkers*? I have the feeling that the 7-stage compressor *BMW 003* never did really come off the ground.

Myhra: Well, yes it did. *Reimar* told me all this about the engines promised to them. The *BMW 003* apparently was up and running, but they were not getting enough thrust out of it, so series production was postponed. Plus the *RLM* in mid 1943 told *BMW* officials to really concentrate on producing their *BMW Model 801* 14-cylinder radial piston engine.

Hopf: Now the *Horten* brothers had to compete with that. The *BMW 801* was to be reserved for high-altitude aircraft fighters.

Wenzel: I had a paper pass from the *RLM* which allowed me access to a damaged aircraft *flugplatz* near Göttingen in order to obtain used aircraft parts. Among the parts *Reimar* and I obtained from this *flugplatz* were the landing gear, and so on. The equipment in the *flugplatz* was very useful and valuable, especially later in the war when new parts were difficult to obtain. If someone needed a generator, landing wheel strut, or whatever, they could be obtained at various damaged aircraft storage areas throughout Germany. These facilities were guarded 24 hours and one had to have permission to enter them. By the way...*Reimar Horten* had a nickname, as did other *Horten* workers. We *Horten* workers called *Reimar* the "*Shek*" meaning someone who is a little eccentric or "nuts", or someone who's really hard to "read" — to know what they are thinking. However, we all liked *Reimar*, but still he was eccentric. Now *Walter Horten* was a more extrovert personality, a wheeler/dealer- horse-trader, an arrogant person, too, and not well liked by the work force. *Walter's* nickname was *"Langer," or* "tall one" and I guess it was given to him by *Galland* during the Battle of Britain. We didn't give him one of our own.

Myhra: So *Reimar* was liked but not *Walter*?

Wenzel: Yes. For example, you could go out at night stealing supplies from *Luftwaffe* depots with *Reimar*, but not *Walter*. There is the difference. *Reimar* was one of us while *Walter* knew he was born into a higher class than we. That's how *Walter* carried on his relationship with us. He wasn't bad but he was different from us.

Myhra: Did you workers call *Reimar* the "*Shek*" to his face?

Wenzel: No. Never!

Myhra: Did you ever see the *Horten Ho 9 V2* fly?

Wenzel: No, I did not even see the *Horten Ho 9 V2* aircraft fully assembled and completed. In fact I left the Göttingen workshop in Autumn, 1944, just after I had finalized modifying the *Horten Ho 9 V2's* center frame to accept the *Junkers Jumo 004s*. After that I worked on the *Horten Ho 8* at another *Horten* workshop . I did not even get to see the *Junkers Jumo 004Bs* placed in the *Horten Ho 9 V2*, much less ever see them operating, and the machine flying with them.

End of Interview

Chapter 04

Fifty years of stealth aircraft designs: the first...the *Horten Ho 9* of 1943 and the latest...the *Northrop B-2* of 1988. These two designs spanning 45 years are surprising similar in planform. What's old is suddenly new again suggesting that there's really nothing new under the sun.

Comment:

Any one with an interest in aviation, especially military aviation, talks about the new "stealth fighter/bomber aircraft designs" as if the concept was discovered yesterday. But stealth is not a new idea. Mother nature has given birds, animals, fishes natural camouflaging via color so that they will better blend into their surroundings to avoid getting caught and eaten prematurely. When talking of military aircraft, camouflaging and decoying aircraft fighters and bombers goes back to World War One. The term "stealth," however, is new and fresh but it still means decoying or hiding an aircraft from the unrelenting searching wave bands of radar. The idea of stealth when applied to military aircraft of today is to give it a shape which will help camouflage it from enemy radar not so much through color (although this is used, too) but by deception. It is hoped an individual watching a radar screen will see a shape that will be mistakenly taken for something other than an aircraft...perhaps a bird. Thus the purpose of modern-day stealth technology is to reduce an aircraft's visual signature to radar and thus avoid detection. In the mid 1940s as now, the main way to detect in-coming military aircraft is by its signature on the radar screen. In the early to mid 1940s the *Horten* brothers knew that if the fledgling British radar could be fooled into thinking what was being scanned was not a military aircraft after all, but a bird, well then, *Luftwaffe* fighters and bombers could go about their business over England all the while evading detection.

When looking at the *Horten* all-wing designs from the mid 1930s to the exotic *Horten Ho 229* of early 1945 none had the tell-tale signature of a conventional aircraft. That is, long fuselage and tail assembly of a vertical rudder and horizontal elevators. The *Horten* brothers were designers all-wing sail and motor-powered aircraft their first all-wing sailplane flew in the Summer of 1934. The *Horten* brothers had experimented with plastic composition which was one of the first attempts in the world to construct and aircraft out of materials other than metal or wood. Their *Horten Ho 9* twin turbojet powered fast bomber had wings of wood. The *Horten Ho 9's* center section was welded up thin wall metal pipe similar to electrical conduit and covered with plywood. Glues used in the wooden panels, conventional wisdom of the day suggested that when mixed with coal dust, a certain amount of radar waves would be absorbed never to be reflected back to an operators radar screen. The shape of the aircraft, *Reimar Horten* believed in 1943, could act as a decoy. The *Horten* brothers had excellent connections in *Nazi* Germany, especially *Walter Horten*. Technical information flowed to them. In the case of radar, *Reimar* who earned a *PhD* after the war in aerodynamic mathematics knew that length of radar waves and an aircraft's cross section were what was important. For example, radars can be set to send out a beam on a certain wave-length. An aircraft cross-section larger than the radar wave would be picked up nicely on an enemies radar screen. However, if the cross section was smaller than the wavelength of the radar then the aircraft would go pretty much undetected being "invisible" to radar. The secret in achieving stealth in 1943 as it is in 1999 is the same. A successful stealth aircraft will be one with the smallest radar cross section (RCS).

The angular *Northrop B-2* of 1988 and the United States' state-of-the-art "black magic"commonly known as stealth technology. The goal is to reduce, eliminate, or scatter even further any reflected radar energy so that radar receivers will not be able to detect what little reflected energy remains.

To obtain "stealth" an aircraft designer must minimize the flat areas presented to radar found on a military aircraft. It has been said that the *Boeing B-52* bomber has an RCS value of 10,764 square feet (1,000 square meters) while the *Northrop B-2* may have an RCS ratio of 5.4 square feet (0.5 square meters). At 5.4 square feet an emery radar might determine that what radar waves are reporting back in nothing more than a small bird whereas the *Boeing B-52* would show up on radar as a very large aircraft. It would not be a stealth aircraft by any means. *Reimar Horten* believed in the

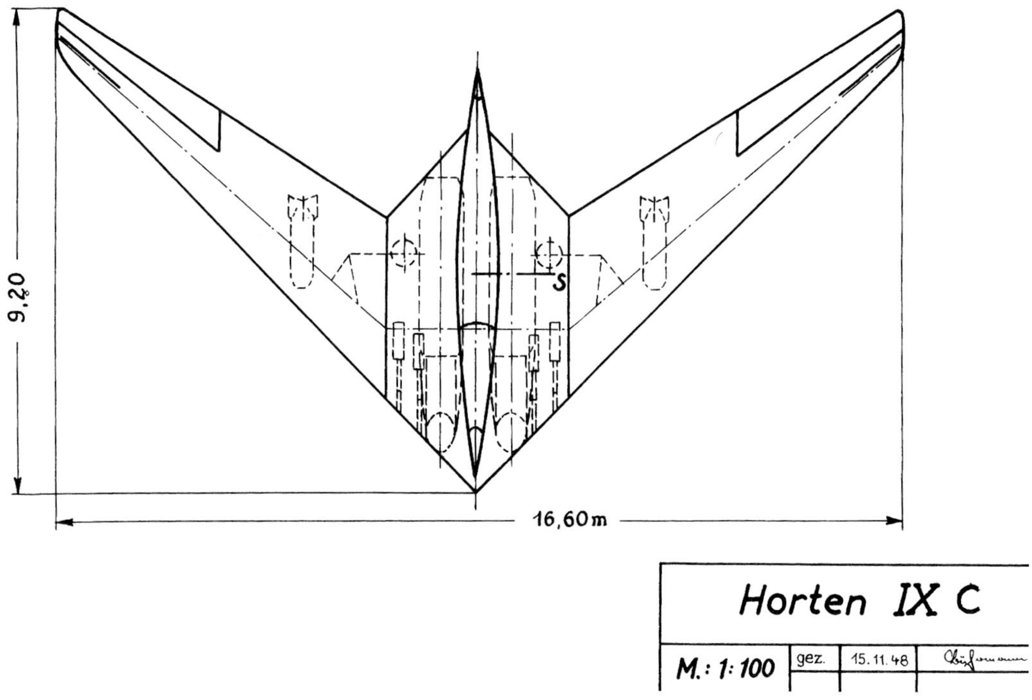

The proposed *Horten Ho 9C* of 1945 showing its sharp external airframe angles which were known from mid 1940s research would be good reflectors of radar energy. The *Horten Ho 9Cs* small flat surfaces with its high aspect ratio wing was thought to be a good way to scatter and disperse British radar.

The *Horten Ho 7* shown in a low-level banking maneuver over the Minden *Flugplatz* in 1943. With its long narrow wing span it would have been highly effective in obscuring less-pronounced radar waves known today as "side lobes" the *Horten Ho 7* is an excellent example of a very small radar cross-section (RCS).

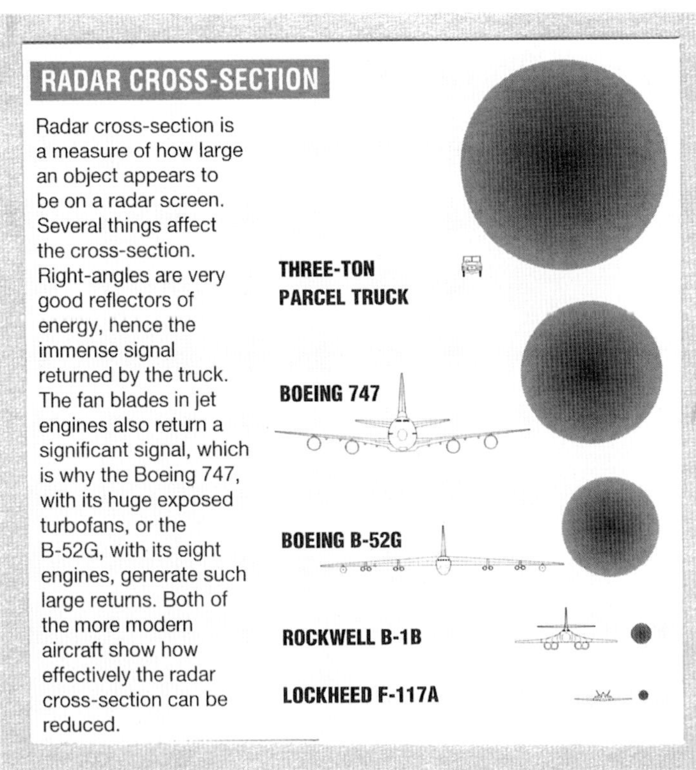

A graphic illustration of radar cross-section. Courtesy: *IMP Lockheed F-117 Nighthawk.*

all-wing planform. A bonus of this planform was its very low RCS and the all-wing, he believed, was a natural for reducing an aircraft's signature. Designers of the *NorthropB-2* forty five years later, also found that the all-wing was an essential planform if one was really serious in reducing visual signatures. The *Horten* brothers in 1943, just like their fellow designers in 1983 took advantage of camouflage coloring. The *Northop B-2* is painted in colors not unlike the older *Horten Ho 9*. They included various shades of gray on the upper surfaces and light blues and grays on the under surfaces.

Finally, reducing detection depends on where and how a turbojet engine is installed. Turbojet engines require huge volumes of air to function so unimpeded air flow is crucial. Yet the amount of metal in a turbine has to be decoyed as well as the hot gases leaving the aircraft in the form of thrust. The *Horten* brothers were among the first aircraft designers in the world who placed their powerplants inside the wing. *Messerschmitt AG*, *Arado Flugzeugbau*, and *Junkers Flugzeugbau*, for example, placed the turbines outside the aircraft with no attempt to reduce its detection. *Ernst Heinkel* placed a turbine inside the fuselage of his *Heinkel He 176*. It didn't perform well because its wing surface was not large enough. On his next turbojet-powered aircraft, the *Heinkel He 280*, his designers placed the turbines in pods one under each wing like the *Messerschmitt Me 262*. The all-wing *Horten Ho 9 V2/229* of the mid, 1940s set itself apart from all its contemporaries in terms of reducing its visual presence to radar. It would be right a home among the *NorthropB-2s* of today.

A lone *Northrop B-2* with its wing-mounted air brakes extended reminds us that stealth in the form of the *Northrop B-2* is not a new idea, perhaps a new name. Stealth means to go about your business undetected. The design similarities between the *Horten Ho 7* airframe of the early 1940s and the *Northrop B-2* of the late 1980s clearly show that regardless of the war then being fought, radar had to be fooled through airframe design.

Walter Horten was keenly aware of British radar and the dangers it posed for *Luftwaffe* fighter and bomber aircraft. The *Horten Ho 9 V1,* its nose starboard side shown, mirrors the 45 year newer *Northrop B-2* to minimize its side view to radar waves so that if they can't see or hear you coming, you'll be operational long enough to deliver all your offensive weapons.

A front, starboard-side view of the large high-tech *Northrop B-2* showing a surprisingly similar side profile as the older radar absorbing, wood-built *Horten Ho 9 V1*.

A front-on view of the wooden *Horten Ho 7* which had a radar signature in 1945 unlike anything seen before. World War Two aircraft had huge RCS values while the *Horten Ho 7* and the twin turbojet powered *Horten Ho 229* would have appeared on British radar screens to be not much larger than a bird.

Front-on view of the *Northrop B-2* showing how its design contributes to its very low RCS values.

A view of the *Horten Ho 7* flying off to starboard and away showing nicely its high aspect ratio wings and small RCS values. It would have been a difficult object to identify on radar screens of today.

The *Northrop B-2* shows its absolutely smooth uncluttered surface. Oh, what if *Reimar* and *Walter Horten* had continued their all-wing work in America? What do you suppose our *Northrop B-2* would have looked like if *Reimar* could have continued to refine his *Horten Ho 7*, *Horten Ho 229*, and so on between 1945 and 1985?

The *Horten Ho 9 V1* rear view demonstrating its smooth overall profile. It is parked out front of its *Junkers* hangar at Göttingen about Spring, 1944.

The *Northrop B-2* showing the same smooth upper surface overall profile as the older *Horten 9* project.

Chapter 05

Horten All-Wing Aircraft Designs Prior To Their Turbojet-Powered *Horten Ho 9 V2*

The *Horten* brothers first piloted all-wing sailplane, the *Horten Ho 1* with a 40.7 foot wingspan. It is shown at the *Bonn Hangalar* (air field) Spring, 1934. The three brothers had tested their all-wing ideas extensively with balsa and wood scale model airplanes. As many as 200 scale models were built and flown before the *Horten's* began their *Horten Ho 1*. In this photo *Walter Horten*, seated in the cockpit, is preparing for a test flight. *Reimar Horten* is standing at the wing's apex assisting his brother prior to flight. Total empty weight of the *Horten Ho 1* was 264 pounds.

The *Hortens* air towed their *Horten Ho 1* to the 1934 *Rhön/Wasserkuppe* Summer sailplane competitions. Although the weather did not permit the *Horten Ho 1* to demonstrate its potential, *Rhön* officials awarded the *Hortens'* 600 *Reich Marks* for the most innovative new aircraft of the summer event. Interesting is the fact that the *Horten Ho 1* carries the *Nazi Party* insignia on its port landing flap and the German national flag on its starboard landing flap. After the competitions were over the *Hortens* were unable to obtain an air tow back to Bonn. The *Horten Ho 1* had been built with its outer wings permanently attached to the center section. Unable to obtain an air tow, the *Hortens* burned their *Horten Ho 1* at the *Rhön/Wasserkuppe*. All future *Horten* sailplanes, both power and non- powered, would be built in three sections: center section and two outer wings which could be detached from its center section for land transport.

Comment:

The *Horten* brothers had been designing all-wing airplanes, powered and sail, for only eight years before they attempted to power one of their designs with the state-of-the-art turbojet engine. Their first all-wing, the *Horten Ho 1* competition sailplane, was designed in 1933 and participated at the *Rhön/Wasserkuppe* annual sailplane competitions of 1934. The *Horten* brothers first powered all-wing was their *Horten Ho 2*. It was designed in 1934 as a sailplane and made its maiden flight in 1935. Afterward, the *Horten* brothers placed a *Hirth* 60 horsepower "pusher" aeroengine in the center section. The conversation was successful. This *Horten Ho 2* would, in 1943, be converted back to its sailplane configuration and highly modified, used as a test-bed to determine the aerodynamics of large round turbine intakes such as those required for the *Junkers Jumo 004* which had to be cut in to the wing's leading edge. Thus, the ancient *Horten Ho 2* was used in the development of the twin turbojet-powered *Horten Ho 9/229*. With the success of mating an aeroengine to their all-wing designs, the *Horten* brothers designed an even larger powered all-wing. These included the twin piston engined *Horten Ho 5* series. Their biggest and most powerful twin piston powered all-wing was the *Horten Ho 7*. It was the *Horten Ho 7* which the *Horten* brothers considered to be their best and strongest air-frame within which to test the several alternative engines then available in late 1941 and early1942 including the *Bramo/BMW 002* turbojet engine, the *Argus As 014* pulse-jet engine of *Dr. Paul Schmidt* and the *HWK 509* bi-fuel liquid rocket drive from *Hellmuth Walter*.

The *Horten Ho 2* sailplane of 1935 with its 54.1 foot wingspan. This aircraft was the first *Horten* sailplane to incorporate detachable outer wings. It did not participate in the *Rhön/Wasserkuppe* summer sailplane competitions of 1935 because it was not quite flight ready when time registration closed. Several versions were constructed. The *Horten Ho 2C* shown in this photo with German civil registration, *D-10-125*, was flown by a *Luftwaffe* sailplane competition team.

Top sailplane: a *Horten Ho 2C* and flown in the prone position. This *Horten Ho 2C* was one of three *Horten Ho 2C's* built at Lippstadt in 1937. Bottom sailplane: a *Horten Ho 3B* with its raised cockpit canopy and one of the estimated 10 *Horten Ho 3B's* built in 1939 in Fürth, Berlin, and other locations throughout *Nazi* Germany. The *Horten Ho 3* sailplane had a wing span of 65.6 feet and an empty weight of 550 pounds.

The port wing of the *Horten Ho 3C* sailplane (*D-12-347*) with its high aspect ratio. This *Horten Ho 3* belongs to sailplane competition flyer *Werner Blech* who favored piloting his *Horten Ho 3C* with a fore-wing to improve flight dynamics. Not entirely a new aerodynamic concept in the 1930s Germany, after all, the *Wright* brothers had incorporated this feature on their history-making bi-wings.

Werner Blech in his *Horten Ho 3C* at the 1938 *Rhön/Wasserkuppe* Annual Summer Competitions. He is being towed aloft by *Walter Horten* piloting a *Focke-Wulf Fw 56. Blech* would lose his life when he flew into a thunder cloud. While in the cloud the *Horten Ho 3C* was lifted up to a higher altitude and the sailplane was pelted by hail stones and destroyed.

A pair of piston-powered *Horten* all-wing aircraft. In the foreground is the *Horten Ho 2B* of 1935 with a 54.1 foot wingspan and powered by a 60 horsepower *Hirth HM 60R* piston engine. Several years later the *Hortens* would modify this machine to test out the feasibility of air intakes cut through the wing's leading edge. Out front is the high-tech *Horten Ho 5A* with its 52.5 foot wingspan. The twin piston powered *Horten Ho 5A* was constructed in 1938 out of a new plastic laminate provided by *Dynamit AG,* unfortunately it crashed on its maiden flight shortly after takeoff due to a miscalculation of its center of gravity by *Reimar* who mistakenly placed it too aft in the center section. The machine was tail-heavy. Both *Hortens* narrowly escaped death and it was the last time the two brothers would test fly one of their aircraft together. The plastic *Horten Ho 5A* was replaced shortly afterward with the *Horten Ho 5B* an identical aircraft in every sense but constructed entirely out of wood.

A front on view of the *Horten Ho 5A.* A two seater it was powered by twin piston pusher-type engines a twin-raised cockpit canopy. It differed from the earlier *Horten Ho 5A* in that the *Horten Ho 5B* had small cockpit canopies where as the *Horten Ho 5A* the pilot and co-pilot sat entirely with in the wing with no protrusions such as a cockpit canopy. This example is another first for the high-tech minded brothers. Its outer wings including the main spar were constructed out of plastic material provided by *Dynamit AG.*

The high aspect ratio *Horten Ho 4A* competition sailplane over Göttingen, 1942. The center section was constructed of welded thin-wall pipe and covered with plywood. The outer wings were constructed entirely out of wood.

The brand new experimental *Horten Ho 5B* research aircraft with its twin separated individual cockpits. The *Horten Ho 5B* shows the general configuration which the *Hortens* were thinking of prior to the design of their first concept *Horten Ho 9* fighter powered by twin *Bramo/BMW 002* turbojet units.

Walter Horten surveying their new twin pusher engined, single-seat *Horten Ho 5C*. This was the *Horten* brothers initial piston-powered effort for a proposed all-wing fighter. Although the *Horten Ho 5C* prototype was underpowered and unarmed, it bears a strong resemblance to the *Horten* brothers twin *Bramo/BMW 002* turbine-powered *Horten Ho 9* 2nd concept fighter prototype. The center section's trailing edge is board across, just it is with the concept *Horten Ho 9*. Later the actual *Horten Ho 9's* center section would have a tapered trailing edge.

The *Horten Ho 7* as seen from below. In this photo, *RLM* official *Oberst Siegfried Knemeyer* is piloting the tandem seat *Horten Ho 7* out of Oranienburg Air Base in the northwest suburbs of Berlin. *Knemeyer* would later go on to request the *Horten* brothers to build a four turbojet-powered all-wing "*Amerika Bomber*" known as the *Horten Ho 18*. The twin-piston engined *Horten Ho 7* with tandem seating had a 131 foot wingspan and an empty weight of 7,050 pounds. The *Hortens* considered their *Horten Ho 7* to be one of their most satisfying powered designs and true pleasure to fly. It was the *Horten Ho 7* which the *Hortens* first thought about attaching *Schmitt-Argus 014* pulse- jet engines or possibly an *HWK 509* bi-fuel liquid rocket drive. These thoughts were abandon because the *Horten's* believed that the *Horten Ho 7* frame would be over stressed for alternative forms of engines, even *BMW 003's* or *Junkers Jumo 004's* turbojets. Sweet though the *Horten Ho 7* was to fly, the *Horten's* could not get the *RLM's* approval for series production. However, with the serial production of the *Horten Ho 9*, some twenty *Horten Ho 7's* were to have been built, too, as trainers for pilots going on to the *Junkers Jumo 004B*-powered *Horten Ho 229*. No examples of the *Horten Ho 7* survived the war.

The ultra high performance *Horten Ho 6* sailplane with a wingspan of 78.7 feet and an empty weight of 550 pounds. The *Horten Ho 6* sailplane had the longest wingspan of any *Horten* sailplane built between 1933-1945. Two *Horten Ho 6's* were started in late 1943 and only one survived the war and it was shipped to the United States. The *Horten Ho 6* shown in this photo is at *Northrop Aviation* 1947-1948 and is being systematically studied by *Northrop* engineers. It is now owned by the National Air and Space Museum and is on loan to the Berlin Technical Museum who gave it a beautiful restoration.

Chapter 06

Horten Ho 9 Surface Colors, Camouflage, Insignia, and National Markings

LUFTWAFFE COLOURS

To reduce the possibility of misinterpreting the colour plates which follow, the official RLM colour number is cross-referenced to two internationally accepted colour 'dictionaries': first, the Methuen *Handbook of Colour,* then (in brackets) to the US publication *Colours* (Federal Standard F.S.595a). An asterisk indicates an approximate match only. The values given are typical averages: it will be appreciated that each falls within an 'envelope' of darker or lighter tones, depending upon age and operational conditions. Most Luftwaffe exterior colours gave a matt, silky finish with a slight sheen, particularly after some service use. For this reason, 'semi-gloss' references have been quoted for the F.S.595a values.

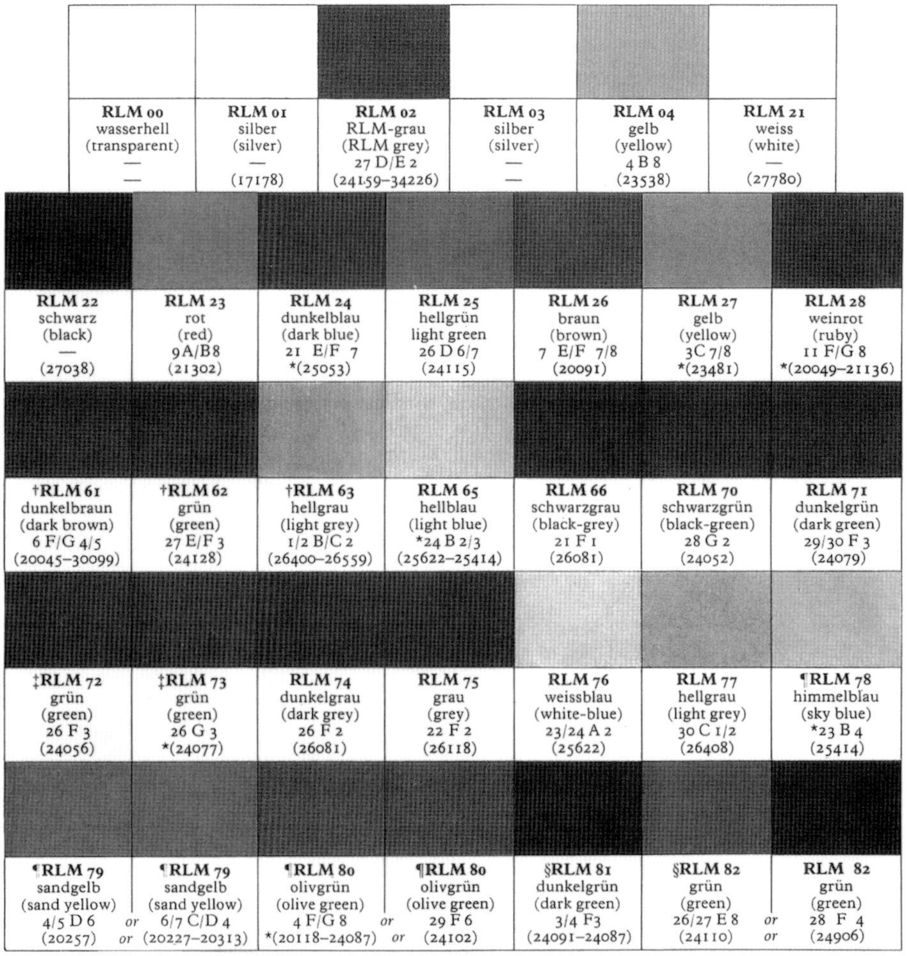

RLM 00 wasserhell (transparent) — —	**RLM 01** silber (silver) — (17178)	**RLM 02** RLM-grau (RLM grey) 27 D/E 2 (24159–34226)	**RLM 03** silber (silver) — —	**RLM 04** gelb (yellow) 4 B 8 (23538)	**RLM 21** weiss (white) — (27780)

RLM 22 schwarz (black) — (27038)	**RLM 23** rot (red) 9A/B8 (21302)	**RLM 24** dunkelblau (dark blue) 21 E/F 7 *(25053)	**RLM 25** hellgrün light green 26 D 6/7 (24115)	**RLM 26** braun (brown) 7 E/F 7/8 (20091)	**RLM 27** gelb (yellow) 3C 7/8 *(23481)	**RLM 28** weinrot (ruby) 11 F/G 8 *(20049–21136)
†RLM 61 dunkelbraun (dark brown) 6 F/G 4/5 (20045–30099)	**†RLM 62** grün (green) 27 E/F 3 (24128)	**†RLM 63** hellgrau (light grey) 1/2 B/C 2 (26400–26559)	**RLM 65** hellblau (light blue) *24 B 2/3 (25622–25414)	**RLM 66** schwarzgrau (black-grey) 21 F 1 (26081)	**RLM 70** schwarzgrün (black-green) 28 G 2 (24052)	**RLM 71** dunkelgrün (dark green) 29/30 F 3 (24079)
‡RLM 72 grün (green) 26 F 3 (24056)	**‡RLM 73** grün (green) 26 G 3 *(24077)	**RLM 74** dunkelgrau (dark grey) 26 F 2 (26081)	**RLM 75** grau (grey) 22 F 2 (26118)	**RLM 76** weissblau (white-blue) 23/24 A 2 (25622)	**RLM 77** hellgrau (light grey) 30 C 1/2 (26408)	**¶RLM 78** himmelblau (sky blue) *23 B 4 (25414)
¶RLM 79 sandgelb (sand yellow) 4/5 D 6 *or* (20257) *or*	**¶RLM 79** sandgelb (sand yellow) 6/7 C/D 4 (20227–20313)	**¶RLM 80** olivgrün (olive green) 4 F/G 8 *or* *(20118–24087) *or*	**¶RLM 80** olivgrün (olive green) 29 F 6 (24102)	**§RLM 81** dunkelgrün (dark green) 3/4 F3 (24091–24087)	**§RLM 82** grün (green) 26/27 E 8 *or* (24110) *or*	**RLM 82** grün (green) 28 F 4 (24906)

† Discontinued gradually from 1938 ; a few older types only remained in these colours up to about the end of 1941.
‡ Maritime aircraft.
¶ North Africa and Mediterranean.
§ Home Defence from 1943.

Color samples of standard *Luftwaffe* exterior colors. Courtesy: *German Aircraft of World War 2 In Colour*, by *Kenneth Munson*, 1978, Blandford Press Limited, Poole-Dorset, England.

Comment:

The first two prototypes of the *Horten Ho 9* were painted in camouflage colors. All upper surfaces were painted in *Gray-Violet 75*, while all lower surfaces received color *Light Blue 76*. The demarcation line between the two colors was soft-edged, with the top color overlapping the leading edge slightly in a uniformly straight line. The wing-walk area, originating on the port rear side of the center section and extending up to the cockpit entrance, was identified by two parallel lines painted in color *Wine Red 28*. Next to the wing-walk entrance was the admonition "*Nicht betreten*" in two lines, also in color *Wine Red 28*. Adjacent to this was the aircraft data block containing eight lines of statistical information such as the aircraft's serial number, weight, and classification. This information was applied color *Black 22*. Over all surfaces were applied a coat of *00 Waterbright*, a clear finish which could be highly polished.

Although the *Ho 229 V3* was never finished nor painted before the war's end, it undoubtedly would have been camouflaged in the new colors then being introduced on day fighters. These colors were *Brown Violet 81*, *Bright Violet 82*, and *Dark Green 83* for upper surfaces, with color *Light Blue 76* reserved for the under surfaces. Unlike most fighters of the period, the *Ho 229* would undoubtedly have used a single color for its upper surfaces. This could have been any one of the three colors mentioned.

German national markings carried by the *Ho 229* were confined to the *Balkenkreuz* on four positions. The *Ho 9 V1* and *V2* used a black and white cross *(B3)* style on both upper and lower surfaces. The *Ho 9 V3* and subsequent aircraft undoubtedly would have used a simplified cross *(B6)* style for upper surfaces while the underwing crosses would have been either the black and white *(B3)* style

Pen and ink drawing of the side and upper wing surface view of the series production *Horten Ho 229 A-1*. Upper surface colors would have been either *Brown Violet 81*, *Bright Violet 82*, and *Dark Green 83* in pairs or singly.

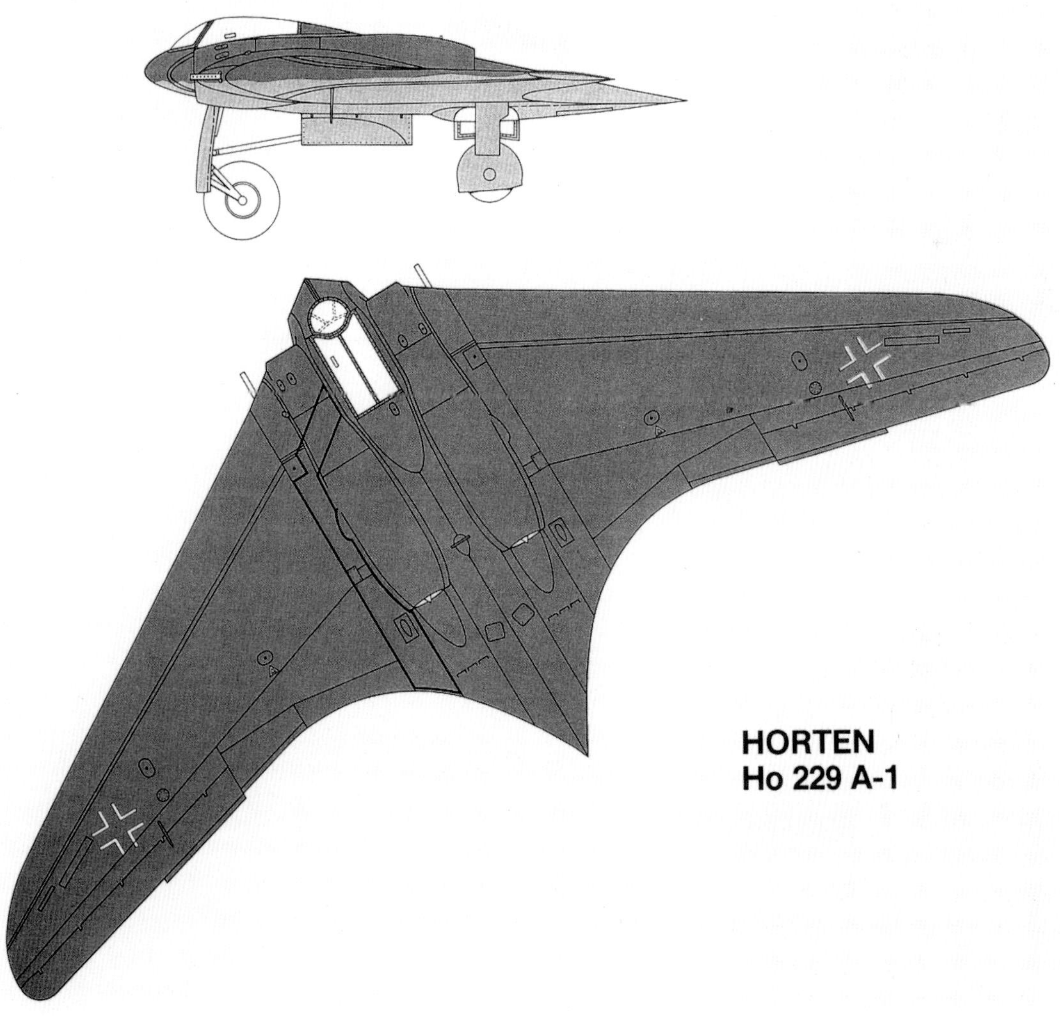

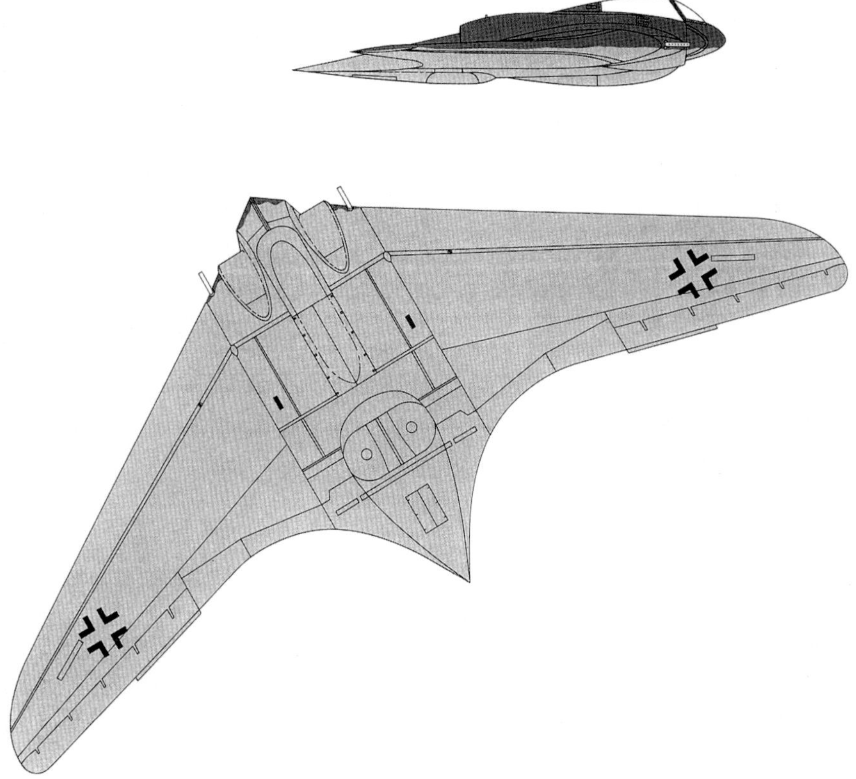

Pen and ink drawing of the side and under surface view of the *Horten Ho 229 A-1*. The under surface color would have been *Light Blue 76.*

The color separation line shown in this photograph of the new *Horten Ho 9 V1's* center section outside the *Horten* workshop at Grone. February, 1944. The under surface is painted *Light Blue 76* while the upper surface appears to be *Bright Violet 82.*

The *Horten Ho 9 V2* (right) and the *Horten Ho 229 V7* (left) painted in camouflage. The paint color line separation is seen just about midway on the leading edge. Scale models by *Reinhard Roeser*.

The proposed *Bramo/BMW 002* powered *Horten Ho 9* concept fighter of 1941 showing the upper and lower paint separation.

The upper and lower surface paint demarcation line of the *Horten Ho 9 V2* shown here under going test flights at Oranienburg Air Base is not so clearly visible. All we can assume is that the *Horten Ho 9 V2* would have carried the same paint scheme as did the *Horten Ho 9 V1*. Very few photographs exist of the *Horten Ho 9 V2* compared to numerous documentation of the *Horten Ho 9 V1* during construction, after construction, and flight testing.

The *Horten Ho 3D* shown fitted with a single *Walter "Micron"* engine at Göttingen, 1942. Its national markings is illustrated by the black and white cross (*B-3*) style on all four wing positions.

A close up view of the black and white cross (*B-3*) style painted on the *Horten Ho 3* ammunition carrier intended for the Russian Front.

The *Horten Ho 7* shown about late 1944 and a painted *Balkenkreuz* of the simplified (*B-4*) style.

The *Horten Ho 7's* upper wing surface. It carries the *Balkenkreuz* of the simplified (*B-6*) style. Notice, too, that this machine has no *Halkenkreuz* painted on it anywhere. It appears that all powered *Horten* aircraft beginning with the *Horten Ho 7* no longer carried the *Swatiska*.

The upper surface of the *Horten Ho 9 V1* in Spring, 1944 and a painted *Balkenkreuz* of the simplified (*B-4*) style.

or the simplified *(B4)* style. Despite the fact that there was no vertical surface to display the *Halkenkreuz* (*Swastika*) the *Hortens* usually applied them anyway on a horizontal surface such as a control flap. The *Hortens* applied the *Halkenkreuz* on several of their all-wing aircraft such as the *Ho 4a* and *Ho 5b*. If the aircraft had a fixed main landing gear such as the *Ho 5c* a *Halkenkreuz* would be applied outboard of each fixed wheel covering. It is interesting that no *Halkenkreuz* appeared on Horten powered aircraft after the *Ho 5c*. There was no *Halkenkruez* displayed on the early *Ho 9 002* turbojet powered concept designs nor the *Ho 9* to be powered by *003s*. Furthermore, there was no *Halkenkruez* on the *Ho 9 V1* at anytime. It is not known if one appeared on the *Ho 9 V2* because there are so few photographs of this machine unlike the *V1* which was extensively documented via photographs. I believe that it is safe to say that the *Ho 9 V2* did not carry the *Halkenkruez*. However, I do not know whether the series produced *Ho 229* would have flown through the skies of German adorned with the *Halkenkruez*...it might have.

Finally, fuel filler points would have been identified by the customary yellow and while equilateral triangles. (Courtesy *Monogram Close-Up #12 — Ho 229* by *David Myhra*, 1983.)

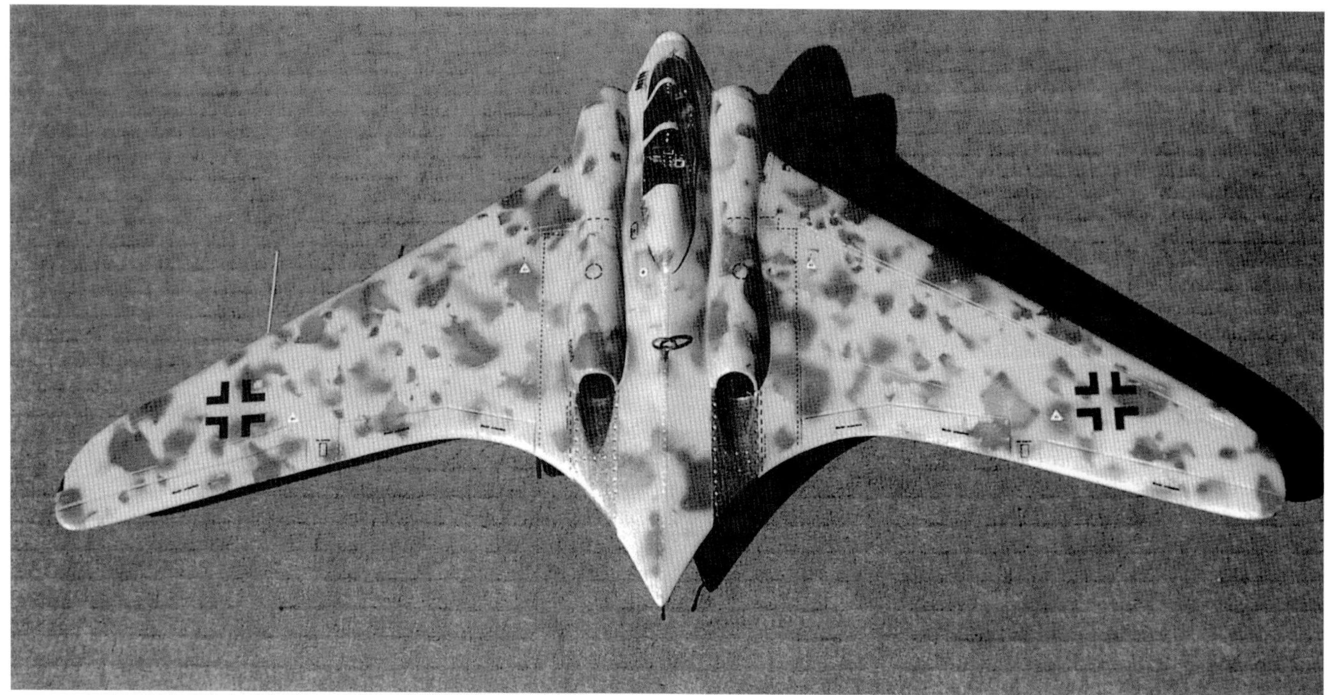

A *Horten Ho 229* two seat radar equipped night fighter painted camouflage and shown with a *Balkenkreuz* of the simplified (*B-6*) style for upper surfaces. Scale model by *Lindsay Charman*.

The first *Horten* flying machine of 1934 carried a painted-on *Halkenkreuz* on its upper and lower port middle flap of the mid to late 1930s style.

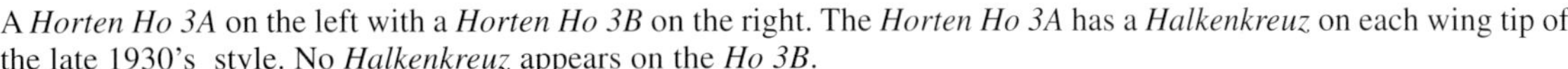

A *Horten Ho 3A* on the left with a *Horten Ho 3B* on the right. The *Horten Ho 3A* has a *Halkenkreuz* on each wing tip of the late 1930's style. No *Halkenkreuz* appears on the *Ho 3B*.

The port side wing tip of *Werner Blech's Horten Ho 3C* showing its *Halkenkreuz* of the old style.

One of several *Horten Ho 4As* built. This one has the *Halkenkreuz* painted on the center section's cockpit fairing near its trailing edge. The *Hortens* did not require a vertical surface to apply the *Halkenkreuz* as has been commonly thought.

The fully assembled *Horten Ho 4A "LA-AK"* out in a grain field in Fall, 1944. This sailplane was given to *Robert Kronfeld* by *Reimar* post war. It was immediately taken to England and later tested by the RAE-Farnborough. It's later style *Halkenkreuz* on the nearly flat upper surface trailing edge is clearly visible.

The *Horten Ho 5B* appearing prior to its maiden flight in 1938 in Cologne-Ostheim Air Base. The *Hortens* said that the *Horten Ho 5B* was their biggest disappointment. The *Horten's* painted the *Halkenkreuz* on the upper surface of the center landing flap.

The *Horten Ho 5B* showing its *Halkenkreuz* on the under side of the center landing flap.

The *Horten Ho 5C* single seat twin piston engine prototype fighter. The two children to the left in the photo are holding the forward detachable portion of the cockpit canopy. Shown is the paint demarcation line with upper surface painted *Bright Violet 82* and the lower surface *Light Blue 76*. Notice that the *Hortens* applied the *Halkenkreuz* (*Swastika*) in black to the vertical surface of the fixed main landing gear. This is the last motorized *Horten* all-wing to have a *Halkenkreuz* applied to any surface...vertical or horizontal. The reason is not known to this author.

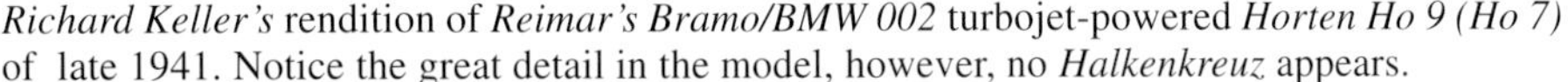

Richard Keller's rendition of *Reimar's Bramo/BMW 002* turbojet-powered *Horten Ho 9 (Ho 7)* of late 1941. Notice the great detail in the model, however, no *Halkenkreuz* appears.

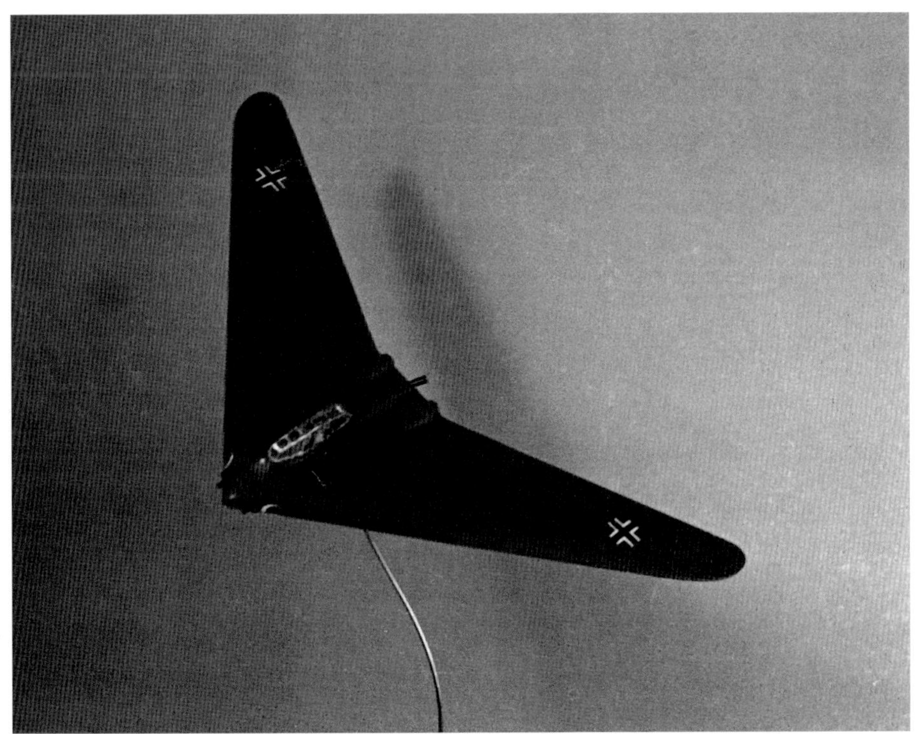

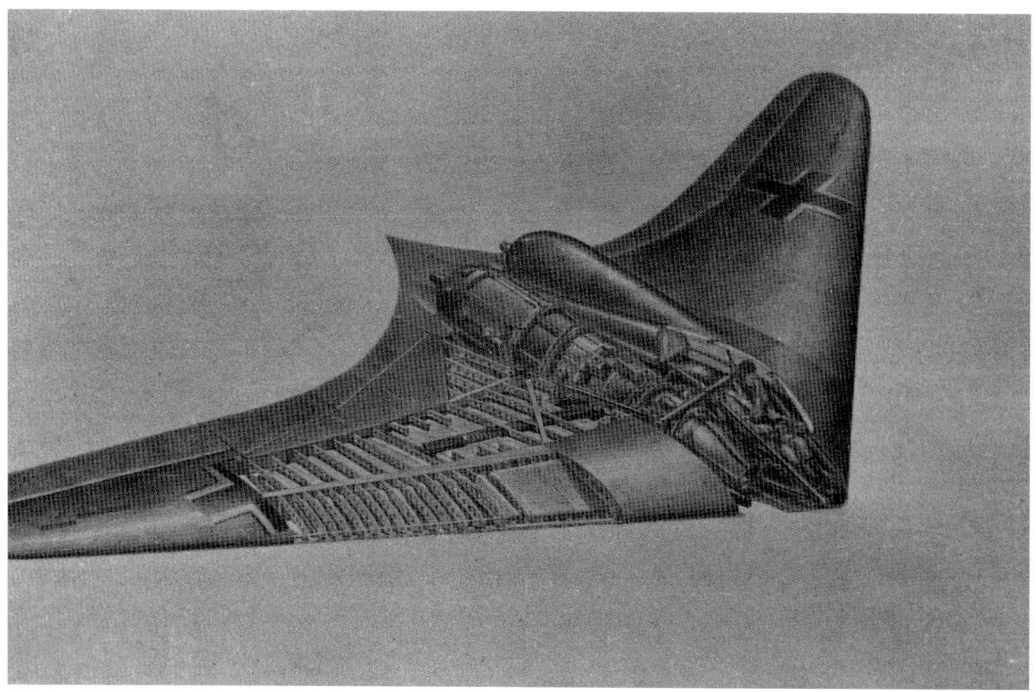

Richard Kellers rendition of *Reimar's BMW 003* turbojet-powered *Horten Ho 9* of early 1942. Notice, too, the great detail built into this "see through" illustration, however, no *Halkenkreuz* appears.

A view of the *Horten Ho 9 V1* as taken from the *Junkers'* hangar roof at *Göttingen* about mid-Summer, 1944. All complete and correctly painted except for any sign of the *Halkenkreuz*.

This is a scale model of the *Horten Ho 9 V2* shown without any *Halkenkreuz*. This author knows of no photographs in existence which shows the painted center section's trailing edge. Therefore we have to assume that the *Horten Ho 9 V2* followed that same painting pattern as all previous *Horten Ho 9* examples...concept as well as the *Horten Ho 9 V1*. Scale model by *Reinhard Roeser*.

The *Horten Ho 229 V3* painted in a desert camouflage and how it might have appeared in the new colors being introduced on all day fighters. These colors were *81*, *82*, and *83* for upper surface with color *Light Blue 76* reserved for the under surfaces. German national markings on the *Horten Ho 229 V3* probably would have continued with the four *Balkenkreuz* on four positions as shown in this photograph. The *Balkenkreuz* would have been the simplified cross (*B-6*) style for upper surface and the black and white (*B-3*) style or (*B-4*) style on the lower surface. Scale model by *Reinhard Roeser*.

As far as it is known to this author, no *Halkenkruez* appeared on the *Horten Ho 7*. There are numerous photographs of the *Horten Ho 7* in existence and none of them show a *Horten Ho 7* with a *Halkenkruez*. Scale model by *Reinhard Roeser*.

The *Horten Ho 229 V3* center section in storage at NASM, Silver Hill, Maryland shows two white *Halkenkruezs*. The *Horten Ho 229 V3* did not come out of Germany with a *Halkenkruez*. Of course the plywood surface was not yet ready for paint, either. It was applied perhaps, by *GIs* after it arrived at Freeman Field from Europe about September, 1945. It's doubtful that a *Halkenkruez* would have been applied, then again, this machine was in series production and pretty much out of the *Horten's* hands and anything was possible.

A scale model of the proposed *Horten Ho 229 V7* two man crew, radar equipped, night fighter. Given the *Horten* practice of applying the *Halkenkruez* on their sailplanes in the past, were the *Halkenkruez* to be applied it in all likelihood been a small double one painted forward of the port and starboard trailing edge as shown in the photo. Then, too, since the *Horten Ho 229 V3* appears now with double *Halkenkruezs* on the center section's trailing edge. scale model-builders assume it to be officially correct. Although non-official this is probably where the *Halkenkreuz* would have appeared, given the *Horten* practice of applying the *Halkenkreuz* on their *Horten Ho 4A* and *Horten Ho 5B*. Scale model by *Reinhard Roeser*.

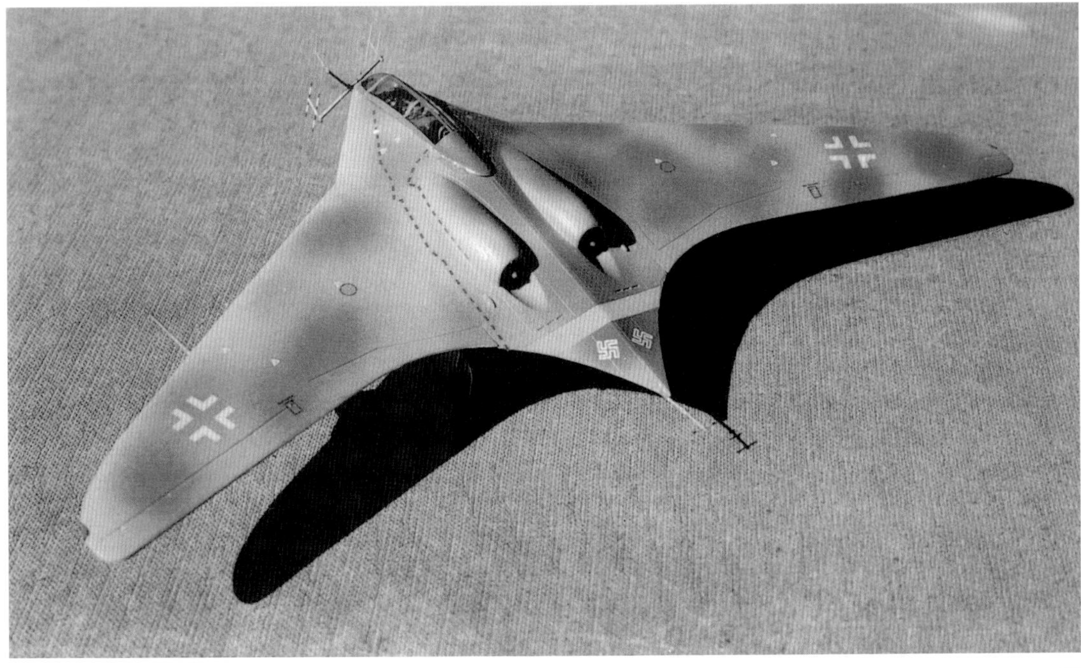

Chapter 07

Horten Ho 9 Weight, Specifications, and Performance Statistics

An overhead view of the new *Horten Ho 9 V1* taken from the roof of its *Junkers* hangar, Göttingen. Summer, 1944.

Comment:

The *Horten Ho 9* project as envisioned by the *Horten* brothers in the summer of 1941 was to be a relatively lightweight high speed fighter aircraft built largely out of wood and constructed quickly by low skilled wood workers at locations throughout Germany. But as the *Horten Ho 9* proceed from design idea to project status it got heavier and heavier. *Reimar* believed that the *Horten Ho 9* fighter could be built almost anywhere just as his popular *Horten Ho 3* sailplane had been prior to the war being constructed by academic flying groups. Although the two aircraft types were worlds apart, *Reimar* felt that once the *Horten Ho 9* project had become standardized components such as outer wings could be constructed by a wing factory group, center section frames by another, and landing gear by yet another, and so on. All these components could then be brought to several assembly locations thus series production of the *Horten Ho 9* fighter could be quickly and efficiently achieved. This was the dream. But with most experimental projects such as the *Horten Ho 9* was in the being, series production can get complicated fast.

Reichsmarshall Hermann Göring had contracted with the *Horten* brothers to construct an experimental machine capable of

Aircraft type		Ho 229 V1
Role		Test Prototype
Seating		1
Wing Area	m^2 (ft^2)	52 (560)
Wing Span	mm (ft-in)	16,760 (54 - 11¾)
Length	mm (ft-in)	7,600 (24 - 11¼)
Height	mm (ft-in)	
Weight Empty	kg (lb)	2,200 (4,850)
Takeoff Weight	kg (lb)	2,400 (5,291)
Engine type		None
Maximum thrust	kg (lb)	
Maximum speed at sea level	km/h (mph)	
Maximum speed at 12 km (39,372 ft)	km/h (mph)	
Cruise speed at 10 km (32,810 ft)	km/h (mph)	
Service ceiling	km (ft)	
Landing speed	km/h (mph)	
Rate of climb	m/min (ft/min)	
Flight duration	hrs	
Armament		None

Design Specifications of the *Horten Ho 9 V1.*

Richard Keller of the *Horten Flugzeugbau*, rendering of the *Horten Ho 9 V2A* to be powered by 6-stage compressor *BMW 003* engines. *BMW* abandoned their *003A* in favor of a 7-stage compressor engine known as the *BMW 003B* creating delay and frustration at the *Horten Flugzeugbau* - Göttingen.

Aircraft type		Ho 229 V2a
Role		Test Prototype
Seating		1
Wing Area	m^2 (ft^2)	52 (560)
Wing Span	mm (ft-in)	16,760 (54 - 11¾)
Length	mm (ft-in)	7,465 (24 - 6)
Height	mm (ft-in)	
Weight Empty	kg (lb)	4,082 (9,000)
Takeoff Weight	kg (lb)	7,938 (17,600)
Engine type		2 x BMW 003 A-1
Maximum thrust	kg (lb)	798 (1,760)
Maximum speed at sea level	km/h (mph)	
Maximum speed at 12 km (39,372 ft)	km/h (mph)	1,046 (650)
Cruise speed at 10 km (32,810 ft)	km/h (mph)	697 (433)
Service ceiling	km (ft)	15.8 (52,000)
Landing speed	km/h (mph)	145 (90)
Rate of climb	m/min (ft/min)	1,311 (4,301)
Flight duration	hrs	4.5
Armament		None

Design specifications of the *Horten Ho 9 V2A*.

3x1000 performance, that is, 1000 kilometer range, 1000 kilometers/hour speed, and 1000 kilogram bomb load. The takeoff weight of the *BMW 003* powered *Horten Ho 9* was 17,600 pounds and top speed was estimated at 650 miles per hour. The *Horten Ho 9 V2* had a takeoff weight of 18,739 pounds and top speed was estimated at 607 miles per hour. For the *Horten Ho 229 V3*, its performance was even lower. Takeoff weight was up to 19,840 pounds...more than 1-ton heavier than the *BMW 003* powered *Horten Ho 9*. The *Horten Ho 229 V3's* top speed was lower, too.

Richard Keller of the *Horten Flugzuegbau*, rendering of the *Horten Ho 9 V2B* to be powered by *BMW 003Bs*, then when they were not ready, powered by *Junkers Jumo 004Bs*. More delays.

Aircraft type		Ho 229 V2b
Role		Test Prototype
Seating		1
Wing Area	m² (ft²)	52 (560)
Wing Span	mm (ft-in)	16,760 (54 - 11¾)
Length	mm (ft-in)	7,465 (24 - 6)
Height	mm (ft-in)	2,810 (9 - 2¾)
Weight Empty	kg (lb)	4,600 (10,140)
Takeoff Weight	kg (lb)	8,500 (18,739)
Engine type		2 x Jumo 004 B-2
Maximum thrust	kg (lb)	900 (1,983)
Maximum speed at sea level	km/h (mph)	950 (590)
Maximum speed at 12 km (39,372 ft)	km/h (mph)	977 (607)
Cruise speed at 10 km (32,810 ft)	km/h (mph)	690 (429)
Service ceiling	km (ft)	16 (52,496)
Landing speed	km/h (mph)	145 (90)
Rate of climb	m/min (ft/min)	1,320 (4,331)
Flight duration	hrs	3.0
Armament		None

Design specifications of the *Horten Ho 9 V2B*.

The *Horten Ho 229 V3*. Digital image by *Mario Merino*.

Aircraft type		Ho 229 V3
Role		Fighter Prototype
Seating		1
Wing Area	m^2 (ft^2)	53 (570.5)
Wing Span	mm (ft-in)	16,800 (55 - 1⅜)
Length	mm (ft-in)	7,465 (24 - 6)
Height	mm (ft-in)	2,810 (9 - 2¾)
Weight Empty	kg (lb)	5,067 (11,170)
Takeoff Weight	kg (lb)	8,999 (19,840)
Engine type		2 x Jumo 004 B-2
Maximum thrust	kg (lb)	900 (1,983)
Maximum speed at sea level	km/h (mph)	949 (590)
Maximum speed at 12 km (39,372 ft)	km/h (mph)	977 (607)
Cruise speed at 10 km (32,810 ft)	km/h (mph)	632 (393)
Service ceiling	km (ft)	15.8 (52,000)
Landing speed	km/h (mph)	156 (97)
Rate of climb	m/min (ft/min)	1,311 (4,301)
Flight duration	hrs	4.5
Armament		None

Design specifications of the *Horten Ho 229 V3*.

Index